PREVENTING AND COUNTERING VIOLENT EXTREMISM AND RADICALISATION
Evidence-Based Policy and Practice

Edited by
Teresa C. Silva and Marzena Kordaczuk-Wąs

P

First published in Great Britain in 2025 by

Policy Press, an imprint of
Bristol University Press
University of Bristol
1–9 Old Park Hill
Bristol
BS2 8BB
UK
t: +44 (0)117 374 6645
e: bup-info@bristol.ac.uk

Details of international sales and distribution partners are available at
policy.bristoluniversitypress.co.uk

© Teresa C. Silva and Marzena Kordaczuk-Wąs 2025

The digital PDF and ePub versions of this title are available open access and distributed under the terms of the Creative Commons Attribution-NonCommercial-NoDerivatives 4.0 International licence (https://creativecommons.org/licenses/by-nc-nd/4.0/) which permits reproduction and distribution for non-commercial use without further permission provided the original work is attributed.

This project has received funding by the European Union's Horizon 2020 research and innovation programme H2020-SU-SEC-2020 under grant agreement no. 101021701.

British Library Cataloguing in Publication Data
A catalogue record for this book is available from the British Library

ISBN 978-1-4473-7092-5 paperback
ISBN 978-1-4473-7093-2 ePub
ISBN 978-1-4473-7094-9 ePdf

The right of Teresa C. Silva and Marzena Kordaczuk-Wąs to be identified as editors of this work has been asserted by them in accordance with the Copyright, Designs and Patents Act 1988.

All rights reserved: no part of this publication may be reproduced, stored in a retrieval system, or transmitted in any form or by any means, electronic, mechanical, photocopying, recording, or otherwise without the prior permission of Bristol University Press.

Every reasonable effort has been made to obtain permission to reproduce copyrighted material. If, however, anyone knows of an oversight, please contact the publisher.

The statements and opinions contained within this publication are solely those of the editors and contributors and not of the University of Bristol or Bristol University Press. The University of Bristol and Bristol University Press disclaim responsibility for any injury to persons or property resulting from any material published in this publication.

Bristol University Press and Policy Press work to counter discrimination on grounds of gender, race, disability, age and sexuality.

Cover design: Andy Ward
Front cover image: 123rf/howdybob

We dedicate this book to every victim and survivor of violent extremism and terrorism. May our work prevent others from experiencing a similar fate.

Contents

List of figures and tables vii
List of abbreviations ix
Notes on contributors x

Introduction 1
Teresa C. Silva and Marzena Kordaczuk-Wąs

PART I Theoretical and epistemological framework

1 Criminological aspects of crime prevention 21
 Jerzy Sarnecki

2 An epistemological framework for evidence- 50
 based crime prevention
 Teresa C. Silva and Gustav Grut

PART II Designing, implementing and evaluating preventing and countering violent extremism initiatives

3 A step-by-step logic model of evidence-based 81
 practice design
 Marzena Kordaczuk-Wąs

4 Evaluation as a standard component of the 122
 evidence-based practice assumptions
 Marzena Kordaczuk-Wąs

PART III The three pillars of evidence-based practice

5 Radicalisation across the community and forensic 163
 units: a systematic literature review on the
 psychology of violent extremism
 Sören Henrich, Jane L. Ireland and Michael Lewis

6	"But what if I get it wrong?" Exploring practitioners' understanding of preventing and countering violent extremism and radicalisation duty guidance *Erin Lawlor*	216
7	Restorative justice for preventing and countering violent extremism: some reflections from the Basque Country *Gema Varona*	244

PART IV Thinking critically about evidence-based practice

8	Role of academic researchers in preventing and countering violent extremism policy and practice *Leena Malkki and Irina van der Vet*	275
9	The Atomwaffen Division: the myth of evidence-based policy on the threat of far-right extremism *Simon Fulgoni and Susanna Menis*	303

Index 333

List of figures and tables

Figures

0.1	Epistemological contextualisation of preventing and countering violent extremism	8
2.1	Proposed epistemological framework for evidence-based crime prevention	53
2.2	Characterisation of an initiative's main and side effects	60
2.3	Stages of initiative design, implementation and evaluation	69
3.1	The main stages of the step-by-step process of evidence-based programme design addressing the issue of radicalisation	93
3.2	The main steps that build the theoretical foundation of an evidence-based programme	94
3.3	The main aspects of diagnosis in building the evidence-based foundation of a preventive programme	97
3.4	The main steps in building the logic model of an evidence-based programme design	99
3.5	Step 2 of the logic model of an evidence-based programme design: selection of programme addresses	100
3.6	Step 6 of the logic model of an evidence-based programme design: formulation of the programme's main objective	102
3.7	Step 6 of the logic model of an evidence-based programme design: formulation of the programme's operational objectives	103
3.8	Step 6 of the logic model of an evidence-based programme design: measuring progress in achieving the programme's main objective	104

3.9	Step 10 of the logic model of an evidence-based programme design: formulation of evaluation from general assumptions	106
3.10	Complementary process of evidence-based programme design	107
4.1	Formative evaluation example	138
4.2	Process evaluation example	139
4.3	Results evaluation example	141
4.4	The main steps in building the logic model of an evidence-based programme design	145
4.5	An example of a definitional indicator that measures programme progress	148
4.6	An example of a correlation indicator that measures programme progress	148
5.1	Flowchart depicting the search process for the systematic literature review	168

Tables

1.1	Typology of crime prevention measures	27
3.1	Standard elements of a preventive programme construction	90
4.1	Selected features, similarities and differences between peer/self-review, measurement, assessment and evaluation	130
4.2	Definition of a long-term prevention programme and the types of evaluation it should be subjected to	136
4.3	Standard elements of the construction of a preventive programme, including evaluation	145
4.4	A sample relation between the indicators measuring the implementation of the main objective, type of evaluation, research procedure and proposed methods, techniques and measurement tools of evaluation	149
5.1	Overview of factors derived from the thematic analysis, listed from most to least empirical support	170

List of abbreviations

AWD	Atomwaffen Division
EBP	evidence-based practice
EDDRA	Exchange on Drug Demand Reduction Action
EFRJ	European Forum for Restorative Justice
EMCDDA	European Monitoring Centre for Drugs and Drug Addiction
EUCPN	European Crime Prevention Network
ISO	International Organisation for Standardisation
MCT	Mass Casualty Terrorism
NSO	National Socialist Order
P/CVE	preventing and countering violent extremism
PRISMA	Preferred Reporting Items for Systematic Reviews and Meta-Analysis
RAN	Radicalisation Awareness Network
RJ	Restorative Justice

Notes on contributors

Simon Fulgoni graduated from the University of Greenwich and completed his postgraduate studies in the field of terrorism and counter-terrorism at Royal Holloway, University of London. His research focuses on international relations, far-right terrorism and White supremacist violent extremism. Simon is a visiting university lecturer and currently works as a civil servant at the Ministry of Justice in London, England.

Gustav Grut studied criminology at Mid Sweden University in Sundsvall and Stockholm University. He is currently a lecturer at Mid Sweden University and has written on corporate harm in the pharmaceutical industry and crime prevention through environmental design. He has also developed and taught courses in evidence-based crime prevention.

Sören Henrich is Lecturer in Forensic Psychology at the Manchester Metropolitan University and a research associate at the Ashworth High-Security Hospital. With a decade of experience working in secure psychiatric settings in Germany and the UK, his expertise is in risk and threat assessment, particularly with high-risk radicalised individuals. The psychological formulation of extremist violence is his key research interest. A multi-study project at the University of Central Lancashire resulted in the Eco-System of Extremist Violence (ES-EV) model. Dr Henrich is now preparing psychologists, counter-terrorism officers and international colleagues to understand group-based violence. He is an active contributor to several academic journals and scientific committees.

Jane L. Ireland is a Forensic Psychologist, Chartered Psychologist and Chartered Scientist. Professor Ireland holds a Professorial Chair at the University of Central Lancashire. She is Violence Treatment Lead within High Secure Services, Ashworth Hospital, Mersey Care NHS Trust and an EMDR (trauma) Europe Accredited Clinical Supervisor/Consultant. She is Editor-in-Chief for *Aggressive Behavior* and publishes widely in the area of aggression, trauma, personality disorder and psychopathology. Professor Ireland has in excess of 150 publications and several handbooks.

Marzena Kordaczuk-Wąs is an experienced advisor in the law enforcement industry with 18 years of work experience in the Polish Police, with particular emphasis on preventing security threats. Currently, she is an expert on preventing radicalisation at the Polish Platform for Homeland Security and co-chair of the Police and Law Enforcement Group of the Radicalisation Awareness Network (RAN). She holds a PhD in social sciences in the field of sociology of security from the University of Wrocław. Hence, her main research interests focus on community policing as a crime prevention tool and social conditions influencing the effectiveness of activities in this area.

Erin Lawlor is a qualified Mental Health Social Worker. She began her PhD at the Centre of Excellence in Terrorism, Resilience, Intelligence and Organised Crime Research (Sheffield Hallam University) in 2022 and is passionate about combining holistic interventions into security practices. Her research focuses on exploring the integration of public health perspectives, frameworks, and theories into radicalisation and deradicalisation work. She has focused on scoping the intersections between policy, practice and theory in both deradicalisation and public health work and believes that front-line radicalisation/deradicalisation work could benefit from integrating public health approaches, for instance, person-centred care, systematic approaches, and service user empowerment.

Michael Lewis is a Chartered Psychologist, Registered Forensic Psychologist, Chartered Scientist and Associate Fellow of the British Psychological Society. He works clinically in secure psychiatric services and leads the MSc Applied Forensic Psychology programme at the University of Central Lancashire,

Preston. His research interests include personality pathology, aggression and psychological trauma.

Leena Malkki is Director of the Centre for European Studies at the University of Helsinki. She is a historian and political scientist specialised in the study of terrorism and violent extremism in Europe. She has extensive experience in cooperating with policy makers and practitioners in the field of preventing and countering violent extremism. Her fields of interest include terrorism and violent extremism in post-war Europe, the development of counter-terrorism policies, transnational diffusion of extremist narratives, and political and societal resilience to terrorism. She is one of the editors of *Routledge Handbook on Radicalisation and Countering Radicalisation* (2023).

Susanna Menis is Lecturer in Law at Birkbeck London University, School of Law. Her research and teaching reflect an interest in law and the humanities, socio-historical and doctrinal approaches to law. She writes and publishes on the historical development of prisons and has carried out several projects addressing legal education, criminal law doctrine within social history, and legal history.

Jerzy Sarnecki was educated at Stockholm University, where he received his doctorate in 1978. Sarnecki worked as a researcher and later as head of investigations at the Swedish Crime Prevention Council in the years 1977–1993. He was a professor of general criminology at Stockholm University in the years 1993–2015. He is currently a senior professor at Gävle University, Mid Sweden University in Sundsvall and at the Institute for Future Studies in Stockholm. Sarnecki's research concerns, among other things, life-course criminology, criminal networks and crime prevention methods. He is the author of several textbooks in criminology. Since 2005, he has been co-chairman of the Jury for the Stockholm Prize in Criminology.

Teresa C. Silva is Associate Professor of Criminology at Mid Sweden University and a member of the European Crime Prevention Network and Project INDEED advisory boards. With a background in psychology and health sciences, since 2016, she has been researching and teaching different areas of evidence-based crime prevention and has published several works on the topic. Furthermore, Dr Silva collaborates with several municipalities and regions in Sweden, advising on the design, implementation and evaluation of crime prevention interventions and strategies.

Irina van der Vet is Research Coordinator at the Centre for European Studies, University of Helsinki. She specialises in researching counter-terrorism policy and prevention of violent extremism and radicalisation in the European Union. For the past eight years, she has been mainly involved in EU-funded research projects on security and the prevention of terrorism, where she has been working between academic research and practice. As part of the University of Helsinki team, she has been leading the development of the model and the tool for evidence-based evaluation of preventive programmes in the framework of the H2020 INDEED project.

Gema Varona is Director of the Basque Institute of Criminology of the University of the Basque Country (Spain), where she is a senior researcher and professor of victimology and criminal policy. Her research interests include human rights, victimhood, prevention and reparation of different forms of violence (interpersonal, organisational, state and corporate violence) and restorative justice. Her most recent publications talk about strategies to connect with victims and the criminalisation of violence against women.

Introduction

Teresa C. Silva and Marzena Kordaczuk-Wąs

As in any crime prevention area, preventing and countering violent extremism (P/CVE) and radicalisation rely on decision-making processes about working methods and approaches and the design and implementation of initiatives and policies. Evidence-based practice (EBP) refers to decision-making processes guided by the best available scientific evidence, relying on the expertise of professionals (practitioners and policy makers) and considering the values and preferences of those it is intended to serve. Strauss and colleagues (2005) outlined EBP as a five-step course of action. The first step involves proposing an answerable question that fulfils the need for information. The question must explicitly state what the professional needs to know or do. In the second step, the professional identifies and gets acquainted with scientific evidence that helps answer the question. Evidence pertains to findings in the scientific literature that are relevant to the intended discovery. In the third step, the selected evidence undergoes critical appraisal to assess its validity, impact and applicability. Determining the quality of the evidence is critical in this process. Every research study has strengths, weaknesses and methodological limitations, and their results must consider these. As a general approach, practitioners and policy makers may initially consider searching for systematic reviews and meta-analytic studies, as they offer the highest level of evidence.

In the fourth step, professionals integrate appraised evidence with their expertise. Many practitioners and policy makers have extensive experience in their field, possessing an unstructured knowledge of what is and is not effective for the populations they serve and in areas where they operate. This knowledge is not disregarded in EBP. On the contrary, it is considered essential, and professionals are encouraged to incorporate it into their practice. Furthermore, the characteristics of the individuals or groups targeted in the decision-making processes, along with the preferences and values of participants, are integrated with the evidence and professional expertise from previous steps. Finally, in the fifth step, the effectiveness and efficiency of initiatives and policies are evaluated. In EBP, evaluation is essential.

In the 1990s, the seed of EBP applied to crime problems was sown when scholars began to debate the importance of evaluating crime prevention initiatives and emphasised the necessity of knowing what works, what does not, and what shows promise. In 1997, a study commissioned by the US Congress systematically reviewed over 500 scientific evaluations of crime prevention interventions to determine if there was enough evidence to support certain types of programmes for funding (Sherman et al, 1998). In the early 2000s, with roots in medical practice and recognising the necessity of efficient resource allocation, the EBP movement for decision-making in crime prevention and criminal policy emerged with the establishment of the Campbell Collaboration, among other initiatives.

Finding what works was deemed essential for a rational practice that would necessarily rely on continuously reviewing the most up-to-date scientific research. However, until recently, the evidence-based model struggled to gain traction and bring about a permanent change in the practices of those involved in developing and implementing crime prevention and P/CVE initiatives and strategies. The results of basic research were often confined to the shelves of universities and research centres, and while disseminated by researchers in scientific meetings, they did not effectively reach professionals who could have consistently and systematically applied them in the field. This resulted in a significant gap between academia and practice, in contrast to what occurred in the medical field, perhaps because scholars working on crime-related subjects did not adopt the same approach as medicine, which wisely anchored medical training in the evidence-based paradigm. In the 1990s, EBP spread through medical schools, and a new generation of physicians emerged who would revolutionise the outdated practice of medicine based on intuition and unsystematic clinical experience to a whole new way of clinical decision-making (Guyatt et al, 1992). The pioneers of the evidence-based medicine movement advocated the need to train medical students in efficient literature-searching skills and the application of formal rules for critically appraising clinical literature (Guyatt et al, 1992). Nowadays, it is unthinkable to treat a medical problem using methods that have not been adequately tested, consistently proven effective through research, and where the benefits outweigh the potential harm to the patient. However, this remains the standard practice in many countries regarding crime prevention and P/CVE. Not only are the outcomes of initiatives often inadequately evaluated, if at all, but many interventions also function as black boxes because their programme theories or theories of change have not been tested.

Notwithstanding, crime prevention practitioners and policy makers have recognised the importance of EBP and have developed a vested interest in adhering to its principles. Evaluation procedures are now frequently expected from those responsible for implementing programmes and policies. Suddenly, there seems to be a rush to change old ways of working, although not always with a clear understanding of what EBP entails. Process and outcome evaluation are necessary but insufficient to bestow an initiative or policy with the scientific rigour that EBP implies. Interventions in which the theory of change has not been properly tested are considered pseudo-scientific despite the fact that they might be deemed effective in addressing the crime problem they were designed for.

In 2020, the European Crime Prevention Network commissioned an inquiry among practitioners in the 27 European member states to ascertain the procedures and methods employed by them or their respective organisations for evaluating initiatives (Silva and Lind, 2020). The authors of the investigation concluded that there was still a long way to go before EBP could be effectively reached in the field of crime prevention. A culture of evaluation had not yet been firmly established, many practitioners lacked the necessary competencies to plan evaluations, and initiatives were inadequately designed, resulting in shortcomings and misalignments between the identified crime problem, the intervention objectives and the activities employed to achieve them. On the other hand, the inquiry revealed that practitioners were generally receptive to adopting a new approach and acknowledged the importance of being supported by updated scientific evidence. Silva and Lind (2020) pointed out that overcoming constraints of time and resources for conducting proper evaluations should be an objective for those involved in planning initiatives and policies.

Solutions to prevent crime are diverse in their approaches, theoretical frameworks, methodologies and scopes. A classification from prevention science divides initiatives into universal, selective and indicated. Universal prevention targets the general population and addresses individual, social and situational factors known as causes or correlates of criminal activity. Selective prevention initiatives target those individuals or groups identified as at risk of committing a crime and typically address more specific factors in the target group. Conversely, indicated prevention works with individuals who have already committed a crime and is directed at preventing reoffending. In the P/CVE and radicalisation field, interventions can focus, for example, on the school population of adolescents between 14 and 16 (universal prevention), groups of adolescents between 16 and 18 in areas with a high level of radicalised individuals (selective prevention) or on those imprisoned for committing violent extremist acts (indicated prevention). P/CVE initiatives may work to hinder the impact of factors such as dysfunctional or inexistent family bonds, justification of violence, political grievances, and recruitment by deviant networks (for example, Wolfowicz et al, 2022). Initiatives and policies may focus on deradicalising beliefs (ideological deradicalisation) or behaviour (disengagement) (Koehler, 2017). Furthermore, they may target enhancing media literacy, political engagement, social skills, social cohesion, integration and self-esteem. Educational-based programmes and mentorship are frequently selected as a general approach.

The efficiency of P/CVE initiatives and policies has been considered unclear in the past (Gielen, 2017), but there have been increased efforts to advance EBP in the field. There are certain methodological difficulties when measuring the effect of such initiatives and policies. Saghal (2018) points out that these difficulties are related to various factors. To begin with, any prevention-oriented intervention (if efficacious) works with non-events. Therefore, evaluating its impact is challenging. The measurement of indicators, in such cases, is entirely hypothetical since it assumes the problem has a level of incidence that, if the initiative works, will not be true. Second, the interconnected web of factors happening in complex environments, as frequently occurs in the case of individuals at risk of radicalisation and violent extremist behaviour, makes it difficult to demonstrate attribution and causality. In this regard, determining what works and what does not is susceptible to being confounded by many variables. Furthermore, in P/CVE and radicalisation, many actors may be involved. When resources for evaluation are limited, it may be challenging to determine who to include when it is impossible to include everyone. Another methodological difficulty relates to when measuring P/CVE initiatives' effects is more appropriate since many are designed for long-term purposes. There are also challenges related to the reliability of the data since, on many occasions, evaluating P/CVE initiatives relies on self-report. There is always a shadow of compromised reliability when dealing with this type of data.

Across Europe, there has been a movement from different organisations to sit practitioners, policy makers and researchers at the same table to discuss and overcome these difficulties and other problems concerning P/CVE so we can move towards settling EBP in the field effectively. For instance, through the Horizon 2020 programme, the European Commission funded the INDEED project, a European consortium constituted to develop an evidence-based model for P/CVE evaluation. The project provides a practical tool tailored for use by various frontline practitioners and policy makers and an open-access repository of documents on factors and pathways leading to preventing social radicalisation.[1] The project has also provided policy recommendations concerning the design, implementation and evaluation of P/CVE and radicalisation initiatives. Moreover, it promotes in-person and e-learning courses and training materials for practitioners and policy makers.

The European Commission also annually funds the Radicalisation Awareness Network (RAN), facilitating the exchange of knowledge, first-hand experiences and approaches to P/CVE among frontline practitioners.² This platform offers a repository housing numerous documents, from general information about violent extremism and radicalisation to more specific guidelines, toolkits and instructions for implementing certain initiatives. As of autumn of 2023, the platform also publicises and promotes expert meetings, training sessions, workshops, conferences and summits, where specific training for some intervention approaches and forums for discussing the state of play regarding evaluating initiatives, ethical guidelines in P/CVE, and legal and policy challenges are offered. Moreover, the RAN facilitates learning and discussions on various themes pertaining to individual, social, technological and other factors essential to consider in violent extremism and radicalisation.

At a national level, some countries have established their own organisations. For example, the Swedish Center for Preventing Violent Extremism was created in 2018 under the auspices of the Swedish National Council for Crime Prevention to serve as a knowledge hub to support local actors.³ Based in The Hague (Netherlands), the International Centre for Counter-Terrorism is an independent foundation established in 2010 due to an initiative that originated in the Dutch parliament. The centre provides research, policy advice and training to enhance counter-terrorism policies and practices worldwide, with a particular focus on Europe, the Middle East and Africa.⁴

Overview of the book

The book aims to give the reader a comprehensive perspective on EBP applied to the P/CVE field. In addition to including technical chapters that specifically address issues related to the design and evaluation of initiatives, we found it essential to frame this work theoretically and epistemologically, revealing the fundamental principles underlying such practice. Furthermore, we illustrate the pillars of EBP by demonstrating how evidence is generated, the complexities of professional expertise, and the necessity of considering the stakeholders' values and preferences. Finally, on the one hand, we discuss the possible contribution of the academic community to P/CVE evidence-based practice, while on the other, we critically highlight eventual biases introduced by academic and political discourses on violent extremist organisations.

Theoretical and epistemological framework

In the first part of the book, we explore and discuss the input of various areas of knowledge to the constitution of P/CVE as a unique discipline. In this regard, we positioned P/CVE within the broader domain of crime prevention, which, in turn, is situated within the broader framework of problem-solving criminology (see Figure 0.1). This approach defines P/CVE as a problem-solving activity that focuses on violent extremism and radicalisation with the specific purpose of preventing harm to individuals and communities.

In Chapter 1, the theoretical and conceptual groundings of crime prevention are presented. It discusses crime and its causes and offers a historical perspective of how communities have sought to protect themselves against it. The author offers an overview of historical changes in the perspective of 'control' and 'treatment' as measures to prevent all types of crime. The state's role in crime prevention efforts is featured. Criminological theories are introduced as they offer a foundation for understanding criminality and the crime problems ultimately targeted for prevention. Understanding criminological theory is the base for developing rational programme theories and theories of change. Moreover, the chapter analyses the concept of crime prevention and the academic definitions that have dominated and evolved to include all those actions that focus on the mechanisms that cause crime to change, situations in which crime is more likely to happen, and how individuals' motivation to commit crime can shift. Current definitions of crime prevention also include reducing fear of crime and its harmful effects. The author proposes a typology based on the level at which the preventative actions operate (that is, primary, secondary and tertiary) and the mechanisms they target. The mechanisms can either centre on internal and external control aspects for crime commission or opportunities that facilitate it. On the other hand, these mechanisms can instead focus on minimising the harm caused by crime.

Figure 0.1: Epistemological contextualisation of preventing and countering violent extremism

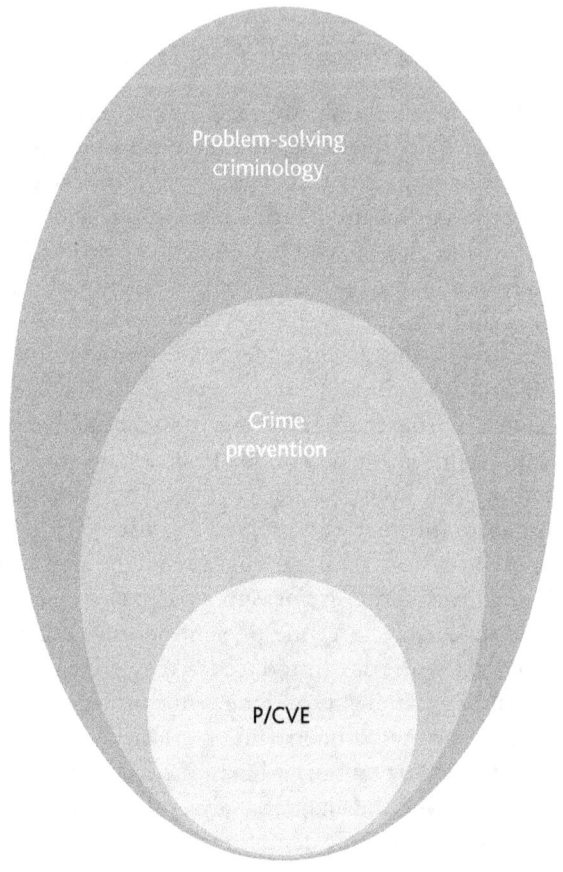

In Chapter 2, an epistemological framework for evidence-based crime prevention and, consequently, for evidence-based P/CVE is proposed. The framework identifies converging areas of knowledge and the diversity of conceptual approaches, methods and theories that contribute to the discipline. The authors situate crime prevention (and P/CVE) at the intersection of three scientific disciplines: design science, prevention science, and the joint group of behavioural and social sciences. Each of these disciplines adds to the unique body of knowledge that constitutes problem-solving criminology, which underlies all efforts to prevent crime.

On one hand, design science delineates a systematic rationale to solve problems. It establishes the process of designing solutions that, in the case of P/CVE, may eventually involve addressing individual antisocial behaviour, social dysfunction or other preventative mechanisms. As the authors see it, the approach to designing a solution parallels that of designing a product. On the other hand, given that the problem for which a solution is sought is none other than crime, the field draws upon theories and research methods from behavioural and social sciences. Finally, prevention science provides a methodology for translating the knowledge produced in academic settings and research centres into practical field applications. The authors delineate the various stages that an initiative's design, implementation and evaluation should follow, from the initial stages of translating basic science into programme theories to the final stages of implementation scale-up and policy change in the making of EBP.

Designing, implementing and evaluating preventing and countering violent extremism initiatives

The second part of the book shifts focus from the general crime prevention framework to specifically address P/CVE and radicalisation initiatives' design and evaluation processes. Significant emphasis is placed on 'programme theory', considered the core of any initiative. Programme theory is an explicit conceptualisation or model of the initiative's working mechanisms. Programme theory explains how and why the chosen activities yield the specific results proposed in the objectives. As Funnell and Rogers (2011) indicated, programme theory should be thoughtfully and strategically developed, represented and used in ways that suit the crime problem and situation. Ultimately, intermediate outcomes are proposed in a sequential chain of reactions that produce the intended results. Programme theory makes explicit the contribution of each link in the chain. It is the basis for accurately interpreting the evaluation results and distinguishing between implementation failure (that is, the expected results were not achieved because the initiative was not implemented according to the implementation design and instructions) and theory failure (when the instructions were followed according to the plan, the initiative was implemented as it should, but it still failed). Knowing what did not work allows those who developed the initiative to propose improvements. Observing failure without understanding what has failed would most likely lead to discarding the work and starting from the beginning.

Programme theory experienced a surge in the 1960s with the work of Suchman, who defended the necessity of adopting a scientific approach to evaluation. According to Suchman (1967), every evaluation should test the hypothesis 'that activity A will attain objective B because it is able to influence process C, which affects the occurrence of this objective. Understanding all three factors—program, objective, and intervening process—is essential to the conduct of evaluation research' (p 177). The logic framework approach, a version of programme theory, was developed later and intended to be used not only in evaluation but also in the initiatives' design (Practical Concepts Incorporate, 1979). The logic framework approach standardises the causal chain into four components:

1. activities, that is, what the initiative does with the resources;
2. outputs, meaning what the initiative 'produces' that others use;
3. purpose, or what is the same, the medium-term outcomes resulting from the use of outputs; and
4. goal, that is, the long-term outcomes resulting from the purpose.

A linear template of five components was developed to display the logic framework (WK Kellogg Foundation, 2004), and it has been widely used for interventions' development and evaluation. The five components are inputs, activities, outputs, outcomes and impact. Impact is defined as the result of the intervention for the broader community beyond the result that it eventually had on those directly targeted and participating in its activities.

Considering these technical aspects, Chapter 3 thoroughly outlines the development of a comprehensive, long-term, evidence-based programme to prevent radicalisation that leads to hate speech. Through this particular example, the author introduces a systematic approach to designing initiatives and explains the design process based on programme theory. The concepts of 'theory of change' and 'logic model' are explained and discussed. The author exemplifies the step-by-step development of a logic model for EBP and debates the importance of standardisation in the design and implementation of initiatives.

Chapter 4 focuses on evaluation procedures and all the technical aspects associated with them. In this case, the author discusses the importance, role and functions of evaluation and details the process of designing and conducting evidence-based evaluations. The differences between 'evaluation' and 'evidence-based evaluation' are explained to the reader, as well as the distinction between 'peer review', 'measurement', 'assessment' and 'evaluation'. Attention is given to the relationship between objectives and indicators when measuring the progress of the initiative's evaluation.

The three pillars of evidence-based practice

In the third part of the book, we selected writings to highlight the three pillars of EBP. As previously indicated, EBP relies on the most current scientific knowledge (first pillar), the expertise of practitioners and decision-makers (second pillar) and considers the values and preferences of participant stakeholders (third pillar). It is out of the scope of this book to explain the different methods used to generate evidence, endow the reader with expertise that comes with years of field experience, discuss the values and preferences of individuals and groups potentially targeted by P/CVE initiatives or the stakeholders involved in their design and implementation. Instead, we deemed it more appropriate to illustrate these aspects with real examples.

Regarding the first pillar, systematic reviews and meta-analyses are important sources of evidence for initiative developers and policy makers. In the field of crime prevention, the Campbell Collaboration is a critical resource available to all. The Campbell Collaboration promotes the production and use of systematic studies. Campbell's systematic reviews focus on synthesising evidence from association studies (risk factors for criminal behaviour) and analyses of interventions' effects, typically randomised trials and high-quality quasi-experimental studies. As of September 2023, 64 systematic reviews in the field of crime and justice, including four specifically focused on violent extremism and radicalisation, were listed on the Campbell Collaboration website. However, the field has generated significantly more extensive work. For example, searching for systematic reviews using the terms 'radicalisation' or 'violent extremism' on PsychoInfo produced 22 other results. The studies mainly focused on the analysis of risk and protective factors (nine studies), psychology of violent extremism (six studies) and risk assessment (three studies). Only two studies analysed prevention strategies but did not specifically include the analysis of complex initiatives like programmes. One study analysed theoretical developments that explain violent extremism, and finally, one study analysed methodological issues in original studies that measured violent extremism and radicalisation. Evidently, the field still lacks a comprehensive body of systematic evidence on the outcomes and impact of P/CVE initiatives.

In Chapter 5, the reader will find a detailed example of how a systematic review is produced. The authors chose to synthesise the scientific literature on radicalisation processes across community and forensic settings. The study's methodology is explained in detail, along with the results of the literature synthesis, which included 96 articles varying in scientific quality. The chapter is a detailed academic product of high value in understanding various factors underlying radicalisation processes that may be targeted for addressing in initiatives, either isolated or taken together. Studies like the one presented in that chapter provide the most robust foundation for informing programme theory in initiatives and constructing a theory of change, thereby increasing the likelihood of success in P/CVE and radicalisation efforts. The reader will find a discussion on the contributing role of factors such as extremism enhancing attitudes, social influences exposing individuals to extremism, mental health issues, content radicalisation cognitions, and impaired functioning in radicalisation.

The second pillar of EBP centres on professional expertise. For those less familiar with the evidence-based paradigm, the concept of professional expertise might appear to have no place within it. After all, the evidence-based movement was born of the rebellion against decision-making based exclusively on the unstructured judgements of professionals and policy makers. For instance, the first proponents of the evidence-based approach in medicine argued that '[e]vidence-based medicine de-emphasizes intuition, unsystematic clinical experience, and pathophysiologic rationale as sufficient grounds for clinical decision making and stresses the examination of evidence from clinical research' (Guyatt et al, 1992, p 2420). However, the authors also pointed out the importance of accounting for professional judgement, considering it a certain type of (low-level) evidence. In subsequent works, the role of clinical expertise in evidence-based medicine was clarified. Sackett et al indicated:

> By individual clinical expertise, we mean the proficiency and judgement that individual clinicians acquire through clinical experience and clinical practice. Increased expertise is reflected in many ways, but especially in more effective and efficient diagnosis and in the more thoughtful identification and compassionate use of individual patients' predicaments, rights, and preferences in making clinical decisions about their care. (Sackett et al, 1996, p 312)

The concept was further refined to incorporate the unique capacity of professionals to heuristically judge the adequacy of interventions given the specific characteristics of the problem, situation, place and individuals involved, as opposed to a mechanical (algorithmic) approach.

The importance of professional judgement was also recognised in other areas. For instance, risk assessment evolved from relying exclusively on actuarial instruments to incorporating professional judgements in evaluations to improve their accuracy. Scholars and practitioners in criminal justice perceived that professional expertise would provide crucial insights not produced by research studies or actuarial tools, and counting on it while doing risk assessment would improve their practice (for example, Hart et al, 2016).

In Chapter 6, policing, healthcare, education and charity professionals were interviewed to determine their understanding of radicalisation. The author considered these professionals' level of training when specifically working in radicalisation and how they perceived their level of expertise. Curiously, many practitioners, especially those outside the police force, reported a lack of confidence in their ability to do P/CVE work despite receiving annual training. The author discusses a multidisciplinary approach that may enable the necessary competence for these professionals to act. A lesson learned in this chapter is that expertise is not only a matter of knowledge but also a self-perception that may reinforce or hinder practice.

The third pillar of EBP considers stakeholders' values, preferences, needs and the environmental and social context in which the work occurs. P/CVE initiatives and policies are not designed and implemented in a vacuum. They are tailored for individuals with particular characteristics living in a specific area at a given time. Different organisations, institutions and authorities may be involved in its design and implementation. The principles and mechanisms of the initiatives' programme theory may require adjustment and customisation to align with the purpose when a specific group is targeted. Furthermore, evidence may be sparse in some areas of practice or when innovation is required. In such cases, considering the stakeholders' perspective is critical to avoid scholarly paternalism. The stakeholders involved must believe in what they are doing and promoting.

Furthermore, and in addition to ethical concerns, implementing a particular initiative or policy without adequately accounting for gender, race, cultural and religious values and beliefs may lead to its failure. Encouraging participants to adopt the goals of initiatives and policies is facilitated by minimising factors that may cause resistance.

To illustrate the third pillar of EBP, Chapter 7 offers a unique perspective on P/CVE work in the Basque Country, a region affected by political terrorism, especially active during the second half of the past century. The author provides a reflection and analysis on restorative justice and the role of society as a stakeholder in fighting against violent extremism, looking at the duality of prevention and reparation. Restorative justice has the capacity for individual and social reconstruction, contingent upon adopting specific values to work. Recognising the challenges and working to overcome them is advantageous.

Thinking critically about evidence-based practice

The book concludes with a call for thinking critically about EBP and P/CVE. Designing and evaluating initiatives and policies to address crime problems is a creative and collaborative endeavour. Practitioners have firsthand field knowledge and encounter real-life problems, a perspective that scholars often lack. Conversely, scholars are well-versed in theories, methodologies, frameworks and approaches, and have access to sources of information that are typically unfamiliar to most practitioners. Policy makers, in turn, are responsible for decisions that academics and practitioners are not. Effectively transitioning from outdated approaches to an effective EBP implies understanding and respecting each other's professional value and working in close collaboration.

In Chapter 8, the authors revisit the academic world's contribution to EBP in the field of P/CVE and outline the ongoing divide between academia and practice, partly because practitioners mistrust academics. Scholars can offer valuable contributions by closing gaps in practice through implementing multidisciplinary approaches or using appropriate methodologies for designing and evaluating interventions. Furthermore, universities and research centres provide a formal structure for developing knowledge that is difficult to achieve in other ways.

On the other hand, understanding limitations and sources of biases can make EBP more efficient. In this regard, deconstructing preconceived ideas, critically appraising the evidence and re-evaluating mainstream discourses is fundamental. Chapter 9 reflects on these issues, using a case study centred on academic and policy literature regarding a political extremist group. The authors identify biases that inflate and sensationalise the threat that this and similar groups pose to communities. Identifying these biases and their original source and dismantling them based on critical, well-founded argumentation will strengthen the P/CVE EBP.

Notes
1. The outcomes of the INDEED project are available at https://www.indeed project.eu/.
2. Further details about the Radicalisation Awareness Network are provided at https://home-affairs.ec.europa.eu/networks/radicalisation-awareness-network-ran_en.
3. A description of the work developed by the Swedish Center for Preventing Violent Extremism can be found on the webpage https://cve.se/omcve/inenglish.4.44140c6e18408651f69bb1.html.

4   More information about ongoing projects and publications by the International Center for Counter-Terrorism can be found on the website https://www.icct.nl/.

References

Funnell, S.C. and Rogers, P.J. (2011) *Purposeful Program Theory: Effective Use of Theories of Change and Logic Models*, San Francisco: Jossey-Bass.

Gielen, A.J. (2017) 'Evaluating countering violent extremism', in L. Colaert (ed) *Deradicalisation: Scientific Insights for Policy*, Brussels: Flemish Peace Institute, pp 101–15.

Guyatt, G., Cairns, J., Churchill, D., Cook, D., Haynes, B., Hirsh, J., et al (1992) 'Evidence-based medicine: A new approach to teaching the practice of medicine', *Journal of the American Medical Association*, 268(17): 2420–5.

Hart, S.D., Douglas, K.S. and Guy, L.S. (2016) 'The structured professional judgement approach to violence risk assessment: Origins, nature, and advances', in D.P. Boer (ed) *The Wiley Handbook on the Theories, Assessment, and Treatment of Sexual Offending*, Boston: Wiley Blackwell, pp 643–66.

Koehler, D. (2017) *Understanding Deradicalization: Methods, Tools, and Programs for Countering Violence Extremism*, Philadelphia: Routledge.

Practical Concepts Incorporate (1979) *Guidelines for Teaching Logical Framework Concepts*, Washington, DC: Practical Concepts Incorporate. Available from https://pdf.usaid.gov/pdf_docs/pnaec576.pdf [Accessed 17 September 2023].

Sackett, D.L., Rosenberg, W.M.C., Gray, J.A.M., Haynes, R.B. and Richardson, W.S. (1996) 'Evidence-based medicine: What it is and what it isn't', *British Medical Journal*, 312(1): 71–2.

Saghal, G. (2018) 'Monitoring and evaluation for CVE: Strategies from STRIVE II', in S. Zeiger (ed) *Expanding the Evidence Base for Preventing and Countering Violent Extremism: Research Solutions*, Abu Dhabi: Hedayah, pp 71–93. Available from https://hedayah.com/app/uploads/2021/09/File-782018161624.pdf [Accessed 10 September 2023].

Sherman, L.W., Gottfredson, D.C., Mackenzie, D.L., Eck, J.E., Reuter, P. and Bushway, S.D. (1998) 'Preventing crime: What works, what does not, what is promising', *Research in Brief: National Institute of Justice*, July: 1–19.

Silva, T. and Lind, M. (2020) 'Experiences of the member states performing evaluations in projects and activities aimed at crime prevention', *MIUN Studies in Criminology No. 1*. Available from https://miun.diva-portal.org/smash/record.jsf?pid=diva2%3A1437033&dswid=5684 [Accessed 5 June 2024].

Strauss, S.E., Richardson, W.S., Glasziou, P. and Haynes, R.B. (2005) *Evidence-Based Medicine: How to Practice and Teach EBM* (3rd edn), New York: Elsevier/Churchill Livingstone.

Suchman, E.A. (1967) *Evaluation Research*, New York: Russell Sage Foundation.

WK Kellogg Foundation (2004) *Logic Model Development Guide*, Michigan: WK Kellogg Foundation. Available from https://www.nj.gov/state/assets/pdf/ofbi/kellogg-foundation-logic-model-development-guide.pdf [Accessed 17 September 2023].

Wolfowicz, M., Hasisi, B. and Weisburd, D. (2022) 'What are the effects of different elements of media on radicalization outcomes? A systematic review', *Campbell Systematic Reviews*, 18: e1244.

PART I

Theoretical and epistemological framework

1

Criminological aspects of crime prevention

Jerzy Sarnecki

Introduction

Crime-related issues consistently feature in public debate worldwide, making crime prevention a constantly relevant topic. However, there is little consensus on what crime prevention means or its most effective methods. This book is about the prevention of violent extremism and radicalisation or, in other words, the prevention of extremes. However, measures aimed at preventing extremism do not differ, in any significant way, from general crime prevention measures. This applies even if all extremist actions are not criminalised in the same way that all deviant behaviour is not punishable. In this chapter, crime prevention is conceptualised in broader terms. Individual worldviews heavily influence the question of which methods lead to crime reduction. For instance, those leaning politically right often advocate for moral integrity and stricter punishments as deterrents, while supporters of liberal or left-wing ideologies emphasise the preventative effects of social interventions and collective solutions. This political polarisation often invites scepticism towards research in this field, posing challenges for objective discussion about crime prevention methods.

Historically, crime prevention has been associated with efforts within the judicial system. Utilitarians such as Beccaria (1764/

1995) and Bentham (1789/1988), often regarded as fathers of our modern legal system, saw crime prevention as the objective of the penal system. Beccaria believed that crime prevention is more important than punishment and that general deterrence is the only acceptable motive for punishment. According to Beccaria, punishment should deter crime, not serve society's desire for revenge. However, general deterrence is one of many approaches to crime prevention discussed today. For example, recent legislation in Sweden (Swedish Ministry of Justice, 2022) entrusts local municipalities with crime prevention. In Sweden, the state, not the local self-government, oversees the police and judiciary. The municipalities' crime prevention responsibility will, therefore, not be about policing or other measures within the judicial system but instead include efforts such as social services, schools and leisure activities.

This chapter aims to discuss definitions of crime prevention and develop a typology of its various measures. The key question is what measures should be included in the concept of prevention. We also discuss the state's role in crime prevention efforts and historical shifts in perspectives on treatment as a crime prevention method. The latter part of the chapter discusses the consequences of criminological theories on the causes of crime for crime prevention.

The state's responsibility for crime prevention

According to Beccaria (1764/1995) and Bentham (1789/1988), the state, through the legal system, has the main responsibility for crime prevention. This idea traces back to the 'original agreement' that citizens historically made with representatives of power. Historically, people sought protection in cities, an arrangement we can still observe in medieval architecture when flying at low altitudes over southern Europe. We can see castles and churches atop hills, with many small buildings huddled close to these two main types of buildings often within a defensive wall. These small houses seem to climb up the hill to get as close as possible to the castle. The rationale behind this architectural arrangement is simple – people flocked to the ruler's dominion for protection from threats like marauding bandits and hostile armies. According to civilisation researcher Norbert Elias (1939/2000), this patronage was not unconditional. The ruler, whether a prince, city or state, dictated that subjects must adhere to the city's laws, a requirement that imposed restrictions on their freedom in terms of conforming behaviour, work performed and tax payments.

Thus, one could argue that protection was the original function of organised state power – protection against external and internal enemies. The modern state has two institutions that fulfil this role: the army and the legal system. As is known, state formations have a different character, sparking intense political debates about the responsibilities of the modern state. The disagreement is usually between the supporters of the welfare state, who believe that the state should have many duties, such as public health and education, and the supporters of a state with as few duties as possible. However, even the supporters of a minimalist state believe that the state should be responsible for justice and external defence. Yet, in many parts of the world there is a trend towards privitisation in parts of these two basic sectors.

Thus, the 'original agreement' between the subjects and power still applies and power (now usually the national state) still has the primary responsibility for the protection of citizens. In a modern state, the judicial system's role is to prevent crime so that citizens are not harmed. If that fails, the state must try to mitigate the damage caused by crime by, among other things, dispensing justice. Such a provision exists in the legislation of many countries, as evident in the Swedish Police Act (Swedish Code of Statutes, 1984:387) and the laws on victims' rights (Swedish Crime Victim Compensation Authority, 2023).

Definitions

The growing interest in crime prevention in recent decades has resulted in many publications addressing how crime prevention should be defined. For example, Ekblom (1994) defines crime prevention as 'interventions in mechanisms that cause crime' (p 194).

However, Wikström and colleagues (1994) define crime prevention as 'measures that reduce the individual's propensity to commit crimes or that reduce the incidence of criminogenic situations' (p 20).

In a later work, Wikström and colleagues (1997) propose the following definition: '[Crime prevention encompasses] interventions in mechanisms (measures) that in the short- or long-term lead to a reduction in the number of crimes by (1) reducing the individual's propensity to commit crimes or (2) reducing the occurrence of situations that contribute to the individual's motivation to commit crime' (p 18). More recently, researchers have also begun to include the prevention of fear of crime in their definition of crime prevention. In the eighth edition of his book *Crime Prevention: Approaches, Practices, and Evaluations*, Lab (2012) proposes the following definition: 'Crime prevention means all measures aimed at reducing the actual level of crime and/or the perceived fear of crime' (p 27).

The fear of crime is a serious social problem that affects many people's lives (Heber, 2007). Nevertheless, we must consider whether measures that reduce the fear of crime can logically belong in a definition of crime prevention. If we include measures against fear in this definition, which, in my view, is reasonable, the question arises as to why other harm caused by crime should not also be included.

In her study on crime prevention as a concept and social phenomenon, Sahlin (2000) emphasises that contemporary discourse influences which measures are perceived as preventive. As this discourse evolves, there is a shift in the meaning of the concept of prevention to include new goals considered urgent today. Given the current focus on victims' issues, it is reasonable that the definition of crime prevention should include measures that minimise all harm caused by crime, including the fear of crime.

Thus, the definition of crime prevention proposed by Sarnecki (2004) is based on Lab's definition but includes all harm caused by crime, as follows: 'Crime prevention are measures and conditions that reduce the likelihood of crime being committed and/or reduce the harmful effects of crime' (p 19).

This is a broad definition, which includes measures to prevent crime and prevent or, alternatively, reduce harm caused by crime. Factors that prevent crime and damages resulting from crimes that do not have the character of measures, such as individual characteristics or social conditions, are also included in the definition.

In modern definitions of crime prevention, including damage caused by crime is common. The United Nations Office on Drugs and Crime (UNODC, 2023) uses the following definition taken from the United Nations Economic and Social Council Resolution 2002/13 (ECOSUC, 2002): 'Crime prevention encompasses strategies and measures aimed at reducing the risk of crime occurring and their potentially harmful effects on individuals and society, including fear of crime, by intervening to influence their many causes' (p 9).

Similarly, the European Crime Prevention Network (EUCPN, nd) defines crime prevention as '[e]thically acceptable and evidence-based activities aimed at reducing the risk of crime occurring and its harmful consequences with the ultimate goal of working to improve the quality of life and safety of individuals, groups and communities' (p 2).

In contrast to Sarnecki, the UN and EUCPN definitions refer only to intentional crime prevention measures and not to the processes that lead to crime reduction resulting from unintentional events. Like Lab, the UN definition specifically mentions fear of crime as an important aspect of damage caused by crime. The EUCPN's definition underlines the ethical and humanistic aspects of crime prevention and points out that crime prevention measures must be evidence-based and thus provide the conditions for success.

Focusing on harm caused by crime also has a practical advantage. It facilitates crime problem mapping and evaluation of the measures taken, using the Cambridge Crime Harm Index (Sherman et al, 2016). This index assigns weights to different crimes according to the estimated harm they cause. This means that crimes can be specified with one measure instead of separate measures for each crime category.

A crime prevention typology

Criminologists Cohen and Felson (1979) based their Routine Activity Theory on the assumption that the character of crime in society is determined by its everyday routines; thus, changes in routine activities lead to changes in crime. They outlined three prerequisites for a crime to occur:

1. a motivated offender;
2. a suitable object; and
3. the lack of capable guardians.

The Routine Activity Theory is a good starting point for crime prevention thinking. Crime can be prevented by eliminating one (or more) of the three preconditions for crime.

Sarnecki (2015) reduces these three conditions to two:

1. opportunity; and
2. control.

'Control' here refers to both external social control (Hirschi, 1969) and internal self-control (Gottfredson and Hirschi, 1990), covering Cohen's and Felson's first and third prerequisites for crime. In this line of reasoning, 'opportunity' has a multifaceted meaning, referring partly to the structure of opportunity in terms of the possibility of committing a crime (for example, Clarke, 1995) but also to the possibility of accessing legitimate tools and the possibility of accessing illicit means (Cloward and Ohlin, 1960). Also, Giordano and colleagues' (2013) reasoning about 'hooks for change', that is, opportunities that can give the individual support for a changed lifestyle, is relevant here.

As mentioned earlier, prevention should also include actions that eliminate or reduce harm caused by crime and are aimed at dispensing justice. The crime prevention typology proposed in this chapter contains three parts:

1. measures aimed at increasing external and internal prosocial control and decreasing antisocial control;
2. measures that reduce opportunities for crime and increase opportunities for a prosocial life;
3. measures to eliminate or reduce the harm caused by crime and provide justice for victims.

The three types of preventive measures can be implemented at three different levels,

- primary prevention (general measures);
- secondary level (measures aimed at at-risk individuals and risk objects);
- tertiary prevention (measures to prevent recidivism and repeat victimisation).

Sarnecki (2015) developed the typology of crime prevention measures depicted in Table 1.1.

Control

This section discusses crime prevention aspects of different types of control at the primary, secondary and tertiary levels. The crime prevention effects of control are well-researched in criminology (for example, Hirschi, 1969; Gottfredson

Table 1.1: Typology of crime prevention measures

	Measures aimed at increasing external and internal prosocial control and decreasing antisocial control	Measures that reduce opportunities for crime and increase opportunities for a prosocial life	Measures to eliminate or reduce damage caused by crime and provide justice to victims
Primary	For example, general deterrence	For example, electronic locks on cars	For example, different types of insurance
Secondary	For example, home visiting programme for vulnerable families	For example, monitoring of vulnerable objects	For example, information about risks of victimisation in connection with alcohol consumption
Tertiary	For example, treatment programmes in prisons	For example, defect programmes for gang members	For example, economic compensation to the victims

and Hischi, 1990; Sampson and Laub, 1993; Laub and Sampson, 2003). In research, one usually talks about different types of control, such as external (control exercised by the social environment) and internal (self-control which is the internalisation of external control), formal control (exercised by representatives of authorities) and informal control (exercised by the social environment). Sarnecki and Carlsson (2021) also write about vertical (exercised by different kinds of superiors) and horizontal control (exercised by equals, for instance, in a group of young people). In this chapter, we assume (in opposition to Hirschi, 1969) that control does not always have prosocial effects (for example, vertical control can be exercised by a Nazi state or by gang leaders, horizontal control can transfer to antisocial norms, values and patterns of action).

Crime prevention using punishment

Threats of punishment can be counted among the previously discussed elements of formal control. This partly refers to general deterrence, an external, primary form of control that eventually turns into self-control in many individuals. In this section, we will also discuss the crime prevention effects of incapacitation, a measure that limits an individual's freedom and thus reduces the individual's ability to commit crimes.

As mentioned earlier, punishment is expected to have a deterrent effect. Through transparent legislation in which various punishments (for instance, infliction of pain, Bentham, 1789/1988) were linked to criminal acts, as well as examples of actual punishment of those individuals who have broken the law, the utilitarians[1] considered that it was possible to maintain obedience to the law. Scholars who further developed these ideas (for example, Träskman, 1984) believe that the general deterrent effects of punishment are related to three elements: severity of the sanction; probability of the sanction; and immediacy of the sanction. Severe punishments alone cannot be expected to affect criminality to a great extent if the likelihood that the crimes will be solved and punished is low and if the penalty is not in temporal connection to the crime (for example, Nagin, 2013). The difficulty here is that increasing the penalty is often politically easy while meeting the other requirements for the effectiveness of the punishment is much more difficult.

However, general prevention is not the only preventive effect of punishment. Punishment can also be expected to have individual effects on the person being sentenced (tertiary prevention). It is usually expected that punishment will discourage the individual from committing further crimes, and certain sorts of sanctions, especially for young people, are designed to deter further crime. These punishments include, among other things, boot camps[2] where young people are subjected to tough military training to deter further crime. However, the effectiveness of that kind of deterrent is questionable (Villettaz et al, 2014).

Another tertiary effect of limitations on freedom is so-called incapacitation. This applies primarily to admissions to various 'Total institutions' (Goffman, 1961), such as prisons, juvenile detention centres or compulsory care in mental hospitals. Even different types of surveillance that limit an individual's freedom have a certain incapacitating effect.

In the literature (for example, Sarnecki, 2015), a distinction is usually made between two forms of incapacitation, general and selective. General incapacitation refers to all individuals sentenced to custodial measures. A general increase in the length of prison sentences increases incapacitation, which leads to fewer cases of recidivism. Such effects have been investigated through natural experiments in Sweden, for instance, when a mandatory release after serving half of a prison sentence was converted to mandatory release after two-thirds of the sentence was served (Ahlberg, 1990). It should be stressed that the effect of general incapacitation is not linear, that is, the number of offences does not decrease proportionately to increasing prison time, regardless of how much the prison time increases. The effects of incapacitation per unit of time are greatest, with small increases in penalties. The greater the increase in sentence length, the smaller the effect per unit of time since crime decreases with increasing age among those convicted (Farrington, 1986). The older a prisoner is, the lower the likelihood that the individual will reoffend after release.

Selective incapacitation means incapacitating individuals with the highest relapse risks (Greenwood, 1982). That kind of incapacitation, purely theoretically, provides opportunities to reduce recidivism without increasing the prison population. The problem, in this case, is the difficulties it implies in predicting recidivism and ethical concerns about punishing crimes that the individual has not (yet) committed.

Treatment

Treatment can be a secondary or tertiary form of prevention. Historically, utilitarians like Bentham (1789/1988) have discussed the possibility of influencing the prisoner's morale during the sentence period. The prison construction proposed by Bentham (the panopticon) would provide opportunities for various morale-influencing activities. This idea has evolved in recent decades, with prison stays often incorporating measures to influence prisoners' propensity to commit crimes. This involves, for example, education and different treatment types adapted to the inmate's needs.

However, optimism regarding the possibilities of preventing crime through different treatment measures decreased sharply when the effects of such measures began to be evaluated. In a classic article from 1974, Martinson asks, 'What works? Questions and answers about prison reform' regarding prison treatment programmes. He answers that, with few exceptions, the treatment programmes he investigated have had no demonstrable effects on recidivism. Martinson believed that his discovery, that prison does not have rehabilitative effects, should lead to less use of the prison sentence in the future. However, his results were interpreted as support for theses of 'tougher measures' and a greater push for incapacitation and deterrence (Miller, 1989).

Lipton and colleagues (1975) were commissioned by the United States Academy of Sciences to review American treatment projects from 1945 to 1967. It turned out that most of these projects were evaluated using low-quality methods or not at all. After excluding all substandard evaluations, 231 studies remained. The analysis covered many different forms of treatment, such as counselling, psychiatric treatment, psychological therapy, various group therapies and social support. This approach was much broader than that of Martinson, who only studied treatment in prisons. But the results were similar. Lipton and others found no significant effects on relapse in most of these projects. Wright and Dixon (1977) and Gensheimer and colleagues (1986) reviewed treatment projects from the mid-1960s (where Lipton and colleagues' review ends) until the mid-1980s. The results were equally disappointing. Most evaluations were flawed, and few indicated a positive effect among those with an acceptable methodological level. Perhaps most disappointingly, the more careful an evaluation was, the less likely the results showed that the interventions reduced relapses (Lab, 2012). Nor does the review of Scandinavian projects carried out by Bondeson in 1974 and Kyvsgaard in 1978 provide a different conclusion.

It could be said that Martinson's article from 1974 and the subsequent results regarding the ineffectiveness of the treatment projects came at the right time in the ongoing debate about society's reaction to crime. They have, therefore, had a significant impact (Pratt et al, 2011). Criticism of these treatment projects was not limited to the lack of evidence of effectiveness but also had a philosophical, not to say ideological, character in terms of legal philosophy. One of the earliest critics of treatment in the Nordic countries was Christie (1960), who argued that Norwegian institutions for treating alcoholism had the character of prisons. The Finnish researcher and later Minister of Justice Anttila (1967) criticised the treatment of offenders for lack of legal certainty. Anttila also pointed out that the treatment approach in this system requires that the individual's delinquency be perceived as something sick. According to Anttila, this assumption must be false when self-report surveys show that most people (especially young people) commit crimes.

The Swedish case

In Sweden, the treatment ideology has gained more influence than in many other countries. According to Träskman (1984), the Swedish criminal code of 1864 was based on the classical school of criminal law, where punishment was proportionate to the harmfulness of the offence. Over time, the classical approach was increasingly abandoned, and the penalties individualised. Interest shifted from the criminal act to the criminal's need for treatment (Träskman, 1984).

A report by a group of young Swedish lawyers (Swedish National Council for Crime Prevention, 1977), titled 'New penal system', had a considerable impact on the Swedish discourse. This report advocated that the principle of justice and proportionality between crime and punishment should apply without looking sideways at the offender's unique treatment needs. It suggested that the treatment ideology creates legal uncertainty and that the penalties are vague and outlined, unrelated to the crimes, and unforeseeable.

This view largely coincides with the classical school of criminal law and has also been termed neoclassicism (Bondeson, 1978). It has also attracted criticism, arguing, among other things, that it rejects the humanist view of the criminal. Yet, advocates of the 'new penal system' counter that plain language in the administration of justice does not necessarily imply 'tougher measures'. On the contrary, they argue punishment can be more humane and lenient than treatment.

The previously referenced criticism resulted in substantial amendments to the Swedish Criminal Code in 1988. Before the reform, the following was provided regarding the choice of penalties by the court, '[w]hen choosing a sanction, the court must, with due regard for what is required to maintain general obedience to the law, pay special attention to the fact that the sanction must be suitable to promote the convict's adjustment in society' (Swedish Code of Statutes [SFS] 1962:700, Chapter 1, Section 7).

After the reform, when all the provisions concerning penalty choices were gathered in Chapters 29 and 30, the wording is as follows:

> Penalties shall be determined, in the interests of uniform application of the law, within the applicable scale of penalties according to the penal value[3] of the offence or the crime. In assessing the value of the penalty, particular account shall be taken of the harm, violation or danger caused by the act, of what the accused knew or ought to have known about it, and of the intentions or motives he had. (Swedish Code of Statutes [SFS] 1988:942)

The judicial reform described earlier thus reduces the direct link between the court's choice of sanction and crime prevention. Although the law still aims to some extent to prevent crime, courts must no longer take preventive considerations into account when choosing sanctions. Instead, penalties should correspond to the offence's severity, that is, harm caused by the crime and the offender's intent.

The gentle return of treatment

Treatment designed for crime prevention is more prevalent in social services, psychiatry and substance abuse care than in corrections. This is usually conducted voluntarily, though treatment is sometimes based on coercive legislation, including within social services.

As noted earlier, Martinson's 1974 article became the starting point for a massive criticism of treatment measures for, among other things, their lack of effectiveness and legal certainty. Just five years later, however, Martinson (1979) nuanced his position and pointed out that there were treatment programmes that gave positive results, but by then, the perception that treatment lacked effects was already widespread. This new article did not attract as much attention as the previous one.[4]

Despite the previously mentioned negative results, various types of treatment continued, some of which have been evaluated in a scientifically acceptable way. As new results have emerged and new meta-analyses have been conducted, the perspective started to shift. First, it has been pointed out that recidivism cannot be the sole criterion for assessing treatment outcomes.[5] Palmer (1975) had previously argued that relapse is a very rough measure of the effectiveness of a treatment programme. According to him, it is also important to investigate whether offences have the same character, whether the offences are equally serious, and whether any offence-free periods between offences have become longer.

Baker and Sadd (1981) evaluated the attempts to prevent further crime by helping offenders find work and found no difference in recidivism between those helped into work and the control group. However, there were differences in how the judicial bodies dealt with crimes committed by juveniles targeted by the project versus control youths. The courts took a more lenient view on reoffending among those participating in the programme.

Gradually, however, it has also begun to be realised that it is possible to influence relapses through treatment. For example, Andrews and colleagues (1990) argue that treatment definitely has positive effects on recidivism. However, the requirement is that the treatment is adapted to the needs of the treated individuals. Early intervention is considered to have particularly good prospects for success (Farrington and Welsh, 2006; Farrington and Koegl, 2015).

The author perhaps most often cited as representing the new, more treatment-positive view, is Mark Lipsey. Lipsey's meta-analysis includes approximately 600 evaluation studies that maintain an acceptable methodological standard. The results show that treatment measures aimed at young offenders often have positive effects though they rarely involve dramatic improvements (Lipsey, 1992, 1995).

Today, many researchers claim that treatment can provide the desired results (in Sweden, Daleflod [1996] and Andreasson [2003] have published reviews of such research). The revised perspective on treatment has led to a reformulation of the conclusion that 'nothing works' into the research question 'what works?' At the same time, it must be pointed out that there is no reason to return to the old, naïve approach, which could be expressed as 'everything works'. For instance, it is unlikely that projects lacking a solid theoretical basis, trained staff and structure, and that are of short duration and not based on a thorough analysis of the targeted group needs, could produce relevant results. Scientific evaluations have thus made it possible to identify treatment methods that are proven to work, those that are proven not to work, and those that lack sufficient evidence of their effectiveness but which can be considered promising; as summed up in the title of a report to the US Congress on crime prevention, 'What works, what doesn't, what's promising?' (Sherman et al, 1998).

An important question is how large an effect the treatment has. When treatment was once again considered to have preventive effects, expectations of the effect's size were significantly downplayed. This is due to well-conducted evaluations showing that crime reduction is often less robust than was hoped during the optimistic treatment period.

It must be noted, however, that most treatment evaluations are made by studying the effects of measures using registered crime. Yet, Farrington and Koegl (2015) remind us that most crimes remain unsolved. This means that we can count on at least ten non-registered for each prevented, registered prosecution. In terms of percentage shares, the preventive effects are still relatively small, but the actual number of crimes is significantly greater than they appear from evaluations using register data. Reasoning in this way is critical when making cost-benefit analyses of the effects of treatment measures. According to Welsh and colleagues (2015), when calculating treatment effects, the actual number of prevented crimes should be counted; otherwise, the benefits of treatment interventions could be grossly underestimated.

It should also be emphasised that measures that restrict individual freedom, whether taken for deterrence, incapacitating or treatment purposes, have significant adverse effects on those exposed to them (Travis et al, 2014). For the vulnerable individual, these measures not only restrict freedom, but also entail the risks of being negatively affected by fellow inmates with various problems, as well as the dissolution of social ties with society outside (that is, the family, the workplace and the local community). Dissolving these ties can often mean returning to a 'normal' life after serving a sentence can be very problematic. The claim that imprisonment prioritises society's interests above the interests of the criminal individual is only partially correct, since imprisonment or other restrictions on freedom are often expensive and require resources that society could use for other purposes, such as crime prevention efforts (Travis et al, 2014).

A dynamic approach to treatment

The control dimension of crime prevention thus refers to various aspects of reducing the individual's propensity to commit crimes and can be used in primary, secondary and tertiary prevention. Planning that kind of prevention must address the issue of the causes of crime. This means that crime prevention has a strong connection to criminology, where several theories have been developed over the past 100 years about the causes of crime. Modern theories see crime, like all other behaviour, as a result of the interplay between individual characteristics and social factors (Sarnecki and Carlsson, 2021). To understand crime and be able to propose adequate measures, a dynamic view is required. This involves insight into the continuous evolution of both the individual and society and their interplay. For crime prevention measures to be effective, they must take account of these changes. Thus, measures that can be expected to affect an individual at a particular stage of development may not work at another stage. Preventive methods must be subject to constant development and adaptation to individual and social changes.

One individual is born with certain characteristics while other qualifications are 'pre-programmed' and will manifest later in the life course. The development of the individual is affected by the environment from the beginning (even before birth[6]). The fact that the individual is constantly changing in terms of individual characteristics means that crime prevention measures (which are part of the environmental impact) must be constantly adapted. The overall research in the field (Sarnecki and Carlsson, 2021) indicates that the greatest conditions for success are measures taken early in the life course. There is also evidence that individuals around the age of 20 may again be susceptible to various preventive measures. The most difficult group appears to be teenagers, that is, individuals who, according to the age-crime curve, are at the peak of their criminal activity and in great need of extensive efforts, but who at the same time show poor susceptibility to these.

Opportunity

The realisation that crime can be prevented by influencing the opportunity structure is old. According to Ankerloo and Henningsen (1987), in the 1600s, there were regulations that forbade young boys from herding cattle without adult supervision. This regulation was intended to prevent opportunities for these boys to commit bestiality, a serious crime punishable by death at the time.

An article by Clarke and Mayhew (1988) has gained considerable influence in modern criminological research. The article is not about crime but the change in the number of suicides in the UK between 1963 and 1975. During this period, the total number of suicides decreased drastically. The reason is that household gas became less toxic and could no longer be used to kill oneself. The critical insight is that restricting access to easy means of committing suicide (or crime) reduces the frequency of the act. People are not always inclined to resort to another less accessible way of committing a particular act. Of course, the reduction is most significant for spontaneous acts, also a characteristic common to many crimes.

Situational crime prevention

In general, measures that reduce the opportunity to commit crimes are considered simpler than those affecting the individual's propensity to commit crimes. Among researchers who have contributed to the development of such methods is Felson (1994), who has developed a model for assessing the vulnerability of different objects to crime (the so-called VIVA model). Felson argues that an attack on an object (for instance, a theft attempt) is preceded by a conscious evaluation of the following characteristics of the object: value, inertia, visibility and accessibility. This model can be directly used (and is already widely used) for preventive purposes. By reducing the object's value to the potential perpetrator and making it difficult to move, find and access, we can protect it against attacks.

Over the last few decades, clear progress has been made in this kind of protection of property, particularly for homes and cars. For example, the reduction in car thefts over the past three decades in Europe is attributed to car manufacturers equipping cars with electronic locks since the 1990s, which are much more difficult to force than mechanical locks. It is worth noting that this change was prompted by an EU directive (Commission Directive 95/56/EC), an interesting example of how crime can be influenced by a completely different type of law than criminal law.

The housing sector deserves special attention regarding situational crime prevention. Research shows that relatively simple measures, such as functioning locks on garages and basements, can significantly reduce crime in a residential area (Ringman, 1997).

In general, the architectural design of residential areas has been shown to be important for both crime (mainly burglary) directed against homes and other types of crime that occurs in residential areas, such as vandalism, assault on persons, attacks on cars and basement burglary. In this context, we are talking about crime prevention through environmental design. In 2005, Clarke and Newman published the book *Designing Out Crime from Products and Systems*, showing how architectural and other designs can reduce crime. In Sweden, Ceccato (2019), among others, has conducted this kind of research.

A problem with the excessive use of situational crime prevention is that it can make everyday life more difficult, and conflicts between different groups may increase. Christie (2005) argues that the reduced solidarity between different groups in the population and the increasing gaps associated with such a development eventually lead to increased crime. In many places, for example, so-called gated communities have been built, where those who can afford it live in communities that are closed off from the surroundings with high walls and guarded gates. Gated communities thus only protect the wealthy and lead to increased segregation.

Another area where environmental design can play an important role in preventing crime is the transport environment (Ceccato, 2014). Different technical measures in traffic can reduce crime. This may involve, for example, making access more difficult for unauthorised persons to various places and security devices in the city's subway network or automatic speed cameras on streets and roads.

In general, technical measures may reduce some (traditional) crimes, but some crimes committed are likely to become more violent. If technical barriers cannot be overcome, some criminals may attack 'soft targets' (that is, people, by kidnapping, hostage-taking, extortion and so on) to get money and other desirable things.

Private people are usually motivated to protect their property and careful not to leave unlocked bicycles in the street and to install alarms, door and window locks and other devices on their homes and cars. However, motivation is not always as high among companies, especially larger ones, and the public sector, though various protective measures are also applied there. Examples include technical safeguards against theft in stores and workplaces, anti-fraud mechanisms, and exit controls. Both the private and public sectors are responsible for protecting society's infrastructure (for instance, energy supply, communications and water supply). A large part of the protection of the infrastructure consists of a combination of technical crime protection and various surveillance. Today, such crime prevention measures against profit or ideologically motivated crime are seen as standard in our society.

As the use of various electronic systems increases, so does cybercrime. This applies, for example, to crime directed against various types of transactions, such as the purchase of goods and services, the transfer of money and the like, taking place over the Internet. Another problem of cybercrime concerns information theft and sabotage. A growing problem in this area, which is difficult to prevent in a democratic society, is various forms of disinformation on a political/ideological basis.

Vulnerability in information technology is significant, affecting not only private individuals but also businesses and the public sector. A major reason for this vulnerability is low awareness of the risks and how to protect oneself. For most people today, it is quite easy to understand how to effectively protect real property, for example, by locking up valuable objects. Using different passwords, encryptions, firewalls and the like is much more difficult to assimilate.

Opportunities for prosocial life

Measures to increase opportunities for prosocial life can also be implemented as primary, secondary and tertiary prevention. At the primary level, a free-of-charge school system accessible to everyone in the country can be expected to have preventive effects. This includes free lunches in schools, opportunities for everyone to receive financial aid for further studies, and so on. At the secondary and tertiary level of prevention through education, it is important to lower entry barriers to higher education and offer educational opportunities for adults who did not manage to complete their schooling earlier in life.

Similar effects can be expected from measures that facilitate the integration of young people (with or, in particular, without qualifications) into the labour market. Such measures include different types of traineeships, financial incentives for employers to hire young people and the like. However, we do not know how effective these measures are in crime prevention because evaluations are usually lacking.

Research also shows that young people who participate in, for example, sports activities or non-profit youth organisations are registered less often for crimes than those who do not (Sarnecki, 1983). This does not automatically mean that it is proven that all such activities prevent crime. Likewise, the low recorded crime rate of participants in certain organised leisure activities may be due to selection. Often, the involvement of young people in leisure activities also requires the involvement of parents, both financially and in terms of time, which is not possible in all families.

An important insight regarding opportunities for prosocial life is that the ability to benefit from these opportunities varies between different ages and individuals. Some individuals mature late, meaning that opportunities to stop antisocial life and enter society must also exist for adults. Examples here include activities that help individuals leave extremist groups or criminal gangs.

Preventing damage caused by crime

A clear advantage of including in the definition crime prevention measures that reduce not only crime but also the harm caused by crime is that this definition also includes measures aimed at crime victims. In criminal policy discourse, victims' interests are often pitted against the needs of potential perpetrators. The argument used in such discourse is that the victims' needs may be secondary in this context, such as when implementing interventions targeting potential perpetrators. This thesis is incorrect because effective crime prevention measures protect potential victims. In addition, all crime prevention must also include measures benefiting crime victims.

The simplest way to mitigate the harm caused by crime is to compensate victims financially. On a general, primary level, these are different types of insurance that compensate individuals for their losses due to crime both directly (lost and destroyed property) and indirectly (for example, treatment costs or income loss due to reduced working capacity). Public health insurance, which provides citizens with the necessary medical care and, where appropriate, sickness benefits and other support, is mainly designed to deal with types of illness and injury other than those caused by crime. However, victims of harm caused by crime also receive help within the framework of public health insurance. At the same time, the needs of people harmed by crime may vary, for example, with some requiring more psychological support than other patient groups.

A parallel discussion can be made regarding efforts within social services and other social security systems. In principle, victims are covered by the general schemes, but they may also have special needs. Social security systems must be prepared to deal with these needs.

To minimise damage caused by crime, one must not forget the state's task of administering justice. This is a form of tertiary prevention that many victims of crime and the public consider central. Legal proceedings resulting in the defendant's conviction often provide restitution for the victim. However, the problem in this context is that most crimes do not lead to prosecution, leaving many victims without redress. The challenge is to identify other means beyond increasing crime detection through which victims can receive redress – methods for this need to be developed. One possibility to compensate for the lack of legal process could be to apply reparative justice to a greater extent and for the state to be generous with financial compensation and other forms (psychological and social) of support for victims of unsolved crimes.

Scientific basis for crime prevention

As mentioned earlier in the chapter, the EUCPN definition of crime prevention highlights that crime preventive measures must be evidence-based. Crucially, most measures labelled as crime prevention lack substantial evidence or rely on weak evidence because evaluating crime prevention measures is still not routine. These evaluations, when conducted, seldom meet high scientific standards. It is essential to shift attitudes towards crime prevention, ensuring all such measures are monitored for goal fulfilment by staff and evaluated by external parties wherever possible. It is also important to widely disseminate the results of evaluations so that they are available to those planning new initiatives.

The chances of achieving the goals of preventive projects increase when measures are based on knowledge of the causes of the crimes they aim to prevent, that is, when these measures are informed by criminological theory and empirical research.

Summary

- Preventing crime and harm caused by crime is one of the state's central tasks.
- Traditionally, the legal system is supposed to prevent crime. Currently, crime prevention involves many actors.
- In addition to reducing the number of crimes, the modern definition of crime prevention also refers to minimising harm caused by crime.
- There is no contradiction between preventive measures aimed at potential perpetrators or crime victims.
- Crime prevention measures can be divided into those that increase control (external and internal), those that reduce opportunities for crime and increase opportunities for prosocial life, and those that mitigate harm from unprevented crimes.
- Crime prevention can refer to general measures (primary prevention), those aimed towards at-risk individuals and risk situations (secondary prevention) and those that prevent the recurrence of crime (tertiary prevention).
- Preventive measures must be based on knowledge of the causes of crime.
- It is necessary that crime prevention measures are followed up by those working with them. Preventive measures of principle interest require scientific evaluation.

Suggested directions for future research

- Future research should characterise the effectiveness of methods in crime prevention and identify their mechanisms of action.

- Evaluating the success of crime prevention measures is, of course, a priority, but it is necessary to move from 'what works' to 'why' a certain measure works.
- More research is necessary to identify key (public and private) stakeholders within each type of crime prevention measure classified according to the typologies and how they should coordinate according to their particular competencies to prevent and reduce the harm produced by crime.

Notes

[1] Bentham and Beccaria are considered utilitarians, followers of a philosophical orientation that advocates the pursuit of the greatest possible happiness for the greatest possible number of individuals.
[2] A form of camp with a harsh military regime often used to deter young lawbreakers in, for example, the United States and Great Britain.
[3] The penal value can be translated to offence severity.
[4] Shortly after publishing the article in 1979, Martinson took his own life.
[5] The requirement in several of the meta-analyses has been that the evaluation should be based on comparisons between treatment and control groups to which individuals are randomly allocated or possibly natural experiments.
[6] For example, the central nervous system of the foetus is affected by maternal nutrition (Rain, 2014).

References

Ahlberg, J. (1990) *Inkapacitering: Effekter av Förändrade Strafftider* [*Incapacitation: Effects of Changed Prison Terms*], Stockholm: Brottsförebyggande Rådet.

Andreasson, T. (2003) *Institutionsbehandling av Ungdomar: Vad Säger Forskningen?* [*Institutional Treatment of Adolescents: What Does the Research Say?*], Stockholm: Gothia Förlag.

Andrews, D.A., Zinger, I., Hoge, R.D., Bonta, J., Gendreau, P. and Cullen, F.T. (1990) 'Does correctional treatment work? A clinically relevant and psychologically informed meta-analysis', *Criminology*, 28(3): 369–404.

Ankerloo, B. and Henningsen, G. (1987) *Häxornas Europa 1400–1700: Historiska och Antropologiska Studier* [*The Witches' Europe 1400–1700: Historical and Anthropological Studies*], Stockholm: Institute for Legal History Research.

Anttila, I. (1967) 'Konservativ och radikal kriminalpolitik i Norden' ['Conservative and radical criminal policy in the Nordic countries'], *Nordisk Tidskrift for Kriminalvidenskab*, 3: 237–51.

Baker, S.H. and Sadd, S. (1981) *Diversion of Felony Arrests: An Experiment in Pretrial Intervention: An Evaluation of the Court Employment Project. Summary Report*, New York: Vera Institute.

Beccaria, C. (1764/1995) *Dei Delitti e Delle Pene* [*On Crimes and Punishments*], reprint, Milan: Mursia.

Bentham, J. (1789/1988) *An Introduction to the Principles of Morals and Legislation*, reprint, Amherst: Prometheus.

Bondeson, U.V. (1974) *Fången i Fångsamhället: Socialisationsprocesser vid Ungdomsvårdsskola, Ungdomsfängelse, Fängelse och Internering* [*The Prisoner in the Prison Society: Socialisation Processes at Community Home, Juvenile Prison, Prison, and Detention*], Malmö: P.A. Nordstedt & Söners Förlag.

Bondeson, U.V. (1978) 'Vad är nytt i nytt Straffsystem?' [What's new in the new Penal System?], *Nordisk Tidsskrift for Kriminalvidenskab*, 65(3): 121–46.

Ceccato, V. (2014) 'Ensuring safe mobility in Stockholm, Sweden', *Municipal Engineer*, 168: 74–88.

Ceccato, V. (2019) 'Fieldwork protocol as a safety inventory tool in public places', *Criminal Justice Studies*, 32(2): 165–88.

Christie, A. (2005) *Social Work Education in Ireland: Histories and Challenges*, Huelva: Portularia. Universidad de Huelva.

Christie, N. (1960) *Tvangsarbeid og alkoholbruk* [*Forced Labor and Alcohol Use*], Oslo: Universitetsforlaget.

Clarke, R.V. (1995) 'Situational crime prevention', in M. Tonry and D.P. Farrington (eds) *Building a Safer Society: Strategic Approaches to Crime Prevention*, Chicago: University of Chicago Press, pp 91–150.

Clarke, R.V. and Mayhew, P. (1988) 'The British gas suicide story and its implications for prevention', *Crime and Justice*, 10: 79–116.

Clarke, R.V. and Newman, G.R. (2005) *Designing Out Crime from Products and Systems*, Monsey: Criminal Justice Press.

Cloward, R.A. and Ohlin, L.E. (1960) *Delinquency and Opportunity: A Theory of Delinquent Gangs*, Glencoe: Free Press.

Cohen, L.E. and Felson, M. (1979) 'Social change and crime rate trends: A routine activity approach', *American Sociological Review*, 44(4): 588–608.

Commission Directive 95/56/EC. 'Euratom of 8 November 1995 adapting to technical progress Council Directive 74/61/EEC relating to devices to prevent the unauthorised use of motor vehicles', *Official Journal of the European Communities*, 29 November. Available from https://eur-lex.europa.eu/legal-content/SV/TXT/PDF/?uri=CELEX:31995L0056&from=EN [Accessed 12 September 2023].

Daleflod, B. (1996) 'Är det möjligt att rehabilitera kriminella ungdomar?' ['Is it possible to rehabilitate criminal youth?'], in B.-Å. Armelius, S. Bengtzon, P.-A. Rydelius, J. Sarnecki and K. Söderholm Carpelan (eds) *Vård av Ungdomar med Sociala Problem: En Forskningsöversikt* [*Care of Adolescents with Social Problems: A Research Overview*], Stockholm: Liber Utbildning/SiS, pp 398–38.

ECOSUC (2002) 'UN Economic and Social Council Resolution 2002/13. Action to promote effective crime prevention', *The Economic and Social Council*. Available from www.unodc.org/documents/justice-and-prison-reform/crimeprevention/resolution_2002-13.pdf [Accessed 12 September 2023].

Ekblom, P. (1994) 'Proximal circumstances: A mechanism-based classification of crime prevention', in R.V. Clarke (ed) *Crime Preventions Studies, Vol 2*, Monsey: Criminal Justice Press, pp 185–232.

Elias, N. (1939/2000) *The Civilizing Process: Sociogenetic and Psychogenetic Investigations* (revised edn), Oxford: Blackwell.

EUCPN (nd) 'Crime prevention: European definition', *European Crime Prevention Network*. Available from https://www.eucpn.org/definition-crimeprevention [Accessed 23 September 2023].

Farrington, D.P. (1986) 'Age and crime', *Crime and Justice*, 7: 189–250.

Farrington, D.P. and Koegl, C.J. (2015) 'Monetary benefits and costs of the stop now and plan program for boys aged 6–11: Based on the prevention of later offending', *Journal of Quantitative Criminology*, 31: 263–87.

Farrington, D.P. and Welsh, B.C. (2006) *Saving Children from a Life of Crime: Early Risk Factors and Effective Interventions*, Oxford: Oxford University Press.

Felson, M. (1994) *Crime and Everyday Life: Insights and Implications for Society*, Thousand Oaks: Pine Forge Press.

Gensheimer, L.K., Mayer, J.P., Gottschalk, R. and Davidson, W.S. (1986) 'Diverting youth from the juvenile justice system: a meta-analysis of intervention efficacy', in S.J. Apter and A.P. Goldstein (eds) *Youth Violence: Programs and Prospects*, Elmsford: Pergamon Press, pp 39–57.

Giordano, P.C., Cernkovich, S.A. and Rudolph, J.L. (2013) 'Gender, crime, and desistance: Toward a theory of cognitive transformation', *American Journal of Sociology*, 107(4): 990–1064.

Goffman, E. (1961) *Asylums: Essays on the Social Situation of Mental Patients and Other Inmates*, New York: Anchor Books.

Gottfredson, M.R. and Hirschi, T. (1990) *A General Theory of Crime*, Stanford: Stanford University Press.

Greenwood, P. (1982) *Selective Incapacitation*, Santa Monica, CA: Rand Corporation.

Heber, A. (2007) *Var Rädd om Dig! Rädsla för Brott Enligt Forskning, Intervjupersoner och Dagspress* [*Look after Yourself! Fear of Crime According to Research, Interviewees, and Daily Press*], doctoral dissertation, Stockholm: Stockholm University, Criminology Institute.

Hirschi, T. (1969) *Causes of Delinquency*, Berkeley: University of California Press.

Kyvsgaard, B. (1978) *Straffesystemets Virkning* [*The Effect of the Penal System*], Master's thesis, Copenhagen: Copenhagen University.

Lab, S.P. (2012) *Crime Prevention: Approaches, Practices and Evaluations* (10th edn), Cincinnati: Anderson Publishing Co.

Laub, J.H. and Sampson, J.R. (2003) *Shared Beginnings, Divergent Lives: Delinquent Boys to Age 70*, Cambridge, MA: Harvard University Press.

Lipsey, M.W. (1992) 'Juvenile delinquency treatment: A meta-analytic inquiry into the variability of effects', in T.D. Cook, D.S. Cooper, D.S. Cordray, H. Hartmann, V. Hedges, R.J. Light, et al (eds) *Meta-Analysis for Explanation: A Casebook*, New York: Russell Sage Foundation, pp 83–127.

Lipsey, M.W. (1995) 'What do we learn from 400 research studies on the effectiveness of treatment with juvenile delinquents?', in J. McGuire (ed) *What Works: Reducing Reoffending: Guidelines from Research and Practice*, New York: John Wiley, pp 63–78.

Lipton, D., Martinson, R. and Wilks, J. (1975) *The Effectiveness of Correctional Treatment: A Survey of Treatment Evaluation Studies*, New York: Praeger.

Martinson, R. (1974) 'What works? Questions and answers about prison reform', *Public Interest*, 35: 22–54.

Martinson, R. (1979) 'New findings, new views: A note of citation regarding sentencing reform', *Hofstra Law Review*, 7(2): 243–58.

Miller, J.G. (1989) 'The debate on rehabilitating criminals: Is it true that nothing works?', *The Washington Post*, March. Available from https://www.prisonpolicy.org/scans/rehab.html [Accessed 12 September 2023].

Nagin, D.S. (2013) 'Deterrence: A review of the evidence by a criminologist for economists', *Annual Review of Economics*, 5(83): 84–105.

Palmer, T.B. (1975) 'Martinson revisited', *Journal of Research in Crime and Delinquency*, 12(2): 133–52.

Pratt, T.C., Gau, J.M. and Franklin, T.W. (2011) *Key Ideas in Criminology and Criminal Justice*, Thousand Oaks: SAGE.

Raine, A. (2014) *The Anatomy of Violence: The Biological Roots of Crime*, New York: Vintage Books.

Ringman, K. (1997) 'Brottsförebyggande åtgärder i en förort: Teori och praktik' ['Crime prevention measures in a suburb: Theory and practice'], *Rapport 1997:1*, Stockholm: Stockholm University, Criminology Institute.

Sahlin, I. (2000) *Brottsprevention* [*Crime Prevention*], Lund: Arkiv Förlag.

Sampson, R.J. and Laub, J.H. (1993) *Crime in the Making: Pathways and Turning Points through Life*, Cambridge, MA: Harvard University Press.

Sarnecki, J. (1983) *Fritid och Brottslighet* [*Leisure and Crime*], Stockholm: Brottsförebyggande Rådet.

Sarnecki, J. (2004) *Kunskapsbaserad Brottsprevention: Teoretiska Utgångspunkter för Brottsförebyggande Arbete i Stockholms Stad* [*Knowledge-Based Crime Prevention: Theoretical Foundations for Crime Prevention in the City of Stockholm*], Stockholm: Stockholms Stad.

Sarnecki, J. (2015) *Introduktion till Kriminologi: Straff och Prevention* [*Introduction to Criminology: Punishment and Prevention*] (2nd edn), Malmö: Studentlitteratur.

Sarnecki, J. and Carlsson, C. (2021) *Introduktion till Kriminologi: Straff och Prevention* [*Introduction to Criminology: Punishment and Prevention*] (2nd edn), Malmö: Studentlitteratur.

Sherman, L.W., Gottfredson, D.C., Mackenzie, D.L., Eck, J.E., Reuter, P. and Bushway, S.D. (1998) 'Preventing crime: What works, what does not, what is promising', *Research in Brief. National Institute of Justice*, July: 1–19.

Sherman, L.W., Neyroud, P.W. and Neyroud, E. (2016) 'The Cambridge Crime Harm Index: Measuring total harm from crime based on sentencing guidelines', *Policing: A Journal of Policy and Practice*, 10(3): 171–83.

Swedish Code of Statutes [SFS] 1962:700. *Brottsbalk [Criminal Code]*, The Swedish Parliament.

Swedish Code of Statutes [SFS] 1984:387. *Polislag [Police Law]*, The Swedish Parliament.

Swedish Code of Statutes [SFS] 1988:942. *Lag om Ändringar i Bottsbalken [Law on Amendments in the Swedish Penal Code]*, The Swedish Parliament.

Swedish Crime Victim Compensation Authority [Brottsoffermyndigheten] (2023) *Lagar och Förordningar om Brottsoffers Rättigheter [Laws and Regulations on Victims' Rights]*. Available from https://www.brottsoffermyndighe ten.se/utsatt-for-brott/brottsoffers-rattigheter/ [Accessed 12 September 2023].

Swedish Ministry of Justice (2022) 'Kommuners ansvar för brottsförebyggande arbete [Municipalities' responsibility for crime prevention work], Prop. 2022/23:43' *Regeringskansliet*. Available from https://www.regeringen.se/rattsliga-dokum ent/proposition/2022/12/prop.-20222343/ [Accessed 12 September 2023].

Swedish National Council for Crime Prevention [Brottsförebyggande Rådet] (1977) 'New penal system: Ideas and proposals', *Brå-Rapport 1977:7*, Stockholm: Liber Förlag/Allmänna Förlaget.

Träskman, P.O. (1984) 'Brottspåföljder och brottsmålsförfarandet: rättsutvecklingen i Finland och Sverige under femtio år' ['Criminal sanctions and the criminal procedure: Legal development in Finland and Sweden over fifty years'], *Svensk Juristtidning*, 1: 826–40.

Travis, J., Western, B. and Redburn, S. (eds) (2014) *The Growth of Incarceration in the United States: Exploring Causes and Consequences*, Washington, DC: The National Academies Press.

UNODC (2023) 'Crime prevention', *United Nations Office on Drugs and Crime*. Available from https://www.unodc.org/unodc/ru/justice-and-prison-reform/cpcj-crimeprevention-home.html [Accessed 12 September 2023].

Villettaz, P., Gilliéron, G. and Killias, M. (2014) *The Effects on Re-Offending of Custodial Versus Non-Custodial Sanctions*, Stockholm: Brottsförebyggande Rådet.

Welsh, B.C., Farrington, D.P. and Goven, R.B. (2015) 'Benefit-cost analysis of crime prevention programs', *Crime and Justice*, 44: 447–516.

Wikström, P.-O.H., Ahlberg, J. and Dolmén, L. (1994) *Brott, Brottsprevention och Kriminalpolitik* [*Crime, Crime Prevention, and Criminal Politics*], Stockholm: Brottsförebyggande Rådet.

Wikström, P.-O.H., Torstensson, M. and Dolmén, L. (1997) *Lokala Problem, Brott och Trygghet i Stockholms Län* [*Local Problems, Crime, and Security/Safety in Stockholm County*], Sörentorp: Polishögskolan.

Wright, W.E. and Dixon, M.C. (1977) 'Community prevention and treatment of juvenile delinquency', *Journal of Research in Crime and Delinquency*, 14(1): 35–67.

2

An epistemological framework for evidence-based crime prevention

Teresa C. Silva and Gustav Grut

Introduction

Evidence-based crime prevention is a specialised area of problem-solving criminology. Preventing and countering violent extremism (P/CVE) and radicalisation is the branch of crime prevention specifically dedicated to finding solutions that may prevent or reduce the harm produced by radicalised individuals and their violent extremist acts. In 2020, the European Crime Prevention Network (EUCPN) reunited a group of experts who collaboratively agreed on a definition to establish the framework for professionals and academics working in the field. According to this definition, crime prevention encompasses all those 'ethically acceptable and evidence-based activities aimed at reducing the risk of crime occurring and its harmful consequences with the ultimate goal of working towards the improvement of the quality of life and safety of individuals, groups and communities' (EUCPN, nd, p 2).

At its core, evidence-based crime prevention uses a problem-solving approach. This means that designing initiatives to prevent crime is methodologically analogous to developing prevention actions in other disciplines, such as health or social care. The design process focuses on identified problems and proposes solutions that must be tested before they are applied in the community and orient policy making. A thorough analysis of the problem at hand is the starting point of designing an initiative that accomplishes principles of evidence-based practice. Afterwards, initiative design follows a series of steps and involves loops of development and evaluation until its effectiveness is demonstrated and its implementation is recommended.

Designing crime prevention initiatives is, at a conceptual level, a process similar to developing a new vaccine. Both endeavours involve several compulsory stages. When the world faced the stresses of a new pandemic at the end of 2019 (COVID-19), scientists worldwide initiated intensive research in their labs, analysing the new virus and collecting all the epidemiological information possible about its behaviour in different human and animal groups. Researchers relied on existing knowledge of similar families of viruses and the most advanced practices in vaccine development to create a new product (research discovery stage) with the capacity to protect the population from disease and death (real-world application and dissemination stage). Despite their efforts, the medical community could not prevent millions from becoming infected and hundreds of thousands dying before vaccines were released in December 2020. As of 29 December 2020, there were 79.2 million confirmed cases worldwide, with 1.7 million deaths due to the virus or associated complications (World Health Organization, 2020). Why did it take so long to release the vaccine to the public? The process was, in fact, very accelerated compared to previous vaccine development timelines until then (for example, Seunghoon, 2015). However, no government or health organisation would risk prematurely releasing the vaccine to the public without proper testing, assuring its efficacy against infection or serious illness, and confidence that the side effects would not outweigh population-level benefits.

The obligatory steps that vaccine development involves[1] must be followed. Following initial research discovery, researchers test the vaccine's ability to induce the desired immune response in laboratory animals. If the vaccine proves effective in significantly reducing infections and deaths, the development process moves forward and is tested on human groups. Only after rigorous testing confirms its effectiveness and safety can the vaccine be licensed and recommended for public use.

In the same way we tackle infectious diseases, problem-solving criminologists seeking effective solutions to combat crime rely on current knowledge of its causes and past successes or failures. When proposing solutions, problem-solving criminologists further determine their efficacy (does it work?), effectiveness (at what level does it work?) and efficiency (what is the cost?) through proper evaluations. This is the same type of working model that design sciences employ when developing a product.

Furthermore, designing and implementing preventive initiatives on a wider scale, whether a simple action, a well-defined programme or a complex strategy, involves a structured sequence of steps. Theoretical and basic research knowledge from labs, research centres and academia must be 'translated' for practical application, which is not always an easy endeavour. However, adopting the knowledge translation framework from prevention science can help problem-solving criminologists achieve the objective of an evidence-based practice.

While design and prevention sciences offer a foundation to structure the process of designing crime prevention initiatives, knowledge from behavioural and social sciences provides the necessary criminological content and research methods for inquiry and analysis. Since the problems to be solved are, in this case, crime-related, problem-solving criminologists rely on theoretical and empirical findings from academic disciplines such as criminology, psychology and sociology (among others).

Consequently, we place evidence-based crime prevention, an activity framed by problem-solving criminology, at the intersection of design science, prevention science, and behavioural and social sciences (see Figure 2.1). In this chapter, we present each discipline's epistemological contribution to design, implement and evaluate evidence-based crime prevention initiatives.

Design science: finding the best solution

Design science has been defined as a body of intellectual analytic, partly formal and partly empirical doctrine about the design process (Simon, 1988). Design science, or the study of the artificial, was first presented in 1961 by Fuller when he proposed that competent design could shift the world's resources from serving 40 to 100 per

Figure 2.1: Proposed epistemological framework for evidence-based crime prevention

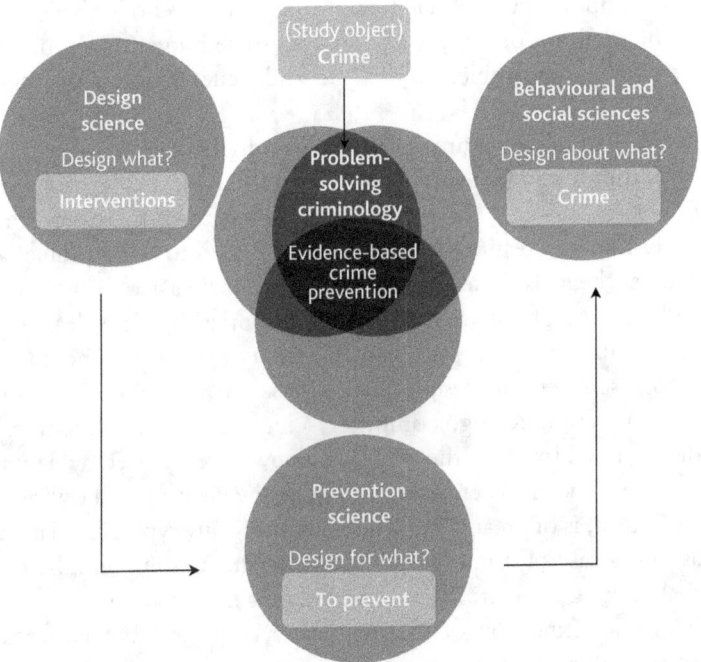

cent of humanity despite continuously dwindling resources (Fuller and McHale, 1963). Fuller integrated sociophysical theories with macro-engineering practices, advocating that scientists should be entrusted with designing human ecology. Design science is considered the third research paradigm. It constitutes one of the three major categories of the systematic study of knowledge (epistemology), along with natural and human sciences (Gregor, 2009). In the natural sciences (chemistry, biology, physics), the discovery process seeks to explain the rules that govern the natural world. Researchers identify natural laws through rigorous measurement and quantitative analytic methods and attempt to determine mathematical (deterministic or stochastic) models for explaining and predicting natural processes. Natural sciences were the dominant scientific paradigm until the late 19th century when, on the one hand, the academic institution of social sciences and, on the other hand, the development of psychodynamic theory spread across Europe, initiating the rise of the human sciences. The human (interpretative) sciences introduced a level of complexity to the methods of inquiry and analysis since human phenomena are not as observable, predictable and generalisable as natural sciences laws.

The natural and human science paradigms concern studying 'how things are'. Conversely, design science concerns 'how things might be' (Simon, 1996). In this third paradigm, researchers study human creations or artefacts developed to solve problems and reach goals. These artefacts can be material objects, tools and instruments, as well as services, activities, living or learning environments, and symbols (Buchanan, 1992). The most recognised fields in design science are architecture, information systems, engineering, computer science and other technical disciplines. However, the general framework employed by design sciences, since it is centred on studying the creation and utility of a solution, is of great value when designing any type of initiative, as in the case of crime prevention. Buchanan (1992) emphasises that seeking a scientific basis for design is not an attempt to turn it into an extension of the neo-positivist project but rather to connect and integrate knowledge from arts and sciences to solve problems of the present. Buchanan (1992) classified the problems that are the object of design science as wicked since they focus on things that 'do not yet exist'. In such cases, researchers must adopt a problem-solving approach in an iterative process of development and evaluation that requires careful consideration of alternative solutions and hypothesised outcomes.

Over the last 20 years, human and design sciences have become more intertwined as the development of actions, programmes, policies, interventions and strategies to solve social and health problems has become more widespread while, at the same time, searching for better methodological approaches based on available scientific evidence. A significant challenge has been the development of a comprehensive framework for crime prevention that incorporates both the rich theoretical and empirical insights from criminology, psychology, sociology and related disciplines and the rational guidance provided by design science. It is within this intersection that problem-solving criminology emerges.

Roschuni (2012) outlined a process with two interlinked cycles for creating solutions. In the first part, data gathered from different sources is analysed to define the problem (problem development cycle or problem definition). Following this, solutions are proposed, and prototypes are tested (solution development cycle or problem solution). Both cycles include iterative feedback loops where information generated during evaluation processes is integrated to refine better problems and solutions. In the problem definition phase, the analytical stage, researchers work to identify all constituent elements (in the case of crime prevention, these may be the factors contributing to the occurrence of crime) and determine the requirements for successful solutions. Conversely, developing a final plan that combines the different elements of a solution is a synthetic process. In design research, constructing a solution entails continuous evaluation, starting from the initial stages of problem identification and extending through the solution's revision over time.

Design affects contemporary life extensively. The traditional concern for functionality, form and appearance of material objects is perhaps the best proof of design's pervasiveness. Tools, instruments, machinery, vehicles, buildings, clothing and everyday items are designed to fulfil specific functions. Designers are also concerned about integrating physical, psychological, social and cultural dimensions into their creations, highlighting the complex relationship between products and human beings. For instance, the physical appearance of objects has long been regarded as a necessary element in their design, addressing environmental requirements while also contributing to group identity. As an illustration, the red-painted wooden houses with steeply inclined black roofs commonly seen in the Swedish countryside are quite different from the low, white-painted houses with simple roofs in Mediterranean regions. Furthermore, design has also developed in the areas of symbolic and visual communication. Advertising a product has become as important as the product itself, leading to many professionals specialising in creating photography, video and digitised images that are integrated into complex messages that engage the target audience.

Design thinking may be applied to any area of human experience (Buchanan, 1992). In this sense, and much like the design of physical objects and advertising, design can be extended to human activities such as health and social initiatives, and policies can be seen as creations strategically planned through logical decision-making to bring about changes in the behaviour of individuals and communities. In this sense, they represent forms of social engineering. Like physical products, they may integrate psychological, social, cultural and historical dimensions to integrate a rational component with the capacity to better serve their purpose. Planning an initiative implies that those participating in its design have a deep understanding of the problem and are competent in using a set of tools for complex problem-solving, a language for communicating the solution's approach, and developing strategies for employing the necessary resources.

According to Hevner and colleagues (2004), when designing a product or solution, design science needs to address two fundamental questions:

1. What is the utility of the new product/solution?
2. How is that utility demonstrated?

If researchers conclude that existing products are adequate to solve the problem at hand, then the new product/solution is irrelevant (unnecessary). If the new product/solution does not solve the problem, it has no utility. If proper evaluation does not demonstrate utility, then it is not possible to claim that the product/solution contributes to anything.

In sum, the design science paradigm uses a problem-solving approach. Employing this framework and following its rational process of action to design crime prevention initiatives and policies strengthens and endows them with rigour and accuracy. The objective is to replace 'black boxes' with transparent and rational mechanisms. For this to take place, problem-solving criminologists work in several stages:

1. Situation analysis or needs assessment. First, it is necessary to understand and describe the crime problem as detailed as possible and its causes and correlates. To begin with, problem-solving criminologists rely on theoretical and empirical background from social and behavioural sciences and the research methods that these sciences employ (referenced later

in the chapter). When defining the problem, the present state is described (for example, individual characteristics, attitudes and perceptions, and life experiences that are risk factors or that can mitigate or prevent radicalisation).
2. Definition of the initiative objectives. Only when the present state is defined can the preferred state (intended to be achieved with the initiative) be defined. For instance, taking the previous example, the objectives of a deradicalisation initiative might be to achieve attitudinal or behavioural changes relevant to disengagement/desistance or to change perceptions of injustice, discrimination and in-group superiority. When defining the objectives, it is crucial to follow the prescriptions of the acronym SMART, meaning that objectives must be 'Specific' (precise, clear, defined by verbs that document an action), 'Measurable' (use a measure to show progress), 'Achievable' (within reach for participants and team, considering available resources and time), 'Relevant' (aligned with goals) and 'Time-bound' (define a reasonable date for achieving the objective).
3. Definition of mechanisms of action. Subsequently, problem-solving criminologists define the mechanisms of action and the activities that constitute the initiative. The activities and objectives must be well aligned, relying on the causal or correlational mechanisms identified during the first stage (situation analysis). Ideally, the initiative designers propose multiple solutions. When a solution is chosen, it should be rationally justified, detailing its advantages and disadvantages.
4. The chosen solution is then tested. The test results may orient to the solution's implementation, necessity of improvement, or the initiative designers may revisit alternative solutions to find a more effective approach for the proposed objectives. At the end of this iterative process, the most effective solution is selected to be implemented at a larger scale.

Prevention science: translating knowledge into practice

Prevention science frames the steps from an initiative's design stage through its large-scale implementation and, eventually, policy change (or creation).

The object of prevention science is the systematic study of initiatives designed to change the occurrence of a disruptive phenomenon in a certain population (for insance, disease, crime, political or religious radicalisation). Prevention science provides problem-solving criminologists with a framework for translating criminological theoretical and empirical knowledge produced in academic settings and research environments into effective practice (knowledge translation). When applied in the field, this knowledge can prevent crime or mitigate its societal impact.

Evidence-based prevention practice draws on the latest evidence about the direct causes of the event it aims to prevent and on those factors that, when present, increase the likelihood that the phenomenon will occur. When the phenomenon is a specific type of crime, pinpointing direct causes is challenging since many unaccounted elements may contribute to it in an intricate web of interrelated factors. For example, in the case of violent extremism, a 2020 meta-analytic study found that while activism, perceived in-group superiority and perceived distance to others played significant roles in radicalisation, factors like lower education level, negative peers and perceived discrimination also had an impact, albeit to a lesser degree (Emmelkamp et al, 2020).

Fishbein and colleagues (2016) proposed a six-stage process to frame knowledge translation for which transdisciplinary collaborations are essential. In Stage 1, basic research findings (produced by different disciplines in laboratory-based and field-based research) are integrated. In the case of crime prevention, it may be useful, for instance, to integrate empirical findings from criminology (for example, criminal group dynamics, criminal networks, case-management in prisons), police studies (for instance, problem-oriented, community, intelligence-led policing), psychology (attitudes, personality, peer relationships and so on), and sociology (for example, institutional powers, policy). If the objective is to prevent crime in a certain area, incorporating evidence from urban studies, specifically Crime Prevention Through Environmental Design, can be beneficial. If the objective is to curb activity in drug markets, it can be beneficial to familiarise oneself with basic economic research to understand drug market dynamics.

Prevention may not be the main objective of basic science discovery. Still, basic research provides insight into the causes and likelihood of a phenomenon. This evidence informs the next stage (applied research).

In Stage 2, initiatives are planned. Designing an initiative implies using the outcomes of integrated basic research (Stage 1) to produce a 'theory' of how the initiative will work (programme theory). In this stage, initiative designers describe the present state of the problem they want to address, define the preferred state they want to achieve, and design the mechanism of change for it to happen. This process is essential to avoid black boxes. In evidence-based practice, programme theory is rational, well-described and tested. In automation, this would be the equivalent of designing the engine and explaining how it works. Problem-solving criminologists might focus on self-esteem and empathy to prevent violent radicalisation (see Feddes et al, 2015). In this case, one possibility for programme theory would be that increasing self-esteem empowers individuals while enhancing empathy for others inhibits narcissistic features, which are two well-known risk factors for violence. Together, it creates resilience against perceived in-group superiority, another factor increasing the probability of radicalisation. In another example, problem-solving criminologists might focus on young people's sense of identity, belonging and political socialisation based on Stage 1 research indicating that adolescents with a strong sense of relative disadvantage and social deprivation are more prone to radicalisation (Schröder et al, 2022).

In Stage 3, the initiatives designed in Stage 2 are applied, ideally in a controlled situation with a small group of individuals. The objective is to determine the initiative's efficacy. This stage seeks to answer questions such as, 'does the initiative work?', 'how significant is the effect?' and 'what are the side effects?'. This research stage is conducted within or near the academic environment. The aim is to verify if the programme theory's predictions worked as planned, thus establishing the initiative's internal validity. Researchers are also interested in determining the resources and costs required for success. This is important because initiatives, even if efficacious, might not always be efficient, might fail to reach those who most need them, could be challenging to implement fully, or may be prohibitively costly.

Figure 2.2: Characterisation of an initiative's main and side effects

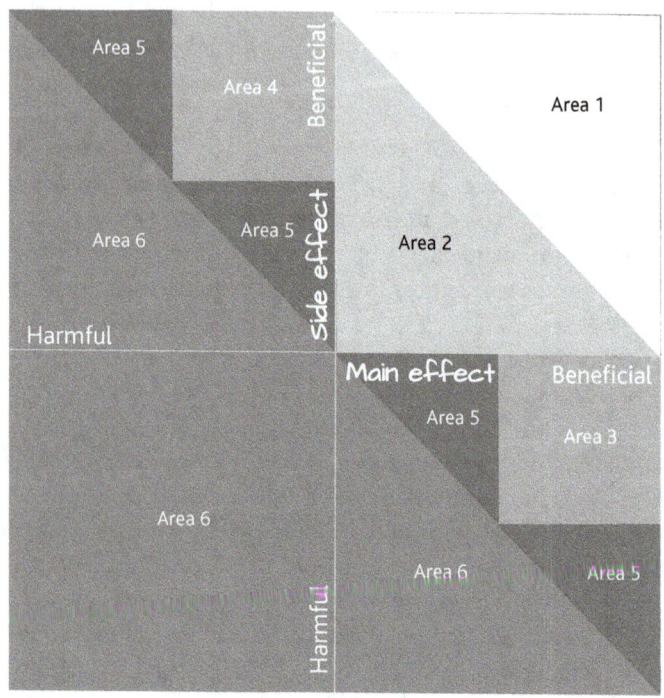

Source: Adapted with permission from Silva and Lind (2020)

Evidence-based practice requires characterising the benefits and harmfulness of the initiative's main and side effects, as displayed in Figure 2.2.

Initiatives in Area 1 effectively prevent crime, and their side effects (if any) are beneficial. Those in Area 2 are not ideally effective and should only be chosen if more effective solutions are unavailable. Eventually, crime prevention managers may decide to implement such an initiative if it has a better cost-benefit ratio than others. Initiatives in Area 3, although highly effective, require strategies to address side effects. For instance, successfully dismantling a radicalised group should not lead to several smaller, hidden groups with the potential for violent crime. If the initiative falls in Area 4, despite its ineffectiveness for the intended purpose, it may serve a different purpose, an important outcome that should not be disregarded. History shows that many outstanding products and solutions have accidentally emerged. Casual findings in problem-solving criminology may inform other initiatives and areas for development.

If the trial results when testing an initiative fall somewhere within Areas 5 or 6, the initiative is not suitable due to the ethical concerns arising from its harmful effects. For instance, mentorship programmes targeting individuals at risk of radicalisation are initiatives developed to boost the confidence and ability of the individual (or groups of individuals) to deal with life challenges, build resilience to the narrative and recruitment efforts from violent extremist groups, create alternative social networks and support, and educate about how violent extremist groups operate (Winterbotham, 2020). This type of initiative aims to change individuals' attitudes and behaviours and may also focus on building self-esteem. However, increasing confidence levels may not prevent problematic behaviour or improve social relationships. On the contrary, Lub (2013) points to evidence that initiatives aiming solely to boost self-esteem encourage narcissism, aggressiveness and antisocial behaviour. Likewise, promoting liberal democratic values as a part of mentoring is potentially ineffective in preventing radicalisation (Lindekilde, 2012).

In another example, a systematic review of educational-focused initiatives revealed that non-tailored ones do not sufficiently address local factors and can do more harm than good (Wallner, 2020). The study concluded that not all local drivers of radicalisation and recruitment can be effectively addressed with this type of initiative. Therefore, choosing appropriate programmes, tailoring them and evaluating their effectiveness is essential. Wallner (2020) concluded that knowledge-based interventions, a particular type of educational-focused initiatives that address historical awareness and civic participation, can positively impact young people but can also be detrimental if used to spread certain narratives of national identity and history that alienate groups or sectors of the population.

In sum, the decision to implement a particular initiative should be based on a comparison of its main effects, side effects and costs.

In Stage 4, an initiative developed in previous stages moves from the academic research setting to real-world application, where conditions are not so controlled, and many variables may interfere with the results. Adopting an effective initiative is intended to overcome the problem in society. The implementation strategy must adhere to the prescriptions of the initiative's design, considering the characteristics of the field where it will be implemented and the populational groups to whom it will be applied. For instance, prison deradicalisation efforts may be constrained by a country's criminal and institutional policy, available resources or the average age of the criminal population. Critical and strategic thinking must address multiple factors that may impact the initiative's implementation in the real world. Evaluating outcomes and cost-benefits establishes the initiative's external validity. In this regard, the initiative must demonstrate its value under the controlled conditions of the previous stage and when it is applied in the field. Replicating the initiative's impact in different settings, cultures, populations and institutions contributes further to its scientific value. For this to occur, researchers, practitioners and policy makers must find appropriate forums to communicate effectively with each other and foster a global community.

Stage 5 is concerned with scaling. The objective of this stage is to make evidence-based initiatives widely available with documented information about their internal and external validity and achieve widespread implementation and documented success. Repositories that index and classify initiatives according to their prescriptions and documented success are very useful, as well as centres that support their dissemination, quality implementation, sustainability and impact. For instance, the Evidence-based Prevention and Intervention Support Center is a collaborative partnership between Pennsylvania State University and the Pennsylvania Commission on Crime and Delinquency. The centre promotes itself as a 'university-based intermediary organisation connecting research, policy and real-world practice to improve outcomes for children and families across Pennsylvania'.[2] The EUCPN has similar objectives for general crime prevention practice in Europe, and the Radicalisation Awareness Network (RAN) specialises in the area of radicalisation and violent extremism. The INDEED project, a European consortium developed to support the evaluation of P/CVE initiatives, also includes a repository of evidence-based initiatives. As Fishbein et al (2016) argued, implementation and scale-up can only be resolved when science is applied (through skilful professional practice).

Finally, in Stage 6, results achieved in the previous stages are translated into policy at the local and national levels to target the problem across different cultures and societies effectively. In this stage, priorities at the international level are set by international agendas. The objective is to globally coordinate efforts to prevent a problem based on sound scientific principles. Preventing radicalisation and violent extremism exemplifies the need for communities to collaborate on successful solutions to implement transnationally across different settings.

This six-stage translational approach to develop and implement evidence-based initiatives that we propose, adapted from prevention science, contrasts with the prevalent fragmented approach in crime prevention, which often fails to adhere to the principles of evidence-based practice (Silva and Lind, 2020).

In many places, practitioners and policy makers who may lack the requisite knowledge are tasked with designing initiatives and strategies to address crime problems in the local community, working in institutions that lack the necessary personnel and resources (Silva, 2018). Often, they attempt to 'reinvent the wheel', overlooking existing evidence and knowledge from others in the field. Often, these local professionals have minimal or no training in design and evaluation and are unfamiliar with existing evidence-based initiatives. To address this situation, we need research that investigates the complex processes and mechanisms of initiatives, their skilful implementation at a large scale and their sustainability. In this regard, it is necessary to improve the currently limited infrastructure and capacity to support evidence-based practice and initiatives' scaling up in crime prevention areas. Unfortunately, limited funding and policy barriers often hinder these efforts.

Behavioural and social sciences: contributing with theory and research methods

While design and prevention sciences offer a rational approach to the design, implementation, evaluation and sustainability of initiatives, problem-solving criminologists must draw from other areas of knowledge that explore the nature and causes of crime, individual and societal risk and protective factors, and the psychology of both offenders and their victims. Social and behavioural sciences serve this purpose. Not only do these sciences offer theories that explain the causes of crime, but problem-solving criminologists also employ their research methods to guide problem analysis and the various evaluations needed for initiative design and implementation.

The contribution of theory

When designing crime prevention initiatives, problem-solving criminologists aim to effect change in individuals, groups or their environment. Relying on theory endows professionals with the rational arguments they need to design the initiatives. Theories provide guidelines to analyse and explain phenomena. For instance, they help understand individuals' antisocial attitudes and criminal behaviour based on their characteristics, how they interact with the environment, and the complex synergies between protective and risk factors present in their lives. Many believe that a theoretical framework is irrelevant to problem-solving criminology, and an evidence-based practice should rely on demonstrating what works by evaluating the initiatives' outcomes. As previously mentioned, evaluation is essential, but programme theory (the initiative's 'engine') must be explained in detail. There are no black boxes in evidence-based practice. In this regard, initiative designers must explain how and why they anticipate the initiative will work. In evidence-based practice, the principles of programme theory (the logic behind the 'how' and 'why') are explicit.

When constructing the programme theory, the initiative designers should also integrate evidence produced by reliable scientific studies concerning the crime problem and any other solutions that, eventually, may have been proposed and tested. Unless there is a strong rationale for why the initiative's design should rely on principles that have already proven ineffective in solving the problem, they should be disregarded.

In the specific area of P/CVE, initiatives are primarily directed at individuals' knowledge, attitudes and behaviours, be it educational-focused projects, exit programmes or initiatives to increase resilience via community engagement. For instance, educational-focused initiatives seek, among other things, to promote values and beliefs that counteract radicalisation, address questions of identity and group belonging and promote empathy for individuals of other groups and victims. Some initiatives specifically address how students interact with each other and are intended to foster dialogue skills and encourage tolerance. Peer-to-peer initiatives assume that young people can more effectively reach their peers at risk of radicalisation than the adults in their environment. Social psychology, particularly group interaction, theoretically supports the development of such initiatives. Principles of social psychology assert that the individual is interlinked with their social environment and explain the behavioural systems and psychological processes occurring within a social group or between social groups.

The assumptions of educational-focused initiatives heavily rely on educational principles. For instance, some programmes focus on students' knowledge (dangers of violent extremism, principles of a secular state and freedom of religions, political education and historical awareness, history regarding terrorism and so on), while others focus on the way students think (for example, critically appraise information, process information, reasoning abilities). On the other hand, some programmes focus on building educators' capacity to convey P/CVE-relevant content, assuming that teachers can deliver it creatively, fostering students' engagement in discussing sensitive and polarising topics.

Wallner (2020) defined five main assumptions for such educational-focused programmes:

1. the educational system can help young people resist violent extremism by promoting historical awareness and civic participation;
2. the education system can make young people more resilient to radicalisation and recruitment by enhancing their critical thinking skills;
3. schools can reduce prejudice between majority and minority group members by facilitating their encounters and interactions on neutral grounds;

4. building teachers' capacity to implement lessons relevant to P/CVE effectively is a factor to consider in education programmes; and
5. teachers are capable of accurately identify signs of radicalisation and recruitment in their pupils.

Behavioural, cognitive and humanistic theories can justify the mechanisms of action implied in these assumptions. Key principles of cognitive theory explain that the way we think has the capacity to elicit emotions. In this regard, while certain thoughts and beliefs lead to adaptive and healthy emotions and behaviours, others lead to disturbed emotions and disruptive behaviour. On the other hand, behavioural theory attributes conduct to the antecedents and consequents present in the environment and the associations the individual acquires through experience. Conversely, humanistic theory emphasises individual uniqueness and focuses on the whole person and their capacity for change. For example, the Tolerance Project, a pedagogical model launched in Sweden in 1995 following the murder of a 14-year-old boy by four other young people, primarily aims to promote positive relationships between students. The programme, designed for schools, focuses on preventing extremist organisations from recruiting adolescents. The programme brings together students with intolerant attitudes who may have caused unrest in school and students who do not show such attitudes and behaviour. The initiative covers topics such as participatory democracy, human rights and citizenship. In this instance, the rationale for initiative is based on attitudes, beliefs, group identity and peer pressure.

On a different note, mentorship is a kind of preventive approach that aims at the specific needs of individuals or groups at risk of radicalisation and recruitment. In mentorships, a bond is established between an individual at risk and an experienced mentor who serves in a supportive role. The mentor can be someone in the community, such as a peer, teacher, sports coach, youth worker or religious leader.

Mentorship intends to develop the individuals' confidence and ability to deal with life challenges, creating a social network of support that can build resilience against the appeal of radicalised discourses and the narrative of violent extremist groups

(Winterbotham, 2020). Mentoring aims to support individuals by offering alternative social networks and connections. This approach helps young people build strong relationships with peers, parents, teachers and other adults in the community, like a 'social immunity' mechanism against radicalisation. In the case of mentoring, social bonds theory and differential association can provide the rational underpinnings for programme theory development. Social bonds theory (Hirschi, 1969) explains that individuals form strong attachments to others and commitments to social norms if they experience a high level of involvement with the social environment. The higher the level of social bonds the individual establishes with the community, the less likely the individual is to commit deviant or destructive behaviour. In turn, differential association theory (Sutherland, 1939) asserts that behaviour is learned in social contexts. Therefore, individuals learn to behave like criminals when they associate with others who commit crimes. According to this theory, learning criminal conduct includes not only specific techniques for committing crimes but motives and attitudes are also conveyed in the learning process. While learning to behave as a criminal, the individual gets closer to others who violate the law and distances themselves from those who live according to the rules.

The contribution of research methods

Another important contribution of behavioural and social sciences to evidence-based crime prevention is their methods of inquiry and analysis. Problem-solving criminologists follow scientific mandates in the collection, analysis and interpretation of data when they collaborate on initiatives' design and evaluation. Problem-solving criminology researchers typically approach their work from a focused perspective. They first search for in-depth information about what the problem at hand is through a situation (problem) analysis. The objective of this analysis is to understand the factors contributing to the problem. Ultimately, researchers are not in charge of designing the initiative, just as those designing the initiative might not be the ones implementing it. Nevertheless, coordination and collaboration are essential, ensuring that information flows back and forth across all stages (see Figure 2.3).

The tasks identified in the lightly shaded boxes require social and behavioural sciences research methods expertise. Information collected during the problem analysis informs about what needs to be done. The objectives are then defined. For instance, if the problem at hand is young people's attitudes and tolerance for a radicalised narrative, it may be important to study in detail certain types of discourse during problem analysis. The objectives define the type of baseline indicators that need to be measured (quantitatively) or qualitatively studied before the initiative is implemented. The same indicators will be assessed after the implementation so that the change sought by the initiative can be effectively known. In this regard, it is crucial to plan the outcome evaluation while the intervention is designed.

The initiative is tested, ideally through an experiment involving small groups of individuals who share characteristics similar to the target population for which it is designed, who should be randomly assigned to the experimental versus control conditions (randomised control trial or RCT). However, it is not always possible or ethical to randomly assign individuals to one group or another. In such cases, researchers may need to collect more information from the experiment participants and factor this into their data analysis.

Problem-solving criminologists occasionally deal not with people but with places (interventions that target the urban environment). For testing such initiatives, they may choose a smaller and more limited space than the one the intervention is designed for. If the test phase proves effective, the initiative may, subsequently, be considered for implementation.

During the implementation stage, information is collected to certify the fidelity to the implementation protocol (detailed instructions on implementation procedures and necessary resources). Any judgement regarding the initiative outcomes needs to consider implementation fidelity. An initiative may fail not because it is ineffective to solve the problem but due to flawed implementation.

In subsequent stages, there are three types of evaluation to be considered. Outcome evaluation assesses the ratio of change in measures taken before and after the implementation to determine

Epistemological framework

Figure 2.3: Stages of initiative design, implementation and evaluation

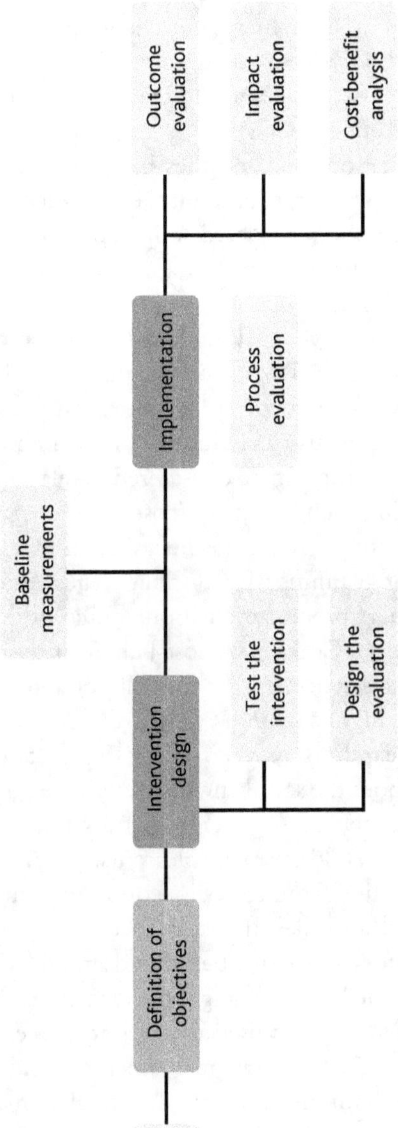

Source: Adapted with permission from Silva and Lind (2020)

the effect of the initiative on the target population. It will answer questions such as 'Was there any change in students' attitudes towards radicalised narratives?' (intervention's efficacy) and 'How much did students' attitudes towards radicalised narratives change?' (intervention's effectiveness).

Impact evaluation, on the other hand, assesses the initiative's capacity to achieve a broader result. For instance, it might answer questions such as, 'What decrease in the number of radicalised individuals has been observed in a certain community after the initiative was implemented?'. Generally, impact effects require more time to achieve, making impact evaluations long-term undertakings (compared to outcome evaluation). The programme's efficiency (how much it costs to achieve such results) is measured through economic analysis. This can be a pure measure of costs (cost analysis) or costs can be considered in relation to the benefit of implementing such initiatives (cost-benefit analysis).

Research methods from the behavioural and social sciences are critical for planning five distinct stages: problem analysis; initiative testing; process evaluation; outcome evaluation; and impact evaluation. Conversely, cost-benefit analysis uses methods from economic science, which we will not address in this text.

When planning a situation analysis for developing a P/CVE initiative, researchers may consider, for instance, collecting information about the social environment in neighbourhoods and schools, factors related to parenting and school achievement in groups of at-risk children and adolescents, use of alcohol or drugs in the community, families' socioeconomic status, or antisocial and radicalised attitudes and beliefs. Researchers will choose relevant indicators to measure before and after the implementation process so that the level of change is objectifiable. If an initiative is intended to decrease radicalised attitudes, it is necessary to measure such attitudes. If it seeks to increase tolerance and dialogue skills, these are selected for measurement. Eventually, an initiative works with more complex objectives and concepts, such as, for instance, decreasing youth vulnerability to recruitment by radicalised groups. In such cases, 'vulnerability' must be operationalised so that its (eventual) change can be measured.

After defining indicators and variables, the researcher decides on the instruments necessary to collect the information. Attitudes are easily measured through self-administered attitudinal scales. One branch of psychology has dedicated many years to developing such scales. To study how young people interact in conflictive situations, classroom observation, for example, maybe a more suitable data collection method. Crime statistics are often employed by problem-solving criminologists to evaluate the initiative's impact.

Researchers decide on the research design, which depends on the nature of the research question, objectives and available resources. Research design is a set of methods and procedures defining how the information is collected and analysed. Ideally, the step of testing an initiative employs an experimental design. In this case, the group of participants is divided into two groups. One group is subjected to initiative (experimental condition) while the other (control group) is not. Sometimes, the researcher may want to test different levels of the experimental condition. For instance, the researcher may want to evaluate the effectiveness of an educational-focused programme applied for three months compared to six months. In this case, participants would be divided into three groups. One group would be assigned to the first experimental condition (three-month intervention delivery), another to the second experimental condition (six-month intervention delivery) and the third group would serve as control. Ideally, participants would be randomly assigned to each group (true experiment or RCT). If participants are divided into groups, but randomisation is not possible, it is a quasi-experimental design.

When conducting problem analysis, instead of an experimental design, the researcher most likely will choose to do an observational study. In this case, the researcher may want to compare the outcome (for instance, vulnerability to recruitment by radicalised groups) between individuals who were (naturally) exposed to certain conditions in their past (for example, parental neglect) and those who were not. This type of research design is considered a 'natural' experiment.

In observational studies, the main objective may be descriptive, making group comparisons unnecessary. If the researcher describes certain characteristics and does not analyse relationships in the data, the study will be descriptive (non-analytical). For instance, reporting about risk factors found in a certain group of radicalised individuals is a descriptive design. However, if the researcher compares the risk factors in radicalised and non-radicalised individuals, it would be an observational analytical study.

Observational research designs are also classified based on the directionality of the study. When individuals are divided into groups based on specific characteristics (for example, radicalised versus non-radicalised), and the researcher examines their past to determine which risk factors were present (for instance, racist values), this is a case-control study. Conversely, if individuals who, at a certain point in time, present a specific risk factor (for example, religiously intolerant parents) and those without are tracked over time to determine who is more likely to be radicalised in the future, this is called a cohort study. If there is no directionality and the researcher only aims to capture data about what is happening at a certain moment, that is a cross-sectional study.

Research studies can also be classified based on the development of the outcome. If the outcome has already occurred (or not occurred for individuals in a control group) and the researcher collects data from records or requests participants to recall their exposure to a certain risk factor in the past, it is called a retrospective study. Conversely, if the research begins before the outcome occurs, and participants are monitored over a period to determine the occurrence of the outcome, then it is called a prospective study. Typically, case-control studies are retrospective, while cohort studies can be prospective or retrospective.

While planning the research design, the researcher determines what data is needed and how to collect it. It may be necessary to use data from registers (for instance, crime suspects), but often, research evaluators need to request information from individuals through surveys and interviews to know their characteristics (attitudes, beliefs, behaviour, level of knowledge in one matter, aspects related to their past, mental health issues and so on). Self-reported data has certain limitations because it relies on individuals' memory and willingness to disclose personal information. Participants are also likely to respond in ways they think are more acceptable or that are expected from them. However, self-reporting is often the only way that the evaluation researcher has to collect information. The researcher may also need to collect data through observation, for instance, sitting in a group discussion to assess how juveniles from different backgrounds interact in controversial matters. Data can also be collected from documents, and in the case of radicalisation, online propaganda is often targeted for analysis. Problem-solving criminology researchers also determine how much data they will need regarding the accuracy of the results that they intend to achieve. The system of data collection will depend on the research objectives and time constraints, resources, and availability, but it is always systematic and according to scientific principles.

In sum, the research design needs to be carefully planned to determine what data is necessary and how to collect it in a systematic and ethical way. Research methods principles borrowed from behavioural and social sciences will guide problem-solving criminology researchers to succeed in this endeavour.

Summary

- Evidence-based crime prevention is a specialised area of problem-solving criminology. Epistemologically, it is situated at the intersections of design science, prevention science and behavioural and social sciences.
- Design science, or the science of the artificial, offers a framework to structure the general procedure when solving crime problems. This procedure involves loops of development and evaluation that continue in time to achieve a sustainable solution.
- Prevention science offers a method of knowledge translation. The knowledge produced in laboratories, research centres and universities by basic science is utilised to produce solutions that can effectively prevent crime from happening in society.
- Knowledge translation is a six-step process initiated by gathering empirical findings from different disciplines useful to understand the problem to be solved. Although basic research may not be concerned with preventing crime, the evidence it produces about why and how crime occurs is crucial information to design preventive initiatives and strategies.
- Knowledge translation involves developing and testing the preventive initiatives at an experimental level to prove their internal validity. Only when problem-solving criminology

researchers have certified that initiatives are effective and harmless to the individuals, groups or society at large should they be implemented on a larger scale.
- Evidence-based initiatives that, besides being effective, have a positive impact in the communities where they are applied may be chosen for widespread implementation in other environments, settings and cultures to verify their external validity.
- Initiatives with proven external validity should be well-documented and available in repositories as a resource for practitioners and policy makers as well as for problem-solving criminologists who can take advantage of the knowledge produced in the development process.
- While design and prevention sciences offer a general framework and methodological approach for initiative design, implementation, evaluation and sustainability, behavioural and social sciences endow the process with theoretical and empirical knowledge in the criminological field.
- Problem-solving criminologists rely on behavioural and social theory to rationally develop programme theories and explain initiatives' mechanisms of action. Evidence-based crime prevention does not include initiatives with unknown mechanisms of action (black boxes).
- Problem-solving criminology researchers employ behavioural and social sciences research methods for problem analysis, initiative testing, and process, outcome, and impact evaluation. Relying on these tools, researchers decide on types of research design and methods of inquiry and data analysis.

Suggested directions for future research

The following questions can orient further research and discussion in the area:

- How can knowledge produced by basic research be effectively translated and inform the design and implementation of crime prevention and, specifically, P/CVE initiatives?

- How should initiative developers demonstrate the levels of crime prevention and P/CVE initiatives' efficacy?
- Is it time to discuss the introduction of a problem-solving criminology framework in university and college educational curricula? How much would practitioners take advantage of such education?

Notes

1. Centers for Disease Control and Prevention webpage provides further reading on vaccine development stages.
2. The Evidence-based Prevention and Intervention Support (EPIS) Centre has a webpage available: https://epis.psu.edu/.

References

Buchanan, R. (1992) 'Wicked problems in design thinking', *Design Issues*, 8: 5–21.

Emmelkamp, J., Asscher, J.J., Wissink, I.B. and Stams, G.J. (2020) 'Risk factors for (violent) radicalization in juveniles: A multilevel meta-analysis', *Aggression and Violent Behavior*, 55: 1–16.

EUCPN (nd) 'Crime prevention: A European definition', *European Crime Prevention Network*. Available from https://eucpn.org/sites/default/files/document/files/2012_Concept%20paper_A4_LR.pdf [Accessed 12 September 2023].

Feddes, A.R., Mann, L. and Doosje, B. (2015) 'Increasing self-esteem and empathy to prevent radicalization: A longitudinal quantitative evaluation of a resilience training focused on adolescents with a dual identity', *Journal of Applied Social Psychology*, 45: 400–11.

Fishbein, D.H., Ridenour, T.A., Stahl, M. and Sussman, S. (2016) 'The full translational spectrum of prevention science: Facilitating the transfer of knowledge to practices and policies that prevent behavioral health problems', *Translational Behavioral Medicine*, 6: 5–16.

Fuller, R.B. and McHale, J. (1963) *World Design Science Decade 1965–1975*, Carbondale: World Resources Inventory Southern Illinois University.

Gregor, S.D. (2009) 'Building theory in the sciences of the artificial', *International Conference on Design Science Research in Information Systems and Technology*. Available from https://api.semanticscholar.org/CorpusID:14759341 [Accessed 9 January 2023].

Hevner, A.R., March, S.T., Park, J. and Ram, S. (2004) 'Design science in information systems research', *MIS Quarterly*, 28: 75–205.

Hirschi, T. (1969) *Causes of Delinquency*, Berkeley: University of California Press.

Lindekild, L. (2012) 'Neo-liberal governing of "radicals": Danish radicalization prevention policies and potential iatrogenic effects', *International Journal of Conflict and Violence*, 6: 109–25.

Lub, V. (2013) 'Polarisation, radicalization, and social policy: Evaluating the theories of change', *Evidence & Policy*, 9: 165–83.

Roschuni, C.N. (2012) *Communicating Research Design Effectively*, doctoral dissertation, UC Berkeley Electronic Theses and Dissertations. Available from https://escholarship.org/uc/item/75f0z49v [Accessed 9 January 2023].

Schröder, C.P., Bruns, J., Lehmann, L., Goede, L.-R., Bliesener, T. and Tomczyk, S. (2022) 'Radicalization in adolescence: The identification of vulnerable groups', *European Journal of Criminal Policy & Research*, 28: 177–201.

Seunghoon, H. (2015) 'Clinical vaccine development', *Clinical and Experimental Vaccine Research*, 4: 46–53.

Silva, T.C. (2018) 'Knowledge and skills needed for successful management of crime prevention strategies', *Journal of Scandinavian Studies of Criminology and Crime Prevention*, 19(1): 113–14.

Silva T.C. and Lind, M. (2020) 'Experiences of the member states performing evaluations in projects and activities aimed at crime prevention', *MIUN Studies in Criminology No. 1*. Available from urn:nbn:se:miun:diva-39125 [Accessed 12 September 2023].

Simon, H.A. (1988) 'The science of design: Creating the artificial', *Design Issues*, 4: 67–87.

Simon, H.A. (1996) *The Sciences of the Artificial* (3rd edn), Cambridge, MA: The MIT Press.

Sutherland, E.H. (1939) *Principles of Criminology*, New York: Lippincott.

Wallner, C. (2020) *Preventing and Countering Violent Extremism through Education Initiatives: Assessing the Evidence Base*, London: Royal United Services Institute.

Winterbotham, E. (2020) *How Effective Are Mentorship Interventions? Assessing Evidence Base for Preventing and Countering Violent Extremism*, London: Royal United Services Institute.

World Health Organization (2020) *Covid-19 Weekly Epidemiological Update*, 29 December. Available from https://www.who.int/publications/m/item/weekly-epidemiological-update---29-december-2020 [Accessed 12 May 2023].

PART II

Designing, implementing and evaluating preventing and countering violent extremism initiatives

3

A step-by-step logic model of evidence-based practice design

Marzena Kordaczuk-Wąs

Introduction

This chapter presents a systematic approach to designing a comprehensive, long-term, evidence-based programme to prevent radicalisation leading to discrimination and hate speech. It introduces the concept of standardisation and guides the reader through developing the standard elements of such an initiative. Starting from building a theoretical framework embedded in a specific scientific discipline and a selected paradigm, through an in-depth diagnosis of the problem to which such a programme is to be devoted, to designing all standard elements building its assumptions, such as the main goal, specific goals, programme process measurement indicators, prevention strategies, planned tasks and all stages of evaluation. The chapter presents the method of combining scientifically justified evidence with the needs of the addressees of the prevention initiative to effectively respond to the security threat diagnosed in the local environment, considering the expectations and values of its potential recipients. Furthermore, the chapter underscores the significance of integrating the theory of change logic model with the programme logic model in the design process, which guides the author step-by-step towards designing an evidence-based initiative.

A systematic approach to design

One of the reasons for preparing material on the step-by-step design of initiatives for prevention and counteracting radicalisation leading to violent extremism was driven by a continued need in this area. Additionally, combined with the need for a comprehensive approach that extends beyond current, security-based and basic counter-terrorism measures to include systematic preventive measures directly addressing the root causes of extremist violence (UN General Assembly, 2015). Another layer to this motivation was created by conclusions from the literature review supported by observations from practice that regardless of the type of social risk, prevention planners are often pushed to implement solutions to urgent problems facing their communities. Meanwhile, research and experience show that for prevention to be effective, it must start with understanding many complex issues in their complex environmental context. To facilitate this understanding, the guide on the strategic prevention framework focused on substance misuse problems highlights that it is necessary to build prevention activities based on well-defined steps and some guiding principles that offer prevention planners a comprehensive approach to understanding and addressing the problems facing their communities (Substance Abuse and Mental Health Services Administration, 2019). Similarly, the disease prevention and health promotion field also underlines that intervention design is a complex process involving careful decision-making on the intended outcomes. This includes, among other things, understanding the many etiological mechanisms, such as risk factors and protective factors that contribute to the behaviour to be modified, strategies that will effectively induce behavioural change, and other important issues. A crucial task in designing initiatives is to develop and apply a thorough understanding of theories about what determines the target behaviours or other outcomes and how to change them (Rohrbach, 2014). Consequently, designing undertakings in the field of prevention, including the domain related to prevention and countering radicalisation leading to violent extremism, requires a systematic approach to organise this process and guide the initiative's author through its necessary steps.

Several models derived from design research describing regularities in design processes were proposed in the 1960s and 1970s, especially with a focus on engineering design (Asimow, 1962; Hubka, 1974; Ullman, 1992; Hubka and Eder, 1996; Pahl et al, 2007). These models have been used as a framework to locate specific design techniques and delineate different types of design, but also to propose guidelines for transforming a set of design goals into the structure of a design solution. One of the most detailed and widely cited normative design models is the systematic approach developed by Pahl and Beitz, describing engineering design as a sequence of four phases:

1. task clarification;
2. conceptual design;
3. embodiment design; and
4. detail design (Pahl et al, 2007).

The first phase involves gathering, formulating and documenting the requirements of the product to be designed. The second aims to define the basic principles and outline the design solution. Then, the third phase enables the project's development into a layout that meets various technical and economic criteria. The last phase finalises the design and prepares production documentation. It should be emphasised that each of the four phases consists of a sequence of actions that can be performed iteratively. After each phase, a 'decision phase' is performed, allowing one to evaluate the results and decide whether the phase needs to be repeated or the next phase can begin (Pahl et al, 2007). The systematic approach concept, initially proposed for use in engineering, should also be applied to the design of preventive initiatives. Providing the main framework to the process by indicating its individual phases that enable logical and cause-and-effect connections leads to the technique of intervention modelling using a logical model for a detailed description of data elements. This approach fosters a visual understanding of all the theoretical, empirical and practical elements, attributes and keys, thanks to which it guides the initiative's author through their relationships, facilitating the creation of a well-designed initiative.

The design process based on a logic model

The use of the theory of change and programme logic models began in the 1970s. Pioneers and champions in the use of logic models in both programme design and evaluation include Carol Weiss (1995), Michael Fullan (2001) and Huey Chen (2005). Although initially, they did not gain much recognition, this changed in 1996 when a publication promoting the structures and vocabulary of logical models appeared (United Way of America, 1996). A logic model can be defined as a visual 'snapshot' of an initiative that illustrates the intended relationship between its individual elements. In simple terms, this model graphically describes the various stages of complex initiatives comprising many interlinking components. It is a tool whose purpose is to describe and articulate programme theory (Savaya and Waysman, 2005) and is often used interchangeably with other names with a similar concept, such as 'plan', 'chain of cause', 'change model', 'programme theory', 'action theory' or 'theory of change' (National Center on Birth Defects and Developmental Disabilities, 2007). In fact, the literature reveals approaches that distinguish between the two models – the theory of change and the programme model – that differ in their level of detail and application but represent the same underlying logic.

These two types of models differ in both appearance and use. In a nutshell, programme logic models contain many more features than change theory models. Thus, theory of change models are more conceptual, while programme logic models have operational functions.

The models also differ in the purpose of their use. Theory of change models presents an idea or initiative in its simplest form using limited information. They are a generic idea outline. On the other hand, programme logic models offer additional information to assist in design, planning, strategy, monitoring and evaluation. They are a more complete version of an idea proposal because they contain much more detail, often including activities, resources, outcomes and other items of interest to those creating and/or implementing an initiative represented by this model. Therefore, they can significantly help in creating action plans (Wyatt Knowlton and Phillips, 2012). Simply put, a theory of change model is simply a general representation of how an author thinks change will happen. The programme logic model, in turn, details the resources, planned activities, and their outputs and outcomes over time that reflect the intended outcomes.

Both models differ in terms of time frame, level of detail, number of elements, display and focus. However, they are similar because they share the same research, theory, practice and/or literature. Essentially, both models can be considered complementary techniques representing views of the same evidence-based logic with a common origin (Wyatt Knowlton and Phillips, 2012). Based on literature interchangeably using the terms logical programme model and theory of change, one can conclude that constructing an initiative following the previously mentioned model enables both detailed consideration and justification of the proposed solutions, as well as an explanation of why certain goals were formulated as such and no other strategies or preventive actions were selected. In addition, it gives the opportunity to clearly describe the assumptions of the initiative, the mechanism of its operation, and the method of measuring progress in achieving the intended goals (National Center on Birth Defects and Developmental Disabilities, 2007). The individual components of the model illustrate the relationship between the planned work and the intended results (WK Kellogg Foundation, 2004). It should be underscored that the programme logic model is also used to prepare the initiative for evaluation as it schematically shows the relationships between its goals, activities, indicators and resources. The extended logic model defines both outcome and process indicators (Dwyer and Makin, 1997). Both described techniques of modelling the process of designing a preventive initiative are not mutually exclusive; rather, they can be seen as complementary. Therefore, later in the chapter, both techniques will be used together to build a comprehensive model of step-by-step logic of evidence-based practice design.

Defining a long-term comprehensive, evidence-based programme

It should be noted that both in the literature and in practice, there are various terms for activities in the field of preventing and counteracting radicalisation, but also concerning other social problems. Terms such as 'measures', 'undertakings', 'initiatives', 'interventions' and 'programmes' often appear; therefore, it is necessary to explain how to define the concept of a programme which will be the subject of further consideration. At the same time, it is not easy to find a clear division of measures to prevent radicalisation into specific categories or typologies.

The key documents guiding these initiatives contain rather general statements about the need to take such measures without specifying them. For example, the Counter-Terrorism Agenda focuses on the need for a more structured and evidence-based approach to knowledge building and transfer, mentioning only the exchange of ideas and experiences, identifying good practices, and recommending the best ways to deal with all forms of radicalisation. It also highlights the funding of projects and initiatives in this field (European Commission, 2020a). Similarly, on a more operational level, Action Plans do not specify tools and define measures. They talk about priority goals, values and their achievement through implementing programmes and actions (European Commission, 2020b). Interestingly, the Radicalisation Awareness Network (RAN) has gathered over 200 practices in the field of preventing and countering violent extremism (P/CVE) in its collection of effective practices. In fact, these are mainly programmes and projects, but without a clear definition. Rather, the terms 'programme' and 'project' are used interchangeably (RAN, 2020). In sum, it should be stated that in preventing and counteracting radicalisation leading to violent extremism, there is practically no typology or categorisation of undertaken activities. There are no definitions explaining these forms of measures, what they mean, how they differ, to what extent they are similar, or how they are structured. Awareness of this situation has contributed to an attempt to systematise the approach to defining the main forms of measures, understood as prevention tools enabling the implementation of tasks in preventing radicalisation, under the INDEED project.[1]

To unambiguously characterise the term 'long-term evidence-based prevention programme' implemented in P/CVE and deradicalisation already in use, it was decided to formulate the so-called conceptual definition (Kojder, 1976). The process was grounded primarily on the concept of evidence-based practice

(EBP) formulated by the consortium based on conducted research.[2] EBP was defined as a decision-making process that integrates:

1. available external evidence;
2. professional knowledge; and
3. values, preferences and circumstances of the client (Klose, 2022).

Then, the process was continued based on a lexicographical corpus searched from the literature and databases available on the Internet (Shoemaker et al, 2004; Podsakoff et al, 2016). Conclusions were drawn from the aggregation of many sources regarding selected definitions related to the terms such as 'program', 'programme' and 'project' (Catalano et al, 2004; Dałkowski et al, 2009; Szymańska, 2012; Project Management Institute, 2013, 2017; Stawnicka, 2013; Boustani et al, 2015; Brolsma and Kouwenhoven, 2017; Kordaczuk-Wąs, 2018). This made it possible to minimise ambiguities and inconsistencies because many definitions considered separately were not fully satisfactory and formulate the following conceptual definition:

> A preventive work tool in the form of a standardised set of interrelated activities constructed in an evidence-based manner and responding to the needs of the community at a specific level (school, local, regional, national, and so on), whose objectives contribute to the implementation of a common long-term goal focused on stopping or at least reducing the diagnosed social/security threat (for example, radicalisation leading to violent extremism) and its causes, taking into account risk and protective factors, addressed to a strictly defined group of recipients at a selected level of prevention (primary, secondary, tertiary), implemented by various competent entities and accordingly evaluated.

This definition helped to eliminate, or at least reduce, the ambiguity and vagueness of this concept. In addition, which is extremely important from the perspective of the systematic approach to programme design, it gave the defined term specific characteristics and content, drawing attention to the elements of the structure of such an initiative. This structure must include standard elements to refer to the initiative as a comprehensive programme and to design it efficiently.

Standardisation in designing and performing prevention programmes

Standardisation refers to the practice of adhering to a standard routine or procedure in operation (Shook, 2022). In management, standardising data elements is essential for creating a unified, integrated and efficient data model (Cong et al, 2013). In computer programming, this involves a series of instructions that tell the computer what to do. Some essential standard elements include statements, functions, variables, operators, objects, properties, methods and comments (McGrath, 2016). In terms of the International Organization for Standardization (ISO), a standard is a document established by consensus and approved for common and repeated use, rules, guidelines or characteristics of activities or their results aimed at achieving an optimal degree of order in each context. These standards are based on the consolidated results of science, technology and experience (ISO, 2019). Following the concept of standardisation allows a practice to be designed systematically, formulating its specific standard elements.

Indications as to the desired and, at the same time, necessary construction elements that will affect the manner and efficiency of preventive activity can also be found in the area related to solving social problems. In the field of counteracting drug addiction, the European Monitoring Centre for Drugs and Drug Addiction (EMCDDA) laid out European quality standards in addiction prevention, indicating the design cycle of the prevention programme consisting of eight stages:

1. needs assessment;
2. resource assessment;
3. programme formulation;
4. intervention design;
5. management and mobilisation of resources;
6. delivery and monitoring;
7. final evaluations; and
8. dissemination and improvement (EMCDDA, 2011, p 55).

Based on the standards of prevention programmes and mental health promotion resulting from the Exchange on Drug Demand Reduction Action (EDDRA) programme, standards and criteria were also prepared and implemented in Poland for assessing the quality of mental health prevention and promotion programmes under the recommendation system.[3] According to this, the main standards for constructing a preventive programme based on the so-called logic model include:

1. problem analysis as a starting point for its construction;
2. use of knowledge about risk factors and protective factors;
3. basing it on theoretical theories (models) with proven effectiveness;
4. selection of strategies and methods of action adequate to the set goal and addressees;
5. care for the quality of programme implementation through obligatory monitoring and professional staff selection;
6. the need to ensure appropriate conditions for implementation; and
7. evaluation of the programme to verify the correctness of the adopted assumptions (Polish National Office for Countering Drug Addiction, 2010, 2011).[4]

The Polish police also implemented the concept of listing the precise standards for the design of prevention programmes. In 2015, the Prevention Office of the National Police Headquarters carried out a review of preventative initiatives, along with a diagnosis of irregularities committed during the construction and classification of police preventive programmes. This review led to the conclusion that police activities were often not completed with a documented process examining their effectiveness, and their construction often lacked elements that would allow to qualify a given initiative as a prevention programme (Kordaczuk-Wąs, 2017b). Also, available research results[5] showed that in the scope of designing police preventive activities in police organisational units, there are no normative standards, and these activities are usually prepared based on one's own intuition and knowledge, decisions, and instructions of the superior, as well as based on decisions and instructions from the superior unit (Kordaczuk-Wąs, 2017a). Due to the diagnosed situation, it was considered necessary to eliminate errors in the design and implementation of prevention programmes. It was assumed that the standardisation process would make it possible to standardise the rules for constructing the programmes in question for the entire police force and conduct a reliable evaluation of implemented social activities.

Based on a detailed analysis of the literature on the subject, attention was paid to the programme recommendation system described earlier, based on the standards of mental health prevention and promotion programmes resulting from the EDDRA programme (EMCDDA, 2011; Polish National Centre for Addiction Prevention, 2023). On this basis, after slight modifications, an initial set of elements standardising the construction of prevention programmes was listed (see Table 3.1), which should be considered already at the design stage.

Moreover, the legitimacy of building evidence-based prevention programmes according to elements arranged in a logical sequence was also confirmed by a study conducted in 2021.[6] According

Table 3.1: Standard elements of a preventive programme construction

1	General data about the programme (name, author, entity responsible for implementation, programme type, implementation period)
2	Description of the phenomenon (problem) with the results of the diagnosis (including causes and risk factors)
3	Target audience (addressees)
4	Level of prevention
5	Adopted scientific theories and preventive strategies
6	Protective factors
7	Objectives and indicators measuring the progress of the programme
8	Planned preventive tasks
9	Partner entities
10	Schedule and implementation methods
11	Ways and dates of evaluation (formative, process and results)
12	Sources of information about the programme and methods of dissemination
13	Programme's expenditure (costs and resources)

Source: Adapted from the Polish Education Development Centre (2015)

to 78 per cent of surveyed and interviewed practitioners dealing with preventing and combating radicalisation leading to violent extremism,[7] ensuring high standardisation of the preventive measures increases their effectiveness. Study participants indicated that the processes and standard elements must be mandatorily included by their organisation/institution in the process of long-term comprehensive programme preparation and implementation. In a multiple-choice questionnaire, among the processes, 38 per cent of respondents pointed to the logical model of programme construction that allows the author to discern the current stage of construction, the next step, and how to achieve it by skilfully combining personal experience with knowledge of the underlying mechanisms of the problem, and 47 per cent indicated the diagnosis and analysis of the problem and its causes as a starting point for programme construction. Then, as many as 61 per cent indicated the need to use knowledge about risk factors and protective factors. Specific groups of recipients of the programme clearly indicated based on local needs diagnosis listed among the standard elements building its structure and assumptions were indicated by 38 per cent of respondents, while theories of proven effectiveness by 33 per cent of them. Both the need to formulate specific objectives that meet the requirements of the SMART acronym (that is, Specific, Measurable, Achievable, Relevant, Time-Bound) and corresponding indicators measuring the programme's progress was indicated by 47 per cent of practitioners. The choice of preventive strategies and methods of operation, adequate to the set objectives and specific groups of recipients, were pointed out by 60 per cent of respondents, followed by a selection of programme implementers resulting from reliable analysis of local environment resources ensuring implementation of the programme objectives, indicated by 40 per cent. Assessment of the quality of the programme's implementation and the results obtained (evaluation) as the standard element of the programme was indicated by 58 per cent of practitioners participating in the study (Kordaczuk-Wąs, 2024).

Although the need to include the previously mentioned elements in the constructed prevention programmes is so important for the effectiveness of undertakings around preventing and counteracting radicalisation, it should be noted that a detailed assessment of the level of preparation of many initiatives and the way of their implementation, unfortunately, shows numerous errors or deficiencies in their construction. This often results from difficulties translating the theory available in the literature and applying it in the form of practical solutions. Therefore, the next chapter contains an attempt at a synthetic description, reduced to simple schemes, of selected stages of the construction of a preventive programme. Of course, it is only a specific proposal for a concise presentation of quite complex issues based on theoretical foundations, drawing knowledge from scientific paradigms and from the methodology of social sciences. However, understanding the concept of standard programme elements can be facilitated by systematically going through the process of designing an evidence-based preventive programme, step-by-step, through all its elements.

Step-by-step logic model of evidence-based programme design

The proposed step-by-step logic model for designing evidence-based programmes combines the two models described earlier in this chapter. This specific combination allows the initiative to be presented, thanks to the theory of change model, in its simplest form using limited information. In turn, the programme logic model provides additional information resulting from the programme design and planning process (Wyatt Knowlton and Phillips, 2012). An explanation of assumptions on which the programme is based was visualised in the schematic representations of the programme (Rush and Ogborne, 1991). It allows for a clear separation of the hierarchy and connections between the individual standard elements of its construction and the steps of the design process.

In addition, it also allows the design process to include all components that make up evidence-based practices, which can be understood as a decision-making process that integrates:

1. available external evidence;
2. professional knowledge; and
3. values, preferences and circumstances of the client (Klose, 2022).

The whole process is presented in the example of an educational programme entitled 'UNDERSTAND = RESPECT' to prevent radicalisation leading to discrimination and hate speech.[8] During the construction of this programme, a logic model was used to 'step-by-step' plan and describe the process of constructing, implementing and evaluating the programme. At the stage of constructing and planning its assumptions, the structure of the logic model helped first to define the expectations towards the programme and then to plan all its parameters (standard elements) affecting the desired and assumed changes between its participants. On the other hand, as an evaluation tool, the logic model made it possible to make appropriate design decisions that influenced the programme evaluation trajectory.

The logic model reads from left to right, thus describing the basics of the programme. This means following the chain of reasoning that connects its individual parts (WK Kellogg Foundation, 2004). The simplified diagram depicted in Figure 3.1 illustrates the main three stages of the step-by-step process of evidence-based programme design arranged in a logical sequence of the design process grounded in the theory of change, followed by the logical model of the programme itself and the use of its individual elements. At the same time, the diagram illustrates the systematic approach to programme design, starting with deriving the programme from a theoretical foundation, followed by diagnosing the specific problem the initiative aims to address, and then, based on the formulated recommendations, laying the groundwork for further design of individual standard elements of the programme.

The preparation of an evidence-based prevention programme requires the adoption of a paradigm that will directly indicate

Figure 3.1: The main stages of the step-by-step process of evidence-based programme design addressing the issue of radicalisation

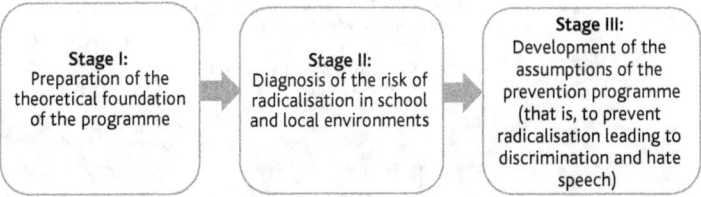

theories, concepts, strategies, as well as methods, techniques and research tools necessary and appropriate from the point of view of the conducted process and later also during the implementation of this initiative. Therefore, the process of preparing a programme preventing radicalisation leading to discrimination and hate speech UNDERSTAND = RESPECT has been grounded in the concept of relational sociology, additionally inscribed in the intellectual space of the paradigm of critical realism, which encourages deep reflection and reconstruction from the roots of both the way of thinking and acting (Porpora, 2015).

The tradition of critical sociology, which encourages orderly and systematic reconstruction of sociological practice based on reflection (Archer, 2013), accompanied the entire process, starting from its first steps in diagnosing the level of actual or potential threat of radicalisation in schools and local communities, through the analysis of the collected research material, to individual steps for constructing all elements of the programme. Therefore, Stage I of the step-by-step process of evidence-based programme design consisted of subsequent logical steps to build the programme's theoretical foundation, as shown in Figure 3.2.

Figure 3.2: The main steps that build the theoretical foundation of an evidence-based programme

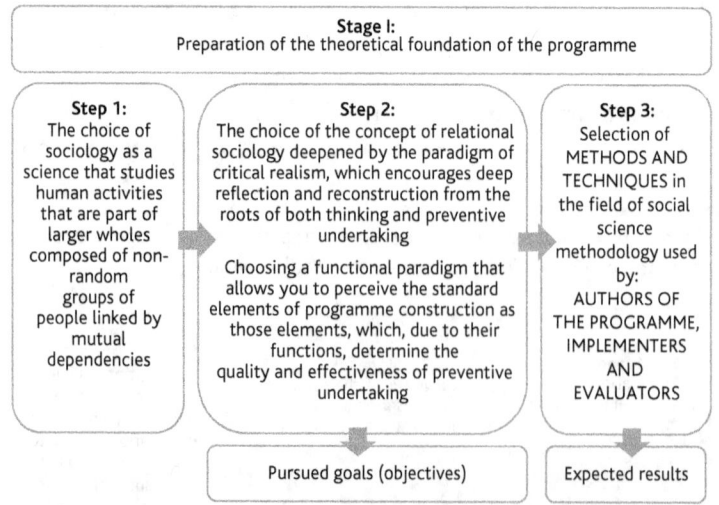

The relational approach to social reality emphasises social interactions and interdependencies and treats both relationships and their objects as equally basic foundations of this reality (Donati, 2011). Therefore, it was recognised that it is reasonable to perceive public problems (radicalisation) and private issues (threats of individuals with radicalisation) relationally and to use the paradigm of relational sociology to develop a methodological, diagnostic and analytical framework for the programme design process that allows both the proper perception and use of these relationships. If the relationship is the beginning of every social fact (Donati, 2007), then this assumption can be applied to the analysis, construction and improvement of preventive undertaking. Thus, the awareness of the existence of this specific relationship between the individual process of radicalisation of individuals and the selection of 'tailor-made', effective forms of preventive activity eliminating or limiting this process made it possible to use the relational paradigm to thoroughly diagnose, analyse and describe the current situation prevailing in schools and local environments,[9] then laying the groundwork for programming and implementing evidence-based preventive measures.

It was also pointed out that the preparation of a comprehensive professional preventive programme should be additionally based on proven standards (elements) of construction, which, on the one hand, determine the improvement of the quality of operation, and on the other hand, enable its coherent and reliable evaluation (Kordaczuk-Wąs, 2017a). Therefore, when creating an interpretative framework for the stage of the process related to designing detailed assumptions (elements) of the programme, the theoretical perspective of the functional paradigm was additionally used (Parsons, 1991). The starting point for such a procedure was the conviction that the aforementioned standard elements of constructing an evidence-based prevention programme are nothing more than specific functional requirements described by Talcott Parsons (1972), which determine the balance of the preventive action system and its effectiveness.

At the same time, the so-called paradigmatic non-contradiction was remembered, which means that both the assumptions underlying the prevention programme and the means of action of the authors, programme implementers and the evaluator should be derived from the concept belonging to the same paradigm (Brzezińska and Brzeziński, 2001), and the adopted paradigms result from one accepted scientific discipline, which for the UNDERSTAND = RESPECT programme is sociology. Figure 3.4 illustrates a method of maintaining paradigmatic consistency.

Designing an evidence-based programme that responds to real social needs then requires gathering knowledge about the undesirable phenomenon (problem), the size and negative effects of which the programme is supposed to limit. The decision to choose a problem should result from reliable, preferably scientifically confirmed, and at the same time, up-to-date information on current threats in the local environment. A detailed and precise diagnosis of the problem indicated as Stage II of the step-by-step process of evidence-based programme design, is of key importance for further decisions made during the process of programme construction.

The new morphogenetic methodology, derived from the paradigm of relational sociology, provides tools for analysing the mutual relations of culture, structure and subjective agency (Archer, 2015), which makes it possible to detect relationships between the components of the preventive system with relational emergent properties perceived as emergent causal forces. In practice, this means the possibility of describing and explaining whether and to what extent individual parts of the school and local social order are at risk of radicalisation leading to discriminatory behaviour or hate speech, how they found themselves in a given relationship with each other, what risk factors (causes) were responsible, and through which prophylactic interactions they can be effectively prevented or at least effectively reduced. In the case of the UNDERSTAND = RESPECT programme, the morphogenetic approach thus made it possible to create a framework for conducting a practical social analysis in the form of a diagnosis and describing the relationship between emergent sociocultural contexts occurring in schools and local communities in two key areas. The first was related to teachers' and students' perception of the degree and type of risk of radicalisation processes, which may lead to discrimination and hate speech. The second, in turn, concerned the needs and expectations of students and teachers regarding preventive measures planned in the described area.

The research population of the diagnosis consisted of two research subpopulations. According to the assumptions of the 'humanistic coefficient' concept, all social facts are always connected with the activities of some people and can only be studied from the perspective of people in whose experiences they occur (Sztompka, 2012). Personal experiences and observations of people are one of the main sources of sociological knowledge (Znaniecki, 2008), while social realism requires the presence of social actors with properties and powers to, on the one hand, monitor their own lives, mediate between the structural and cultural properties of society, and contribute to the social transformation of social reality (Archer, 2015). Therefore, the diagnosis voiced the opinions and expectations of both teachers perceived as collective social actors responsible for constructing and implementing preventive measures, as well as students, that is, individual actors who, as potentially at risk of radicalisation, are currently or will be recipients of relevant measures.[10] The main aspects covered by this diagnosis are presented in the diagram in Figure 3.3.

It should be emphasised that the diagnosis conducted during the preparation of the UNDERSTAND = RESPECT programme combined two elements from the defined evidence-based practice, namely evidence and practical expertise (Klose, 2022). Through a scientifically prepared and conducted study and its results, it

Figure 3.3: The main aspects of diagnosis in building the evidence-based foundation of a preventive programme

Stage II: Diagnosis of the risk of radicalisation in school and local environments provided information on:	
The current state of radicalisation issue (that is, types and scale of discriminatory behaviour, as well as other manifestations of radical behaviour; risk factors (causes) leading to or potentially leading to the occurrence of radicalisation processes)	The essential details for designing the individual standards/components/elements of preventive programme (that is, target groups; types and forms of preventive tasks; key prevention strategies and protecting factors; recommended partner entities)

Confirmed the legitimacy of constructing and implementing a comprehensive preventive programme focused on preventing radicalisation leading to discrimination and hate speech

confirmed the conclusion formulated by experts working in preventing and combating radicalisation, who, based on their own practice experience, believed that a comprehensive long-term programme in preventing radicalisation leading to discrimination and hate speech was needed in Poland.

The diagnosis confirmed the legitimacy of constructing and implementing a comprehensive prevention programme to prevent discrimination and hate speech. In addition, it provided information on the types of discriminatory behaviour and other manifestations of radical behaviour that have occurred or are present in the school and local environment. It explained how students understand and what they associate with the term 'radicalisation' and how they assess the scale of manifestations of radical behaviour leading to discrimination and hate speech at school. Furthermore, the diagnosis identified risk factors leading to radicalisation, discrimination and hate speech present in the school or local environment. The diagnosis also provided information relevant to constructing individual components of the prevention programme to prevent radicalisation leading to discrimination and hate speech. It answered, among other things, the question of what activities in preventing discrimination are currently implemented in schools, indicated those undertakings that need strengthening, identified the target groups that the anti-radicalisation programme should cover, and measured students' interest in participating in such a programme (Kordaczuk-Wąs, 2023).

The diagnosis results were used in Stage III of the step-by-step process of the UNDERSTAND = RESPECT programme design and translated into components of its structure, described in detail in its assumptions. Based on the conducted research, analysis of the collected results and formulated recommendations, it is possible to proceed to design the assumptions of the prevention programme, successively completing all the standard elements of building an evidence-based programme. The scheme depicted in Figure 3.4 shows the individual steps that made up the design process and translated into the already mentioned standard elements of the structure of the designed programme building the programme logic model (Rush and Ogborne, 1991; Wyatt Knowlton and Phillips, 2012).

A detailed description of the mechanism for designing individual elements of the programme and the links between them, as

Figure 3.4: The main steps in building the logic model of an evidence-based programme design

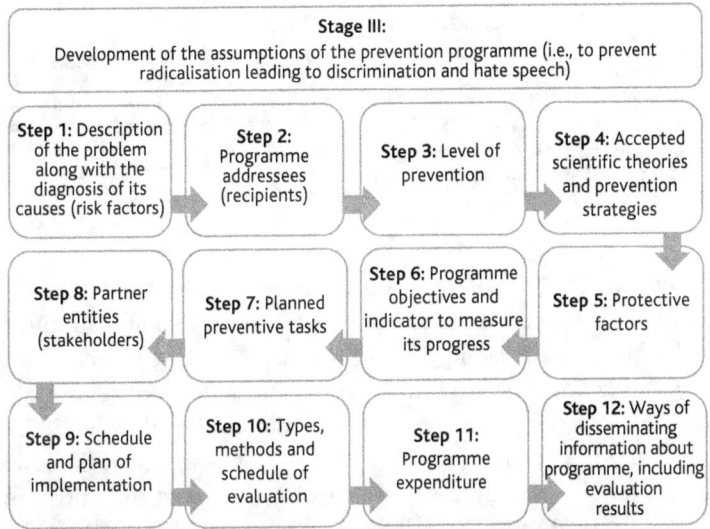

well as the steps that the programme must take to introduce the expected change, is too extensive to include comprehensively in this chapter. However, it is worth showing at least briefly how the selected elements were designed, deriving them from the diagnosis and, at the same time, from the selected design elements.

As it has been repeatedly emphasised, starting work on the programming of preventive undertakings requires a Step 1 dedicated to the description of the diagnosed problem. The diagnosis must show not only what problem we are dealing with in the local environment but also what its causes are. This description is the starting point for formulating the programme's main and specific objectives and then for further stages of programme design. However, the study results revealed many other key elements necessary to build a long-term evidence-based programme. For instance, as presented in a simplified way in Figure 3.5, Step 2 allows for the selection of groups of addressees (recipients) of the programme.

In the next step (Step 3) of designing the programme, a decision was made on the level of prevention. Again, it was not accidental and directly resulted from the diagnosis, which made it possible to

Figure 3.5: Step 2 of the logic model of an evidence-based programme design: selection of programme addresses

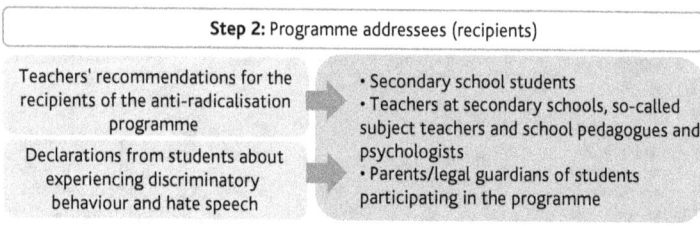

determine the type of the existing threat (problem) and the scale of its occurrence. According to the diagnosis, manifestations of radical behaviour leading to discrimination and hate speech occur at school; however, according to the most frequent assessment of students, they occur 'sometimes' (see Kordaczuk-Wąs, 2023, for details). Therefore, the programme was designed at the level of universal prevention, which aims to counteract the initiation of school youth into risky behaviours (Szymańska, 2012) in the form of discrimination and hate speech by providing appropriate information on radicalisation leading to these behaviours, reducing risk factors and strengthening protective factors. The described characteristics of universal prevention were then reflected in the adopted theories, strategies and proposed preventive actions.

The programme has been based on proven concepts and scientific theories, as well as preventive strategies, which, on the one hand, explain the mechanisms of emergence and development of the diagnosed problems, and on the other hand, allow for the formulation of indications for the planned preventive actions (Gordon, 1983). In Step 4 of the design process for the programme, strategies based on the theory of resilience, the theory of problem behaviour and the theory of social learning were used (Bernard, 2004; Jessor, 2014; Polish National Office for Countering Drug Addiction, 2021). Bearing in mind that the selection of appropriate prevention strategies determining the form of the adopted preventive actions is one of the key stages in designing a professional, comprehensive prevention programme, teachers were also asked about the leading strategies that should become the basis of the programme preventing discrimination and hate speech. Moreover, in Step 5, protective factors have been adopted for the programme. They are understood in science as certain features, situations, conditions or events that reduce the likelihood of problems. Therefore, selecting protective factors, derived from the adopted concepts and strategies, was the next step in preparing the prevention programme. Following the assumptions of the accepted resilience theory, the UNDERSTAND = RESPECT programme focuses on strengthening the protective factors that make it possible to weaken the diagnosed risk factors. The initial selection of key protective factors adopted for the programme was based on the achievements of the resilience theory (Masten and Obradovic, 2008). Then, the selection was supplemented with specific factors protecting against radicalisation, which, according to the surveyed teachers, should be emphasised in the prevention programme preventing discrimination and hate speech.

As previously mentioned many times, based on the results of the diagnosis of the problem and its causes, in the next step (Step 6), it was possible to determine the main objective (aim) and specific operational objectives of the programme. Collected results made it possible to distinguish three main categories of problematic behaviours, discriminatory behaviours and signs of hate speech, as well as other radical behaviours observed in schools by teachers and students. The statements of the surveyed students made it possible to additionally indicate the threats they directly experienced. The knowledge about the diagnosed problem allowed the formulation of the programme's main goal. While formulating the programme's main and specific objectives, the process of evolution of preventive programmes and the transition from the traditional to the modern model of their construction were also considered. The programme was prepared in accordance with a modern model, in which the purpose of the planned activities focuses mainly on promoting behaviour free from the diagnosed problem instead of only combating it (Ostaszewski, 1996). As the programme was included in the trend of positive prevention, it also had an impact on the assumed main as well as operational prevention goals (Szymańska, 2012). The simplified brief schemes in Figure 3.6 show how the main and selected operational objectives (goals) derived from the diagnosis.

Then, the specific objectives of the programme were formulated, derived from diagnosed protective factors that could weaken the

Figure 3.6: Step 6 of the logic model of an evidence-based programme design: formulation of the programme's main objective

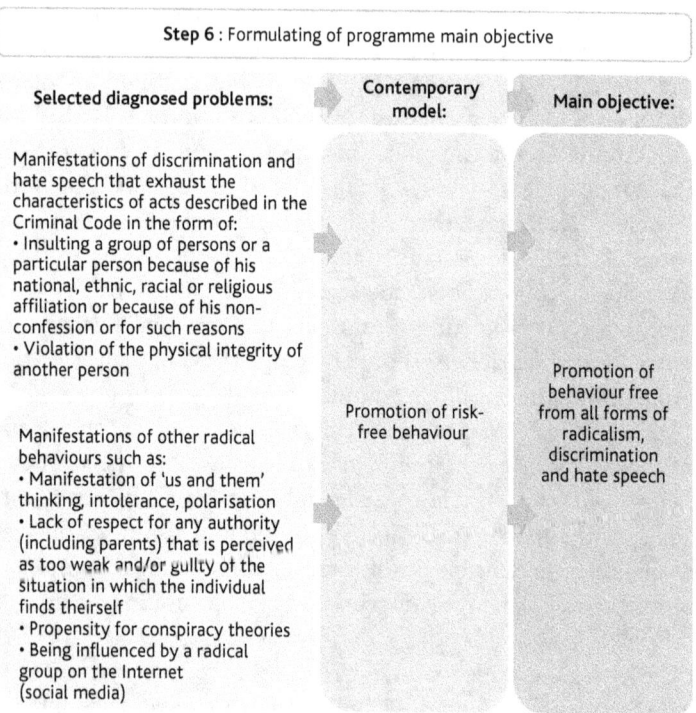

diagnosed risk factors understood as the causes of radicalisation leading to discrimination and hate speech, the implementation of which will translate into the achievement of the adopted programme's main aim. Moreover, to correctly formulate the programme's objectives, the most common manifestations of radicalisation protective factors were related to the leading theories and prevention strategies adopted. The scheme in Figure 3.7 illustrates the process of formulating selected objectives in a simplified way.

Formulated main and operational objectives are measurable and, what is extremely important, consider the accepted scientific theories and the resulting preventive strategies. What is more, at this stage of programme construction, close attention was also paid to the fact that the effectiveness of the implemented prevention programme is determined based on monitoring the

Figure 3.7: Step 6 of the logic model of an evidence-based programme design: formulation of the programme's operational objectives

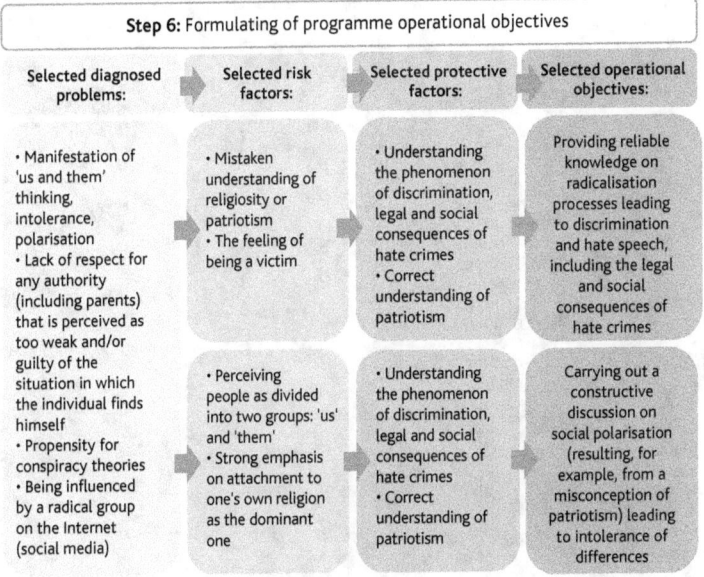

implementation of the assumed prevention goals (objectives) (Kordaczuk-Wąs, 2018). For this purpose, indicators have been adopted to determine whether the objectives have been achieved in full, in part, or not following the adopted assumptions. They are a signpost for the correct implementation of the programme. They allow accountability for the progress in its implementation and determine the success of the activities to be carried out (Polish National Office for Countering Drug Addiction, 2010). The scheme in Figure 3.8 illustrates the process of formulating indicators, together with the evaluation procedure, that is, the research method and technique resulting from the theoretical foundation of the programme, adopted for the main objective of the UNDERSTAND = RESPECT programme.

The programme was tailor-made, which means responding not only to the actual threats of radicalisation but also to the needs related to the programme's content to prevent these threats. At the same time, its assumptions reflect both the expectations of students as potential recipients of the designed preventive measure, as well as

Figure 3.8: Step 6 of the logic model of an evidence-based programme design: measuring progress in achieving the programme's main objective

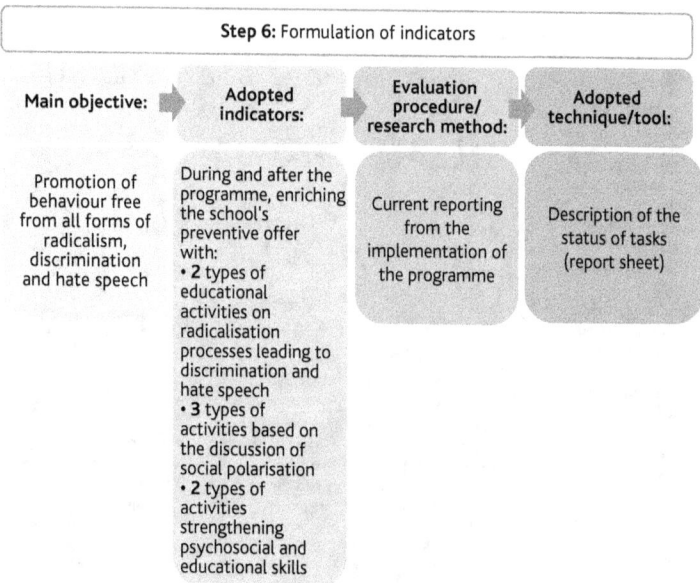

teachers treated as recipients, and in the longer term, also potential implementers of activities aimed at preventing radicalisation leading to discrimination and hate speech. To prepare this tailor-made programme, teachers were asked during the diagnosis about tasks that needed strengthening in their school. The answers provided by teachers allowed, in Step 7, the identification of the forms of preventive tasks that would be strengthened through the activities designed in the programme. Then, when designing the programme, students' preferences were also considered, and in this way, a set of preventive tasks was designed to be implemented as part of the programme.

The selection of partner entities for the programme should also not be accidental, nor should it be based only on the entity's availability in the local environment. Therefore, in the next step (Step 8) of designing the UNDERSTAND = RESPECT programme, the planned programme activities were compared with the results of the diagnosis regarding the types of entities with which schools most often cooperate to implement preventive measures. In addition, the suggestions of students and teachers regarding entities from their local communities to invite for cooperation in the programme preventing radicalisation leading to discrimination and hate speech were considered. Then, in Step 9, a programme schedule was prepared based on the diagnosed needs regarding the types and forms of preventive activities. Additionally, all activities were derived from accepted scientific theories, prevention strategies, diagnosed protective factors and adopted prevention goals.

In the next step (Step 10), it was time for the initial evaluation design. The UNDERSTAND = RESPECT programme covered all its types, starting from formative evaluation, enabling the assessment of the correctness of the action programming, through evaluation of the process, that is, monitoring its progress, to the evaluation of results carried out after the completion of the pilot implementation of the programme. The methodology of the evaluation study, that is, the methods, techniques and tools used to carry it out, was derived from the theoretical foundation adopted for the programme and the paradigms described in detail in Stage I. The scheme in Figure 3.9 shows how to design the general assumptions of evaluation.

In Steps 11 and 12, a complete calculation of expenditures on the programme was carried out, including financial, personnel and material expenditures to be incurred by its implementers. At the design stage, these were the estimated costs of all planned preventive and administrative tasks, while the current version is supplemented during the long-term implementation of the initiative in consultation with partner entities. Planning ways of disseminating information about the programme, that is its assumptions, but also its current implementation, course and results, was also an important step in the prevention programme's design process. This made it possible to include the most convenient channels of communication about the programme and communication between current and potential producers and recipients.

The scheme depicted in Figure 3.10 shows the complementary process of designing the UNDERSTAND = RESPECT programme. It integrates a change theory model showing the three main stages of this process in its simplest form using limited

Figure 3.9: Step 10 of the logic model of an evidence-based programme design: formulation of evaluation from general assumptions

Step 10		
Type of evaluation:	Area under assessment:	Methods, techniques of research:
Formative evaluation	Evaluation of the correctness of programming the assumptions of the programme, the scope of implementation of planned tasks, discussion of changes, additions, etc.	• Consultations with the implementation team • Consultations with school representatives (teaching council, parents' council) • Discussion
Process evaluation	Ongoing programme monitoring (including indicators planned to be achieved during the implementation of the programme – according to the schedule)	• Evaluation surveys (for individual preventive actions) • Face-to-face interviews • Analysis of the degree of achievement of indicators measuring program progress • Examination of documents (reports from the implementation of completed tasks)
Results (outcomes) evaluation	Assessment of the degree of achievement of the assumed preventive objectives (goals); as well as evaluation of the programme by recipients and implementers	• Analysis of the degree of achievement of indicators measuring programme progress • Survey study • Examination of documents • Face-to-face interviews

information; with the programme logic model, which provides additional information to help in designing and planning, and then clearly describing the assumptions of the initiative, the mechanism of its operation and how to measure progress in achieving the intended goals. It also shows the importance and usefulness of scientific evidence from the diagnosis of radicalisation in schools and local communities in the steps of designing almost all standard elements of the structure of this evidence-based programme.

Logic model layouts are as diverse as the programmes they represent and can be applied to initiatives carried out in P/CVE and other crime prevention domains. As constructing a prevention programme is an iterative process, it should be emphasised that stakeholders can correct each model whenever necessary. Also, in the case of the UNDERSTAND = RESPECT programme, any

A step-by-step logic model

Figure 3.10: Complementary process of evidence-based programme design

---

The main stages of the step-by-step process of evidence-based programme designing addressing issue of radicalisation

| Stage I: Preparation of the theoretical foundation of the programme | Stage II: Diagnosis of the risk of radicalisation in school and local environment | Stage III: Development of prevention programme assumptions (that is, to prevent radicalisation leading to discrimination and hate speech) |

The main steps that build the theoretical foundation of an evidence-based programme

Stage I: Preparation of the theoretical foundation of the programme

Step 1: The choice of sociology as a science that studies human activities that are part of larger wholes composed of non-random groups of people linked by mutual dependencies

Step 2: The choice of the concept of relational sociology deepened by the paradigm of critical realism, which encourages deep reflection and reconstruction from the roots of both thinking and preventive undertaking. Choosing a functional paradigm that allows you to perceive the standard elements of program construction as those elements, which due to their functions, they determine the quality and effectiveness of preventive undertaking

Step 3: Selection of METHODS AND TECHNIQUES in the field of social science methodology used by:
- AUTHORS OF THE PROGRAMME,
- IMPLEMENTERS AND EVALUATORS

Pursued goals (objectives) | Expected results

Stage II:
Diagnosis of the risk of radicalisation in school and local environments provided information on:

| The current state of radicalisation issue (that is, types and scale of discriminatory behaviour, as well as other manifestations of radical behaviour; risk factors (causes) leading to or potentially leading to the occurrence of radicalisation processes) | The essential details for designing the individual standards/components/elements of preventive programme (that is, target groups; types and forms of preventive tasks; key prevention strategies and protecting factors; recommended partner entities) |

Confirmed the legitimacy of constructing and implementing a comprehensive preventive programme focused on preventing radicalisation leading to discrimination and hate speech

---

Stage III:
Development of the assumptions of the prevention programme (that is, to prevent radicalisation leading to discrimination and hate speech)

Step 1: Description of the problem along with the diagnosis of its causes (risk factors)

Step 2: Programme addressees (recipients)
- Declarations from students about experiencing discriminatory behaviour and hate speech
- Declarations from students about experiencing discriminatory behaviour and hate speech

- Secondary school students
- Teachers of secondary schools, so-called subject teachers and school pedagogues and psychologists
- Parents/legal guardians of students participating in the programme

Step 3: Level of prevention

Step 4: Accepted scientific theories and prevention strategies

Step 5: Protective factors

Figure 3.10: Complementary process of evidence-based programme design (continued)

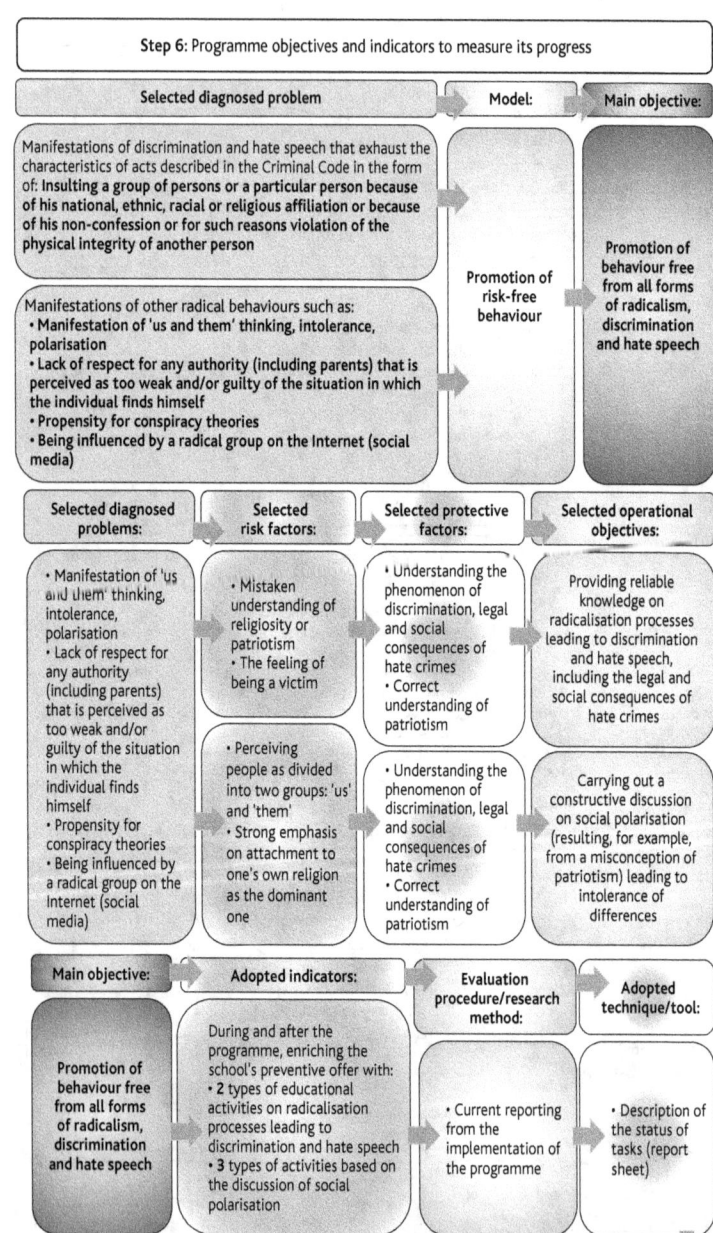

Figure 3.10: Complementary process of evidence-based programme design (continued)

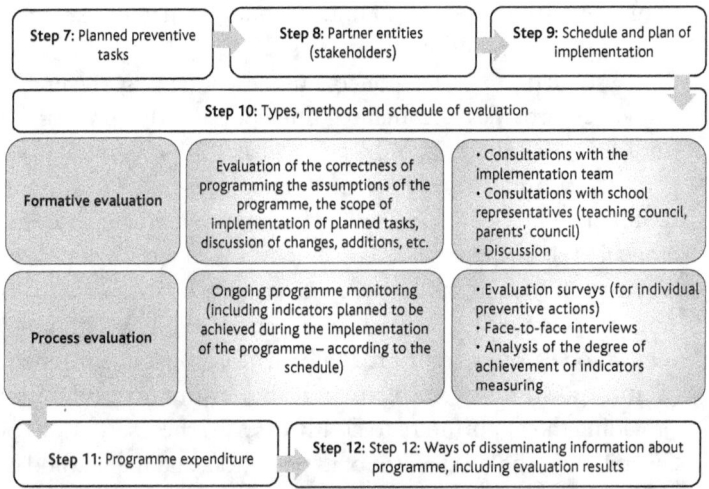

change to the assumptions is described in the current programme documentation, characterising in full detail all standardised elements building the assumptions of the programme as well as its implementation.

Using a practical example, the proposed simplified logical model for designing an evidence-based long-term programme visualises sequences of processes and activities leading through successive stages and steps, enabling building the programme's structure and leading to the intended changes resulting from these activities. It explains step-by-step the principles and procedures for designing and planning the P/CVE initiative using knowledge from scientific diagnosis. Thus, it can encourage professionals and decision-makers to adopt the evidence-based paradigm into their daily practice.

Summary

- In P/CVE, there is an observed need for a more comprehensive approach that includes not only current, security-based and basic counter-terrorism measures but also systematic, effective preventive measures directly addressing the root

causes of extremist violence based on well-defined steps and some guiding principles that offer prevention planners a comprehensive approach to understanding and addressing the problems facing their communities.
- The systematic approach concept used in designing preventive initiatives provides the main framework for the process by outlining its individual phases that enable logical and cause-and-effect connections. Furthermore, it leads to the technique of initiative modelling by using a logical model that allows for a detailed description of data elements.
- Theory of change models present an idea or initiative in its simplest form using limited information, while programme logic models offer additional information to assist in design, planning, strategy, monitoring and evaluation, thereby providing the opportunity to clearly describe the assumptions of the initiative, the mechanism of its operation, and the method of measuring progress towards the intended goals. Both techniques of modelling the design process of a preventive initiative are not mutually exclusive but can be seen as complementary.
- In the area of preventing and counteracting radicalisation leading to violent extremism, there is a lack of typology or categorisation of undertaken activities. The literature and practice mention implementing a range of PC/VE 'interventions', 'programmes', 'actions' and 'projects' among these activities. However, there are no definitions explaining these measures, what they mean, how they differ, to what extent they are similar, and how they are structured.
- EBP integrates three core components: (1) available external evidence; (2) professional knowledge; and (3) the values, preferences and circumstances of the client; a key challenge for implementing EBP is to create a robust evidence base that addresses the needs and concerns of practitioners (Klose, 2022).
- A long-term preventive programme is a preventive work tool in the form of a standardised set of interrelated activities constructed in an evidence-based manner and responding to community needs at a specific level (school, local, regional, national and so on), whose objectives contribute to the implementation of a common long-term goal focused on stopping or at least reducing the diagnosed social/security

threat (for instance, radicalisation leading to violent extremism) and its causes, taking into account risk and protective factors, addressed to a strictly defined group of recipients at a selected level of prevention (primary, secondary, tertiary), implemented by various competent entities and accordingly evaluated.
- Standardisation allows for a systematic approach to designing a practice or routine to follow, guided by specified standard elements, which can be considered the most important requirements for both creators and implementers of preventive activities by modern science.
- Standard elements constitute the programme's description, outline its structure and act as specific steps that guide programme authors through the design process.
- At the stage of constructing and planning programme assumptions, the logical model's structure first helps to define the expectations towards the programme and then to plan all its parameters (standard elements) that influence the desired and anticipated changes among its participants.
- The main three stages of the step-by-step process for evidence-based programme design, arranged in a logical sequence, present the systematics of thinking about the need to derive the programme from (1) a theoretical foundation, progressing through (2) the process of diagnosing the problem to which the proposed initiative relates, and then, based on the formulated recommendations, (3) laying the groundwork for further design of individual standard elements of the programme.
- The preparation of an evidence-based prevention programme requires the adoption of a paradigm that will directly indicate theories, concepts, strategies, as well as methods, techniques and research tools necessary and appropriate for both the design process and the subsequent implementation of the initiative.
- Designing an evidence-based programme to address real social needs requires gathering knowledge about the undesirable phenomenon (problem), its scope, and the negative effects the programme aims to mitigate. Choosing a problem should be based on reliable, preferably scientifically confirmed, and at the same time, up-to-date information on current threats in the local environment. A detailed and precise diagnosis of

the problem is critical for subsequent decisions made during the process of evidence-based programme design.

Suggested directions for future research

The following questions can orient further research and discussion in the area:

- How to define, create typologies and categorise initiatives undertaken in the area of crime prevention, including preventing and counteracting radicalisation leading to violent extremism, such as 'interventions', 'programmes', 'actions' and "projects" in a way that explains what they mean, how they differ, and to what extent they are similar?
- What are the standard elements of such security threat prevention initiatives as (1) policies and strategies, (2) long-term prevention programmes and (3) short-term actions, which outline the structure and act as concrete steps guiding authors through the process of their logical and evidence-based design, and implementers through the process of their implementation and evaluation?
- What are the conditions for the effective use in practice of the scientifically grounded concept of a comprehensive 'systematic approach' to planning and designing preventive initiatives, allowing practitioners to model initiatives using a logical model derived from the diagnosis of the root causes of security threats and describing in detail the individual elements of the initiative (such as goals and indicators measuring progress, target groups, tailored activities, types and methods of evaluation, and so on)?

Notes

[1] Project on 'Strengthening a comprehensive approach to preventing and counteracting radicalisation based on a universal evIdeNce-based moDEl for Evaluation of raDicalisation prevention and mitigation' (acronym INDEED). This project aims to use evidence-based approaches to strengthen first-line practitioners' and policy makers' knowledge, capabilities, and skills for designing, planning, implementing and evaluating Preventing Violent Extremism, Countering Violent Extremism and deradicalisation initiatives, such as policies and strategies, long-term programmes, short-term actions and ad-hoc interventions, in an effective and proven manner. This project received funding from the European Union's Horizon 2020 Research and

Innovation Programme under grant agreement No. 101021701 and is managed by the Polish Platform for Homeland Security (PPHS) with Dr Marzena Kordaczuk-Wąs as Coordinator. The project's duration is 36 months (September 2021–August 2024) – more at https://www.indeedproject.eu/.

2   The entire Work Package 1 of the INDEED project was devoted to the scientific recognition of what evidence-based practice means and how evidence-based evaluation should be understood. More details on this topic are available in Klose (2022).

3   Polish standards and criteria for assessing the quality of preventive and mental health promotion programmes under the recommendation system were developed by the National Bureau for Drug Prevention in cooperation with the Institute of Psychiatry and Neurology, the Education Development Center and the State Agency for Solving Alcohol Problems.

4   In turn, referring to the disturbing results of research on the quality of school prevention programmes, the Laboratory of Youth Prevention 'Pro-M' of the Institute of Psychiatry and Neurology, together with the State Agency for Solving Alcohol Problems, also pointed to certain standards that properly constructed prevention programmes should meet. These standards include (1) knowledge of protective and risk factors, (2) the use of effective preventive strategies, (3) logical structure of the programme containing specific objectives meeting the requirements defined by the SMART acronym (that is, Specific, Measurable, Adequate, Realistic and Timely), (4) programme implementers, (5) methods of programme implementation, (6) intensity of activities and (7) evaluation methods (Borucka et al, 2013; more on the topic in Koczurowska, 2002). The presented lists of standards for the construction of prevention programmes are largely consistent, although the most comprehensive and exhaustive is undoubtedly the recommendation system proposed by the Center for Education Development.

It contains standards and criteria for evaluating prevention programmes implemented by schools and other educational institutions before inclusion in the pool of so-called recommended programmes. These standards include: (1) General information about the programme (name, author, entity responsible for implementation, type of programme), (2) Programme implementation period, (3) Description of the phenomenon (problem) along with the diagnosis, (4) Programme objectives (general and specific), (5) Programme assumptions, (6) Recipients of the programme (target group), (7) Indicators measuring programme progress, (8) Planned activities (type, length and intensity), (9) Outlays on the programme (material and personal), (10) Method of implementation (supervision, evaluation, introduction of changes, training of implementers, cooperation with institutions and the local community), (11) Process evaluation, and (12) Sources of information about the programme and methods of dissemination (Polish Education Development Centre, 2015, pp 10–15). The system evaluates programmes in mental health promotion, addiction prevention (drug addiction prevention, prevention of alcohol problems) and programmes for the prevention of other problem (risk) behaviours of children and youth. Standards enable the examination of programmes both in terms of meeting the detailed requirements relating to the quality of the programme as a whole, as well as the individual stages of its implementation, that is, the stage of diagnosis and assessment of needs, selection of the target group, planning goals and methods of their implementation, ensuring the quality of implementation, as well as monitoring and evaluation effects of the programme during the evaluation (more details in Polish National Centre for Addiction Prevention, 2023).

[5] The survey was conducted in 2012 as part of the preparation for a doctoral dissertation on a sample of 185 police officers responsible for implementing preventive measures in 12 counties randomly selected from all over Poland for the study. Read more in Kordaczuk-Wąs (2017a, pp 325–344).

[6] A study on standardisation and an evidence-based approach to preventing radicalisation and other security threats conducted in 2021 on a sample of 57 practitioners and policy makers registered as experts working in P/CVE in the Radicalisation Awareness Network database. More about methodology, course of the study and its results in Kordaczuk-Wąs (2024).

[7] It is worth adding that the respondents included representatives from law enforcement agencies, educational and social care systems, local authorities such as municipalities, community and non-governmental organisations, the probation system, and the penitentiary, correctional and policy sectors.

[8] An evidence-based educational programme to prevent radicalisation leading to discrimination and hate speech called 'UNDERSTAND = RESPECT' was developed, on the level of primary prevention, according to a logic model grounded in social science and based on evidence from a diagnosis of the threat of radicalisation and the need for its prevention, conducted by teachers and students in Poland in 2020. The Polish Platform for Homeland Security implemented the pilot in cooperation with the 1st High School in Gorzow Wielkopolski from December 2021 to June 2022. More about the programme here: https://ppbw.pl/en/preventiveprogram/.

[9] An in-depth description of the theoretical framework and a detailed description of the diagnosis forming the basis for developing the assumptions of the programme can be found in Kordaczuk-Wąs (2023).

[10] One hundred and forty respondents from all over Poland participated in the teacher survey conducted between May and June 2020. In turn, the survey addressed to students, conducted from 10–30 November 2020, 279 students attending grades 1–3 of a general high school. For a detailed description of the diagnosis carried out, the results of which became the basis for developing the assumptions of the programme, see Kordaczuk-Wąs (2023).

References

Archer, M.S. (2013) 'Morfogeneza społeczeństwa: gdzie pasuje Człowieczeństwo' ['The morphogenesis of society: Where humanity fits'], in M.S. Archer (ed) *Człowieczeństwo. Problem Sprawstwa* [*Humanity: The Problem of Agency*], Kraków: Wydawnictwo Nomos, pp 125–39

Archer, M.S. (2015) 'Morfogeneza – ramy wyjaśniające realizmu' ['Morphogenesis – an explanatory framework for realism'], *Uniwersyteckie Czasopismo Socjologiczne*, 10: 40–3.

Asimow, M. (1962) *Introduction to Design*, Hoboken, NJ: Prentice-Hall.

Bernard, B. (2004) *Resiliency: What We Have Learned*, San Francisco: WestEd.

Borucka, A., Pisarska, A. and Frączek, R. (2013) 'Kluczowe kryteria oceny programów profilaktycznych' ['Key criteria for assessing preventive programmes], *Świat Problemów*, 21(1): 15–21.

Boustani, M.M., Frazier, S.L., Becker, K.D., Bechor, M., Dinizulu, S.M., Hedemann, E.R., et al (2015) 'Common elements of adolescent prevention programs: Minimizing burden while maximizing reach', *Administration and Policy in Mental Health and Mental Health Services Research*, 42(2): 209–19.

Brolsma, D. and Kouwenhoven, M. (2017) *PRINCE2 Edition Foundation Courseware English* (2nd edn), Hertogenbosch: Van Haren Publishing.

Brzezińska, A. and Brzeziński, J. (2001) 'Metodologiczne problemy ewaluacji programów profilaktycznych stosowanych wobec młodzieży' ['Methodological problems in the evaluation of preventive programmes for young people'], in J.Ł. Grzelak and M.J. Sochocki (eds) *Ewaluacja Profilaktyki Problemów Dzieci i Młodzieży* [*Evaluation of the Prevention of Children and Youth Problems*], Warszawa: Pracownia Profilaktyki Problemowej, pp 117–45

Catalano, R.F., Berglund, M.L., Ryan, J.A.M., Lonczak, H.S. and Hawkins, J.D. (2004) 'Positive youth development in the United States: Research findings on evaluations of Positive Youth Development Programs', *Annals of the American Academy of Political and Social Science*, 591: 98–124.

Chen, H. (2005) *Practical Program Evaluation: Assessing and Improving Planning, Implementation, and Effectiveness*, Thousand Oaks: SAGE.

Cong, L., Yang, Y., Zhu, D., Yin, M. and Li, J. (2013) 'Definition and standardization of data elements' attributes in land and resources management', in D. Li and Y. Chen (eds) *Computer and Computing Technologies in Agriculture VI, CCTA 2012, IFIP Advances in Information and Communication Technology*, vol 393, Berlin: Springer, pp 309–20

Dałkowski, B., Staśto, L. and Zalewski, M. (2009) 'NCB National Competence Baseline', *Polskie Wytyczne Kompetencji IPMA, Wersja 3.0* [*Polish IPMA Competence Guidelines, Version 3.0*], Warszawa: Stowarzyszenie Project Management Polska.

Donati, P. (2007) *Che Cos' è la Sociologia Relazionale? Breve Itinerario di Conoscenza della Teoria Relazionale in Sociologia* [*What is Relational Sociology? Brief Itinerary of Knowledge of Relational Theory in Sociology*]. Available from https://www.docsity.com/it/la-sociologia-relazionale-di-p-donati/780904/ [Accessed 20 November 2020].

Donati, P. (2011) *Birth and Development of the Relational Theory of Society: A Journey Looking for a Deep 'Relational Sociology'*. Available from https://www.relationalstudies.net/uploads/2/3/1/5/2315313/donati_birth_and_development_of_the_relational_theory_of_society.pdf [Accessed 20 November 2020].

Dwyer, J.J.M. and Makin, S. (1997) 'Using a program logic model that focuses on performance measurement to develop a program', *Canadian Journal of Public Health*, 88: 421–5.

EMCDDA (European Monitoring Centre for Drugs and Drug Addiction) (2011) *European Drug Prevention Quality Standards: A Manual for Prevention Professionals*, Lisbon: EMCDDA.

European Commission (2020a) *A Counter-Terrorism Agenda for the EU: Anticipate, Prevent, Protect, Respond*. Available from https://home-affairs.ec.europa.eu/system/files/2020-12/09122020_communication_commission_european_parliament_the_council_eu_agenda_counter_terrorism_po-2020-9031_com-2020_795_en.pdf [Accessed 20 May 2023].

European Commission (2020b) *Action Plan on Integration and Inclusion 2021–2027*. Available from https://eur-lex.europa.eu/legal-content/EN/TXT/?uri=CELEX%3A52020DC0758&qid=1632299185798 [Accessed 20 May 2023].

Fullan, M. (2001) *The New Meaning of Educational Change* (3rd edn), New York: Teachers College Press.

Gordon, R.S. (1983) 'An operational classification of disease prevention', *Public Health Reports*, 98(2): 107–9.

Hubka, V. (1974) *Theorie der Maschinensysteme* [*Theory of Machine Systems*], Berlin: Springer.

Hubka, V. and Eder, W.E. (1996) *Design Science: Introduction to the Needs, Scope and Organization of Engineering Design Knowledge*, London: Springer.

ISO (International Organization for Standardization) (2019) *Good Standardization Practices*, Geneva: International Organization for Standardization. Available from https://www.iso.org/files/live/sites/isoorg/files/store/en/PUB100440.pdf [Accessed 15 June 2020].

Jessor, R. (2014) 'Problem behavior theory: A half-century of research on adolescent behavior and development', in R.M. Lerner, A.C. Petersen, R.K. Silbereisen and J. Brooks-Gunn (eds) *The Developmental Science of Adolescence: History through Autobiography*, London: Psychology Press, pp 239–56.

Klose, S. (2022) 'Report outlining identified, analysed and recommended research approaches, methods and tools for evidence-based evaluation cComing from the area of PVE/CVE and de-radicalisation and other selected disciplines', *INDEED*. Available from https://www.indeedproject.eu/wp-content/uploads/2022/09/INDEED-D1.2-resub.pdf [Accessed 12 September 2023].

Koczurowska, J. (2002) 'Konstruowanie programów profilaktycznych' ['Constructing preventive programs'], in G. Świątkiewicz (ed) *Profilaktyka w Środowisku Lokalnym* [*Prevention in the Local Environment*], Warszawa: KBPN, pp 87–106.

Kojder, A. (1976) 'Definicje i definiowanie w socjologii' ['Definitions and defining in sociology'], *Studia Socjologiczne*, 3(62):287–303

Kordaczuk-Wąs, M. (2017a) *Społeczne Uwarunkowania Policyjnych Działań Profilaktycznych* [*Social Determinants of Police Preventive Activities*], Warszawa: Wydawnictwa Drugie.

Kordaczuk-Wąs, M. (2017b) 'Założenia i przebieg procesu standaryzacji policyjnych programów profilaktycznych' ['Assumptions and course of the process of standardization of police preventive programs'], *Kwartalnik Policyjny*, 3: 82–6.

Kordaczuk-Wąs, M. (2018) *Działania Profilaktyczne, Planowanie i Realizacja* [*Preventive Actions, Planning and Implementation*], Warszawa: Wydawnictwa Drugie.

Kordaczuk-Wąs, M. (2023) *Diagnoza Zagrożenia Radykalizacją Oraz Potrzeb Dotyczących Kluczowych Aspektów Programu Profilaktycznego Opartego na Dowodach* [*Diagnosis of the Risk of Radicalization and Needs Regarding Key Aspects of an Evidence-Based Prevention Program*], Warszawa: Wydawnictwo Oh Book!

Kordaczuk-Wąs, M. (2024) Standardization and an evidence-based approach to preventing radicalisation and other security threats (manuscript in preparation).

Masten, A.S. and Obradovic, J. (2008) 'Disaster preparation and recovery: Lessons from research on resilience in human development', *Ecology and Society*, 13(1): Article 9. Available from https://www.ecologyandsociety.org/vol13/iss1/art9 [Accessed 11 February 2021]

McGrath, M. (2016) *Visual Basic in Easy Steps* (4th edn), Warwickshire: In Easy Steps Limited.

National Center on Birth Defects and Developmental Disabilities (2007) 'Logic models for planning and evaluation: A resource guide for the CDC state birth defects surveillance program cooperative agreement', *National Center on Birth Defects and Developmental Disabilities*. Available from https://www.cdc.gov/ncbddd/birthdefects/models/Resource1-Evaluation-Guide-508.pdf [Accessed 11 February 2021].

Ostaszewski, K. (1996) 'Tradycyjne i współczesne programy profilaktyki uzależnień' ['Traditional and contemporary addiction prevention programs'], *Serwis Informacyjny. Narkomania*, 5/1996.

Pahl, G., Beitz, W., Feldhusen, J. and Grote, K.-H. (2007) *Engineering Design: A Systematic Approach* (3rd edn), London: Springer.

Parsons, T. (1972) *Szkice z Teorii Socjologicznej* [*Sketches of Sociological Theory*], Warszawa: Wydawnictwo PWN.

Parsons, T. (1991) *The Social System*, London: Routledge.

Podsakoff, P.M, MacKenzie, S.B. and Podsakoff, N.P. (2016) 'Recommendations for creating better concept definitions in the organizational, behavioral, and social sciences', *Organizational Research Methods*, 19(2): 159–203.

Polish Education Development Centre [Ośrodek Rozwoju Edukacji, ORE] (2015) *System Rekomendacji. Standardy i Kryteria Oceny Jakości Programów Profilaktycznych i Promocji Zdrowia Psychicznego w Ramach Systemu Rekomendacji [Recommendation System. Standards and Criteria for Assessing the Quality of Preventive and Mental Health Promotion Programs Within the Recommendation System]*, Warszawa: ORE.

Polish National Centre For Addiction Prevention [Krajowe Centrum Przeciwdziałania Uzależnieniom] (2023) 'O systemie rekomendacji' ['About the Recommendation System], *Krajowe Centrum Przeciwdziałania Uzależnieniom*, [online]. Available from https://programyrekomendowane.pl/strony/o-systemie-rekomendacji,116 [Accessed 18 April 2023]

Polish National Office for Countering Drug Addiction [Krajowe Biuro Przeciwdziałania Narkomanii, KBPN] (2010) 'System rekomendacji UE' ['Recommendation system UE'], *Krajowe Biuro Przeciwdziałania Narkomanii*. Available from https://kbpn.gov.pl/portal?id=107298 [Accessed 10 September 2023].

Polish National Office for Countering Drug Addiction [Krajowe Biuro Przeciwdziałania Narkomanii, KBPN] (2011) 'System standardy profilaktyki' ['System standards of prevention'], *Krajowe Biuro Przeciwdziałania Narkomanii*. Available from https://kbpn.gov.pl/portal?id=106145 [Accessed 10 September 2023].

Polish National Office for Countering Drug Addiction [Krajowe Biuro Przeciwdziałania Narkomanii, KBPN] (2021) 'Metody i Strategie Profilaktyczne' ['Prevention methods and strategies'], *Krajowe Biuro Przeciwdziałania Narkomanii*. Available from https://programyrekomendowane.pl/strony/artykuly/strategie [Accessed 10 September 2023].

Porpora, D.V. (2015) *Reconstructing Sociology: The Critical Realist Approach*, Cambridge: Cambridge University Press.

Project Management Institute (2013) *A Guide to Project Management Body of Knowledge* (5th edn), Newtown Square, PA: Project Management Institute.

Project Management Institute (2017) *Guide to Project Management Body of Knowledge* (6th edn), Newtown Square: Project Management Institute.

Radicalisation Awareness Network (2020) 'Collection of inspiring practices', *RAN*. Available from https://home-affairs.ec.europa.eu/networks/radicalisation-awareness-network-ran/collection-inspiring-practices_en [Accessed 5 January 2023].

Rohrbach, L.A. (2014) 'Design of prevention interventions', in Z. Sloboda and H. Petras (eds) *Defining Prevention Science: Advances in Prevention Science*, Boston: Springer, pp 275–91.

Rush, B. and Ogborne, A. (1991) 'Program logic models: Expanding their role and structure for program planning and evaluation', *The Canadian Journal of Program Evaluation*, 6(2): 95–106.

Savaya, R. and Waysman, M. (2005) 'The logic model', *Administration in Social Work*, 29(2): 85–103.

Shoemaker, P.J., Tankard, J.W. and Lasorsa, D.L. (2004) *How to Build Social Science Theories*, Thousand Oaks: SAGE.

Shook, J. (2022) *How Standardized Work Integrates People with Process*, Lean Enterprise Institute Inc. Available from https://www.lean.org/the-lean-post/articles/how-standardized-work-integrates-people-with-process/ [Accessed 6 June 2024].

Stawnicka, J. (2013) *Dialogiczny Wymiar Bezpieczeństwa: Rzecz o Polskiej Policji* [*Dialogic Dimension of Security: About the Polish Police*], Katowice: Wydawnictwo Uniwersytetu Śląskiego.

Substance Abuse and Mental Health Services Administration [SAMHSA] (2019) 'A Guide to SAMHSA's Strategic Prevention Framework', *SAMHSA*. Available from https://www.samhsa.gov/sites/default/files/20190620-samhsa-strategic-prevention-framework-guide.pdf [Accessed 30 October 2023].

Sztompka, P. (2012) *Socjologia. Analiza Społeczeństwa* [*Sociology. Society Analysis*], Kraków: Wydawnictwo Znak.

Szymańska, J. (2012) *Programy Profilaktyczne, Podstawy Profesjonalnej Psychoprofilaktyki* [*Prevention Programs, Basics of Professional Psychoprevention*], Warszawa: Wydawnictwo Ośrodek Rozwoju Edukacji.

Ullman, D.G. (1992) *The Mechanical Design Process*, New York: McGraw-Hill.

UN General Assembly (2015) 'Plan of action to prevent violent extremism. Report of the Secretary-General A/70/674', *UN General Assembly*. Available from https://www.thegctf.org/Portals/1/Documents/Foundational%20Documents/UN/UNSG%20Plan%20of%20Action%20to%20Prevent%20Violent%20Extremism%202015.pdf?ver=2020-01-14-094451-673 [Accessed 15 April 2023].

United Way of America (1996) *Measuring Program Outcomes: A Practical Approach*, Alexandria: United Way of America.

WK Kellogg Foundation (2004) 'Evaluation handbook: Philosophy and expectations', *WK Kellogg Foundation*. Available from https://heller.brandeis.edu/cyc/pdfs/wkkelloggfoundationevaluationhandbook.pdf [Accessed 15 January 2022].

Weiss, C.H. (1995) *Evaluation* (2nd edn), Upper Saddle River: Prentice Hall.

Wyatt Knowlton, L. and Phillips, C.C. (2012) *The Logic Model Guidebook: Better Strategies for Great Results* (2nd edn), Thousand Oaks: SAGE.

Znaniecki, F. (2008) *Metoda Socjologii [Sociologic Method]*, Warszawa: PWN.

4

Evaluation as a standard component of the evidence-based practice assumptions

Marzena Kordaczuk-Wąs

Introduction

This chapter focuses on the process of designing, planning and conducting an evidence-based evaluation. It explains the importance of basing the evaluation of prevention initiatives on research evidence and will focus on the main types of evaluation. At the same time, it explains the difference between social research and programme evaluation. The chapter also explains why evaluation should be considered an integral part of the overall prevention initiative-building process and how to derive its objectives and methodology from the inherent standard elements of a long-term comprehensive prevention programme. Furthermore, special attention is paid to the issue of links between programme objectives, indicators measuring its progress and evaluation, as integral parts of the logical model of the programme.

Importance, role and functions of evaluation

As noted in Chapter 3, the concept of systems approach provides the main framework for the process of designing preventive initiatives such as long-term comprehensive programmes by identifying its individual phases that allow for a logical and cause-and-effect linking of the process. This is also a technique for modelling an initiative using a logical model that allows a detailed description of data elements. Elements are described as standard construction components of a preventive initiative, among which an important place is occupied by evaluation. However, it should also be emphasised that this important element is still quite often omitted or limited, both in the structure of the initiative's assumptions or at the stage of their implementation.

In the meantime, evaluation is an important part of many processes. For example, in the teaching-learning process, it helps teachers and students to improve their teaching and learning. It helps to shape students' value judgements, educational status and achievement, and whatever form it takes, it is inevitable because evaluation is necessary in all areas of educational activity (Ifeoma, 2022). Evaluation in education is also conducted to determine the relative effectiveness of the programme in terms of student behavioural outcomes; to make sound decisions regarding education planning; to determine the value of time, energy and resources invested in the programme; or to help teachers determine the effectiveness of their teaching techniques and learning materials. Finally, evaluation in education also serves to provide education administrators with relevant information about teacher effectiveness and school needs, identify problems that may hinder or prevent the achievement of the set goals, anticipate the general trend in the development of the teaching-learning process, and ensure economical and efficient management of resources (Manichander, 2016). The purpose of evaluation is to provide information on which many educational decisions are made. However, Disha (2020) also outlines the functions of evaluation in teaching and learning, which emphasises its importance for the entire process. This is important because evaluation functions indicate the aspects to be assessed throughout the process that can easily be applied not only to the teaching-learning process but also to other areas related to human-based social activities.

Disha (2020) lists among them the following: (1) the 'placement function' of evaluation helps in undertaking special curricula and conducting individualised teaching, (2) the 'instructional function' helps in establishing and developing ways, methods and techniques of teaching; helps formulate and reformulate appropriate and realistic learning objectives; to improve curricula and evaluates various educational practices; to determine the extent to which learning objectives can be achieved; to improve teaching procedures and the quality of teachers; and helps to plan appropriate and relevant learning strategies. In turn, (3) the 'diagnostic function' makes it possible to diagnose the weak points of the curriculum, propose an appropriate recovery programme, adapt instruction to the different needs of students and assess progress. Moreover, the author also draws attention to (4) the 'administrative function' of evaluation that help guide better education policy and decision-making, including assessing supervisory practice and sound planning. In addition, he points out its (5) 'developmental function' that provide reinforcement and feedback on teaching and learning processes, help modify and improve teaching strategies and learning experiences, and help achieve goals and educational goals. (6) The 'research function' helps provide data for generalising research and clarifying ambiguities for further studies and research. Finally, Disha also points out (7) the 'communication function' that help communicate progress results, to support the process of informing parents about the results of progress, and dissemination of school progress results (Disha, 2020). The functions of evaluation in education justify the necessity of its use. Since these functions are basically universal, their legitimacy is validated in the teaching-learning process and other areas of social life related to human activity and there is a need to ensure their effectiveness, particularly regarding prevention and countering radicalisation that leads to violent extremism and deradicalisation.

The central and universal purpose of evaluation is to promote accountability. The United Nations Evaluation Group has noted that evaluation aims to understand why and to what extent intended and unintended results are achieved. In addition, it allows one to analyse the implications of the results. It can assist in planning, programming, budgeting, implementation and reporting, and can contribute to evidence-based policy making, development effectiveness and organisational efficiency (United Nations Evaluation Group, 2016). Similarly, in the process of improving the quality of work, employee performance evaluation is an important element (Shaout and Yousif, 2014). An effective employee performance evaluation session helps the leaders of a given organisation to make the right decisions for the employee's success and development (Long et al, 2013). Using employee evaluation data can help leaders stimulate, motivate and guide team members, as the higher the motivation of team members, the better the team and organisation perform (Kirovska and Qoku, 2014). Therefore, evaluation enables assessment of the organisation's performance, including individual employee assessment, and also verification, correction or creation of new action plans. Evaluation also allows and should evaluate these action plans as well. In this regard, significant emphasis is placed on the economic aspects of the activity, which the evaluation allows one to assess.

As evidence emerged of the positive impact of social programmes and policies on society, the focus on the aforementioned responsibility expanded to include evaluating the economic return on social investment (Haskins and Margolis, 2015; Steuerle and Jackson, 2016). Increasingly, the public and legislators demand that public funds be spent on initiatives such as programmes and policies where the public benefits outweigh their costs. Therefore, using economic evidence derived from evaluation as an important element of policy making now has considerable support (Steuerle and Jackson, 2016). Moreover, most evaluators agree that programme evaluation can have both a formative function, that is, helping to improve the programme, and a summative function, enabling the decision to continue the programme. Other opportunities offered by programme evaluation include, for example, participation in making decisions about programme installation; participation in decisions regarding its programme continuation, extension or 'certification'; participation in making decisions about programme modifications; or obtaining evidence to gather support for or opposition to the programme (Worthen, 1990).

The Radicalisation Awareness Network (RAN) has noted the importance of evaluation for activities aimed at preventing and combating radicalisation that leads to violent extremism and deradicalisation. In its studies, the RAN highlights the growing importance of evidence-based research and policy in Europe.

Both academics and practitioners require an evaluation of existing programmes and empirical evidence of their effectiveness, as well as an evaluation of the assumptions about the mechanisms of radicalisation on which these programmes are based. Meanwhile, programme evaluation remains a significant gap. In addition to the fact that a limited evidence base supports these programmes, there is also almost no evaluation of their effectiveness. Most of them have descriptions of programmes or their quantitative summaries. Practitioners working in the RAN's areas of operation, such as prison and probation, note that most programmes are not evaluated, and those that are, do not assess their impact and are not made public. Practitioners of counter-narrative campaigns also report a lack of evaluation of these activities (Pisoui and Ahmed, 2016). At the same time, the RAN adds that practitioners still often struggle with how to enable evaluation in a practical, feasible way (RAN, 2019). Following this statement, it is worth adding that research from the INDEED[1] project reveals the main problems for which evaluation is either neglected or inadequately conducted.

As the project emphasises, effective evaluation of initiatives implemented in the field of preventing and countering violent extremism (P/CVE) and deradicalisation and prevention of other security threats (policies and strategies, long-term programmes, short-term actions, ad hoc interventions and so on) is affected by various gaps and bad practices. These bad practices are common across all sectors, undermining their judgements, quality and the impact of their initiatives. Practitioner surveys show, among other things, that in all sectors, 'bad planning' is a persistent practice which manifests in many forms, for instance, lack of early planning, insufficient knowledge of the project/initiative being evaluated, inadequate explanation, and common/shared language around P/CVE evaluation and the deradicalisation domain. In addition, the lack of an effective evaluation methodology, often due to time and financial pressure, affects the design and implementation of evaluations. In most sectors, the methodology is replicated across multiple initiatives without considering the context, purpose and objectives of each initiative/programme. Most importantly, from the perspective of this chapter, the survey shows that most of the sectors covered by INDEED's study do not provide accurate, timely and adequate knowledge of evaluation prior to implementation. This leads to confusion, wrong methodology and weak cooperation between stakeholders. Therefore, the study report emphasises that a well-informed evaluation provides support for evaluation and utilisation of its results (Sahar and Raven, 2022). Due to this situation, it is necessary to prepare practitioners for the design and effective implementation of the evaluation of their activities. It is necessary to explain the mechanisms of its design, as well as the principles that facilitate its implementation. However, to make this possible, it is necessary to start by distinguishing evaluation from other aspects related to performance assessment.

Differences between peer review, measurement, assessment and evaluation

When discussing evaluation, practitioners still often mistakenly or interchangeably use terms such as peer review, measurement and assessment, treating them as evaluation. It is therefore necessary to consolidate the proper definition, understanding and practical use of the concept of evaluation, starting with explaining the differences between evaluation and the other terms mentioned in the subtitle. Although closely connected, peer review, measurement, assessment and evaluation have different meanings and definitions.

Peer or self-review differs from evaluation, as it is intended for internal reflection on the activities carried out to improve the quality of work performed. Importantly, the results are only used internally and are not intended to be published. However, peer/self-review can support evaluation and even be part of it. Peer/self-review and evaluation also differ in their scope of assessment. Whereas a review mainly focuses on casework and management, an evaluation, while fulfilling the same objective, can also consider the 'big picture' and address structural challenges related to funding, workload or strategic issues. Evaluation can and even should provide empirically grounded answers about the effectiveness of the applied solutions. Meanwhile, peer/self-review will never provide such objective reviews because, as already noted, it is based on self-reflection. However, it has an advantage over evaluation because it allows practitioners to develop their skills.

Moreover, a definite strength of the review is that it consists of reflecting on one's own daily practical activities (Van de Donk et al, 2019). To sum up, it can be said that the main purpose of self-assessment and peer review is to revise and improve one's performance (Stancic, 2020; see also Doch et al, 2006; Van den Berg et al, 2006). While the peer or self-review concerns the entire process of reflective thinking about the undertaken or completed initiative and differs in scope and subject from a comprehensive evaluation, measurement and assessment are rather activities by means of which this evaluation can be made or supported.

It is important to emphasise that the measurement is always numeric as it refers to units, symbols, percentages, ranks or raw scores. According to the dictionary, 'measurement' means finding out the exact size or quantity, or something that has a certain size (Turner, 2006). Measurement also means the process of assigning numbers or characteristics to individuals according to certain rules. It is also possible to say that measurement is a quantitative description of someone's performance. An additional simplification of the term allows it to be defined as the process of quantifying the degree to which someone or something possesses a given feature, that is, quality, characteristics or features (Ebel and Frisbie, 1991). However, it is the process of assigning numbers to items, quantities or events to give quantitative meaning to such characteristics. Measurement, therefore, ends with the attribution of quantity but not the evaluation of achievements (Manichander, 2016).

By contrast, assessment can be defined as a systematic procedure for collecting information that can then be used to make inferences about the characteristics of people or things, as well as the process of collecting evidence and drawing conclusions about results (American Educational Research Association, 1999). Assessment is the process of collecting data and then shaping it into an interpretable form, which enables informed judgement. This activity consists of establishing facts that describe the conditions existing at a particular time. While assessment often involves measurements to collect data, its domain is to organise measurement data into interpretable forms based on multiple variables. While assessment may describe progress towards a given goal at a given point in time, it does not address the underlying causes or make recommendations for further action. Following the opinions formulated by some educators comparing assessment with evaluation, one can express the opinion that evaluation is generally used when the subject is not individuals or groups of people but the effectiveness of the course, curriculum or teaching method. On the other hand, assessment is usually used to measure or define personal attributes (for example, learning environment, achievements). Different quantitative data collection instruments, such as tests, inventories, questionnaires, observation schedules and so on, are used to obtain measurement data from different sources. All these sources provide data that is structured to show evidence of change and the direction of change (Manichander, 2016). The literature on the subject emphasises that assessment has a broader meaning than measurement but a narrower meaning than evaluation.

Evaluation adds an element of value judgement to the assessment. Its value lies in the application of findings resulting from an evaluation of the effectiveness, social utility or desirability of a product, process or progress in terms of carefully defined and agreed goals or values. Importantly, it is a qualitative measure of the prevailing situation and often includes recommendations for further constructive action. Thus, evaluation is an estimation of the value of things, processes or programmes to make sensible decisions concerning them (Manichander, 2016). Evaluation is a systematic process of collecting and analysing data to determine whether and to what extent objectives have been or are being achieved. And very importantly, it leads to decision-making (Ebel and Frisbie, 1991). It enables critical examination of key assumptions and formulation of potential solutions that may respond to hidden and visible assumptions held by various stakeholders (Mertens, 2016). Evaluations of programmes, projects or other activities, such as those implemented in P/CVE, therefore allow for the collection of empirically based assessments of their results. The result of an evaluation is, therefore, an assessment of some aspect of the programme, project or measure under examination, accompanied by conclusions for further action. Thus, it serves to inform the project management, funder or decision-makers on issues such as its usefulness and effectiveness, and in many cases, the evaluation results are also published in

Table 4.1: Selected features, similarities and differences between peer/self-review, measurement, assessment and evaluation

Feature	Measurement	Assessment	Peer/self-review	Evaluation
Type of activity	Process of assigning numbers or characteristics to objects or individuals	Process of collecting and organising measurement data into interpretable forms	Process of reflective thinking about the undertaken or completed action based on self-reflection	Empirically grounded objective process related to the initiative assumptions, its implementation and results
Scope	Quantitative description of performance or characteristics	Enables informed judgement	Intended for internal reflection on the activities carried out to improve the quality of work performed	Critical examination of key assumptions and formulation of potential solutions leading to decision-making
Placement in activity	Ends with the attribution of quantity; a set of activities supporting assessment, self-review and evaluation	Establishing facts that describe the conditions existing at a particular time; a set of activities supporting self-review and evaluation	After implementation of an initiative; a set of activities supporting evaluation	Before, during and/or after implementation of an initiative by measuring, assessing, self-reviewing and objective conclusions

publicly available reports (Van de Donk et al, 2019). Table 4.1 summarises the key features and differences between the terms discussed earlier.

The differences between peer/self-review, measurement, assessment and evaluation are significant; thus, it is important that practitioners designing and/or implementing prevention initiatives for preventing and combating radicalisation that leads to violent extremism and in other areas related to crime prevention understand them. A proper understanding of evaluation is essential for its correct design and implementation in practice.

Therefore, before indicating the place of evaluation in the process of designing prevention initiatives and before explaining in more detail how to plan and design evaluation, it is necessary to start with its clear definition.

Defining evaluation

In the literature on the subject, we read that the problem with the definition of evaluation has persisted for decades, and many definitions of evaluation have been proposed over the years. Noteworthy is the definition given by Scriven (1991) and later adopted by the American Evaluation Association (2014), according to which evaluation means a systematic process of determining merit, worth, value or significance. Picciotto notes that this definition is generally supported by most researchers (Picciotto, 2011) and is probably the closest to consensus on the matter, as almost all evaluation theorists assume that evaluation is about merit and worth (Shadish, 1998). For instance, Asuru sees evaluation as dealing with goodness, worth, utility, effectiveness, adequacy and so on. Additionally, he emphasises that it answers questions such as how well a given initiative has been implemented and how effective, satisfactory and adequate it was. The answers to these evaluation questions are expressed in qualitative terms such as pass, fail, excellent, good, satisfactory, poor, advancement, repetition, withdrawal, success and failure, among others. Thus, qualitative statements indicate a judgement based on specific criteria (Ifeoma, 2022) adopted in the evaluation procedure.

However, the evolution of the definition of evaluation is not limited to Scriven's legacy. Other evaluators defining evaluation have drawn attention, at least in part, to its decision-making purpose (Rossi et al, 2004; Russ-Eft and Preskill, 2009; Yarbrough et al, 2010) or as a participatory endeavour (Patton, 2008; Yarbrough et al, 2010). Following other aspects of evaluation from the point of view of this chapter, the definition formulated by the Joint Committee on Standards for Educational Evaluation deserves attention. It sees evaluation as a systematic examination of the quality of programmes, projects and their components for the purpose of decision-making, judgements and new knowledge in response to the needs of identified stakeholders, leading to improvements or accountability and ultimately contributing to organisational or societal value (Yarbrough et al, 2010). Focusing on programme evaluation, it can be described as a process of systematic collection of empirical data and contextual information about the programme. In particular, answers to evaluation questions like 'what', 'who', 'how', 'if' and 'why' aid in the programme's planning, implementation and effectiveness assessment (Chen, 2015). Therefore, it is evident that this understanding brings evaluation closer to the empirical process of collecting data on a planned, constructed or implemented programme about its assumptions, and the method of implementation, and its results. Thus, this understanding tends towards evidence-based evaluation.

However, before explaining what evidence-based evaluation means, it is necessary to focus on the difference between programme evaluation and research in applied social sciences. As Levin-Rozalis (2003) notes, in fieldwork, evaluators often encounter a lack of awareness of the essence of evaluation in general, and in particular the difference between evaluation and research. This difficulty in distinguishing between them comes at the expense of evaluation. Also, some evaluators do not see the difference between applied social research and programme evaluation, simply stating that evaluation itself is applied research (Barker et al, 2016). Others agree that while evaluation uses social science methodology, it differs from social science research (Montrosse-Moorhead et al, 2017). That is why it is so important to understand what evaluation is and recognise its distinctness from research. Research is broader in scope than evaluation research (Vedung, 2004). They also differ in purpose, where research generates knowledge to inform the research base, whereas evaluation generates knowledge for a specific programme/client and provides information for decision-making/learning. The primary audience is also different because in research, it consists of researchers, and in the case of evaluation, it is internal and external customers. What is also very important is that researchers decide on the topic, methods, design and so on in research. On the other hand, evaluation is a matter of clients, and funders often play a large role in determining the research subject. Moreover, in research, the researcher determines the schedule, and the budget is supported by research grants or university funds. In contrast, in evaluation, the timeline is constrained by the time frame requirements of the organisation or funder, and the evaluation is funded by the client or funder organisation. An additional, very important difference concerns value judgements. Research provides value neutrality, and evaluation provides an assessment of value and often provides additional recommendations (Wanzer, 2021). Therefore, it should be emphasised again that evaluation, especially evidence-based evaluation, benefits from the support of social sciences and methods of implementing research in this area, however, it is identical to scientific research.

Evidence-based evaluation

It is also essential in the evaluation material to explain what evidence-based evaluation means. In recent times, a lot of attention has been given to it, although at the same time, it is not fully understood what it means. This is important because effective public policy and practice must be evidence-based. This approach has been adopted in medicine and other fields dedicated to improving society. The call for services to ensure that their programmes and practices are based on well-conducted, relevant, evidence-based research has been going on for years (Midgley, 2009). And although it is not a standard usually adopted in crime prevention and criminal justice (Sherman et al, 2002), it certainly needs to be.

The quality of the evaluation is assessed based on the credibility of the evidence collected as part of it and then the use of the collected evidence in improving policies and programmes (Newcomer et al, 2015). It is important to emphasise that only systematic evaluation can capture the evidence and criteria on which the evaluative judgement is based and limit sources of bias (Shaw et al, 2006). A strong basis for evidence-based evacuation has been derived from medicine. Evaluation of interventions in this area is complex (Pagliari, 2007), context-dependent (Bahati et al, 2010), considers differences in epistemological beliefs about interventions in clinical trials, and considers social aspects (Bates and Wright, 2009; Catwell and Sheikh, 2009). Understanding evidence-based medicine allows one to understand the importance of evidence in health-related interventions. Evidence-based medicine is the diligent, unambiguous and judicious use of the best current evidence in making decisions about the care of individual patients. This practice entails combining individual clinical knowledge with the best available external clinical evidence from systematic research (Sackett et al, 1996). Another essential element of evidence-based evaluation also concerns examining the needs of the recipients of a given initiative. The evidence-based movement in this domain advocates professional decision-making that integrates the best scientific evidence with clinical expertise and the unique values and circumstances of the patient (Strauss et al, 2019). Such evaluation is not limited to medicine, however. Certainly, it is possible and even necessary to use its advantages and experiences in other areas where human activities should be evaluated. Therefore, it also applies to the field of social action, including prevention, countering radicalisation leading to violent extremism and deradicalisation.

In this area, it is worth referring to the understanding of evidence-based evaluation developed by the INDEED[2] project consortium based on the conducted research, which suggests that the principles of evidence-based practice can be usefully applied in the field of evaluation. Consequently, based on the understanding of evidence-based practice, it initially introduces evidence-based evaluation as 'a process of planning and implementing evaluation that integrates available external evidence, professional expertise and the values, preferences, and circumstances of stakeholders' (Klose, 2022, p 40). As this definition will be the guiding understanding of evaluation later in this chapter, it should also be emphasised by INDEED that three key principles guide evidence-based evaluation. First, evidence-based evaluation commits evaluation practitioners to seek, assess, engage and consider available external evidence in planning and implementing evaluations. These may include research on the evaluation as well as evaluation projects, methods and tools. Second, planning and implementing an evaluation requires serious consideration of the client's (and, more broadly, the stakeholder's) values, preferences and circumstances. As such, it requires evaluating practitioners to adopt a contextual and participatory approach in which stakeholders can voice their preferences and concerns and in which assessment procedures and outcomes are clearly presented and discussed. Finally, third, it requires them to develop their professional expertise and rely on their skills and professional judgement during the assessment process to decide on a course of action, considering and integrating available external evidence and the stakeholder's values, preferences and circumstances (Klose, 2022). All the listed values are relevant to planning, designing and conducting an evidence-based evaluation. Hence, references to these will also appear later in the chapter, describing how to design such an evaluation as a standard component of the evidence-based practice assumptions.

Types of evaluation

Before discussing the place of evaluation in the process of designing an initiative, it is also necessary to refer to the three main types of evaluation, the design of which will be discussed. It can be seen in the literature that there are many different types of evaluation, and each type has its own set of processes and/or rules. The categorisation of common types of evaluation is often based on criteria, which include the purpose of the evaluation, its function, who is carrying out the evaluation, when the evaluation is carried out, the general approach used, the nature of references/interpretations, and cross-cutting topics. Depending on these criteria, formative, summative, external, internal or self-evaluation, joint, peer, participatory, end-of-phase, ex-post, real-time, process, impact, theory-based evaluation, and others are listed as the different types of evaluation (ActionAid, 2016; Ifeoma, 2022). A closer analysis, however, shows that many of them coincide in terms of general assumptions and purpose (function) and differ only in the implementation method or timing. Therefore, it is more appropriate to narrow down the typology of evaluation to the one proposed by Chen.

The conceptual framework Chen created allows for a more complete classification of evaluation types. He proposes a typology created by crossing two evaluation functions, that is, 'improvement' and 'assessment', with two stages of the programme, which are 'process' and 'result'. As a result, he proposes four basic types of evaluation that can be considered comprehensive enough to cover the wide range of evaluations practitioners encounter. At the same time, it provides a framework that can accommodate mixed-type evaluations (Chen, 1996). Building on this concept, this chapter lists three main types of evaluation necessary for a proper and comprehensive programme evaluation. Considering the assessment function, which is assessment and improvement, as well as programme stages, attention was paid to process evaluation (monitoring), as well as evaluation of programme results. However, regarding improvement, it was referred not only to the final effects but also to the assumptions of the programme before or immediately after its implementation. Therefore, formative evaluation is added to this set. These three types of evaluation will be the subject of further consideration regarding evaluation as an inherent part of programme assumptions. From the very definition of the evaluated initiative, it is possible to deduce the types of evaluation that should be applied to it to check its quality, the way it is conducted and the effects it achieves or has achieved. This is presented in Table 4.2, an example of a long-term comprehensive prevention programme formulated for the needs of the INDEED project.[3]

Thus, the definition not only makes it possible to organise thinking and communication, which we understand uniformly as a 'long-term prevention programme', but also gives the defined term specific characteristics and content. But what is very important is that it also draws attention to the elements

Table 4.2: Definition of a long-term prevention programme and the types of evaluation it should be subjected to

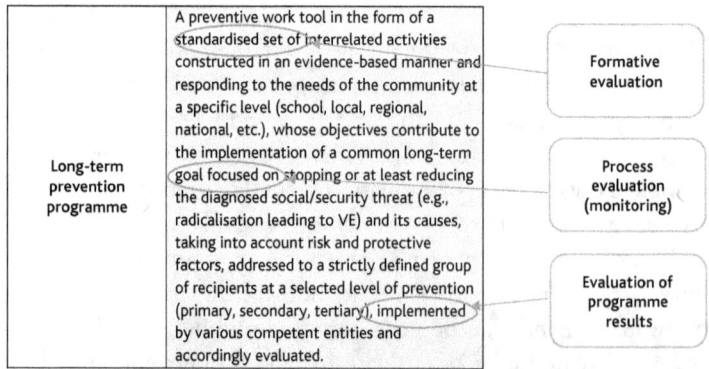

of the structure of such a programme and, at the same time, indicates which aspects of the programme should be evaluated. As a result, it is easier to determine what type of evaluation should be applied to the programme. The three types of evaluation mentioned earlier, due to their functions and the stages of the programme at which they should be used, allow for checking the correctness of programme assumptions, monitoring its progress, and assessing the achieved and achieved results, that is, the goals set for this programme.

The literature indicates that in the domain of teaching-learning, the purpose of formative evaluation is, among others, to determine areas needing modifications or improvement of the teaching-learning process (Manichander, 2016). In the more general field of project and programme implementation, formative evaluation is usually carried out during a project or programme, often halfway through. The purpose of formative evaluation is to help shape the future of a project or programme and thus enable it to improve its results. Formative evaluation is more focused on learning and management than accountability (ActionAid, 2016). This evaluation ensures that the whole programme or specific activity is viable, appropriate and acceptable before it is fully implemented. It is usually carried out when a new programme or activity is developed or when an existing one is adapted or modified (Salabarría-Peña et al, 2007). Therefore, already during the design of the programme, it is necessary to check on an ongoing basis whether the adopted solutions are consistent with the decisions made within the framework of the theoretical concepts, strategies and programme objectives. It is also necessary to check whether the programme's assumptions form a coherent (logical) whole and the potential impact of the proposed activities, both previously planned and unforeseen, on the direct and indirect recipients of the programme. This is also the purpose of formative evaluation. It may take the form of:

1. discussion with programme partners about the prepared assumptions before the programme is implemented;
2. pilot implementation of the programme to check on a smaller group of recipients whether the assumptions of the programme have been designed and planned properly; and

3. consultations with recipients during the programme to gauge views on its quality or effectiveness of the implemented measures (Kordaczuk-Wąs, 2018).

Formative evaluation can be carried out by an external evaluator, but also by an evaluator appointed by the programme partners. It certainly serves to verify and, if necessary, to improve the designed assumptions of the programme. An example of formative evaluation, along with its function, purpose, methods and techniques, is shown in Figure 4.1.

Process evaluation, on the other hand, focuses specifically on internal project or programme issues. This may include assessing whether activities have been carried out, as well as evaluating the quality of work performed, the impact of internal management practices on work, and any other internal issues relevant to the implementation process and the initiative (ActionAid, 2016). Process evaluation (monitoring) tracks variables such as funds received, products and services provided, payments made, and other resources contributed to and disbursed by the programme. It also allows for control of the programme's operation and adherence to the adopted deadlines (Centers for Disease Control and Prevention, 1999, 2008). Some authors note that process evaluation is the most important form of evaluation of undertaken actions, and its task is to assess a specific process. The area of interest of this evaluation includes activities (planned and unplanned)

Figure 4.1: Formative evaluation example

| Formative evaluation allows to answer the question whether the adopted forms of action allow you to achieve the assumed goals. And if not, what modifications should be made to the assumptions of the programme | This type of evaluation is used to optimise the activities planned or implemented and to improve their quality | Both qualitative and quantitative methods and techniques are used to carry it out | Examples:
• Moderated discussion with the partners of the programme on its assumptions
• Interview with representatives of programme implementers on the process of incorporating proactive measures into the assumptions of the programme to prevent hate speech
• A survey followed by a focus group interview with students to find out their opinions on the 'Say no to hate speech' Guidebook |

related to the actual process undertaken for the implementation of this process, as well as the activities of employees, recipients and other people involved in this process (Sochocki, 2006). This type of evaluation determines whether programme activities have been implemented as intended and have produced the desired results. It can be performed periodically throughout the programme and starts with a review of the activities and output components of the logic model (Salabarría-Peña et al, 2007). Process evaluation can also be understood as programme monitoring and, like formative evaluation, can be carried out by an external evaluator or an evaluator appointed by the programme partners. An example of process evaluation, along with its function, purpose, methods and techniques, is shown in Figure 4.2.

There are typologies in the literature that distinguish the final evaluation of a programme into four different types. The first is a summative evaluation that is carried out at the end of a project or programme. It aims to assess what has been achieved and how. It is often carried out when a project or programme has ended or is about to end, and it is no longer possible to make changes, but lessons can still be learned that can help shape future initiatives (ActionAid, 2016). The second is the outcome evaluation, which measures the effects of the programme on the target population by

Figure 4.2: Process evaluation example

| Process evaluation, or in other words monitoring of the implementation of both planned and unplanned programme activities | This type of evaluation is used to collect data on the course of the programme, however it can be also used to modify it | The activities of the programme authors, its implementers (partners) and recipients are monitored | Process evaluation is conducted during the duration of the programme based on the verification of indicators for measuring the progress of the programme using both qualitative and quantitative research methods and tools.
Examples:
• Analysis of the content of the report in terms of introducing at least three types of new leisure activities for young people at risk of radicalisation into the local prevention offer
• Analysis of the quality of the Guidebook developed under the programme |

evaluating progress towards the objectives which the programme addresses (Salabarría-Peña et al, 2007). The third is the impact evaluation, which assesses the programme's effectiveness in achieving its ultimate goals (Salabarría-Peña et al, 2007). It aims to assess the impact of a given work. While most evaluations aim to assess impact to a greater or lesser extent, an impact evaluation is usually an evaluation with a clear and robust quantitative and qualitative methodology, or both, designed to determine change and causation (contribution to that change) (ActionAid, 2016).

Finally, the fourth type of final evaluation mentioned in the literature is the ex-post evaluation, which is also performed after the completion of the project. Long-term effects are usually studied in this type of evaluation. On the one hand, effectiveness is examined, that is, the degree of achievement of the goals set at the project planning stage, as well as efficiency, that is, a comparison of the resources used with the results obtained (Kisielnicki, 2017). At the same time, a follow-up evaluation is distinguished, carried out immediately after the project is closed and carried out sometime after the project (Trocki, 2012). The ex-post evaluation shows to what extent the project results justify the costs incurred. In addition, during this evaluation, factors of success or failure are examined (Trocki, 2013). However, it is obvious that all these types of evaluation have many things in common, such as similar functions, goals and time. Therefore, it is justified to take a holistic approach to the final evaluation of the programme and treat it jointly as an evaluation of the programme results. Of course, this includes simultaneous consideration of aspects like the assessment of the degree of implementation of the programme's objectives, implementation of tasks, quality, effectiveness, efficiency, and its impact on the programme's recipients. Additionally, it is worth noting that evaluation of programme results, just like formative and progress evaluations, can be conducted by an external evaluator or an evaluator appointed by the programme partners. Figure 4.3 shows an example of results evaluation, along with its function, purpose, methods and techniques.

Later in this chapter, the roles of the three evaluation types – formative, process and results evaluation – will be explained within the framework of a long-term comprehensive, evidence-based prevention programme. The significance of incorporating

Figure 4.3: Results evaluation example

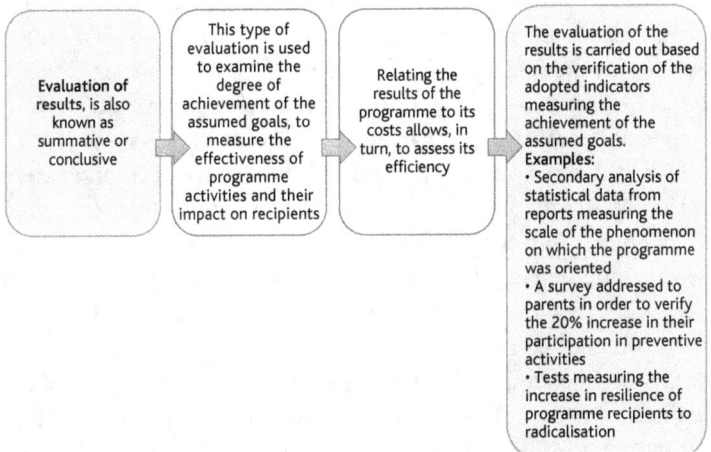

evaluation from the programme's design phase will also be discussed.

The place of evaluation in evidence-based practice assumptions

The literature on the theoretical foundation of evaluation emphasises that evaluation results can be used to maintain or improve programme quality and ensure that future planning can be more evidence-based. It also emphasises that evaluation is integral to the ongoing cycle of programme planning, implementation and improvement (Patton, 1987). Having an evaluation plan in place is crucial, and it is best to have it ready when the programme starts. Therefore, keeping evaluation in mind when designing a programme can help ensure the success of future evaluations because evaluation can be difficult or even impossible if stakeholders do not plan evaluation during initial programme development (Martin, 2015). Embedding the evaluation process into programme design during programme development also helps to ensure that the data collected throughout the programme lifecycle is meaningful to stakeholders and will thus be used to continuously improve the programme.

Such a procedure also allows for demonstrating responsibility for specific tasks set for various interested parties. Partners have clear task assignments and an understanding of how to monitor and check the quality and effectiveness of implementing of these tasks. However, any shortcomings or unmet goals would not lead to negative evaluation of partners. Instead, the focus would be on collaborative consideration of possible corrective or improvement activities. Consequently, this provides an opportunity to build a common understanding of the programme's purpose as well as the intended results from the outset – from the moment of designing its standardised assumptions, including the evaluation methods and plan.

Meanwhile, evaluation still seems to be the most difficult of the elements (standards) that make up the construction of a prevention programme. While authors and implementers of the projects assess the mere planning and evaluation activities as feasible, the very process of evaluating the status of programme implementation and results often seems impossible to implement. As a result, this crucial element is often overlooked during construction or implementation, leading to quality loss in prevention programmes. Meanwhile, it happens that programme implementers carry out activities evaluating individual stages of the implementation of their initiatives but do not treat these as evaluation activities. This is often due to an insufficient understanding of what evaluation is (Kordaczuk-Wąs, 2017). The previously mentioned report prepared by the INDEED project emphasises that strengthening the evidence base in preventing and countering radicalisation that leads to violent extremism and deradicalisation requires the expansion of theory-based and stakeholder-oriented evaluation projects, which are currently lacking, as shown in several recent (systematic) reviews. The implementation of evidence-based practice in the mentioned area requires, above all, measures facilitating the application of robust evaluation practices (Klose, 2022). Also, in other areas related to preventing other forms of crime, most evaluations are conducted with little regard for methodological reliability (Ekblom and Pease, 1995). This makes it necessary to create clear procedures, mechanisms, tools or concepts that help practitioners acquire the necessary knowledge in the field of evaluation, teach and improve the necessary practical skills, and facilitate the design, planning and implementation of evaluation. Including evaluation in the process of designing a preventive programme can serve this purpose.

The need for strategic investments in the development of technical and human expertise and skills and the creation of an evaluation culture within or across institutions/sectors is underlined by the INDEED programme consortium. The conducted research indicates that structured, standardised and conscious approaches, frameworks and tools will help decision-makers and practitioners conduct evaluation effectively (Klose, 2022). As mentioned in the previous chapter, programmes are complex phenomena, usually created based on experience and professional knowledge (Weiss, 1998). The importance of deriving the construction of a preventive programme from theoretical foundations and combining all elements building the assumptions of the programme into a logical sequence was also emphasised as the way to build structured, standardised and conscious approaches to programme designing and its evaluation. The importance of programme theory is also noted by Weiss. He notes that prevention programme stakeholders usually want to know if what they are doing is working and how they can improve their initiative. Furthermore, he states that the evaluation of programme theory alone can often provide this kind of information. He defines programme theory as the intermediary mechanisms between the delivery (and receipt) of a programme and the emergence of results of interest (Weiss, 1998). Theory-based evaluation is an approach that pays attention to the theories of programme managers or other stakeholders that are logically related. Conceptually, theory-based evaluations express the theory of a programme. Empirically, theory-based evaluations aim to test that theory, examining whether, why or how programmes achieve their intended or observed outcomes (Leeuw, 2012). It must be strongly emphasised that theory-based evaluation is not the same as the logical framework of a programme (Astbury and Leeuw, 2010). At the same time, not applying programme theory to evaluation creates a 'trap' of discrepancies between this theory and (empirical) evaluation carried out without paying attention to this theory (Funnell and Rogers, 2011).

Logical modelling is generally presented in the evaluation literature to better understand the causal mechanisms (Renger and Titcomb, 2002; Renger and Hurley, 2006). At the same time, it should be emphasised that although the logical model of the programme is the basis for a better understanding of the mechanisms of its operation (WK Kellogg Foundation, 2004; Silverman et al, 2007; Wyatt Knowlton and Phillips, 2012), it still cannot replace evaluation. The theory of the programme shows the mechanisms that operate between the implementation of the initiative and the intended results, not the way in which the intervention brings the intended results. Therefore, the chain of standard elements building the programme based on a theoretical foundation still needs to include specific evaluation activities related to individual programme elements and related goals as the inherent part of the programme logic model.

Again, referring to the previous chapter, such a solution is the proposal to build prevention programmes based on the proposed list of standards of construction elements that create a logical model of a prevention programme. Using it during the designing process as a template containing a concise description of all elements that must be included in the construction of a standardised prevention programme will certainly facilitate the inclusion of all necessary elements in its assumptions, including evaluation (Kordaczuk-Wąs, 2017). Table 4.3 illustrates the logical model built from the previously mentioned standard elements that a comprehensive long-term prevention programme should consist of.

These elements indicate what elements should be designed and the steps to be taken in the design process (Figure 4.4) to determine the logical model of the prevention programme. This helps the authors in design and helps implementers and partners in the next stages in joint understanding and implementation of such an initiative.

Attempting to evaluate something formally involves tackling a series of abstract concepts, such as value, growth, value, criteria, standards, goals, needs, norms, audience, metrics, reliability, objectivity, practicality, meaning, process, product and impact. Evaluators need to explain what they mean when they work.

Table 4.3: Standard elements of the construction of a preventive programme, including evaluation

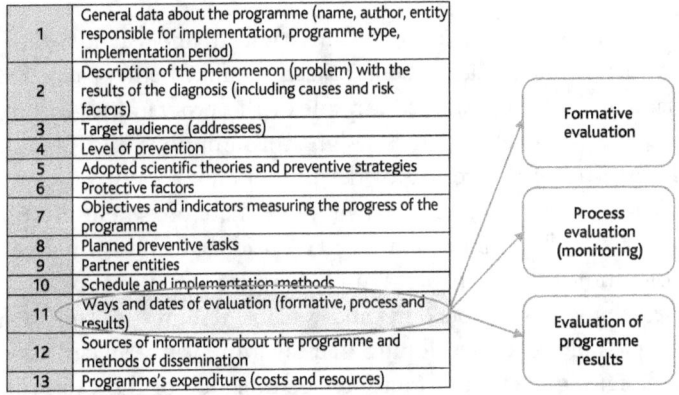

Figure 4.4: The main steps in building the logic model of an evidence-based programme design

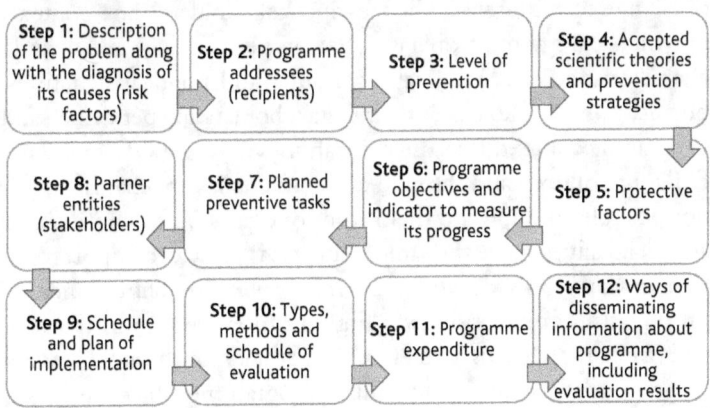

Evaluation can never be a one-time activity, and conceptualisation can never be static (Madaus et al, 2012). Therefore, the assumptions of the evaluation must be closely related to the assumptions and course of the prevention programme. Tips on how to derive assumptions about what, when and how to evaluate directly from the process of designing such a programme are described in the next section.

The relationship between objectives, indicators measuring the progress of the programme and evaluation

Conducting a final evaluation means trying to understand whether the programme has achieved its objectives and whether participant changes can be considered a result of the programme. In turn, evaluation that checks the designed assumptions and ongoing monitoring of the course of the programme affects the degree to which these goals can be achieved. Therefore, the evaluation must be well planned, that is, it considers the links between programmed and non-programmed factors and uses appropriate research methods, procedures and available resources to collect the best possible data. Developing an evaluation plan at an early stage of designing an initiative ensures compliance of the evaluation schedule with the course of implementation and key decisions of authors, implementers and evaluators.

The programme works in different ways and sometimes for different people, which means it can trigger different mechanisms of change for different audiences and stakeholders. The contexts in which a programme operates affect its performance and include characteristics such as social, economic and political structures, organisational context, programme stakeholders and personnel, and geographic context. Because programmes may work differently in different contexts and through different change mechanisms, it is not possible to duplicate them from one context to another and automatically achieve the same results. It is therefore important to know 'what works for whom, in what contexts and how', and one of the tasks of evaluation is to find out more about this (Pawson and Sridharan, 2010). Therefore, it is crucial for the achievement of programme results to formulate programme objectives based on a diagnosis of the situation prevailing in the local environment. However, the correctness of this formulation is also important for evaluation. For a reliable evaluation to be possible, these objectives must be correctly formulated as they determine the selection of the content of the impact on the addressees and affect the selection of appropriate strategies and forms of preventive action.

Meanwhile, those elements of the structure of the prevention programme that often cause difficulties for authors include prevention goals and indicators that measure progress in implementing the programme and achieving its assumed goals. The analysis of the construction of police prevention programmes shows that their goals often do not refer to real problems diagnosed in local communities. It happens that despite the preparation of a reliable diagnosis and its description in the programme, preventive goals concern other problems that do not result from this diagnosis, or they are formulated in a way that makes it difficult or even impossible to achieve them (Kordaczuk-Wąs, 2017). Therefore, the first step to planning and carrying out a reliable evaluation is to correctly formulate the objectives of the programme at the stage of initiative design. This means that the previously mentioned objectives should be related to the main problem diagnosed in the local environment and then to the diagnosed causes of the described situation. The diagnosed problem indicates the main goal of the preventive programme being constructed. An example of the process of correctly formulating the main and operational objectives of the programme was presented in the previous chapter.

An important element, especially from the point of view of evaluation, related to the objectives are indicators measuring the progress of the programme. They were briefly discussed in the previous chapter, however due to their importance for designing, planning and carrying out evaluations, they deserve a little more attention. Monitoring the implementation of the assumed preventive goals serves, in turn, to assess the effectiveness of the preventive programme being implemented. To achieve this, indicators are designed to make it possible to determine whether these objectives have been achieved in whole, in part, or whether they have not been achieved in accordance with the adopted assumptions. The indicators are used to indicate whether the programme's main and operational objectives are effective and thus constitute a 'signpost' for its proper implementation. They allow one to account for the progress in implementing the programme and the success of the activities carried out (JAC, 2008). According to Nowak's (2011) definition, an indicator of an event 'Z' is an event 'W' such that the statement of its existence, appearance or degree of intensity is used as a premise that, in certain cases, the event 'Z' occurred with certainty, with a certain probability, or at least with a probability higher than average. In addition, the importance of linking indicators to the assumptions and logical model of the programme should be underscored.

As emphasised in the literature, the logical starting point for developing the most appropriate indicators is to create a model or theory of the programme. Without a formulated programme theory, indicators may be less relevant, overly inclusive or poorly related to the programme activities they are intended to measure (Birleson et al, 2001). Lindgren (2001) also shows how problematic performance measurement can be when indicators are developed and applied without regard to the (richness of) programme theory. Indicators measuring the programme's progress, like the objectives, should relate to the programme's target group, be formulated as measurable results and represent expected changes, and also be realistic, that is, achievable, and have a defined timeframe (Polish Education Development Centre, 2015). An example of one of the types of indicators proposed in the methodology of scientific research is shown in Figure 4.5. This is known as a definition indicator, which is either included in the definition of the indicated phenomenon or fully coincides with it (Nowak, 2011).

Among the indicators measuring the programme's progress is also a correlation indicator, in which there is an identity relationship between the indexed phenomenon and its indicator (Nowak, 2011). Figure 4.6 shows an example of such an indicator.

Figure 4.5: An example of a definitional indicator that measures programme progress

| There is an identity relation between the indicator phenomenon and its indicator | Main objective: Reducing the number of cases of radicalism, discrimination and hate speech | Indicator: Number of cases of radicalism, discrimination and hate speech will be reduced by 10% |

Figure 4.6: An example of a correlation indicator that measures programme progress

| If the number of activities promoting behaviour free from all forms of radicalisation, discrimination and hate speech increases, the number of such negative behaviours will be reduced | Main objective: Promotion of behaviour free from all forms of radicalism, discrimination and hate speech | Indicator: 3 types of activities based on the discussion of social polarisation |

To sum up, the important role of evaluation in the assumptions of a prevention programme should be emphasised once again. It is one of its standard elements, and it should be designed and planned already at the design stage of the initiative design. This is because it maintains the important relationship between the programme authors' intended outcomes, its implementation, and the evaluators' verification of whether the programme has achieved the assumed goals. In addition, for the proper design of the evaluation, the relationship between the programme's objectives, indicators measuring its progress and the type of evaluation is particularly important. Table 4.4 summarises these correlations using the example of an evidence-based, long-term comprehensive educational programme, UNDERSTAND = RESPECT, preventing radicalisation leading to discrimination and hate speech.[4]

The programme's logic model offers a visual representation of the standard elements, or assumptions, of the evidence-based programme, how it should work and achieve its purpose, goals and objectives, and describes how its activities are linked to their intended effects. On this basis, therefore, it is easier to prepare an evaluation plan that adequately defines the objectives of future evaluations and the questions that evaluations should answer

Table 4.4: A sample relation between the indicators measuring the implementation of the main objective, type of evaluation, research procedure and proposed methods, techniques and measurement tools of evaluation

Programme objective	Indicators	Type of evaluation	Evaluation procedure/research method	Technique/tool
Promotion of behaviour free from all forms of radicalism, discrimination and hate speech	During and after the program, enriching the school's preventive offer with: • 2 types of educational activities on radicalisation processes leading to discrimination and hate speech • 3 types of activities based on the discussion of social polarisation • 2 types of activities strengthening psychosocial and educational skills	Process evaluation (monitoring) Results evaluation	• Current reporting from the implementation of the programme • Evaluation surveys (for individual preventive activities) • Analysis of the degree of achievement of indicators measuring programme progress • Examination of documents • Face-to-face interviews	• Description of the status of tasks (report sheet) • Survey questionnaire • Statistical data • Reports from programme implementation • Interview questionnaire

(Martin, 2015). The presented ways of thinking about evaluation as an inherent standard element of an evidence-based prevention programme are only an example, but they can be used as practical guidelines to facilitate the process of developing evaluation assumptions. They have been derived from the assumptions of the social sciences methodology, thanks to which they can contribute to properly constructing such important elements of the programme structure as the formulation of preventive goals and programme progress indicators, which directly affect the method and quality of evaluation of preventive activities. Undoubtedly, they are worth using because constructing programmes reliably and professionally, based on specific standards, on the one hand, determines the improvement of the quality of undertaken activities and, on the other hand, enables their coherent and reliable evaluation.

Summary

- Evaluation is an important part of many processes, in the teaching learning process as well as the other domains related to human-based social activities, including crime prevention as well as prevention and countering of radicalisation leading to violent extremism and deradicalisation. Evaluation performs functions such as instructional, diagnostic, administrative, developmental and communication.
- The primary and universal purpose of evaluation is to promote accountability, as it aims to understand why and to what extent a specific activity's intended and unintended outcomes have been achieved. It can help with planning, programming, budgeting, implementation and reporting, and can contribute to evidence-based policy making, development effectiveness and organisational efficiency.
- Programme evaluation remains a significant gap. The RAN shows that initiatives such as programmes have a limited evidence base, and there is hardly any evaluation of their effectiveness. At the same time, the Network adds that practitioners still often face the problem of being able to enable evaluation in a practical and feasible way.
- Research shows that 'bad practices' in the field of evaluation include lack of early planning; insufficient knowledge about the

evaluated initiative/programme; inadequate explanations and no common language for assessing the field; lack of effective evaluation methodology; failure to take due account of the context, purpose and objectives of each initiative/programme; and lack of accurate, up-to-date, and adequate knowledge of evaluation prior to its implementation.
- While activities such as peer or self-reviewing, measuring, assessing and evaluating are closely related, they have different meanings and definitions.
- In the literature on the subject, the challenge of defining 'evaluation' has persisted for several decades, and many definitions have been proposed over the years. The consensus among most scholars is that evaluation refers to a systematic process used to determine merit, worth or importance. However, evaluators have also noted its role in aiding decision-making.
- Evaluation and research are distinct fields. While research encompasses a wider scope than evaluation research, their primary objectives set them apart. Research aims to generate knowledge contributing to the research base, while evaluation aims to generate knowledge tailored to a specific programme or client and provides information for decision-making or learning.
- Based on the understanding of evidence-based practice, evidence-based evaluation can be understood as a process of planning and implementing an evaluation that integrates available external evidence, professional expertise, and stakeholder values, preferences and situations.
- The categorisation of common types of evaluation is often based on - criteria, which include the purpose of the evaluation, its function, who carries out the evaluation, when the assessment is carried out, the general approach used, the nature of references/interpretations, and cross-cutting topics. A closer analysis, however, shows that many of them are similar in terms of general assumptions and purpose (function) and differ only in the implementation method or timing. Based on this concept, three main types of evaluation are necessary for a proper and comprehensive programme evaluation. Considering the evaluation function, which is evaluation and improvement, as well as programme stages, it is necessary to use

process evaluation (monitoring) and evaluation of programme results. However, when it comes to improving the programme by revising its assumptions before or immediately after its implementation, one must also consider formative evaluation.
- Evaluation is an integral part of the continuous cycle of programme planning, implementation and improvement. Having an evaluation plan in place is crucial, and it is best to have it ready at the beginning of the programme. Therefore, incorporating evaluation into programme design can help ensure the success of future evaluations. The theory of the programme shows the mechanisms that operate between the implementation of the initiative and the intended results and not how the intervention brings the intended results. Therefore, the chain of standard elements building a programme based on theoretical foundations must include specific evaluation activities regarding individual elements of the programme and related goals as an inherent part of the programme logic model.
- Therefore, already at the programme design stage, it is necessary to check on an ongoing basis whether the adopted solutions are consistent with the decisions made regarding theoretical concepts, strategies and programme objectives. The entire project should be assessed to ensure that it forms a coherent (logical) whole and to evaluate the potential impact of the prepared activities on its direct and indirect recipients. To achieve this, evaluation must accompany activities from the outset. Effective evaluation is not an 'event' that occurs at the end of a project but an ongoing process that helps authors, implementers, decision-makers and evaluators better understand the project and its impact on participants.

Suggested directions for future research

The following questions can orient further research and discussion in the area:

- What are the typologies and categorisations of evidence-based evaluation that organise approaches to planning, designing and implementing

evaluation in terms of the function it serves for the undertaken action, making it effective and pragmatic?
- What are the determinants of creating the ability to plan, design and implement scientifically based evaluation principles in a practical and feasible way by first-line practitioners and policy makers?
- How to understand, obtain and apply in practice 'evidence' as an inherent element of 'evidence-based practice'?

Notes

1. Project on 'Strengthening a comprehensive approach to preventing and counteracting radicalisation based on a universal evIdeNce-based moDEl for Evaluation of raDicalisation prevention and mitigation' (acronym INDEED). The project aims to use evidence-based approaches to strengthen first-line practitioners' and policy makers' knowledge, capabilities, and skills for designing, planning, implementing and evaluating Preventing Violent Extremism, Countering Violent Extremism and deradicalisation initiatives, such as policies and strategies, long-term programmes, short-term actions and ad-hoc interventions, in an effective and proven manner. This project has received funding from the European Union's Horizon 2020 Research and Innovation Programme under grant agreement No. 101021701 and has been managed by the Polish Platform for Homeland Security with Dr Marzena Kordaczuk-Wąs in the role of coordinator. The duration of the project is 36 months (September 2021–August 2024). More at: https://www.indeed project.eu/.
2. The INDEED project consortium summarises the key findings of its research before outlining a framework to strengthen the use of robust evaluation designs in P/CVE and deradicalisation (and beyond). This framework revolves around the initial conceptualisation of the term 'evidence-based assessment', which is at the heart of the INDEED project. More in Klose (2022).
3. The definition of a long-term prevention programme was prepared by Dr Marzena Kordaczuk-Wąs for the needs of the INDEED project, together with definitions of terms of other prevention initiatives such as 'policies and strategies', 'short-term actions' and 'ad hoc interventions'.
4. Evidence-based educational programme to prevent radicalisation leading to discrimination and hate speech called 'UNDERSTAND = RESPECT' was developed by Dr Marzena Kordaczuk-Wąs, on the primary prevention level, according to a logic model grounded in social science and based on evidence from a diagnosis of the threat of radicalisation and the need for its prevention, conducted in Poland in 2020 among teachers and students. The Polish Platform for Homeland Security implemented the pilot in cooperation with the 1st High School in Gorzow Wielkopolski from December 2021 to June 2022. More about the programme here: https://ppbw.pl/en/preventiveprogram/. An in-depth description of the theoretical

framework and a detailed description of the diagnosis forming the basis for developing the assumptions of the programme can be found in Kordaczuk-Wąs (2023).

References

ActionAid (2016) 'Types of evaluation', *Intrac for Civil Society*. Available from https://www.intrac.org/wpcms/wp-content/uploads/2017/01/Types-of-Evaluation.pdf [Accessed 23 September 2023].

American Educational Research Association (1999) *Standards for Educational and Psychological Testing*, Washington, DC: AERA.

American Evaluation Association (2014) 'What is evaluation? *American Evaluation Association*. Available from https://www.eval.org/p/bl/et/blogaid=4 [Accessed June 2023].

Astbury, B. and Leeuw, F.L. (2010) 'Unpacking black boxes: Mechanisms and theory-building in evaluation', *American Journal of Evaluation*, 31(3): 363–81.

Bahati, R., Guy, S., Bauer, M. and Gwadry-Sridhar, F. (2010) 'Where's the evidence for evidence-based knowledge in e-health systems?', In *Proceedings of the Developments in E-systems Engineering (DESE)*, London, September, pp 29–34.

Barker, C., Pistrang, N. and Elliott, R. (2016) *Research Methods in Clinical Psychology: An Introduction for Students and Practitioners* (3rd edn), Malden: John Wiley and Sons.

Bates, D.W. and Wright, A. (2009) 'Evaluating eHealth: Undertaking robust international cross-cultural eHealth research', *PLoS Med*, 6(9): 1–5.

Birleson, P., Brann, P. and Smith, A. (2001) 'Using program theory to develop key performance indicators for child and adolescent mental health services', *Australian Health Review*, 24(1): 10–21.

Catwell, L. and Sheikh, A. (2009) 'Evaluating eHealth interventions: The need for continuous systemic evaluation', *PLoS Med*, 6(8): 1–6.

Centers for Disease Control and Prevention (1999) 'Framework for program evaluation in public health, morbidity and mortality', *Weekly Report*, 48: 1–40.

Centers for Disease Control and Prevention (2008) *Introduction to Process Evaluation in Tobacco Use Prevention and Control*, Atlanta: U.S. Department of Health and Human Services.

Chen, H.T. (1996) 'A comprehensive typology for program evaluation', *Evaluation Practice*, 17(2): 121–30.

Chen, H.T. (2015) *Practical Program Evaluation: Theory-Driven Evaluation and the Integrated Evaluation Perspective* (2nd edn), Thousand Oaks: SAGE.

Disha, M. (2020) 'Education in teaching and learning process in education', *Your Article Library*. Available from https://www.yourarticlelibrary.com/statistics-2/evaluation-in-teaching-and-learning-process-education/92476 [Accessed 23 September 2023].

Doch, F., Segers, M. and Sluijjsmans, D. (2006) 'The use of self-, peer and co-assessment in higher education: A review', *Studies in Higher Education*, 24(3): 331–50.

Ebel, R.L. and Frisbie, D.A. (1991) *Essentials of Educational Measurement* (5th edn), Englewood Cliffs: Prentice-Hall.

Ekblom, P. and Pease, K. (1995) 'Crime and justice', *The University of Chicago Press Journals*, 19. Available from www.journals.uchicago.edu [Accessed 23 September 2023].

Funnell, S. and Rogers, P. (2011) *Purposeful Program Theory: Effective Use of Theories of Change and Logic Models*, San Francisco: Jossey Bass.

Haskins, R. and Margolis, G. (2015) *Show Me the Evidence: Obama's Fight for Rigor and Evidence in Social Policy*, Washington, DC: Brookings Institution Press.

Ifeoma, E.F. (2022) 'The role of evaluation in teaching and learning process in education', *International Journal of Advanced Academic and Educational Research*, 13(5): 120–9.

JAC (2008) 'Standardy programów promocji zdrowia i profilaktyki' ['Standards for health promotion and prevention programs'], *Remedium*, 6(184): 26–8.

Kirovska, Z. and Qoku, P.N. (2014) 'System of employee performance assessment: Factor for sustainable efficiency of organization', *Journal of Sustainable Development*, 5(11): 25–51.

Kisielnicki, J. (2017) *Zarządzanie Projektami. Ludzie – Procedury – Wyniki* [*Project Management. People – Procedures – Results*], Piaseczno: Wydawnictwo Nieoczywiste.

Klose, S. (2022) 'Deliverable 1.2 D1.2 Report outlining identified, analyzed and recommended research approaches, methods and tools for evidence-based evaluation coming from the area of PVE/CVE and De-radicalisation and other selected disciplines', *INDEED*. Available from https://www.indeedproject.eu/wp-content/uploads/2022/09/INDEED-D1.2-resub.pdf [Accessed 23 September 2023].

Kordaczuk-Wąs, M. (2017) 'Projektowanie wybranych elementów programu profilaktycznego' ['Designing selected elements of a preventive program'], *Kwartalnik Policyjny*, 3: 86–94.

Kordaczuk-Wąs, M. (2018) *Działania Profilaktyczne, Planowanie i Realizacja* [*Preventive Actions, Planning and Implementation*], Warsaw: Wydawnictwa Drugie.

Kordaczuk-Wąs, M. (2023) *Diagnoza Zagrożenia Radykalizacją Oraz Potrzeb Dotyczących Kluczowych Aspektów Programu Profilaktycznego Opartego na Dowodach* [*Diagnosis of the Risk of Radicalization and Needs Regarding Key Aspects of an Evidence-Based Prevention Program*], Warsaw: Wydawnictwo Oh Book!

Leeuw, F.L. (2012) 'Linking theory-based evaluation and contribution analysis: Three problems and a few solutions', *Evaluation*, 18(3): 348–63.

Levin-Rozalis, M. (2003) 'Evaluation and research: Differences and similarities', *Canadian Journal of Program Evaluation*, 18(2): 1–31.

Lindgren, L. (2001) 'The non-profit sector meets the performance-management movement: A programme-theory approach', *Evaluation*, 7(3): 285–303.

Long, C.S., Kowang, T.O., Ismail, W.K.W. and Rasid, S.Z.A. (2013) 'A review on performance appraisal system: An ineffective and destructive practice', *Middle East Journal of Scientific Research*, 14(7): 887–91.

Madaus, G.D., Scriven, M. and Stufflebeam, D.L. (2012) *Evaluation Models: Viewpoints on Educational and Human Services Evaluation*, Berlin: Springer.

Manichander, T. (ed) (2016) *Evaluation in Education*, Raleigh: Laxmi Book Publication.

Martin, A.B. (2015) 'Plan for program evaluation from the start', *National Institute of Justice Journal*, 275: 24–8.

Mertens, D.M. (2016) 'Assumptions at the philosophical and programmatic levels in evaluation', *Evaluation and Program Planning*, 59: 102–8.

Midgley, N. (2009) 'Editorial: Improvers, adapters and rejecters. The link between "evidence-based practice" and "evidence-based practitioners"', *Clinical Child Psychology and Psychiatry*, 14(3): 323–7.

Montrosse-Moorhead, B., Bellara, A.P. and Gambino, A.J. (2017) 'Communicating about evaluation: A conceptual model and case example', *Journal of Multi-Disciplinary Evaluation*, 13(29): 16–30.

Newcomer, K.E., Hatry, H.P. and Wholey, J.S. (2015) *Handbook of Practical Program Evaluation*, New York: John Wiley and Sons.

Nowak, S. (2011) *Metodologia Badań Społecznych [Social Research Methodology]*, Warsaw: Wydawnictwo Naukowe.

Pagliari, C. (2007) 'Design and evaluation in eHealth: challenges and implications for an interdisciplinary field', *Journal of Medical Internet Research*, 9(2): e15.

Patton, M.Q. (1987) *Qualitative Research Evaluation Methods*, Thousand Oaks: SAGE.

Patton, M.Q. (2008) *Utilization-Focused Evaluation* (4th edn), Thousand Oaks: SAGE.

Pawson, R. and Sridharan, S. (2010) 'Theory-driven evaluation of public health programmes', in A. Killoran and M. Kelly (eds) *Evidence-Based Public Health Effectiveness and Efficiency*, Oxford: Oxford University Press, pp 42–62.

Picciotto, R. (2011) 'The logic of evaluation professionalism', *Evaluation*, 17(2): 165–80.

Pisoui, D. and Ahmed, R. (2016) 'Radicalisation research: Gap analysis', *RAN: Centre of Excellence*, December. Available from https://home-affairs.ec.europa.eu/system/files/2020-09/201612_radicalisation_research_gap_analysis_en.pdf [Accessed 23 September 2023].

Polish Education Development Centre [Ośrodek Rozwoju Edukacji, ORE] (2015) *Standardy i Kryteria Oceny Jakości Programów Profilaktyki i Promocji Zdrowia Psychicznego w Systemie Rekomendacji [Standards and Criteria for Quality Assessment of Mental Health Prevention and Promotion Programs in the Recommendation System]*, Warsaw: ORE.

RAN (Radicalisation Awareness Network) (2019) 'EX POST PAPER monitoring and evaluating counter- and alternative narrative campaigns', *RAN: Centre of Excellence*, 21–22 February. Available from https://home-affairs.ec.europa.eu/system/files_en?file=2019-04/ran_cn_ex_post_evaluating_campaigns_berlin_210219_22_en.pdf [Accessed 23 September 2023].

Renger, R. and Titcomb, A. (2002) 'A three-step approach to teaching logic models', *American Journal of Evaluation*, 23(4): 493–503.

Renger, R. and Hurley, C. (2006) 'From theory to practice: Lessons learned in the application of the ATM approach to developing logic models', *Evaluation and Program Planning*, 29(2): 106–19.

Rossi, P.H., Lipsey, M.W. and Freeman, H.E. (2004) *Evaluation: A Systematic Approach*, Thousand Oaks: SAGE.

Russ-Eft, D. and Preskill, H. (2009) *Evaluation in Organizations: A Systematic Approach to Enhancing Learning, Performance, and Change*, New York: Basic Books.

Sackett, D.L., Rosenberg, W.M., Gray, J.A., Haynes, R.B. and Richardson, W.S. (1996) 'Evidence based medicine: what it is and what it isn't', *Clinical Orthopaedics and Related Research*, 455: 3–5.

Sahar, A. and Raven, A. (2022) 'D2.6 baseline report of gaps, needs and solutions', *INDEED Project*. Available from https://www.indeedproject.eu/wp-content/uploads/2022/12/INDEED-D2.6-Baseline-Report-of-Gaps-Needs-and-Solutions_v1.0.Submitted.pdf [Accessed 23 September 2023].

Salabarría-Peña, Y., Apt, B.S. and Walsh, C.M. (2007) *Practical Use of Program Evaluation among Sexually Transmitted Disease (STD) Programs*, Atlanta: Center for Disease Control and Prevention.

Scriven, M. (1991) *Evaluation Thesaurus*, Thousand Oaks: SAGE.

Shadish, W.R. (1998) 'Evaluation theory is who we are', *American Journal of Evaluation*, 19(1): 1–19.

Shaout, A. and Yousif, M.K. (2014) 'Performance evaluation: methods and techniques survey', *International Journal of Computer and Information Technology*, 3(5): 966–79.

Shaw, I., Greene, J.C. and Mark, M.M. (2006) *The SAGE Handbook of Evaluation*, Thousand Oaks: SAGE.

Sherman, W., Farrington, D.P., Welsh, B.C. and MacKenzie, D.L. (2002) *Evidence-Based Crime Prevention*, London: Routledge.

Silverman, B., Mai, C., Boulet, S. and O'Leary, L. (2007) 'Logic models for planning and evaluation: A resource guide for the CDC State Birth Defects Surveillance Program Cooperative Agreement', *Centres for Disease Control and Prevention*. Available from https://www.cdc.gov/ncbddd/birthdefects/models/Resource1-Evaluation-Guide-508.pdf [Accessed 15 September 2020].

Sochocki, J. (2006) 'Ewaluacja jako dyskurs – wybrane aspekty ewaluacji projektów realizowanych przez organizacje pozarządowe' ['Evaluation as a discourse – selected aspects of evaluation of projects implemented by non-governmental organizations'], *Trzeci Sektor*, 7: 90.

Stancic, M. (2020) 'Peer assessment as a learning and self-assessment tool: A look inside the black box', *Assessment and Evaluation in Higher Education*, 46(6): 852–64.

Steuerle, E. and Jackson, L.M. (eds) (2016) *Advancing the Power of Economic Evidence to Inform Investments in Children, Youth, and Families*, Washington, DC: National Academies Press.

Strauss, S.E., Glasziou, P., Richardson, W.S. and Haynes, R.B. (2019) *Evidence-Based Medicine: How to Practice and Teach EBM* (5th edn), London: Elsevier.

Trocki, M. (ed) (2012) *Nowoczesne Zarządzanie Projektami* [*Modern Project Management*], Warsaw: PWE.

Trocki, M. (ed) (2013) *Ocena Projektów – Koncepcje i Metody* [*Project Assessment – Concepts and Methods*], Warsaw: Oficyna.

Turner, B. (2006) *Cambridge Dictionary of Sociology*, Cambridge: Cambridge University Press.

United Nations Evaluation Group (2016) 'Norms and standards for evaluation', *United Nations Evaluation Group*, June. Available from https://www.iom.int/sites/g/files/tmzbdl486/files/about-iom/evaluation/UNEG-Norms-Standards-for-Evaluation-2016.pdf [Accessed 23 September 2023].

Van de Donk, M., Uhlmann, M. and Keijzer, F. (2019) 'Peer and self-review manual for exit work', *RAN Centre of Excellence*, 17 January. Available from https://home-affairs.ec.europa.eu/system/files/2020-04/ran_exit_peer_self_review_manual_for_exit_work_en.pdf [Accessed 23 September 2023].

Van den Berg, I., Admiraal, W. and Pilot, A. (2006) 'Peer assessment in university teaching: evaluating seven course designs', *Assessment and Evaluation in Higher Education*, 31(1): 19–36.

Vedung, E. (2004) 'Evaluation research and fundamental research', in R. Stockmann (ed) *Evaluationsforschung: Grundlagen und Ausgewahlte Forschungsfelder* [*Evaluation Research: Basics and Selected Fields of Research*], Opladen: Leske + Budrich, pp 111–34.

Wanzer, D.L. (2021) 'What is evaluation? Perspectives of how evaluation differs (or not) from research', *American Journal of Evaluation*, 42(1): 28–46.

Weiss, C.H. (1998) *Evaluation Methods for Studying Programs and Policies*, Hoboken, NJ: Prentice Hall.

WK Kellogg Foundation (2004) 'Evaluation handbook: Philosophy and expectations', *WK Kellogg Foundation*, January. Available from https://heller.brandeis.edu/cyc/pdfs/wkkelloggfoundatio nevaluationhandbook.pdf [Accessed 15 January 2022].

Worthen, B. (1990) 'Program evaluation', in H. Walberg and G. Haertel (eds) *The International Encyclopedia of Educational Evaluation*, Toronto: Pergammon Press, pp 42–7.

Wyatt Knowlton, L. and Phillips, C.C. (2012) *The Logic Model Guidebook: Better Strategies for Great Results*, Thousand Oaks: SAGE.

Yarbrough, D.B., Shula, L.M., Hopson, R.K. and Caruthers, F.A. (2010) *The Program Evaluation Standards: A Guide for Evaluators and Evaluation Users* (3rd ed), Thousand Oaks: Corwin Press.

PART III

The three pillars of evidence-based practice

5

Radicalisation across the community and forensic units: a systematic literature review on the psychology of violent extremism

Sören Henrich, Jane L. Ireland and Michael Lewis

Introduction

Over the past years, research has fostered a deeper understanding of radicalisation, with scholars agreeing that a universal psychosocial pathway towards extremist violence can be assumed (Sageman, 2008; Borum, 2012a), determined by various factors (King and Taylor, 2011). However, the literature relating to preventing and countering violent extremism (P/CVE) often relates to the psychological escalation of individuals only within the community. Little is known about radicalisation in secure forensic settings like prisons or forensic hospitals, leading authors like Mulcahy and colleagues (2013) to frame prisons as so-called 'breeding grounds for terrorists' (p 4). Adding to the challenges in these settings is that risk factors relevant to extremist violence appear to overlap considerably with risk factors for general violence (for example, Dhumad et al, 2020). Nevertheless, more recently, Silke and colleagues (2021) reviewed 29 publications from 2017 onwards and found that prisons can serve as a disruption to the pathway, aiding rehabilitation efforts. With tentative insight into the wider rehabilitation system (Christmann, 2012; Feddes and Gallucci, 2015), empirical evidence becomes arguably more inconclusive when exploring radicalisation in forensic hospitals. This is due to the unclear role of mental health issues and protective factors in developing violent extremism (for example, Gill and Corner, 2017).

Other areas of uncertainty include the role of ideology and sociodemographic features (for instance, age, socioeconomic status, education) in the radicalisation process. For both, research has failed to yield conclusive findings (Kruglanski and Fishman, 2006; Borum, 2015), for example, leading governmental guidance to exclude ideology as a requirement when referring individuals to preventative initiatives (Patel and Hussain, 2019). These and other challenges faced in P/CVE make a continuous, up-to-date overview of the currently available empirical evidence necessary. This chapter therefore produces a systematic review of the psychology of extremist violence, exemplifying one of the ways evidence is produced to inform policy and practice regarding prevention interventions. Systematic reviews, jointly with meta-analytic studies, are considered the highest level of evidence-synthesis methods and a key to evidence-based practice.

However, methodological issues and limited generalisability impact some of the currently available systematic reviews. Out of the wealth of overviews (for example, Christmann, 2012; Schmid, 2013; Feddes and Gallucci, 2015; Scarcella et al, 2016; Lösel et al, 2018; Gøtzsche-Astrup and Lindekilde, 2019; Vergani et al, 2020; Silke et al, 2021), only the reviews by Scarcella et al (2016), Lösel et al (2018), Vergani et al (2020) and Silke et al (2021) followed the guidelines of the Preferred Reporting Items for Systematic Reviews and Meta-Analysis (PRISMA; Moher et al, 2009). These four publications appear to be the only ones reporting the search process in detail; for example, Scarcella et al (2016) explicitly presented a detailed quality appraisal of the reviewed studies. Furthermore, all reviews present some differences in the included studies, likely due to the reviews' varying theoretical outlooks. Some overviews include research that is not directly related to radicalisation.

Hence, the present review aims to summarise the relevant factors for an individual's psychological development towards extremist violence. The literature search focused on understudied areas, like the radicalisation of forensic patients, the role of mental health issues in the process, protective factors, and factors discussed to be relevant for more than one ideology. Following best practices, the systematic literature review employed methodology from earlier examples, which included defining a clear research question, summarising empirical evidence and evaluating study quality. The goal is to offer an updated perspective to support P/CVE efforts.

It is expected that:

1. A multitude of competing concepts will be highlighted (King and Taylor, 2011), with most of the research focused on group processes (for example, Sageman, 2008) and the role of ideology (Patel and Hussain, 2019). However, the latter will yield inconclusive findings (for example, Borum, 2015).
2. There will be limited insight into radicalisation in forensic mental health populations (Al-Attar, 2020; Trimbur et al, 2021).
3. Studies exploring sociodemographic profiles will present contradictory findings (Kruglanski and Fishman, 2006). Similarly, risk factors for radicalisation will yield inconclusive findings, overlapping considerably with risk factors for general violence (for example, Dhumad et al, 2020).
4. There will be limited considerations of mental health issues and protective factors (for example, Gill and Corner, 2017).

Methodology

Adhering to the best practice examples outlined, the current systematic literature review followed the PRISMA standards (Moher et al, 2009). The process included establishing a clear research rationale, followed by transparent inclusion and exclusion criteria for search strings, outlined databases and quality appraisal. All steps are explained in detail in the following sections.

Data search

A publication was included in the final set of studies when it met all the following criteria:

1. the paper had to present factors that influence the radicalisation process;
2. the presented factors had to be distinct;
3. the presented factors had to be individual, not social or organisational, factors;[1] and
4. the publication had to provide measurable and verifiable evidence for the presented factors.

Papers were excluded if they did not offer any quantifiable empirical evidence, which was the case for guidelines or commentaries. Furthermore, articles were not included when they were reviews, as they represented already synthesised knowledge. Lastly, publications addressing aspects not directly linked to the psychological process of radicalisation, such as organisational or sociopolitical factors, were not part of the final set of papers. While studies outlining the effects of deradicalisation programmes technically do not reflect the radicalisation process itself, they were viewed as valuable additions as they could reference mitigating influences on extremist violence and, thus, were included.

Three different iterations of search strings were used, exploring only English-language articles published until April 2019, with a second updated search conducted to capture literature until April 2023: Radicali*ation OR terrorism OR extremis*. These keywords were combined separately with one of the following three search strings in the respective search:

- AND (vulnerability OR victim)
- AND (prison OR criminal OR offender*)
- AND (assessment OR risk assessment OR screening)

All resulting search strings also outlined exclusion criteria at the end: NOT legislation OR law* OR regulation OR policy OR eco* OR history OR cancer OR injury OR metaboli* OR chem*. All search strings were also tested in reverse to ensure that no larger sections of the literature were excluded despite meeting the inclusion criteria. The search was conducted using the following databases: PsycINFO, PsycARTICLES, MEDLINE, Criminal Justice Abstracts, SocINDEX, and International Security and Counter Terrorism Reference Center.

Quality appraisal

Per PRISMA suggestions, each included study's quality was classified as 'good', 'fair' or 'poor' (Moher et al, 2009). Therefore, the Quality Assessment Tool for Observational Cohort and Cross-Sectional Studies checklist and the Quality Assessment of Case-Control Studies checklist (National Heart, Lung, and Blood Institute, nd) were merged into a 15-item checklist to capture the predominant methodology in the reviewed papers most appropriately. Additionally, some changes were made on the content level to represent the counter-terrorism literature more appropriately. These changes included the presence of explicit definitions, review of multiple ideologies and level of statistical analyses.

Analysis

The Grounded Theory Approach (Martin and Turner, 1986) structures data in an inductive manner (that is, the synthesis of general principles based on specific observations), as opposed to a hypothetico-deductive approach (that is, proposing a falsifiable hypothesis by using observable data). The reason for its utilisation lies in the recency of the academic enquiry into counter-terrorism. It can be divided into four stages, all of which we applied to the current analysis. First, the data were assigned codes. This was achieved in conjunction with the second step, in which some codes were summarised with the concepts so that they were all related. Next, all concepts derived from the data set were summarised in categories. Finally, these categories were related to each other to propose new insights.

Results

Entering the search strings in the databases resulted in 6,849 articles, of which 2,608 were duplicates. Further, 3,630 articles were removed because their titles were deemed irrelevant to the aims of the current study. An additional 458 articles were removed based on their abstracts. For the remaining 153 articles, full-text copies were obtained and screened regarding the inclusion criteria in more detail. As a result, 69 articles were removed, with 28 being case studies and not reporting any statistically relevant empirical data. Twelve articles were added due to a hand search of the full-text references. The final set of 96 articles was subjected to a quality appraisal. Fifty-four were labelled 'good', 31 were labelled 'fair' and ten were labelled 'poor' (see Figure 5.1). The reference list for the 96 articles is provided in Appendix 5A.2.

Figure 5.1: Flowchart depicting the search process for the systematic literature review

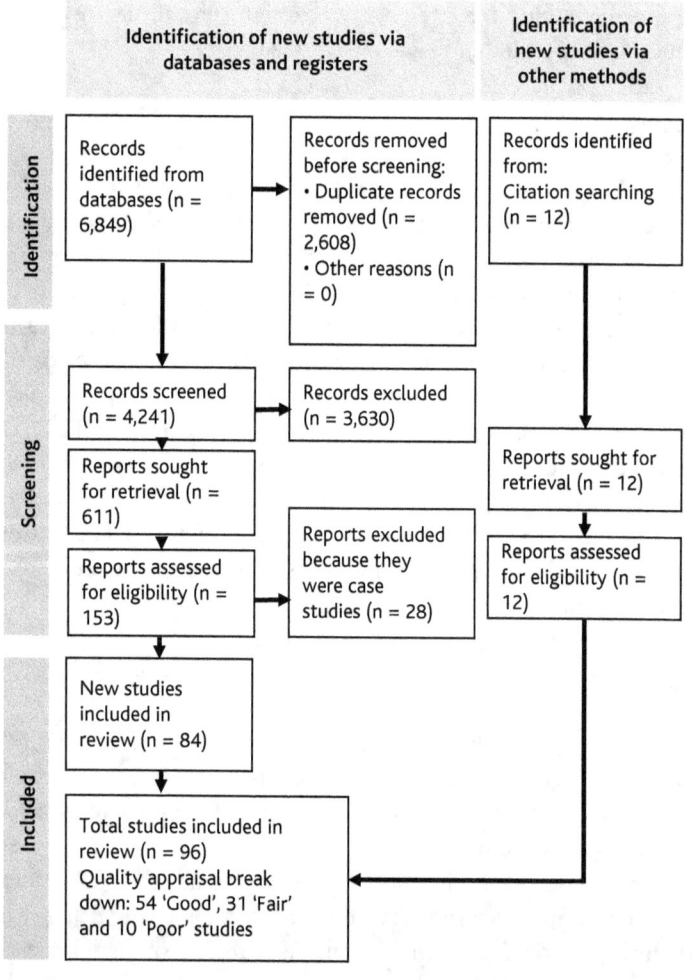

A second independent assessor randomly reviewed 10 per cent of the articles from the abstract and text stage, achieving an interrater agreement of 92.5 per cent. Furthermore, another assessor independently appraised the quality of all 96 included articles, resulting in an interrater agreement of 87.7 per cent. Minor discrepancies on item level were resolved via discussion.

Characteristics of included studies

In 24 instances, an unspecified international focus was employed (see Appendix 5A.1). Most were US publications ($n = 28$), followed by the UK, with nine publications. Articles from non-Western countries (including Palestine, Israel, Russia, Thailand, Kenya, Indonesia and Iran) made up 14 of the 93 included studies.[2]

Seventy-three articles reported quantitative methodology, ten reported qualitative methodology and 12 used a mixed-method approach. The most common study format was surveys ($n = 24$), followed by interviews ($n = 16$), case files ($n = 28$) and publicly available information ($n = 12$). However, 12 articles used multiple data collection methods, meaning that the total count of the methods listed exceeds 63. Case files and public information were most often used when studying terrorist samples ($n = 27$) and lone actors ($n = 15$). Other types of participants and data sources were students and adolescents ($n = 14$) and members of Muslim communities ($n = 8$). Again, it should be noted that some studies utilised several different sample types, resulting in an overlap between articles. Only two studies explored practitioners working in the field to deduce relevant factors of radicalisation.

Themes based on the grounded theory approach

Based on the previously described analysis, 27 subordinate themes were found in the 96 included articles (see Table 5.1). These were summarised in eight themes:

1. extremism enhancing attitudes;
2. criminogenic indicators impacting on offence risk;
3. social influences exposing individuals to extremism;

4. conflicting findings of the contribution of mental health issues to radicalisation;
5. aversive events/circumstances obstructing individuals' prosocial goal obtainment;
6. impaired functioning facilitating extremist attitudes and/or violence;
7. conflicting findings regarding the utility of sociodemographic characteristics in the prediction of radicalisation; and
8. content of radicalisation cognitions.

Table 5.1: Overview of factors derived from the thematic analysis, listed from most to least empirical support

Factor	No. of studies covering the factor	Good quality	Fair quality	Poor quality
Extremism enhancing attitudes	41	24	14	3
Ideology	25	15	9	1
Religion	12	7	3	2
Political attitude	2	1	1	0
Political engagement	1	1	0	0
Worldview	1	0	1	0
Criminogenic indicators impacting offence risk	39	23	11	5
History of violence	11	7	2	2
Past offence characteristics indicating preparedness	16	9	6	1
Protective factors countering extremism	9	6	2	1
Factors motivating engagement with extremism	3	1	1	1
Social influences exposing individuals to extremism	36	20	13	3
Group process	20	10	7	3
Presence of delinquent peers	11	7	4	0
Prison experience	5	3	2	0

Table 5.1: Overview of factors derived from the thematic analysis, listed from most to least empirical support (continued)

Factor	No. of studies covering the factor	Good quality	Fair quality	Poor quality
Conflicting findings of the contribution of mental health issues to radicalisation	31	17	13	1
Depression	10	6	3	1
Non-specific mental health difficulties	10	5	5	0
Personality disorder	5	2	3	0
Anxiety	3	2	1	0
Early childhood memories	2	1	1	0
Substance use	1	1	0	0
Aversive events/circumstances obstructing individuals' prosocial goal obtainment	29	21	6	3
Strain	18	12	4	3
Discrimination	11	9	2	0
Impairment functioning facilitating extremist attitudes and/or violence	21	15	5	1
Cognitive impairment	10	6	4	0
Emotional impairment	7	6	1	0
Impulsiveness	4	3	0	1
Conflicting findings regarding the utility of sociodemographic characteristics in the prediction of radicalisation	17	7	8	2
Sociodemographic characteristics	12	5	5	2
Gender	5	2	3	0
Content of radicalisation cognitions	15	11	4	0
Loss of significance	7	4	3	0
Mortality salience	4	4	0	0
Moral considerations	3	2	1	0
Revenge	1	1	0	0

Each theme and its related sub-ordinate themes are presented next, commencing with the concepts that appear to be studied most often.

Extremism enhancing attitudes

The first emerging theme researched the most often ($n = 41$) relates to 'ideological' ($n = 25$), 'religious' ($n = 12$) or 'political' attitudes ($n = 2$). Both 'political engagement' and 'worldview' were researched once. These concepts do not appear distinct (for example, Bartlett et al, 2010) and are debated as not being equally important. For example, Schils and Verhage (2017) doubt ideology is the main driver. The attitudes entail mostly good-quality studies ($n = 24$) and fair-quality studies ($n = 14$). Ideology appears to have been studied the most frequently, utilising mostly good-quality methodology ($n = 15$). 'Religion' ($n = 7$) and 'political' beliefs ($n = 2$) have been less frequently studied, but also with good-quality methodology. 'Political engagement' presented with one good study and general 'worldview' inclusion has been rated as fair. These attitudes often appear to serve as prosocial legitimisation for violence (Trujillo et al, 2009; Stankov, Higgins et al, 2010; Cohen, 2016). They likely inform pre-offence behaviour (Capellan, 2015), such as target selection (Speckhard and Ahkmedova, 2006; Coid et al, 2016). However, complex relationships have been observed recently between radical beliefs and several other factors, such as social control and peer presence, have been observed (Becker, 2021).

As such, they appear to hold predictive power (Bhui et al, 2014a; Pauwels and De Waele, 2014; Kerodal et al, 2016; Schils and Pauwels, 2016; Challacombe and Lucas, 2019; Obaidi et al, 2022) and, hence, are studied in the context of threat assessments (Laor et al, 2006; Loza, 2010; Doosje et al, 2013; Meloy et al, 2015; Meloy and Gill, 2016; Groppi, 2017).

On a content level, 'religion' appeared to facilitate radicalisation, especially when extremists used spirituality to subscribe meaning to their crisis (Speckhard and Ahkmedova, 2006; Askew and Helbardt, 2012), emphasising collective as opposed to individual strain (Adamczyk and LaFree, 2019). Hence, religion is hypothesised to be a recruitment tool (Speckhard and Ahkmedova,

2006). Linked to this, extremist leadership derives authority from their perceived closeness to divine power (Stankov, Higgins et al, 2010). However, generalisability is limited, as most studies focused on Islamist terrorism (Loza, 2010).

Bhui et al (2016) found that political engagement appears to reduce the likelihood to sympathise with political violence in their sample of South Asian immigrants living in the United Kingdom. Nevertheless, political activism can be an effective predictor of extremist violence in screening instruments (Egan et al, 2016). This is discussed in conjunction with social influences in the next sections. Furthermore, a worldview presenting general disgust with society can contribute to radicalisation (Stankov, Saucier et al, 2010).

Criminogenic indicators impacting offence risk

The second most researched theme (n = 39) represents factors directly linked to the risk of an offence, including recidivism (that is, the risk of reoffending). This included 'history of violence' (n = 11), 'past offence characteristics indicating preparedness' (n = 16), 'protective factors countering extremism' (n = 9) and 'factors motivating engagement with extremism' (n = 3). The studies present mostly good-quality studies (n = 23), followed by fair-quality studies (n = 11) and five poor studies. Violence appears to be studied mainly using good-quality research (n = 7), while past offence characteristics and other motivations exhibit roughly equal amounts of good and fair studies. Lastly, protective factors seemed to show mostly good empirical evidence (n = 6).

A history of general violence was consistently found to increase the risk for radicalisation (for example, Liem et al, 2018), likely because it indicates psychological capability for violence (Gill et al, 2017). While Thijssen et al (2023) found that 60 per cent of 82 convicted extremists in a Dutch prison had been convicted of violent crimes in the past, Bronsard et al (2022) observed less likelihood for prior convictions when comparing radicalised minors to teenagers convicted of non-extremist delinquency. Violence was also operationalised as violent rhetoric (Egan et al, 2016). The readiness can express itself as self-defence (Bartlett et al, 2010) or as a need for excitement (for example, Askew and Helbardt, 2012). Certain forms of violence, such as previous use of weapons, seem predominantly used by lone actors (McCauley et al, 2013). Those offenders might be better captured with psychological dynamics related to school shooters (McCauley et al, 2013).

A general history of criminal activity also appeared to increase the risk of radicalisation (Gill et al, 2017). This is captured in offence characteristics, including the pre-offence phase. Factors included leakage (that is, disclosing plans to others) and attack location familiarity (Gill et al, 2017, 2021; Kupper and Meloy, 2021; Clemmow, Gill et al, 2022). Others included familiarity with past victims, use of weapons, number of victims, the presence of additional offenders (Gruenewald et al, 2013; Liem et al, 2018; Schuurman et al, 2018), as well as lethality and level of planning (Pitcavage, 2015). Most factors are used in threat assessment as they have been found as feasible predictors of extremist violence (for example, Meloy et al, 2015; Egan et al, 2016; Meloy and Gill, 2016; Challacombe and Lucas, 2019). On the content level, offence motivation is often found relevant (for example, Cohen, 2016). Some offenders offered prosocial motivations for joining an extremist organisation (Cohen, 2016) or popularity (Peddell et al, 2016). However, female offenders especially provided antisocial reasoning such as revenge or personal vendetta (Jacques and Taylor, 2008).

Variables mitigating radicalisation are summarised under protective factors. Symptoms of depression were indirectly negatively associated with violence, as they impacted general psychopathology (Coid et al, 2016). Similarly, community-based narratives countering recruitment (Joosse et al, 2015), a combination of resilience and self-control (Merari et al, 2010), prosocial engagement and social control (Becker, 2021), and critical adverse life events (Bhui et al, 2016) decreased the risk for extremism. The latter are discussed as surprising (Bhui et al, 2016), given that grievance is usually framed as a contributing factor to radicalisation (to be discussed later). However, in combination with political engagement, it appeared to foster social connectedness, protecting individuals from radicalisation (Bhui et al, 2014a, 2016). Overall, the findings emphasise the importance of structured psychological interventions (Jensen et al, 2020; Cherney and Belton, 2021).

Social influences exposing individuals to extremism

Thirty-six studies explored the social environment of radicalised individuals, namely 'group processes' ($n = 20$), 'presence of delinquent peers' ($n = 11$) and 'prison experience' ($n = 5$). Most studies exhibited good-quality ($n = 13$), followed by fair-quality studies ($n = 8$) and three poor-quality studies. Both group processes ($n = 10$) and the presence of delinquent peers ($n = 7$) present mostly good-quality research, while the prison experience entails good ($n = 3$) and fair-quality methodology ($n = 2$) in nearly equal parts.

On a collective level, strong group identity (Arndt et al, 2002; Victoroff et al, 2012), conformity to group norms (Askew and Helbardt, 2012), fraternity, participating in a hierarchy (Speckhard and Ahkmedova, 2006; Trujillo et al, 2009; Horgan et al, 2018), and active involvement in an extremist group online or offline (Weinberg and Eubank, 1987; Blazak, 2001; Berko and Erez, 2006; Holt and Bolden, 2014; Schils and Verhage, 2017) were considered linked to radicalisation. The latter was also shown to improve the use of predictive instruments, among other factors (Egan et al, 2016). On a content level, peer pressure and exploitation within extremist groups were utilised to recruit suicide bombers, especially female extremists (Jacques and Taylor, 2008). Furthermore, the perception of the in-group being threatened appeared to have an energising effect on individuals, consequently engaging in extremist violent behaviour (Dillon et al, 2020; Yustisia et al, 2020; Ebner et al, 2022; Pfundmair et al, 2022).

Generally, the presence of delinquent peers, such as gang members, contributed to radicalisation (Gruenewald et al, 2013; Pauwels and De Waele, 2014; Egan et al, 2016; Jasko et al, 2017; Schuurman et al, 2018; Becker, 2021). Especially when they are viewed as worthy of being imitated (Bartlett et al, 2010) or when they share pro-violent attitudes, for example, in families (Weinberg and Eubank, 1987; King et al, 2011; Schils and Verhage, 2017; Dhumad et al, 2020).

This is also applicable to peer influences in prison settings (Trujillo et al, 2009), especially when radicalised individuals are not separated from the extremist in-group (Jensen et al, 2020). Radicalisation appears more likely in these environments when individuals are disillusioned or cynical about prosocial engagement with the criminal justice system. Overall, LaFree et al (2020) demonstrated that prison stays – and particularly the occurrence of radicalisation within these settings – is a reliable predictor for future extremist violence (Thijssen et al, 2023).

Conflicting findings of the contribution of mental health issues to radicalisation

This theme encapsulated 'depression' ($n = 10$), 'personality disorder' ($n = 5$), 'anxiety' ($n = 3$), 'early childhood memories' ($n = 2$), 'substance use' ($n = 1$) and 'non-specified mental health difficulties' ($n = 10$). Most studies exhibited good- ($n = 17$) or fair-quality ($n = 13$), with depression displaying the best-quality research ($n = 6$). Personality disorders, in turn, exhibited a fair evidence basis ($n = 3$).

Several studies have linked general psychiatric symptomatology to an increased risk of radicalisation (Gruenewald et al, 2013; Chermak and Gruenewald, 2015; Meloy et al, 2015; Coid et al, 2016; Meloy and Gill, 2016; Liem et al, 2018; Challacombe and Lucas, 2019; Corner et al, 2019). However, they do not explicitly name them in their design. More specifically, depression- and anxiety-related symptomatology appeared to make an individual more vulnerable to radicalisation (Bhui et al, 2016), like rumination (Bhui et al, 2014a). This was considered likely related to death-related thoughts (Taubman-Ben-Ari and Noy, 2010). These aspects appeared to be researched most frequently in the context of suicide bombings (Speckhard and Ahkmedova, 2006; Merari et al, 2010; Brym and Araj, 2012). However, the extent to which suicidality contributes to radicalisation in those cases is unclear. Bhui et al (2014b) found no association between depression or anxiety with extremist violence but extremist sympathies (Bhui et al, 2020), and Coid et al (2016) found a negative relationship between depression and extremism.

Additionally, some personality disorder symptoms were found to contribute to radicalisation, including self-concept instability, like narcissism (Dechesne, 2009), antisocial personality disorder (Dhumad et al, 2020; Candilis et al, 2021), or any diagnosis relating to cluster C personality disorders of the Diagnostic and Statistical Manual of Mental Disorders (DSM-IV; Merari et al, 2010). Merari and Ganor (2022) concluded that psychopathology amplified the assailants' motivation to escape their lives, resulting in terrorist attacks.

Krout and Stagner (1939) explored early positive and negative childhood memories in the context of psychodynamic theories. They found that abandonment led to antagonism and, subsequently, extremism. These findings were not replicated by Dhumad et al (2020), who compared 160 terrorists with 65 murderers and a non-criminal control group (n = 88). Their findings suggest that both criminal groups were less likely to be subjected to harsh treatments in childhood. However, terrorists exhibited higher levels of disobedience when younger.

Only one study by Gill et al (2021) explicitly explored the relation of substance use to extremist violence. They observed a higher likelihood of mass shooters having a history of substance use when compared to lone actors, likely impacted by how they cope with stress.

Aversive events/circumstances obstructing individuals' prosocial obtainment of goals

Twenty-nine studies explored this theme, including 'strain' (n = 18) and 'discrimination' (n = 11). The former was divided into individual and collective strains. Both strain (n = 12) and discrimination (n = 9) seemed equally well supported by good-quality research. However, the latter exhibited no poor-quality studies, while the former counted three poor-quality studies.

On an individual level, violence may emerge because of struggle (Pauwels and De Waele, 2014), especially in combination with other personal variables. These included a lack of resilience (Dechesne, 2009), experiencing disillusionment related to mainstream culture (Klausen et al, 2020), and when an individual faced a situation threatening their control or predictability

(McCauley et al, 2013; Ebner et al, 2022). Again, these factors were proven useful for threat assessment (Meloy et al, 2015, 2021; Meloy and Gill, 2016; Challacombe and Lucas, 2019; Kupper and Meloy, 2021). Collectively, relative deprivation[3] (Peddell et al, 2016), nationalistic struggles (Jacques and Taylor, 2008) and generational divisions (Blazak, 2001) appeared relevant to radicalisation. However, this seemed likely only for individuals already holding pro-violent ideas (Nivette et al, 2017). Meanwhile, Groppi (2017) found no significant link between economic disparity and being of Muslim faith supporting violence.

Linked to strain was discrimination, which is often framed as a separate concept (Pauwels and De Waele, 2014). This is operationalised as perceived injustice and group threat (Victoroff et al, 2012; Doosje et al, 2013; Schils and Verhage, 2017; Yustisia et al, 2020), individuals' reactions to stereotypes (Kamans et al, 2009), and social exclusion or poor social inclusion (Pauwels and De Waele, 2014; Schils and Pauwels, 2016; Pretus et al, 2018). The subjective perception appears more important than actual victimisation, for example, explored in conjunction with the Alt-Right movement (Boehme and Isom Scott, 2020). However, discrimination only appears to support radicalisation in conjunction with other factors (for example, distorted worldview, presence of delinquent peers) and does not distinguish terrorists from others (for example, Bartlett et al, 2010).

Impaired functioning facilitating the development of extremist attitudes and/or violence

This theme comprised 21 articles addressing 'cognitive impairment' ($n = 10$), 'emotional impairment' ($n = 7$) and 'impulsiveness' ($n = 4$). Cognitive impairment was nearly equally displaying good ($n = 6$) and fair evidence ($n = 4$), while emotional impairment was mainly supported by good-quality studies ($n = 6$). Impulsiveness had been explored by mostly good-quality studies ($n = 3$) and one poor study.

Cognitive impairment is related to impacted intellectual functioning, including reduced cognitive flexibility (Baele, 2017) and increased cognitive rigidity (Cohen, 2012). Vice versa, cognitive flexibility and high levels of emotional expression appear unrelated to extremist views (Muluk et al, 2020). However, higher cognitive abilities were also related to conservatism if the relationship was influenced by low political involvement (Kemmelmeier, 2008). It appears extremists cannot integrate complex cognitions into their political ideas, often expressed as pronounced black-and-white thinking (Savage et al, 2014). Other functions related to radicalisation were the increased need for cognitive closure (Webber et al, 2018) and impaired social cognitions and/or failure to affiliate with others (Challacombe and Lucas, 2019). The latter appeared to have predictive utility in threat assessment (Meloy et al, 2015; Meloy and Gill, 2016), but only in combination with other impaired functions (Baez et al, 2017).

This could include the second subordinate theme, emotional impairment. It appeared that difficulty in emotional recognition distinguished between terrorists and other non-criminal combatants (Baez et al, 2017). Similarly, a lack of empathy was more commonly associated with radicalised individuals than other violent behaviours (Bronsard et al, 2022). Additionally, terrorists exhibited higher levels of proactive aggression (Baez et al, 2017). Baele (2017) found that extremists, especially lone actors, appeared to have generally higher levels of negative emotions. Emotion dysregulation and the expression of aggression, grievance and general negative emotions were successfully utilised in threat assessment (Meloy et al, 2015; Meloy and Gill, 2016; Challacombe and Lucas, 2019).

Radicalisation was also linked to impulsiveness, specifically failures in impulse regulation (Egan et al, 2016) and participation in general risk-seeking behaviour (McCauley et al, 2013; Pauwels and De Waele, 2014). Pauwels and De Waele (2014) concluded that thrill drove the radicalisation process more than impulsivity. However, in a more complex analysis of the same data set, a lack of self-control appeared directly linked to extremist violence (Schils and Pauwels, 2016).

Conflicting findings regarding the utility of sociodemographic characteristics in the prediction of radicalisation

Seventeen studies explored several sociodemographic characteristics (for example, ethnicity, education, income; $n = 12$) and specifically gender ($n = 5$) regarding radicalisation or extremist violence. Studies relating to inconsistencies reported equally good and fair quality in methodology (each $n = 5$) and two poor studies. Gender was studied in three fair-quality studies, followed by two good-quality studies.

Overall, sociodemographic features resulted in inconsistent findings (Coid et al, 2016). Groppi (2017) found no significant link between economic disparity and other common sociological variables. Similarly, Klausen et al (2016) found no significant links between early school dropouts and radicalisation. Comparing suicide bombers with the Palestinian public also yielded no significant differences (Brym and Araj, 2012). They noted that most offenders were unmarried, with 40 per cent being students and 5 per cent unemployed (Brym and Araj, 2012). Lone actors also do not seem different to non-ideological active shooters (Capellan, 2015). But Gruenewald et al (2013) found in their review of the Extremist Crime Database that lone actors were more likely to be younger when following a right-wing ideology, especially when having a university degree (Hollewell and Longpré, 2022). These findings were partially replicated by Chermak and Gruenewald (2015), who found that terrorists following White supremacists, Islamists or left-wing ideology exhibited significantly different age and relationship status profiles. For example, Islamists tended to be older, and Islamists and White supremacists were less often in a committed relationship (Chermak and Gruenewald, 2015). Similarly, Liem et al (2018) showed that 60 per cent of investigated lone actors were single, which made them comparable to homicidal offenders, among other factors (for instance, employment status and level of education).

However, only two studies significantly distinguished radicalised individuals from the general public. Sociodemographic stress indicators, such as unemployment or loss of a relationship, linked a sample of mass murderers to extremism (Gill et al, 2017). Similarly, distressing events and the responses of various age groups, genders and education levels were linked to radicalisation (Webber et al, 2017). Some studies focused exclusively on gender. For example, Berko and Erez (2007) interviewed 14 female Palestinian terrorists and found that most women did not join extremist movements to experience empowerment. Instead, Jacques and Taylor's

(2008) findings suggest female suicide bombers were motivated by personal vendettas. When exploring ideologies, González et al (2014) reviewed the Extremist Crime Database and showed that women seem more likely to join left-wing causes or causes linked to eco-activism. However, they were less likely to actively participate in a terrorist offence or become a lone actor (González et al, 2014).

Content of radicalisation cognitions

Fifteen studies investigated thoughts and perceptions linked to radicalisation, summarised as 'loss of significance' ($n = 7$), 'mortality salience' ($n = 4$), 'moral considerations' ($n = 3$) and 'revenge' ($n = 1$). Here, most included studies were rated as presenting with good quality ($n = 11$).

Losing significance (for example, employment loss) or needing more significance (for instance, due to narcissism), increased vulnerability to radicalisation (Jasko et al, 2017; Webber et al, 2017, 2018; Pfundmair et al, 2022). This could result from isolation, as suggested by findings of ten interviews with ex-members of right-wing movements (Bérubé et al, 2019). Dhumad et al (2020) did not directly study the loss of significance, but in their interpretation, they contextualised deprivation and other justifications brought forward by the investigated offenders ($n = 160$) with the task of reinstating an individual's significance. This central driving dynamic appears to be a significant factor for individuals on the pathway towards an extremist offence compared to those who merely endorse extremist views (Dillon et al, 2020).

Similarly, thoughts regarding an individual's mortality could lead to extremist views (Arndt et al, 2002; Pfundmair et al, 2022). Underlying mechanisms could be a combination of escalating political conditions and low perceived personal vulnerability (that is, how political conditions would affect their personal lives or that of their loved ones [Hirschberger et al, 2009]). However, individuals with war experience only endorsed political violence when considering additional adversary rhetoric (Hirschberger et al, 2009). Ruminations about the self also increased the accessibility of mortality-related thoughts, which triggered the individual's focus on perceived social transgressions to their group (Taubman-Ben-Ari and Noy, 2010). This resulted in unfavourable opinions regarding other groups, likely contributing to radicalisation.

Moral considerations were shown to increase the likelihood of extremism. For example, individuals supporting violence focused merely on the outcome (Baez et al, 2017). Furthermore, Nivette et al (2017) showed in their sample of 1,675 Swiss pupils that individuals who experienced strain were more likely to support extremist violence when also exhibiting a high level of moral and legal neutralisation techniques (that is, morally disengaging from an argument or idea to justify violence, for instnace, by reframing own harmful behaviour as honourable or heroic).

Lastly, one study explored revenge as a motivating factor for extremist violence (Tschantret, 2021). When comparing right-wing terrorists ($n = 12$), Islamist terrorists ($n = 12$) and texts from a control sample ($n = 9,660$), it was observed that right-wing ideology appears to be preoccupied with themes of revenge, including vengeance, and causing chaos.

Discussion

The systematic literature review offered an overview of relevant factors influencing the risk of radicalisation while also reflecting on the quality of the empirical evidence. Eight themes emerged: extremism enhancing attitudes; criminogenic indicators impacting on offence risk; social influences exposing individuals to extremism; conflicting findings of the contribution of mental health issues to radicalisation; aversive events/circumstances obstructing individuals' prosocial goal obtainment; impaired functioning facilitating extremist attitudes and/or violence; conflicting findings regarding the utility of sociodemographic characteristics in the prediction of radicalisation; and content of radicalisation cognitions. These themes confirmed the first prediction that a multitude of factors determine radicalisation. However, only limited insight was gathered about radicalisation in forensic populations, with only five publications (Trujillo et al, 2009; Decker and Pyrooz, 2020; Jensen et al, 2020; LaFree et al, 2020; Thijssen et al, 2023) researching the prison context. This confirmed the second prediction that only limited insight into the radicalisation of forensic mental health populations would be yielded, replicating findings from Mulcahy and colleagues (2013), who criticised the lack of research in this area.

Instead, most research is related to attitudes, justifications and aversive events, all key components of risk assessments. These represent central constructs of risk assessments. The popularity of these themes might stem from their apparent face validity. For example, it is reasonable to conclude that strains like discrimination push individuals away from mainstream culture towards fringe movements. The frequent coverage of these themes could also be due to their accessibility. For example, the exploration of factors like ideology and religion is predominantly comprised of publications that utilise publicly available information about extremist offenders (for example, Capellan, 2015; Challacombe and Lucas, 2019). In these cases, it is arguably simpler to discern the presence of these factors than to uncover more complex features requiring access to secure data.

The influence of ideology on radicalisation was a frequently examined theme, though the review revealed mixed results about its impact. This inconsistency reflects the ongoing debate in literature and aligns with our predictions. Recent developments suggest that ideology is not necessarily a prerequisite for radicalisation, with scholars such as Borum (2015) and Vergani and colleagues (2020) arguing that not every radicalised individual must present with an understanding of ideological agendas. This notion ties into the more recent distinction between cognitive and behavioural radicalisation as distinct outcomes (Vidino, 2010; Neumann, 2013), with only the former associated with ideological preoccupation, while the latter is more closely related to extremist violence.

Furthermore, the review highlighted sociodemographic characteristics as equally contested. No consistent findings could be found which would constitute a terrorist profile. This reflects conclusions by Kruglanski and Fishman (2006), who refuted the search for sociodemographic root causes. The inconsistent findings are likely due to two reasons. First, the theme subsumed the most fair- and poor-quality studies of this review compared to their good-quality studies. The predominant use of correlational designs was likely unable to detect underlying mechanisms not represented in an individual's sociodemographic characteristics. Second, the reviewed studies found an overlap between terrorists and other violent offenders, for example, murderers (for example, Gill et al, 2017).

This and the overlap of criminogenic indicators for radicalisation with factors for general violence affirm the prediction that neither sociodemographic profiles nor risk factors for radicalisation will yield conclusive findings. These indicators are the second most researched aspect in this review, likely due to scholars exploring factors well-established for other risk assessments (for example, HCR-20 by Douglas et al, 2013). Like the general violence literature (De Ruiter and Nicholls, 2011), protective factors also appeared understudied in this review. Some mitigating influences seemed to represent inverted risk factors; for example, violence-triggering critical life events were found to aid prosocial reorientation (Bhui et al, 2016).

However, this review yielded distinct factors separating radicalisation research from general violence discourse. In line with the prediction that most research will emphasise group processes, factors like group identity were well-substantiated. The fact that the presence of delinquent peers was linked to an increased risk of radicalisation confirms the notion of this process as inherently social (for example, Borum, 2012b). The tentative findings are promising – these influences presented consistently good-quality studies, especially compared to other themes. Similarly, the review found that the content of cognitions appeared to distinguish radicalised individuals from general violence. The studies utilised the most experimental designs of the included publications, such as written scenarios, to elicit emotional or moral responses (for example, Hirschberger et al, 2009; Baez et al, 2017). Further research is needed to explore whether those cognitions can be naturally observed.

The prediction was confirmed that mental health issues would yield inconclusive findings. While the review found many publications, no single diagnosis could be empirically linked to radicalisation. This was likely due to the consistently poor-quality study designs, for example, not specifying the explored psychopathology. Similarly, the review yielded no consistent findings for impaired functioning. Again, aspects like impulse control deficits, antisocial personality style or emotional dysregulation are also considered relevant for some offenders of general violence (for example, Douglas et al, 2013). The lack of specificity arguably impacted the understanding of its influence on radicalisation. Overall, this reflects scholars' concerns about the empirical evidence in the field (for example, Gill and Corner, 2017; Al-Attar, 2020), urging for further exploration of these facets.

In sum, several trends are observable in the literature. The more recent studies appear more consistently of good quality than earlier research. For example, studies include more causal inferences rather than purely correlational designs and are more frequently gaining access to primary data. This is also reflected in the explored factors, seemingly focusing more on underlying mechanisms that explain the radicalisation process (for instance, group processes, grievances and protective factors) than outwardly observable factors, such as openly endorsed ideology or sociodemographic features. However, the new possible explanations for the origins of extremist violence are only tentative. Overall, the radicalisation process appears well understood, seemingly encouraging scholars to explore more complex presentations, such as the impact of mental health issues on extremist violence or the radicalisation of complex forensic populations. Again, more research is required to aid future P/CVE initiatives successfully.

In conclusion, several factors were identified as crucial and empirically well-supported in the radicalisation process. However, some influences present considerable overlap with the general violence literature (that is, history of violence, preparedness, and sociodemographic features like income, education or gender). Additionally, the review yielded little insight into the radicalisation of forensic populations, especially when they present with complex needs, as mental health issues appear understudied. As the literature seems particularly limited in this context, the next step must gather insight into groups in secure services. This should combine professionals' views on these dynamics, like the research by Trujillo et al (2009) and primary data, such as interviews with radicalised individuals or case files on their presentation in secure settings. Among other aspects, the primary data would allow for further exploration of the uncertain areas and especially the overlap of risk factors of radicalisation with factors related to general violence. As a result, the current review emphasised the need for a formulation approach to support P/CVE, for example, through care pathway planning or risk assessment and management.

The current study is a reminder of the importance of synthesising knowledge based on the critical reflection of how evidence is produced and its integral contribution to continuously improving evidence-based practice. Overviews of this kind allow the identification of areas that require increased research intention in the future but also offers reassurance to practitioners about well-established concepts and approaches. Currently, it appears that the psychology of P/CVE has fully captured the presence of factors relevant to the radicalisation process. Now, renewed efforts must be made to understand their relevance for the development of extremist violence.

Limitations

The review is limited in several ways. The study only considered English language articles. Hence, alternative empirically substantiated influences in other countries are not included. It is unclear what additional relevant factors for radicalisation might be well established in other cultural settings, limiting the generalisability of the summarised findings. The review only focused on research directly investigating radicalisation and extremism, discarding findings of similar dynamics based on other schools of thought. Some mechanisms, for example, the violence-strain link, have been well-researched for other offence types. Hence, a broader perspective might elicit more empirical support for the factors listed here. Lastly, only a qualitative synthesis of the findings was conducted utilising thematic analysis. This approach restricts insight into the extent of empirically well-established evidence as opposed to more elaborate methods like meta-analyses that, for example, weigh effect sizes against the study qualities.

Summary

- The most well-established influences on radicalisation appear to be aversive events and attitudes which endorse extremism.

- A lack of empirical evidence was identified pertaining to the role of mental health issues, protective factors and radicalisation in forensic populations.
- The role of ideology is inconclusive in the radicalisation process and is suspected to be of only minor importance.
- Sociodemographic characteristics alone appear unhelpful in explaining the radicalisation process, echoing the field's shift away from utilising profiles.
- Risk factors supported by the most empirical evidence appear to be the same factors discussed for general violence without any radicalisation indication.
- However, tentative findings based on good-quality studies suggest that social processes, such as group socialisation, might uniquely influence the development towards an extremist violent offence.
- Overall, it appears that the research quality has improved over the last ten years as the field has explored more nuanced facets of radicalisation.

Suggested directions for future research

- Future research should prioritise discerning the overlap of risk factors present in both extremist violence cases and general violent offending behaviour. Exploring interactions between these factors is further suggested, as their presence during the radicalisation pathways has been well-established.
- It is necessary to conduct an in-depth analysis of the impact of mental health issues on radicalisation and violent extremist behaviour, particularly among forensic populations with complex needs. This endeavour presents a valuable opportunity to gain a comprehensive understanding of the underlying causes that drive individuals towards violent extremism.
- Further research is necessary utilising primary data, meaning insights based directly on research with radicalised individuals, instead of accounts about this population. The latter appears to dominate the current literature, which impacts current insight in the field.

Appendix 5A.1: Study characteristics of all reviewed English-language publications of research

Reference	Quality	Country	Central constructs	Study design	Participants demographic
Adamczyk and LaFree, 2019	Good	International	Religion, sociodemographic	QNT; cross-sectional survey	N = 45,923 survey participants
Altier et al, 2021	Good	International	Recidivism, risk factors	QNT; cross-sectional	N = 87 autobiographical accounts of individuals involved in terrorism
Arndt et al, 2002	Good	United States	Mortality salience, psychological distancing, group identification	QNT; randomised experimental trial in two studies	N_1 = 47 students N_2 = 91 students
Askew and Helbardt, 2012	Poor	Thailand	Motivation	QUL; analysis of interviews, case files and propaganda	N = 3 Patani warriors
Baele, 2017	Good	International	Emotions, cognitive flexibility	QNT; linguistic analysis of written texts	N_1 = 11 lone actors N_2 = 3 peaceful political figures N_3 = thousands of texts as baseline
Baez et al, 2017	Good	United States	Intellectual and executive functioning aggression emotion recognition moral judgement	QNT; comparison of surveys and experiment with matched control group	N_1 = 66 right-wing terrorists N_2 = 66 community-based participants
Bartlett et al, 2010	Good	International	Social and personal characteristics, religion and ideology	QNT, QUL; interviews and case files	N_1 = 58 Islamist terrorists N_2 = 28 radical Muslims (no conviction) N_3 = 71 young Muslims

Reference	Quality	Country	Central constructs	Study design	Participants demographic
Becker, 2021	Good	United States	Social control, social learning, sociodemographic	QNT; cross-sectional	N = 1,757 domestic extremists
Berko and Erez, 2006	Fair	Palestine	Gender, recruitment, prison experience	QUL; interviews	N = 14 women detained for security offences
Bérubé et al, 2019	Fair	Canada	Radicalisation trajectories	QUL; interviews	N = 10 former members of violent right-wing extremist groups
Bhui et al, 2014a	Good	United Kingdom	Psychosocial adversity, social capital, mental health	QNT; cross-sectional survey	N = 608 of Pakistani or Bangladeshi origin (18–45 years old)
Bhui et al, 2014b	Good	United Kingdom	Health, anxiety, depression	QNT; cross-sectional survey	N = 608 of Pakistani or Bangladeshi origin (18–45 years old)
Bhui et al, 2016	Good	United Kingdom	Life events, political engagement, depression	QNT; cross-sectional survey	N = 608 of Pakistani or Bangladeshi origin (18–45 years old)
Bhui et al, 2020	Good	United Kingdom	Depression, dysthymia, anxiety, post-traumatic stress	QNT; cross-sectional survey	N = 618 of Pakistani or Bangladeshi origin (18–45 years old)
Blazak, 2001	Poor	United States	General Strain Theory	QUL; interviews	N = 65 skinheads
Boehme and Isom Scott, 2020	Good	United States	Perceived victimhood	QNT; cross-sectional survey	N = 754 White Americans

Reference	Quality	Country	Central constructs	Study design	Participants demographic
Bronsard et al, 2022	Good	France	Several sociodemographic, clinical and psychological variables, including empathy and suicidality	QNT; comparison group	N_1 = 31 convicted terrorists; N_2 = 101 teenage delinquents
Brookes and McEnery, 2020	Fair	United Kingdom	Ideological struggle	QNT, QUL; correlational, thematic analysis	N = unspecified; texts by British Islamist terrorists
Brym and Araj, 2012	Poor	Palestine	Sociodemographic details, depression	QUL; interviews	N_1 = NR; relatives of suicide bombers
Candilis et al, 2021	Good	Iraq	Sociodemographic factors, motivation, attitudes, psychopathology	QNT; Latent Class Analysis	N = 160 convicted terrorists
Capellan, 2015	Fair	United States	Sociodemographic details, role of ideology	QNT; comparison of case files and public information with control group	N_1 = 40 incidents of ideologically motivated shooters; N_2 = 242 incidents of non-ideologically motivated shooters
Challacombe and Lucas, 2019	Good	United States	TRAP-18: personal pathway, fixation, identification, novel aggression, energy burst, leakage, last resort, threat, grievance and moral outrage, ideology, failure to affiliate with extremist	QNT; comparison of case files and public information with control group	N_1 = 30 violent individuals; N_2 = 28 non-violent individuals both associated with sovereign citizen movement

Reference	Quality	Country	Central constructs	Study design	Participants demographic
Chermak and Gruenewald, 2015	Good	United States	Sociodemographic details, criminogenic conditions, offender type and timing	QNT; comparison of case files & public information	N_1^A = 637 right-wing extremists N_2^A = 182 left-wing extremists N_3^A = 155 Al-Qaeda members
Cherney and Belton, 2021	Good	Australia	Deradicalisation intervention	QNT; cross-sectional	N = 14 convicted terrorists
Clemmow et al, 2022a	Good	United States	Propensity, situation, preparatory, leakage, network	QNT; cluster analysis	N = 183 lone actors
Clemmow et al, 2022b	Good	UK	Risk Analysis Framework	QNT; psychometric network modelling	N = 1,500 members of public
Cohen, 2012	Fair	United States	Cognitive rigidity	QNT; cross-sectional comparison of text analyses	N = 483 students
Cohen, 2016	Fair	Palestine	Reasoning, motivation	QNT; cross-sectional comparison of thematic text analyses	N = 211 suicide bombers

Reference	Quality	Country	Central constructs	Study design	Participants demographic
Coid et al, 2016	Good	United Kingdom	Attitude, psychiatric morbidity, ethnicity, religion	QNT; cross-sectional survey	$N = 3,679$ men, 18–34 years old
Corner et al, 2019	Fair	International	Psychopathology, religion	QNT; cross-sectional comparison of sequential analyses	$N^B = 125$ lone actors
Cramer et al, 2023	Good	United States	Hate-Motivated Behaviour Checklist (HMBC); demographic information, Hate-Motivated Behaviour, social-political characteristics	QNT; cross-sectional survey, factor analysis	$N = 463$ students
Dechesne, 2009	Fair	United States	Violence, struggle, narcissism	QNT; randomised experimental comparison	$N = 128$ students
Decker and Pyrooz, 2020	Good	United States	Imprisonment-extremism nexus	QNT, QUL; interviews, cross-sectional	$N = 802$ released inmates
Dhumad et al, 2020	Good	Iraq	Childhood, family, personality (Significance Quest Theory)	QNT; survey and interviews for comparison with control-groups	$N_1 = 160$ convicted terrorists $N_2 = 65$ convicted murders $N_3 = 88$ community members without criminal history
Dillon et al, 2020	Fair	International	In-group, societal grievances, pursuit for significance	QNT, QUL; thematic analysis, cross-sectional	$N_1 = 14$ violent foreign fighters; 2,000 posts $N_2 = 18$ non-violent supporters; 2,000 posts

Reference	Quality	Country	Central constructs	Study design	Participants demographic
Doosje et al, 2013	Fair	The Netherlands	Perceived procedural justice, emotional uncertainty, perceived group threat, ideology	QNT; cross-sectional online questionnaire	N = 131 Muslims (12–21 years)
Ebner et al, 2022	Good	International	Linguistic categories related to threat, in- versus out-group thinking, role models, hopelessness	QNT, QUL; correlational, ethnographic	N = 200,000 QAnon messages unspecified violent and non-violent control groups
Egan et al, 2016	Good	United Kingdom	Identifying Vulnerable People (IVP) guidance, religious/cultural/social isolation, risk taking behaviour, sudden changes in religious practice, violent rhetoric, deviant peers (view reference for all 16 items)	QNT; cross-sectional analysis of public available data	N = 157 convicted terrorists
Gill et al, 2017	Fair	United States	Sociodemographic details, development, antecedent attack, attack preparation, commission properties	QNT; cross-sectional comparison of case files with codebook	N_1 = 115 lone actors
Gill et al, 2021	Good	International	Demographic, psychologic, behavioural	QNT; bivariate and multivariate statistical analyses	N_1 = 71 lone-actor terrorists N_2 = 115 public mass murderers

Reference	Quality	Country	Central constructs	Study design	Participants demographic
González et al, 2014	Fair	United States	Gender	QNT; comparison of case files with control-group	N_1^A = 49 far-right female lone actors N_2^A = 36 eco female lone actors N_3^A = 244 far-right male lone actors N_4^A = 135 eco male lone actors
Groppi, 2017	Fair	Italy	Sociodemographic details, attitudes, grievance, ideology, identity crisis	QNT, QUL; survey, interviews, focus groups with cross-sectional comparison	N = 440 Muslims
Gruenewald et al, 2013	Fair	United States	Sociodemographic details, psychopathology, victim characteristics, relationship	QNT; cross-sectional analysis of case files	N^A = 96 far-right lone actors
Hirschberger et al, 2009	Good	Iran	Mortality salience, perceived adversary intent, personal vulnerability	QNT; randomised and comparison with control-group experiment	Study 1 N = 80 students Study 2 N = 308 students Study 3 N_1 = 114 students with exposure to war N_2 = 116 students without exposure to war

Reference	Quality	Country	Central constructs	Study design	Participants demographic
Hollewell and Longpré, 2022	Fair	International	Emotional regulation, self-esteem, impulsiveness, self-motivation, trait empathy, Facebook engagement, action and participation, uses and gratification, positive online experiences, social context, extremist attitudes	QNT; cross-sectional	N = 499 online users
Holt and Bolden, 2014	Poor	International	Technological skills	QUL; thematic analysis of written communication	N = 60 online threads of White supremacists (a total of 117 users)
Horgan et al, 2018	Good	United States	Behavioural mapping of recruiters, supporters, actors	QNT; cross-sectional comparison of case files and public information	N = 183 convicted terrorists
Jacques and Taylor, 2008	Good	International	Gender, motivation, recruitment, attack outcome	QNT; comparison of public information with control group	N_1 = 30 female suicide bombers N_2 = 30 male suicide bombers
Jasko et al, 2017	Good	United States	Economic and social loss of significance, presence of radicalised others	QNT; cross-sectional profile comparison	N = 1,496 terrorists (varying ideologies)
Jensen et al, 2020	Fair	United States	Protective factors	QNT, QUL; life-course narrative, group comparison	N = 50 far-right extremists

Reference	Quality	Country	Central constructs	Study design	Participants demographic
Joosse et al, 2015	Poor	Canada	Counter-narratives regarding recruitment	QUL; cross-sectional comparison with interviews	N = 118 individuals with Somalian background
Kamans et al, 2009	Good	The Netherlands	Negative meta-stereotypes	QNT, QUL; cross-sectional interviews and surveys	N = 88 teenagers with Moroccan background
Kemmelmeier, 2008	Fair	United States	Cognitive abilities, political attitudes	QNT; cross-sectional survey	N_1 = 7,279 students; N_2 = NR; participants from all states
Kerodal et al, 2016	Fair	United States	Offence types, commitment to ideology	QNT; comparison of case files with control groups	N_1^A = 142 far-right homicides; N_2^A = 103 far-right financial schemes; N_3 = 27 homicide; N_4 = 33 financial schemes
Khazaeli Jah and Khoshnood, 2019	Fair	International	Sociodemographic, criminogenic indicators, psychopathology, modus operandi	QNT; cross-sectional	N = 37 lone-actor terrorists
King et al, 2011	Fair	Indonesia	Attitudes, family support	QNT, QUL; cross-sectional interviews and surveys	N = 20 immediate relatives of 16 Jema'ah Islamiyah members
Klausen et al, 2016	Poor	United States	Age–crime curve	QNT; cross-sectional case file comparison	N = 600 Islamist terrorists
Klausen et al, 2020	Good	United States	Sociodemographic, New York Police Department four-phase model	QNT; behavioural sequencing	N = 130 case files of homegrown jihadists

Reference	Quality	Country	Central constructs	Study design	Participants demographic
Krout and Stagner, 1939	Fair	United States	Early childhood memories	QNT; survey comparison with control group	N_1 = 153 members of extremist movement (Young People's Socialist League and Young Communist League) N_2 = 97 individuals from the community
Kupper and Meloy, 2021	Good	International	TRAP-18	QNT; correlational comparison	N = 30 manifestos of committed or planned attacks
LaFree et al, 2020	Good	United States	Prison	QNT; matched comparison	N = 675 convicted terrorists
Laor et al, 2006	Good	Israel	Ideology, resilience, family, trauma responses	QNT; cross-sectional surveys	N = 1,105 adolescents exposed to terrorism
Liem et al, 2018	Good	Europe	Event characteristics, sociodemographic details, psychological background, violence	QNT; matched comparison of case files	N_1 = 98 lone actors N_2 = 300 homicides; 3 matched to each in N_1
Loza, 2010	Poor	Canada	Political views, attitudes towards women, attitudes towards Western culture, religiosity, condoning fighting	QNT; cross-sectional assessment	N = 89 incarcerated offenders
McCauley et al, 2013	Poor	United States	Grievance, unfreezing, status- and-risk-seeking, history of weapons use, violence	QNT; comparison of governmental reports with control group	N_1 = 83 lone actors N_2 = 41 school shooters

Reference	Quality	Country	Central constructs	Study design	Participants demographic
Meloy and Gill, 2016	Fair	International	TRAP-18	QNT; cross-sectional comparison of case files	N^B = 111 lone actors
Meloy et al, 2015	Good	Europe	TRAP-18	QNT; cross-sectional comparison of public information	N = 22 lone actors
Meloy et al, 2021	Good	International	TRAP-18	QNT; time sequence analysis	N = 125 lone-actor terrorists
Merari and Ganor, 2022	Fair	Palestine	Psychotic background, severe personality disorder, suicidality	QUL; interviews	N = 45 convicted terrorists
Merari et al, 2010	Fair	Palestine	Ego strength, psychopathic deviation, personality style	QNT; assessment comparison with control group	N_1 = 15 thwarted suicide bombers; N_2 = 12 prisoners due to political violence; N_3 = 14 prisoners due to ordering suicide bombings
Muluk et al, 2020	Good	Indonesia	Cognitive flexibility, emotional expression	QNT, QUL; ethnographic	N = 66 convicted terrorists
Nivette et al, 2017	Good	Switzerland	Collective strain, moral/legal constraints	QNT; cross-sectional and longitudinal comparison with interviews	N = 1,214 students aged 15–17

Reference	Quality	Country	Central constructs	Study design	Participants demographic
Obaidi et al, 2022	Good	United States	Extremist Archetypes Scale	QNT; factor analysis	N_1 = 307 White majority members N_2 = 308 White majority members N_3 = 317 Muslim minority members
Pauwels and De Waele, 2014	Good	Belgium	Social integration, discrimination, procedural justice, beliefs/attitudes, peer delinquency	QNT; cross-sectional comparison with surveys	N = 2,879 adolescents
Peddell et al, 2016	Poor	United Kingdom	Vulnerabilities, motivation, mechanisms	QUL; thematic analysis of focus group	N = 5 counter-terrorism practitioners
Pfundmair et al, 2022	Fair	International	Personality factors, individual processes, group processes	QNT; comparitve frequency	N = 81 case files of Islamist extremists
Pitcavage, 2015	Poor	International	Ideological composition, lethality	QNT; cross-sectional comparison with data bases	N = 35 lone actors
Powis et al, 2021	Good	United Kingdom	ERG22+	QNT; factor analysis	N = 171 Islamist extremists
Pretus et al, 2018	Good	Spain	Social exclusion	QNT; comparison with randomised experimental allocation to fMRTs	N = 38 Sunni Muslim Moroccan men vulnerable to radicalisation

Reference	Quality	Country	Central constructs	Study design	Participants demographic
Savage et al, 2014	Fair	Kenya	Integrative complexity of ideology	QNT; cross-sectional comparison of verbal data	$N = 24$ Kenyan and Somali men vulnerable to radicalisation
Schils and Pauwels, 2016	Good	Belgium	Extremist propensity, exposure to violent extremism, perceived injustice, social integration, perceived alienation, perceived procedural justice, religious authoritarianism	QNT; cross-sectional comparison with surveys	$N = 6,020$ adolescents
Schils and Verhage, 2017	Good	Belgium	Injustice, identity, ideology, social environment, active involvement, online versus offline	QUL; cross-sectional comparison with interviews	$N = 12$ adolescents
Schuurman et al, 2018	Fair	International	Personal background, social context, attack planning, attack preparation, operational security, leakage, postoperation activities, other activities	QNT; cross-sectional comparison of public information (supplemented with primary data where possible)	$N^B = 55$ lone actors
Shortland et al, 2022	Good	United States	Short-term psychological consequences of exposure to extremist material on extremist cognitions	QNT; between-group experimental design	$N = 1,112$ participants

Reference	Quality	Country	Central constructs	Study design	Participants demographic
Speckhard and Ahkmedova, 2006	Fair	Russia	Organisational motivation, community support for suicide attacks, individual motivation, political aspects, religious aspects, foreign influences, ideology, martyrdom, seeking answers, fraternity	QNT, QUL; cross-sectional comparison with interviews	$N = 32$ relatives of 51 suicide terrorists
Stankov et al, 2010a	Fair	International	Justification of violence, religious reasoning, blaming Western legislations	QNT, QUL; cross-sectional comparison with linguistic analyses and thematic analyses	Study 1 $N = 132$ extremists' statements Study 2 $N = 452$ students
Stankov et al, 2010b	Fair	International	Pro-violence, Vile World, Divine Power	QNT; cross-sectional comparison with survey	$N = 2,424$
Taubman-Ben-Ari and Noy, 2010	Good	Israel	Death-related thoughts, rumination about self-consciousness, cultural worldviews	QNT; cross-sectional comparison with survey	Study 1 $N = 56$ students Study 2 $N = 212$ students
Thijssen et al, 2023	Fair	The Netherlands	Sociodemographic, criminogenic indicators, psychopathology	QNT; correlational	$N = 82$ convicted terrorists
Trujillo et al, 2009	Good	Spain	Group hierarchy, group identity, legitimisation of violence, religion	QNT; cross-sectional comparison with survey	$N = 192$ prison officials

Reference	Quality	Country	Central constructs	Study design	Participants demographic
Tschantret, 2021	Good	International	Personality factors	QNT; between-group	N_1 = 12 right-wing terrorists N_2 = 12 Islamist terrorists N_3 = 9,660 controls
Victoroff et al, 2012	Fair	International	Justification of suicide bombings, discrimination, difficulties being Muslim, group identity	QNT; cross-sectional comparison with survey	N_1 = 1,627 European Muslims N_2 = 1,050 US Muslims
Webber et al, 2017	Good	International	Loss of significance, threat of significance, opportunity for significance gain, ideology, group processes, sociodemographic details	QNT; cross-sectional comparison of public information	N = 219 suicide bombers
Webber et al, 2018	Good	International	Loss of significance, cognitive closure	QNT; cross-sectional comparison with survey	Study 1 N = 74 incarcerated members of a Philippine terrorist organisation Study 2 N = 237 incarcerated members of Sri Lankan terrorist organisation Study 3 N = 196 US participants from general public

Reference	Quality	Country	Central constructs	Study design	Participants demographic
					Study 4 $N = 344$ US participants from general public
Weinberg and Eubank, 1987	Fair	Italy	Role in organisation, gender, family relationships, relationships with other terrorists	QNT; comparison of case files with control group	$N_1 = 451$ incarcerated female terrorists $N_2 = 2{,}512$ incarcerated male terrorists
Yustisia et al, 2020	Good	Indonesia	Perception of threat, quantity of social contact	QNT; cross-sectional	$N = 66$ convicted terrorists

Note: QNT = quantitative methodology; QUL = qualitative methodology; NR = not reported.

Appendix 5A.2: References of studies included in the systematic review of research

Adamczyk, A. and LaFree, G. (2019) 'Religion and support for political violence among Christians and Muslims in Africa', *Sociological Perspectives*, 62(6): 948–79.

Altier, M.B., Leonard Boyle, E. and Horgan, J.G. (2021) 'Returning to the fight: An empirical analysis of terrorist reengagement and recidivism', *Terrorism and Political Violence*, 33(4): 836–60.

Arndt, J., Schimel, J., Greenberg, J., Pyszczynski, T. and Solomon, S. (2002) 'To belong or not to belong. that is the question: Terror management and identification with gender and ethnicity', *Journal of Personality & Social Psychology*, 83(1): 26–43.

Askew, M. and Helbardt, S. (2012) 'Becoming Patani warriors: Individuals and the insurgent collective in southern Thailand', *Studies in Conflict & Terrorism*, 35(11): 779–809.

Baele, S.J. (2017) 'Lone-actor terrorists' emotions and cognition: An evaluation beyond stereotypes', *Political Psychology*, 38(3): 449–68.

Baez, S., Herrera, E., García, A.M., Manes, F., Young, L. and Ibáñez, A. (2017) 'Outcome-oriented moral evaluation in terrorists', *Nature Human Behaviour*, 1(6): 1–9.

Bartlett, J., Birdwell, J. and King, M. (2010) 'The edge of violence: A radical approach to extremism', *Demos*: 5–75.

Becker, M.H. (2021) 'When extremists become violent: Examining the association between social control, social learning, and engagement in violent extremism', *Studies in Conflict & Terrorism*, 44(12): 1104–24.

Berko, A. and Erez, E. (2007) 'Women in terrorism: A Palestinian feminist revolution or gender oppression?', *Intelligence*, 30(6): 1–14.

Bérubé, M., Scrivens, R., Venkatesh, V. and Gaudette, T. (2019) 'Converging patterns in pathways in and out of violent extremism', *Perspectives on Terrorism*, 13(6): 73–89.

Bhui, K., Everitt, B. and Jones, E. (2014) 'Might depression, psychosocial adversity, and limited social assets explain vulnerability to and resistance against violent radicalisation?', *Plos One*, 9(9): e105918.

Bhui, K., Warfa, N. and Jones, E. (2014) 'Is violent radicalisation associated with poverty, migration, poor self-reported health and common mental disorders?', *PloS One*, 9(3): e105918.

Bhui, K., Silva, M.J., Topciu, R.A. and Jones, E. (2016) 'Pathways to sympathies for violent protest and terrorism', *The British Journal of Psychiatry*, 209(6): 483–90.

Bhui, K., Otis, M., Silva, M.J., Halvorsrud, K., Freestone, M. and Jones, E. (2020) 'Extremism and common mental illness: Cross-sectional community survey of White British and Pakistani men and women living in England', *The British Journal of Psychiatry*, 217(4): 547–54.

Blazak, R. (2001) 'White boys to terrorist men: Target recruitment of Nazi skinheads', *American Behavioral Scientist*, 44(6): 982–1000.

Boehme, H.M. and Isom Scott, D.A. (2020) 'Alt-white? A gendered look at "victim" ideology and the alt-right', *Victims & Offenders*, 15(2): 174–96.

Bronsard, G., Cohen, D., Diallo, I., Pellerin, H., Varnoux, A., Podlipski, M.A., et al (2022) 'Adolescents engaged in radicalisation and terrorism: A dimensional and categorical assessment', *Frontiers in Psychiatry*, 12: 2585.

Brookes, G. and McEnery, T. (2020) 'Correlation, collocation and cohesion: A corpus-based critical analysis of violent jihadist discourse', *Discourse & Society*, 31(4): 351–73.

Brym, R.J. and Araj, B. (2012) 'Are suicide bombers suicidal?', *Studies in Conflict & Terrorism*, 35(6): 432–43.

Candilis, P.J., Cleary, S.D., Dhumad, S., Dyer, A.R. and Khalifa, N. (2021) 'Classifying terrorism: A latent class analysis of primary source socio-political and psychological data', *Behavioral Sciences of Terrorism and Political Aggression*, 15(1): 1–18.

Capellan, J.A. (2015) 'Lone wolf terrorist or deranged shooter? A study of ideological active shooter events in the United States, 1970–2014', *Studies in Conflict & Terrorism*, 38(6): 395–413.

Challacombe, D.J. and Lucas, P.A. (2019) 'Postdicting violence with sovereign citizen actors: An exploratory test of the TRAP-18', *Journal of Threat Assessment and Management*, 6(1): 51–9.

Chermak, S. and Gruenewald, J.A. (2015) 'Laying a foundation for the criminological examination of right-wing, left-wing, and Al Qaeda-inspired extremism in the United States', *Terrorism and Political Violence*, 27(1): 133–59.

Cherney, A. and Belton, E. (2021) 'Evaluating case-managed approaches to counter radicalization and violent extremism: An example of the Proactive Integrated Support Model (PRISM) intervention', *Studies in Conflict & Terrorism*, 44(8): 625–45.

Clemmow, C., Bouhana, N., Marchment, Z. and Gill, P. (2022) 'Vulnerability to radicalisation in a general population: A psychometric network approach', *Psychology, Crime & Law*, 29(4): 1–29.

Clemmow, C., Gill, P., Bouhana, N., Silver, J. and Horgan, J. (2022) 'Disaggregating lone-actor grievance-fuelled violence: Comparing lone-actor terrorists and mass murderers', *Terrorism and Political Violence*, 34(3): 558–84.

Cohen, S.J. (2012) 'Construction and preliminary validation of a dictionary for cognitive rigidity: Linguistic markers of overconfidence and overgeneralization and their concomitant psychological distress', *Journal of Psycholinguistic Research*, 41(5): 347–70.

Cohen, S.J. (2016) 'Mapping the minds of suicide bombers using linguistic methods: The corpus of palestinian suicide bombers' farewell letters (CoPSBFL)', *Studies in Conflict & Terrorism*, 39(7–8): 749–80.

Coid, J.W., Bhui, K., MacManus, D., Kallis, C., Bebbington, P. and Ullrich, S. (2016) 'Extremism, religion and psychiatric morbidity in a population-based sample of young men', *The British Journal of Psychiatry*, 209(6): 491–7.

Corner, E., Bouhana, N. and Gill, P. (2019) 'The multifinality of vulnerability indicators in lone-actor terrorism', *Psychology, Crime & Law*, 25(2): 111–32.

Cramer, R.J., Cacace, S.C., Sorby, M., Adrian, M.E., Kehn, A. and Wilsey, C.N. (2023) 'A psychometric investigation of the hate-motivated behavior checklist', *Journal of Interpersonal Violence*, 38(7–8): 5638–60.

Dechesne, M. (2009) 'Explorations in the experimental social psychology of terrorism: The struggle-violence link and its predictors', *Revue Internationale De Psychologie Sociale*, 22(3–4): 87–102.

Decker, S.H. and Pyrooz, D.C. (2020) 'The imprisonment-extremism nexus: Continuity and change in activism and radicalism intentions in a longitudinal study of prisoner reentry', *PLoS One*, 15(11): e0242910.

Dhumad, S., Candilis, P.J., Cleary, S.D., Dyer, A.R. and Khalifa, N. (2020) 'Risk factors for terrorism: A comparison of family, childhood, and personality risk factors among Iraqi terrorists, murderers, and controls', *Behavioral Sciences of Terrorism and Political Aggression*, 12(1): 1–17.

Dillon, L., Neo, L.S. and Freilich, J.D. (2020) 'A comparison of ISIS foreign fighters and supporters social media posts: An exploratory mixed-method content analysis', *Behavioral Sciences of Terrorism and Political Aggression*, 12(4): 268–91.

Doosje, B., Loseman, A. and Van Den Bos, K. (2013) 'Determinants of radicalization of Islamic youth in the Netherlands: Personal uncertainty, perceived injustice, and perceived group threat', *Journal of Social Issues*, 69(3): 586–604.

Ebner, J., Kavanagh, C. and Whitehouse, H. (2022) 'The QAnon security threat: A linguistic fusion-based violence risk assessment', *Perspectives on Terrorism*, 16(6): 62–86.

Egan, V., Cole, J., Cole, B., Alison, L., Alison, E., Waring, S., et al (2016) 'Can you identify violent extremists using a screening checklist and open-source intelligence alone?', *Journal of Threat Assessment and Management*, 3(1): 21–36.

Gill, P., Silver, J., Horgan, J. and Corner, E. (2017) 'Shooting alone: The pre-attack experiences and behaviors of US solo mass murderers', *Journal of Forensic Sciences*, 62(3): 710–14.

Gill, P., Silver, J., Horgan, J., Corner, E. and Bouhana, N. (2021) 'Similar crimes, similar behaviors? Comparing lone-actor terrorists and public mass murderers', *Journal of Forensic Sciences*, 66(5): 1797–804.

González, A.L., Freilich, J.D. and Chermak, S.M. (2014) 'How women engage homegrown terrorism', *Feminist Criminology*, 9(4): 344–66.

Groppi, M. (2017) 'An empirical analysis of causes of Islamist radicalisation: Italian case study', *Perspectives on Terrorism*, 11(1): 68–76.

Gruenewald, J., Chermak, S. and Freilich, J.D. (2013) 'Distinguishing "loner" attacks from other domestic extremist violence: A comparison of far-right homicide incident and offender characteristics', *Criminology & Public Policy*, 12(1): 65–91.

Hirschberger, G., Pyszczynski, T. and Ein-Dor, T. (2009) 'Vulnerability and vigilance: Threat awareness and perceived adversary intent moderate the impact of mortality salience on intergroup violence', *Personality and Social Psychology Bulletin*, 35(5): 597–607.

Hollewell, G.F. and Longpré, N. (2022) 'Radicalization in the social media era: Understanding the relationship between self-radicalization and the Internet', *International Journal of Offender Therapy and Comparative Criminology*, 66(8): 896–913.

Holt, T.J. and Bolden, M. (2014) 'Technological skills of white supremacists in an online forum: A qualitative examination', *International Journal of Cyber Criminology*, 8(2): 79–93.

Horgan, J., Shortland, N. and Abbasciano, S. (2018) 'Towards a typology of terrorism involvement: A behavioral differentiation of violent extremist offenders', *Journal of Threat Assessment and Management*, 5(2): 84–102.

Jacques, K. and Taylor, P.J. (2008) 'Male and female suicide bombers: Different sexes, different reasons?', *Studies in Conflict & Terrorism*, 31(4): 304–26.

Jasko, K., LaFree, G. and Kruglanski, A. (2017) 'Quest for significance and violent extremism: The case of domestic radicalization', *Political Psychology*, 38(5): 815–31.

Jensen, M., James, P. and Yates, E. (2020) 'Contextualizing disengagement: How exit barriers shape the pathways out of far-right extremism in the United States', *Studies in Conflict & Terrorism*, 46(3): 1–29.

Joosse, P., Bucerius, S.M. and Thompson, S.K. (2015) 'Narratives and counternarratives: Somali-Canadians on recruitment as foreign fighters to Al-Shabaab', *British Journal of Criminology*, 55(4): 811–32.

Kamans, E., Gordijn, E.H., Oldenhuis, H. and Otten, S. (2009) 'What I think you see is what you get: Influence of prejudice on assimilation to negative meta-stereotypes among Dutch Moroccan teenagers', *European Journal of Social Psychology*, 39(5): 842–51.

Kemmelmeier, M. (2008) 'Is there a relationship between political orientation and cognitive ability? A test of three hypotheses in two studies', *Personality and Individual Differences*, 45(8): 767–72.

Kerodal, A.G., Freilich, J.D. and Chermak, S.M. (2016) 'Commitment to extremist ideology: Using factor analysis to move beyond binary measures of extremism', *Studies in Conflict & Terrorism*, 39(7–8): 687–711.

Khazaeli Jah, M. and Khoshnood, A. (2019) 'Profiling lone-actor terrorists: a cross-sectional study of lone-actor terrorists in Western Europe (2015–2016)', *Journal of Strategic Security*, 12(4): 25–49.

King, M., Noor, H. and Taylor, D.M. (2011) 'Normative support for terrorism: The attitudes and beliefs of immediate relatives of Jema'ah Islamiyah members', *Studies in Conflict & Terrorism*, 34(5): 402–17.

Klausen, J., Morrill, T. and Libretti, R. (2016) 'The terrorist age-crime curve: An analysis of american islamist terrorist offenders and age-specific propensity for participation in violent and nonviolent incidents', *Social Science Quarterly*, 97(1): 19–32.

Klausen, J., Libretti, R., Hung, B.W. and Jayasumana, A.P. (2020) 'Radicalization trajectories: An evidence-based computational approach to dynamic risk assessment of "homegrown" jihadists', *Studies in Conflict & Terrorism*, 43(7): 588–615.

Krout, M.H. and Stagner, R. (1939) 'Personality development in radicals', *Sociometry*, 2(1): 31–46.

Kupper, J. and Meloy, J.R. (2021) 'TRAP-18 indicators validated through the forensic linguistic analysis of targeted violence manifestos', *Journal of Threat Assessment and Management*, 8(4): 174–99.

LaFree, G., Jiang, B. and Porter, L.C. (2020) 'Prison and violent political extremism in the United States', *Journal of Quantitative Criminology*, 36: 473–98.

Laor, N., Wolmer, L., Alon, M., Siev, J., Samuel, E. and Toren, P. (2006) 'Risk and protective factors mediating psychological symptoms and ideological commitment of adolescents facing continuous terrorism', *Journal of Nervous and Mental Disease*, 194(4): 275–8.

Liem, M., van Buuren, J., van Zuijdewijn, J.R., Schönberger, H. and Bakker, E. (2018) 'European lone actor terrorists versus "common" homicide offenders: An empirical analysis', *Homicide Studies: An Interdisciplinary & International Journal*, 22(1): 45–69.

Loza, W. (2010) 'The prevalence of Middle Eastern extremist ideologies among some Canadian offenders', *Journal of Interpersonal Violence*, 25(5): 919–28.

McCauley, C., Moskalenko, S. and Van Son, B. (2013) 'Characteristics of lone-wolf violent offenders: A comparison of assassins and school attackers', *Perspectives on Terrorism*, 7(1): 4–24.

Meloy, J.R. and Gill, P. (2016) 'The lone-actor terrorist and the TRAP-18', *Journal of Threat Assessment and Management*, 3: 37–52.

Meloy, J.R., Roshdi, K., Glaz-Ocik, J. and Hoffmann, J. (2015). 'Investigating the individual terrorist in Europe', *Journal of Threat Assessment and Management*, 2(3–4): 140–52.

Meloy, J.R., Goodwill, A., Clemmow, C. and Gill, P. (2021) 'Time sequencing the TRAP-18 indicators', *Journal of Threat Assessment and Management*, 8(1–2): 1–19.

Merari, A. and Ganor, B. (2022) 'Interviews with, and tests of, Palestinian independent assailants', *Terrorism and Political Violence*, 34(8): 1595–616.

Merari, A., Diamant, I., Bibi, A., Broshi, Y. and Zakin, G. (2010) 'Personality characteristics of "self martyrs"/"suicide bombers" and organizers of suicide attacks', *Terrorism and Political Violence*, 22(1): 87–101.

Muluk, H., Umam, A.N. and Milla, M.N. (2020) 'Insights from a deradicalization program in Indonesian prisons: The potential benefits of psychological intervention prior to ideological discussion', *Asian Journal of Social Psychology*, 23(1): 42–53.

Nivette, A., Eisner, M. and Ribeaud, D. (2017) 'Developmental predictors of violent extremist attitudes: A test of general strain theory', *Journal of Research in Crime and Delinquency*, 54(6): 755–90.

Obaidi, M., Skaar, S.W., Ozer, S. and Kunst, J.R. (2022) 'Measuring extremist archetypes: Scale development and validation', *Plos One*, 17(7): e0270225.

Pauwels, L. and De Waele, M. (2014) 'Youth involvement in politically motivated violence: Why do social integration, perceived legitimacy, and perceived discrimination matter?', *International Journal of Conflict & Violence*, 8(1): 135–53.

Peddell, D., Eyre, M., McManus, M. and Bonworth, J. (2016) 'Influences and vulnerabilities in radicalised lone-actor terrorists: UK practitioner perspectives', *International Journal of Police Science & Management*, 18(2): 63–76.

Pfundmair, M., Aßmann, E., Kiver, B., Penzkofer, M., Scheuermeyer, A., Sust, L. and Schmidt, H. (2022) 'Pathways toward jihadism in western Europe: An empirical exploration of a comprehensive model of terrorist radicalization', *Terrorism and Political Violence*, 34(1): 48–70.

Pitcavage, M. (2015) 'Cerberus unleashed: The three faces of the lone wolf terrorist', *American Behavioral Scientist*, 59(13): 1655–80.

Powis, B., Randhawa, K. and Bishopp, D. (2021) 'An examination of the structural properties of the Extremism Risk Guidelines (ERG22+): A structured formulation tool for extremist offenders', *Terrorism and Political Violence*, 33(6): 1141–59.

Pretus, C., Hamid, N., Sheikh, H., Ginges, J., Tobeña, A., Davis, R., Vilarroya, O. and Atran, S. (2018) 'Neural and behavioral correlates of sacred values and vulnerability to violent extremism', *Frontiers in Psychology*, 9: 2462.

Savage, S., Khan, A. and Liht, J. (2014) 'Preventing violent extremism in Kenya through value complexity: Assessment of being Kenyan being Muslim', *Journal of Strategic Security*, 7(3): 1–26.

Schils, N. and Pauwels, L.J.R. (2016) 'Political violence and the mediating role of violent extremist propensities', *Journal of Strategic Security*, 9(2): 72–93.

Schils, N. and Verhage, A. (2017) 'Understanding how and why young people enter radical or violent extremist groups', *International Journal of Conflict & Violence*, 11(1): 1–17.

Schuurman, B., Bakker, E., Gill, P. and Bouhana, N. (2018) 'Lone actor terrorist attack planning and preparation: A data-driven analysis', *Journal of Forensic Sciences*, 63(4): 1191–200.

Shortland, N., Nader, E., Thompson, L. and Palasinski, M. (2022) 'Is extreme in the eye of the beholder? An experimental assessment of extremist cognitions', *Journal of Interpersonal Violence*, 37(7–8): NP4865–NP4888.

Speckhard, A. and Ahkmedova, K. (2006) 'The making of a martyr: Chechen suicide terrorism', *Studies in Conflict & Terrorism*, 29(5): 429–92.

Stankov, L., Higgins, D., Saucier, G. and Knežević, G. (2010) 'Contemporary militant extremism: A linguistic approach to scale development', *Psychological Assessment*, 22(2): 246–58.

Stankov, L., Saucier, G. and Knežević, G. (2010) 'Militant extremist mind-set: Proviolence, vile world, and divine power', *Psychological Assessment*, 22(1): 70–86.

Taubman-Ben-Ari, O. and Noy, A. (2010) 'Self-consciousness and death cognitions from a terror management perspective', *Death Studies*, 34(10): 871–92.

Thijssen, G., Masthoff, E., Sijtsema, J. and Bogaerts, S. (2023) 'Understanding violent extremism: Socio-demographic, criminal and psychopathological background characteristics of detainees residing in Dutch terrorism wings', *Criminology & Criminal Justice*, 23(2): 290–308.

Trujillo, H.M., Jordán, J., Gutiérrez, J.A. and González-Cabrera, J. (2009) 'Radicalization in prisons? Field research in 25 Spanish prisons', *Terrorism and Political Violence*, 21(4): 558–79.

Tschantret, J. (2021) 'The psychology of right-wing terrorism: A text-based personality analysis', *Psychology of Violence*, 11(2): 113–22.

Victoroff, J., Adelman, J.R. and Matthews, M. (2012) 'Psychological factors associated with support for suicide bombing in the Muslim diaspora', *Political Psychology*, 33(6): 791–809.

Webber, D., Klein, K., Kruglanski, A., Brizi, A. and Merari, A. (2017) 'Divergent paths to martyrdom and significance among suicide attackers', *Terrorism and Political Violence*, 29(5): 852–74.

Webber, D., Babush, M., Schori-Eyal, N., Vazeou-Nieuwenhuis, A., Hettiarachchi, M., Bélanger, J.J., et al (2018) 'The road to extremism: Field and experimental evidence that significance loss-induced need for closure fosters radicalization', *Journal of Personality and Social Psychology*, 114(2): 270–85.

Weinberg, L. and Eubank, W.L. (1987) 'Italian women terrorists', *Terrorism*, 9(3): 241–62.

Yustisia, W., Shadiqi, M.A., Milla, M.N. and Muluk, H. (2020) 'An investigation of an Expanded Encapsulate Model of Social Identity in Collective Action (EMSICA) including perception of threat and intergroup contact to understand support for Islamist terrorism in Indonesia', *Asian Journal of Social Psychology*, 23(1): 29–41.

Notes

[1] As only factors relating directly to the individual's decision-making process are deemed beneficial for formulation efforts (for example, Taylor and Horgan, 2006).
[2] In the literature, it is often discussed that research increased after 9/11 (for example, Schmid, 2013). However, publications presenting empirical data, which is the focus of this systematic literature review, only notably increased from 2009 onwards, with 83 of 96 articles published since then; only two articles published before the 2000s met the inclusion criteria.
[3] The individual's perception of the level of deprivation their group faces compared to other groups in a given society (Peddell et al, 2016).

References

Al-Attar, Z. (2020) 'Severe mental disorder and terrorism: When psychosis, PTSD and addictions become a vulnerability', *The Journal of Forensic Psychiatry & Psychology*, 31(6): 950–70.

Borum, R. (2012a) 'Radicalization into violent extremism I: A review of social science theories', *Journal of Strategic Security*, 4(4): 7–36.

Borum, R. (2012b) 'Radicalization into violent extremism II: A review of conceptual models and empirical research', *Journal of Strategic Security*, 4(4): 37–62.

Borum, R. (2015) 'Assessing risk for terrorism involvement', *Journal of Threat Assessment and Management*, 2(2): 63–87.

Christmann, K. (2012) 'Preventing religious radicalisation and violent extremism: A systematic review of the research evidence', *Youth Justice Board for England and Wales*. Available from https://assets.publishing.service.gov.uk/government/uploads/system/uploads/attachment_data/file/396030/preventing-violent-extremism-systematic-review.pdf [Accessed 12 September 2023].

De Ruiter, C., and Nicholls, T.L. (2011) 'Protective factors in forensic mental health: A new frontier', *International Journal of Forensic Mental Health*, 10(3): 160–70.

Dhumad, S., Candilis, P.J., Cleary, S.D., Dyer, A.R. and Khalifa, N. (2020) 'Risk factors for terrorism: A comparison of family, childhood, and personality risk factors among Iraqi terrorists, murderers, and controls', *Behavioral Sciences of Terrorism and Political Aggression*, 12(1): 1–17.

Douglas, K.S., Hart, S.D., Webster, C.D. and Belfrage, H. (2013) *HCR-20V3: Assessing Risk for Violence: User Guide* [measurement instrument], Burnaby: Mental Health, Law, and Policy Institute, Simon Fraser University.

Feddes, A.R. and Gallucci, M. (2015) 'A literature review on methodology used in evaluating effects of preventive and de-radicalisation interventions', *Journal for Deradicalization*, 5: 1–27.

Gill, P. and Corner, E. (2017) 'There and back again: The study of mental disorder and terrorist involvement', *American Psychologist*, 72(3): 231–41.

Gøtzsche-Astrup, O. and Lindekilde, L. (2019) 'Either or? Reconciling findings on mental health and extremism using a dimensional rather than categorical paradigm', *Journal of Forensic Sciences*, 64(4): 982–8.

Jacques, K. and Taylor, P.J. (2008) 'Male and female suicide bombers: Different sexes, different reasons?', *Studies in Conflict & Terrorism*, 31(4): 304–26.

King, M. and Taylor, D.M. (2011) 'The radicalization of homegrown jihadists: A review of theoretical models and social psychological evidence', *Terrorism and Political Violence*, 23(4): 602–22.

Kruglanski, A.W. and Fishman, S. (2006) 'The psychology of terrorism: "Syndrome" versus "tool" perspectives', *Terrorism and Political Violence*, 18(2): 193–215.

Lösel, F., King, S., Bender, D. and Jugl, I. (2018) 'Protective factors against extremism and violent radicalization: A systematic review of research', *International Journal of Developmental Science*, 12(1–2): 89–102.

Martin, P.Y. and Turner, B.A. (1986) 'Grounded theory and organizational research', *The Journal of Applied Behavioral Science*, 22(2): 141–57.

Moher, D., Liberati, A. and Tetzlaff, J. (2009) 'Preferred reporting items for systematic reviews and meta-analysis: The PRISMA statement', *PLoS Medicine*, 6(7): e1000097.

Mulcahy, E., Merrington, S. and Bell, P.J. (2013) 'The radicalisation of prison inmates: A review of the literature on recruitment, religion and prisoner vulnerability', *Journal of Human Security*, 9(1): 4–14.

National Heart, Lung, and Blood Institute (nd) 'Study quality assessment tools', *National Heart, Lung, and Blood Institute*. Available from https://www.nhlbi.nih.gov/health-topics/study-quality-assessment-tools [Accessed 8 July 2019].

Neumann, P.R. (2013) 'The trouble with radicalization', *International Affairs*, 89(4): 873–93.

Patel, M. and Hussain, M. (2019) 'Channel in practice' [presentation], Faculty of Forensic Clinical Psychology Autumn Meeting 2019, 'Extremism: The Role of Applied Psychology with Individuals, Services and Systems', Liverpool, UK, October.

Sageman, M. (2008) 'A strategy for fighting international Islamist terrorists', *The Annals of the American Academy of Political and Social Science*, 618(1): 223–31.

Scarcella, A., Page, R. and Furtado, V. (2016) 'Terrorism, radicalisation, extremism, authoritarianism and fundamentalism: A systematic review of the quality and psychometric properties of assessments', *PloS One*, 11(12): e0166947.

Schmid, A.P. (2013) 'Radicalisation, de-radicalisation, counter-radicalisation: A conceptual discussion and literature review', *The International Center for Counter-Terrorism*, 4(2) .

Silke, A., Morrison, J., Maiberg, H., Slay, C. and Stewart, R. (2021) 'The Phoenix Model of Disengagement and Deradicalisation from Terrorism and Violent Extremism', *Monatsschrift für Kriminologie und Strafrechtsreform*, 104(3): 310–20.

Talyor, M. and Horgan, J.G. (2006) 'A conceptual framework for addressing psychological process in the development of the terrorist', *Terrorism and Political Violence*, 18: 585–601.

Trimbur, M., Amad, A., Horn, M., Thomas, P. and Fovet, T. (2021) 'Are radicalization and terrorism associated with psychiatric disorders? A systematic review', *Journal of Psychiatric Research*, 141: 214–22.

Vergani, M., Iqbal, M., Ilbahar, E. and Barton, G. (2020) 'The three Ps of radicalization: Push, pull and personal. A systematic scoping review of the scientific evidence about radicalization into violent extremism', *Studies in Conflict & Terrorism*, 43(10): 854–85.

Vidino, L. (2010) 'Countering radicalization in America', *United States Institute of Peace*. Available from https://www.usip.org/sites/default/files/resources/SR262%20-%20Countering_Radicalization_in_America.pdf [Accessed 12 September 2023].

6

"But what if I get it wrong?" Exploring practitioners' understanding of preventing and countering violent extremism and radicalisation duty guidance

Erin Lawlor

Introduction

In 2017, the United Kingdom Department of Education published a report named 'Safeguarding and radicalisation' (Chisholm et al, 2017, p 30), which documented the stress, worries and misgivings felt by Local Authority Children's Social Care staff when approaching preventing and countering violent extremism (P/CVE) and radicalisation work. The UK's approach to dealing with radicalisation/people that have been radicalised is laid out in the national counter-terrorism strategy, titled CONTEST. Nowhere in CONTEST does it say that every frontline practitioner needs to be an expert on P/CVE and radicalisation, but, enshrined in the preventative thread of CONTEST (also known as PREVENT) is an expectation that specified practitioners will have a basic knowledge of radicalisation. CONTEST states that '[w]here there are signs that someone has been or is being drawn into terrorism, the healthcare worker can interpret those signs correctly, is aware of the support which is available and is confident in referring the person for further support' (Home Office, 2018, p 83).

This directive lays out the three areas that the UK Home Office expects practitioners to be able to act upon: first, being able to interpret the signs of a person being drawn into terrorism; second, awareness of the different support offerings available to said person and, finally, the most contentious part of this directive, is that they must feel confident in reporting these signs to the correct authority. The 2017 report puts forward that practitioners are unsure, unhappy and lack confidence in this area. One social worker told researchers:

> The child protection structure is not built [to deal with the risk of radicalisation], it's absolutely not built for that, and we need to be really clear. ... Social Workers aren't trained for that. So, it's very easy for the Government to think you can shove it all in [to your workload], but you can't, you absolutely can't, and it will become more of a mess. [Social Worker, Non-priority Area]. (Chisholm et al, 2017, p 30)

In 2021 the Department of Education updated their report, however, it does nothing to assuage these worries, or provide evidence that much has changed in the interim years. It confirms that rather than providing opportunities for Social Care staff to learn about radicalisation, practitioners' confidence is mainly based upon previous experience dealing with such cases (Langdon-Sheeve et al, 2021). This research only brings in opinions and data from Social Care services and does not involve any of the other organisations that also have responsibility to uphold the directives laid out in the PREVENT strategy. Namely, teachers, medical professionals, third sector organisations, charities (or not-for-profits) and policing and probation staff (His Majesty's Government, 2015).

To create a sound evidence base for the current confidence levels/efficacy of P/CVE and radicalisation work, a cross-section of professionals from all industries who are listed within the PREVENT guidance has been surveyed. Those interviewed for this chapter are from organisations such as the police, charities, healthcare staff and teachers. The data was collected via semi-structured interviews. Common themes have then been extracted and discussed, with a particular focus on the narratives that practitioners have created around radicalisation. Either through experience of working with those that have been radicalised or the training they have received, while acknowledging the outside stimulus they encounter daily, such as media reporting, social media and other colleagues' experiences. It is important to note that this chapter is only comprised of data taken from practitioners based within the UK, and so are most of the structures, frameworks and organisations discussed within it. The general findings and learnings will apply, however, across a global context.

Within this volume, there have been explorations of evidence-based practice (EBP) and its theoretical groundings alongside EBP's utilisation within P/CVE work. It is important to explore and gauge the theoretical background to radicalisation, and it is also vital to understand the reality of what is happening in practice. If we are to invoke change, we must survey and detail the landscape we are attempting to influence, and so, this chapter focuses on giving voice to those who have incidentally ended up as agents in this field. The teachers that could have students in their class engaging with extremist content, the doctors who might be treating the mental health of a person who is saying that they are worried about their own actions, or the police officers who are currently attempting to reintegrate those that have committed acts of violence back into the community.

The language of radicalisation

There are lexicons dedicated to how words come into being and how definition is then ascribed to them. According to Sartori (1984), 'denotative definitions' (p 30) perform three functions. First, they establish boundaries of the object being defined. Second, they manage group membership by deciding which object or objects are referred to by a term. Finally, they manage 'marginal entities' by identifying which objects are to be referred to by the term and which are not (Sartori, 1984).

It has been suggested that before we can comment on the effects of language, we must first know that language (Shepherd,

2010). The term 'extremism' entered UK policy discourse in 2005 as a direct result of the July bombing attacks in London. Its first iteration was utilised within the UK government's counter-terrorism strategy, CONTEST. No explanation was offered as to what extremism meant, or in fact the defining characteristics of an extremist. Since then, extremism and terrorism have become even more inextricably linked and interwoven, therefore, being deemed as an extremist, and holding extremist views, will lead to acts of terrorism (Elahi and Hargreaves, 2022). There have been attempts to offer clarity on the definitions of extremism, such as J.M. Berger's work *Extremism* (2018), in which extremism is denoted as '[t]he belief that an in-group's success can never be separated from the need for hostile action against an out-group' (Berger, 2018, p 33).

This working definition was then used by the Commission for Countering Extremism (Cabinet Office and Her Majesty the Queen, 2017), along with the 'A shared future' report which was published in the wake of the 2018 Manchester Arena bombing (Greater Manchester Combined Authority, 2018).

Once the link between extremism and terrorism had been developed, it then became the responsibility of governments and security services to establish policies, interventions and strategies to protect the nation from said risk (Heath-Kelly et al, 2015). The concept of radicalisation became the lens through which the journey of a 'normal' person was viewed as changing into a person who ascribes to an extremist belief system, and finally would then go on to commit 'abnormal' terrorist acts. The UK government in its online training for professionals goes so far as to say that '[t]errorism begins with radicalisation. It's the name given to the process that moves a person to legitimise their support of violence' (GOV.UK, nd).

There are innate issues with attempting to understand, retrospectively, the actions of those that commit actors of terror. Horgan discusses in his 2014 work that once a dramatic event has happened, we approach the understanding of the perpetrator from an already biased viewpoint of that person. Given that, normally, those that write media and scholarly accounts of such events were not present, there is a level of interpretation and often drama added to the proceedings to gain readership. These narratives focus on the 'abnormal' nature of those that would commit heinous acts of violence, incidentally (for the most part) medicalising and pathologising said perpetrators (Horgan, 2014).

It is hard to pitch research and coverage of terrorists without this vilifying narrative, due to the worries of being seen as a terrorist sympathiser (Heath-Kelly et al, 2015). In the wake of the events of 9/11 governments worldwide were left to develop strategy out of a space of fear due to the ongoing unrest and the threat from Al-Qaeda. The concept of radicalisation offers an opportunity to create a trackable, interruptible and correctable journey allowing security services to surveil and prevent transitions to violence. Radicalisation has allowed politicians to externalise and personify the causes of extremist ideologies, by ascribing blame to a person a villain is then created, directing focus to a tangible character, as opposed to looking at the internal factors that may have attributed to their story. Instead of the act of terror being a statement against the political power in charge due to a multitude of socioeconomic inequalities, systemic racism or oppression, it becomes a religious and ideological 'other' who can be pursued, 'cured', surveilled and, in some cases, punished (Heath-Kelly et al, 2015).

Returning to Sartori and the construction of language, when looking at the definitions discussed within CONTEST it becomes apparent that, while there was a need to create language quickly around a growing phenomenon, in a post-9/11 world, the term 'extremism' lacks boundaries of how it is defined. Instead, it is a fuzzy concept that affected the agenda of the ruling government of the time and its priorities (Schmid, 2018). The conditions of group membership that is ascribed to extremism or radicalisation is equally unclear within UK law. As discussed earlier, Berger looks at in-groups and action against out-groups, but no clear identifiers are placed upon how said groups are determined. Finally, the terms radicalisation and extremism have become so watered down within the cultural zeitgeist, that defining a person as an extremist is down to opinion, politics and whether they express opinions against the populus of 'reasonable individuals' (Schmid, 2014, p 11). To know the language of extremism and terrorism is difficult when governing bodies, academics and social commentators struggle to agree upon definitions for key phrases. Elahi and Hargreaves (2022) argue that it is not even desirable to achieve a universal definition of extremism due to the complex, multifaceted nature of extremism.

It is beyond the scope of this chapter to consider whether radicalisation as a concept is flawed, real or workable. Radicalisation exists as it is enshrined in UK law, therefore, due to the responsibilities placed on policy makers and practitioners, there must be workable frameworks developed to enable practitioners to support those under their services in the best way possible.

The practicalities of radicalisation

The UK government launched its counter-terrorism strategy, CONTEST, in July 2011, with updates and revisions coming into force in 2018. In CONTEST, His Majesty's government describes its plans to tackle the threat of Al-Qaeda, and notably (on the first page) mentions radicalisation as one of the four tactics allowing the continued growth of terrorist groups (Home Office, 2018). The four strands that make up CONTEST are PURSUE, PREVENT, PROTECT and PREPARE. The objective that non-specialised staff are involved in is PREVENT. PREVENT aims to work with a wide range of sectors, with primary focus on education, criminal justice, faith, health and charities. PREVENT aims to help these sectors 'understand their obligations' (His Majesty's Government, 2015, p 63), and effectively respond to noticing either the signs of a person becoming radicalised or one person radicalising another.

By naming these sectors, HM government has given these organisations a responsibility to be able to, as a starting point, show awareness and understanding of the risks of radicalisation, be confident in spotting the signs of and know the procedures to report these worries. As discussed earlier, a 2017 report published by the Department for Education details how the local authority social workers view their role within radicalisation work. The overwhelming response was that they have little to no confidence in their ability to enact this role, as summarised by one social worker:

> There's no information out there, you know, if you suspect, who do you call? What do you do? What are

the symptoms, because I wouldn't know the symptoms of radicalisation. And I think [this local authority] definitely needs even if it's just a one-day training, we have training on all sorts of other subjects, I think it would make a good training subject. [Social Worker, Non-priority area]. (Chisholm et al, 2017, p 20)

A secondary report from the same department was published in 2021. While this secondary report acknowledges that in the years between the 2017 and 2021 no major progress was achieved in certain areas, there have been some notable improvements, namely, that staff in areas that have lower numbers of referrals to PREVENT appear to have a better understanding of radicalisation as a form of harm that could benefit from treatment as another safeguarding issue (Langson-Shreeve et al, 2021). However, the report does not offer statistics, exploration or direct quotes from staff members to corroborate this claim, and itself acknowledges that while this may the case, it then does not translate into action. In the UK, radicalisation policies are most often embedded within overarching safeguarding policies. Safeguarding is a UK-centric catch-all phrase that has become distilled from its root in protecting children and 'vulnerable' adults, arguably, it no longer addresses the needs of survivors or communities in which abuses have taken place (Sandvik, 2019). Safeguarding policies cover the need to protect people from a range of violent acts, such as modern slavery and human trafficking, domestic abuse, sexual abuse, and mental capacity issues. Instead of the nuanced interventions needed for responses to such personal experiences of violence, often shaped by intersecting societal factors (gender, race, class and so on), a generalised safeguarding response produces a generic, formulaic framework for practitioners to externalise responsibility and knowledge to so-called safeguarding 'experts' (Daoust and Dyvik, 2020).

Most organisations do provide some very basic training on spotting the signs of radicalisation and the different ideologies that the UK Home Office deem serious enough to warrant the need to inform practitioners of. The course usually consists of a click-through online training session lasting around 45 minutes to one hour. In the 2018 revision of the CONTEST strategy, it reads that their training has been completed over 'one million times' (Home Office, 2018, p 36). In 2022, in England and Wales, there are over 1.27 million full-time equivalent staff members working in the National Health Service in the UK (DHCS Media Team, 2023), over 468,371 full-time equivalent teachers (GOV. UK, 2023), 169,093 registered charities (Charity Commission for England and Wales, 2023) and an estimated 227,649 policing staff (Home Office, 2023). Over 1 million times is not enough to cover those with a law-bound responsibility.

The training opens with a two-minute video reiterating that working with radicalisation is simply another form of safeguarding. Subsequently, there are sections on PREVENT, what makes a person susceptible to radicalisation, terrorism and its *Notice, Check, Share* directive (GOV.UK, nd). Practitioners are instructed that the definition of extremism is 'the vocal or active opposition to fundamental British values' (GOV.UK, nd), and that the ideologies that practitioners should be concerned with are: Islamist terrorist ideology, extreme right-wing terrorist ideology, left-wing, anarchist and single-issue ideologies. It does acknowledge that the current threat to the UK is dominated by individuals or small groups acting outside of these prescribed terrorist networks (in opposition to the claims made in the Home Office mandated review of PREVENT, in which William Shawcross states practitioners are 'not doing enough to counter Islamist non-violent extremism' [Shawcross, 2023, pp 6–7]). It then introduces the *Notice, Check, Share* directive, which summarises the main warning signs for professionals to take note of, such as spending more time online, talking to extremist groups and displaying signs of violence. Practitioners are instructed to check these signs with a colleague, the PREVENT lead or their local Designated Safeguarding Lead and finally how the information must be shared with PREVENT.

The training exists, therefore the next logical question is, does it help practitioners fulfil the demand of having the 'appropriate level' of training? (Home Office, 2018). While radicalisation cases are not the bulk of a practitioner's caseload (Langdon-Shreeve et al, 2021), when practitioners are not prepared, the effects can be devastating. In 2019, after being released from prison after eight years of continuous supervision, assessment and intervention,

Usman Khan killed two people and injured many more in an incident known as 'Fishmongers Hall'. The UK security service (MI5) was aware that Khan was showing signs of recidivism and yet these concerns were never shared with those that were involved in his rehabilitation, and yet, when the media covered the story, it was those practitioners that received the brunt of the backlash. Preti Taneja was one of the professionals involved in the delivery of a deradicalisation programme to Khan and, in her book *Aftermath*, details the horrifying impact that this had on her life, career and confidence. In a harrowing passage she writes:

> You are shattered and still leaving the house. Propelled by your training to mask any damage that only those who lived with this (or any forensic psychologists) might recognise. Did you recognise it, as dangerous compliance in him. You keep going in circles, if only to keep going, as if dissembling for your own survival. (Taneja, 2022, p 68)

It is a sobering reminder that unless information sharing is prioritised and professionals are given the tools they need, even though radicalisation cases do not make up the bulk of a caseload, the ripple effects that a case like this can have affect staff on all levels.

While there is sector-specific research being done in organisations around how well radicalisation work is currently being enacted (Hall, 2022), there is little work and no evidence base that unites the different multidisciplinary organisations mentioned in the PREVENT duty guidance. The PREVENT guidance focuses on the importance of multidisciplinary communication, information sharing and clarity around cases where a person is being drawn into extremism, however, nowhere is this being translated into offering support or frameworks for these organisations to be able to enact this. There are still major blockades for the police being able to share details with professionals around potentially dangerous people; there is still a lack of trust from allied professionals about getting their service users 'in trouble' (a worry so pervasive that it is in fact mentioned on the first slide of HM government's PREVENT training [GOV.UK, nd]) and a veil of mystery around what work PREVENT officers actually do.

There is also little work examining practitioners and policy makers' understanding of radicalisation as a concept. As researchers we are taught concepts of 'bias' and 'questioning one's internal narratives' in relation to the subjects we research. Yet, there is an expectation on practitioners to be able to walk into the office and abandon preconceived ideas, even when the world's media produces daily headlines reminding them of the 'dangers' (Bayoumi, 2021) of certain societal groups. It is vital to explore practitioner opinions around divisive topics and develop effective training accordingly to ensure the end users, whether those in education, in healthcare services or in the probation and penal system receive fair and effective care.

Researching radicalisation

The results presented in this chapter represent the initial findings from a series of interviews. Interviews have been chosen as a methodological approach due to the broad spectrum of topics that can be discussed, such as radicalisation as a global concept, but also the minutiae of their own personal experiences of radicalisation. One of the goals of qualitative research is to offer a range of perspectives from those with a lived experience of a phenomenon (Hill Bailey and Stephen, 2002). Radicalisation as a phenomenon, so far, has evaded being encapsulated or distilled into a one-size-fits-all framework, and so the ability to allow practitioners the freedom to create their own meaning and interpretation allows for the analysis of different repeating narratives and the ability to build a wide-ranging evidence base. The principle feature of narrative research is the usage of stories as data (Savin-Baden and Van Niekerk, 2007). Stories are collected as a means of understanding experience, both as lived experiences and those that are consciously told and shared (Bell, 2002). When locating narrative work within research methods, it is a qualitative method and utilises reflexivity, interpretation and representation as primary features (Savin-Baden and Van Niekerk, 2007).

An obstacle that radicalisation researchers have come across is the idea that deradicalisation/radicalisation interventions are offering 'excuses' (Heath-Kelly, 2013) for terrorists. In the aftermath of 9/11, terrorism became something inexplicable, it was labelled an 'evil ideology' which not only didn't require exploration, but was rooted in the pathology of mental illness (Kundnani, 2012). The 'otherness' of terrorism (Horgan, 2014) meant that research had to be carefully aligned with security forces so as not to appear sympathetic to the terrorist cause. Working with narrative forces the researcher to question their own place within the narrative, allowing for discussions of bias and fear to be acknowledged and dealt with early in the research. This is also important when interviewing professional peers due to the possibility of a transference of feelings from interviewee to interviewer and vice versa. Therefore, continuously questioning professional opinions is vital.

There are many opportunities when utilising narrative as a springboard for academic discussion (O'Kane and Pamphilon, 2015). Medical educators and practitioners argued that narrative allows them to recognise and comprehend the singular and particular within illness alongside the pathological and psychological (Hurwitz and Charon, 2013). This exploration allowed practitioners to not only focus on the patient as the singular but the systems in which they exist, such as the family network, creating a rich picture of how illness can interrupt systems (Launer, 2002). It encourages researchers to not only focus on one moment of the story, such as a static interview, but look at the participants as having storied lives, as by compiling these stories repeatedly over the span of the data collection period it will allow for comparison of the stories told at the beginning and end of the project. The researcher's role is to interpret the stories in order to collate a series of narratives, some of which may be conscious to the story-teller, some of which may not be (Riley and Hawe, 2005).

With the purpose of writing this chapter, interviews were conducted with a mixture of policy makers and professionals within a range of organisations. There were seven healthcare staff (of varying professional backgrounds, including doctors, nurses and mental health practitioners), two teachers (one inner-city secondary school and one private religious institution), two policing staff (mixed departments), two police officers (one PREVENT office and one senior management) and one charity sector staff member (charity working with clients deemed as vulnerable to radicalisation). The singular inclusion criterion was that the professional must work for an organisation that has a reporting duty to PREVENT within the UK.

The range of experiences canvassed both in terms of industry and management level ensured that a comprehensive evidence base could be presented to effectively assess the impact of current radicalisation policy and training on practitioner confidence. While there is a heavier weighting towards healthcare staff, this group represents a wide range of healthcare staff from psychiatrists, GPs, nurses and administrative staff, all of whom have varying experiences and opinions. The interviews were recorded both in person and via Microsoft Teams, and subsequently transcribed and anonymised. Throughout the chapter, direct quotes will be referred to using the sector name in which the interviewee works for (for example, 'charity sector professional'), allowing for anonymity while giving context for the person discussing their views, opinions and experiences. Due to the mixture of practitioners and policy makers, throughout the chapter those being interviewed will be referred to as interviewees.

All interviews followed the same basic structure. Beginning with a personal summary, allowing the interviewee to explain their journey to their current role, the context in which they work and any other information they wanted to share. This created a comfortable opening where interviewees could relax, share and reflect on the way that their role shapes opinions and affects their feelings towards radicalisation. It was important to form questions based on the experiences of those being interviewed. Interviews with those in policy-making roles focused more on the policy-making questions and interviews with practitioners focused more on the effect that policy had on their work. Open-ended questions were utilised to encourage interviewees to share their experiences, for example, "Do you think radicalisation and violence are always linked?" followed with "Could you expand on that?", offering the interviewer opportunities to delve further within the interviewee's answer, inviting shared reflection.

The issue with interviewing is time, both in the sense that professionals are time-poor, but also as radicalisation can be an uncomfortable topic to discuss, it often took interviewees time to relax into the interview. Despite it being written in the participant handbook beforehand, 11 interviewees out of 12 offered clarifications before we began that they 'didn't know a lot', which implied an air of tension around the interview. These initial reactions are interesting to note and offer an opportunity to explore the atmosphere that discussing radicalisation creates.

The practitioner's perspective

If, before we can comment on the effect of language, we must first know language, then, before we can discuss the effects of radicalisation pressures and policies on practitioners, we must first understand their view of radicalisation as a concept. This was the focus for the opening section of the interview and formed the foundation of later questioning, such as whether radicalisation and violence are inherently linked, whether they felt radicalisation was relevant to their role and then onto who should be responsible for radicalisation interventions.

When asked about their understanding of radicalisation as a concept, there were general commonalities that could be picked out regardless of what industry participants were from. Eleven of the 12 professionals interviewed located the vulnerability to radicalisation within an individual. They described an individual who was already starting from a place of societal deficit or dealing with issues such as loneliness (most common, with ten out of 12 interviewees mentioning this at least once), isolation, ostracisation from a social group, unhappiness/depression and youth and its upheavals/changes/difficulties.

Interestingly, only one practitioner mentioned having diagnosable medical issues such as attention deficit/hyperactivity disorder, autism or a learning difficulty as a precursor to being vulnerable to radicalisation (healthcare professional). Notably, medical/mental ill-health and its link to vulnerability to radicalisation is mentioned frequently in academic discussions about those who commit acts of 'lone wolf violence' (Bael, 2014). A policing staff member disclosed that according to a study they were involved with, 66 per cent of people referred to PREVENT had links to domestic abuse, either as a perpetrator, victim or witness, a percentage greatly different from findings in the general population. In the UK, one in four women and one in six/seven men will experience domestic violence, with domestic abuse-related crimes increasing 7.7 per cent in 2023 from 2022 (National Centre for Domestic Violence, 2023). Studies such as this are vital in offering the potential link for previous trauma to those that are vulnerable to radicalisation.

During analysis it became clear that radicalisation, according to the interviewees, could be broken down into four phases: exposure, acceptance, idée fixe and dissemination. These phases have similarities to other academic models of radicalisation such as the three-stage phase approach (sensitivity, group membership and action) created by Doosje and colleagues (2016), along with the Rational Agent Model put forward by Martha Crenshaw in her chapter of *Conflict After the Cold War: Arguments on Causes of War and Peace* (as cited in Betts, 2017), or the 'cognitive opening' described by Wikotowicz (2005, p 5). While there are a range of critiques for all these models, through these interviews it is obvious that the idea that radicalisation is a staged approach has filtered down into the general populus' understanding of radicalisation.

Exposure

Exposure was described as the initial phase of radicalisation, in which a person who has vulnerabilities is "preyed upon" (charity sector professional) or "provided information" (teaching professional) by an outside source. Examples interviewees provided were religious groups and specifically their leaders (healthcare professional), Internet gaming websites (teaching professional), Internet chat forums (teaching professional) and gang leaders (healthcare professional). This outside force offers the vulnerable individual an alternative narrative, or as one policing professional said, a way out of the "no man's land" in which they may be currently. This alternative narrative provides solutions to their perceived deficits, such as: a shared enemy, a group to be part of, a family, hope. Four out of 12 interviewees mentioned the similarity of this process to grooming, with two defining the person vulnerable to radicalisation as a "victim" (healthcare and charity sector professionals), for example, a charity sector professional said, "[t]he person who has been radicalised becomes damaged in some way and is in need of healing" (charity sector professional).

Acceptance

In the next stage on the radicalisation journey, the vulnerable person moves into acceptance of a previously unsubscribed ideology, the person is "fed more and more of this viewpoint" (healthcare professional) until they hold these same views. Practitioners found it difficult to described from experience what 'acceptance' would look like in terms of presentation, behaviours or thoughts, however one healthcare professional described that they would deem a person radicalised once "they stopped questioning", and that a person would believe "anything that groups said to them" (healthcare professional). When discussing what ideologies and beliefs would be deemed as radically dangerous or extremist, one teaching professional described their own experience by saying, "[y]ou're considered moderate if you are not considered sexist, racist or anything -ist. Essentially, if you're not willing to say that anything's wrong, that's moderate. If you disagree with anyone, you are extremist" (teaching professional).

While this view is unspecific about what makes a view extremist, it shows a tendency to assume that those that hold extremist views feel as if out-groups are doing things that are "wrong" (healthcare professional).

Idée fixe

Idée fixe is a phrase that summarises the focus that an individual has when they have transitioned from a person that is vulnerable to radicalisation to a person that is radicalised. It was described in phrases such as "brain-washed" (teaching professional) and "indoctrinated" (healthcare professional), as opposed to it simply being an interest or change in belief system and is a view that begins to "impact on everyday life" (healthcare professional). To summarise, it was felt as if a person could be defined as radicalised when their new ideology had become their "overwhelming focus" (healthcare professional) and the beliefs were so strong that they would be willing to act against those who did not hold the same views. These acts do not always present themselves as violence. No practitioner said that radicalisation and physical violence were innately linked, but when asked to elaborate why, nine out the 12 interviewees said that they did feel radicalisation was inherently linked to negative outcomes, whether that is physical, mental, emotional violence or closing of the mind to factions of society, for example, one teaching professional discussed that parents belonging to a certain religious group had told their children that they didn't need to listen to her, due to her being a woman.

Dissemination

Although not mentioned by every interviewee, six out of 12 interviewees mentioned a final feature of those that are radicalised: the desire to disseminate their new ideology. It is not simply enough for an individual to hold the belief, they must champion the cause and become a "radicaliser" (education professional) themselves.

In general, the discussion around radicalisation was incredibly negative. A policing professional described feeling as if for some groups radicalisation was "almost preordained" (policing professional) due to the societal deficits their communities were in. While most interviewees initially said radicalisation was not inherently linked to physical violence, as already discussed, most then went on to detail how it is a negative construct. However, while it may be from a surprising source, a policing official did offer a hopeful take on being radical, they said:

> 'This is where I'll start talking about Bob Dylan, and forgetting who I am again. ... There is nothing more natural than a young person believing everything their parents said when they were dependent, but then, becoming a teenager and gaining independence and thinking: "This older generation have screwed this up ... I want to change the word ... I want to be radical". I want my young people to be radical, but I want them to do it peacefully and lawfully.' (Policing professional)

The gut feeling

"Would we find what to do? Yes, of course. Could I tell you off the top of my head? No" (healthcare professional, also safeguarding lead for their organisation). While it may sound flippant, the previous statement summarises the general feeling of practitioners towards radicalisation work. The only person who felt certain in their ability to proactively support someone who had been radicalised was a policing practitioner; however, radicalisation is the major focus of their work. In contrast, radicalisation is not listed in the job descriptions of any of the other interviewees. Other practitioners had undertaken basic PREVENT training, which is mandatory for those that work for organisations with a reporting duty to PREVENT. However, 11 of the interviewees said that this training had not led to an increase in confidence in spotting the signs of radicalisation or confidence in supporting someone who had been or someone who currently was radicalised: "I wouldn't call it training, I would call it watching a video about radicalisation. And to be fair to the trainer, they made sure that it wasn't just about Islam, which I felt like took some effort" (charity sector professional).

Another professional expressed, "I certainly can't remember it. I know it was exactly the same program the last two years that we've had to do it" (healthcare professional). The consensus among interviewees was that, first, if a practitioner were to deal with radicalisation within their day job, they would consult safeguarding procedures or report it to the safeguarding lead, and second, that they would rely on their personal intuition of "feeling like something was off" (teaching professional), or a "gut feeling" (charity sector professional). In summary, their strategies were either externalisation of the issue or a reliance upon professional judgement. Healthcare staff stated that while radicalisation isn't a major part of their role, they did all feel some responsibility to be able to know if a patient was becoming radicalised, however time was a barrier to engaging with this responsibility. Within education there was more a focus on radicalisation being seen as a part of their role, but barriers included working with other services, in particular children's social services, and conflicting priorities.

When discussing how they would define whether PREVENT had been successful in its goal, one professional said that while success would be if that person didn't become further radicalised, they also said:

'You have damaged yourself, you have lost part of that humanness that connects us to one another, because you have to feel like everyone else is evil. So, to take a step towards actual violence, you have to objectify people. And I think that that that coming back from that requires healing.' (Charity sector professional)

Other signs of success against radicalisation were that a person has stopped being "a risk to other people" (healthcare professional), that they would be able to "meet and work with regular people" (healthcare professional) or as one teaching professional eloquently said, "Lead a normal, quiet life without fear" (teaching professional). The focus was on harm reduction, and the ability to be able to understand the nuance within their chosen ideology. Regaining the ability to critically examine their ideology and choose which aspects they agreed with rather than blind acceptance. Interestingly, nobody mentioned the promotion of 'British values' (Home Office, 2018).

Policy versus practitioner

Since interviewees did not necessarily feel as if their training had equipped them with the necessary tools to help with their duty around radicalisation, the next step was to explore whether their organisation's policy offered more clarity on the subject. Eleven practitioners were aware that their organisation had a policy regarding their duty to report radicalisation and could locate it within the organisation's safeguarding policy document. There were mixed views on the need/efficacy of policy in general. This could be due to the mixture of policy- and non-policy-making interviewees within the group. Out of the 12, five were with policy makers and seven with non-policy makers, that is, practitioners.

Of the five policy makers, three said that they felt as if policy was helpful, particularly due to the protection that it offers staff. For instance, without having a policy there is no way to have an "audit trail" (policing professional). It was a common theme mentioned throughout the policy discussion, that unspoken worries exist and that when 'things go wrong' blame must be ascribed somewhere. Hence, if there is an evidence-based policy in place, a practitioner on any level can defend their actions by saying that they followed the policy. One policy maker stated having a policy did not make them feel supported within their role at all as they were the "one that had to design it all" (charity sector) and so could see the potential flaws but acknowledged that it had a positive impact on their staff, offering accountability and support. They further emphasised that they didn't hire staff on their ability to follow policy, but on their skills. The final policy maker was more indifferent, claiming they had never really needed to refer to a policy when dealing with an issue, as they would "normally turn to colleague and discuss the matter informally" (healthcare staff).

The reaction to policy from practitioners was more varied. There were those that felt as if policy gave them a "safety net" (healthcare professional) to land in times of trouble, and it was therefore something they referred to often. One practitioner expressed their frustration that often policies were designed by people "who do not work with it" (teaching professional), which led to policies being tokenistic in nature as opposed to being easily applied to practice. Finally, one healthcare professional described an aversion to all policy, stating "I think it takes creativity from everything" (healthcare professional).

In terms of radicalisation policy, it was described as embedded within the organisation's safeguarding policy (healthcare and teaching professional), and one healthcare professional said they thought it "described some of the basic signs of radicalisation" and their duty to then report it to PREVENT. No practitioner or policy maker interviewed said it made them feel more confident in their ability to undertake their PREVENT duty. Those questioned on what would make them feel confident offered examples such as "discussing it over coffee with a colleague" (healthcare professional), "definitely my own experience, once I've seen it once, I know what I'm looking for" (teaching professional) or utilising the Internet to learn and find examples (healthcare professional).

Where does the buck stop?

When discussing their role within radicalisation work, only one interviewee (teaching professional), outside of the police, said that they believed their role lent itself to leading on working with radicalisation. Their rationale for this was that within their role, as a teacher, they spent "most of that child's waking hours" (teaching professional) with them, they knew them best and therefore any form of intervention should be led by them, they said, "I want to know it wasn't for nothing. All the care, all the work, pounding away at these times tables, I need to know it was for something" (teaching professional).

Nine interviewees, with varying degrees of reticence, that they would be willing to be part of a multidisciplinary team, attend meetings, "do their part" (healthcare professional) or input into the ongoing care of someone who had been radicalised. The question of leadership was less clear, as a charity sector professional summarised:

> 'I think that's a really difficult thing to say when you say, "who should be responsible" because I genuinely don't even think that we know as a society how to even fix these people. And so ... who should be responsible becomes a non-question because it doesn't matter who's responsible, they're not going to do a good job. ... I don't know how to fix these people. I know how to fix victims – because victims wanna be fixed.'
> (Charity sector professional)

A common theme in all areas of questioning was the idea that practitioners would find someone who had more experience. They would want someone who "knew what they were doing" (healthcare professional) to take the lead. Due to the undeniable securitisation around radicalisation and its inherent link with terrorism, it has fallen to the police to lead on radicalisation cases. While it may seem to make sense, this was not reflected in the viewpoints of any of the interviews, only one practitioner committed to the idea that the police should lead on radicalisation cases. This practitioner was a police officer. Every other interviewee put forward a joint approach, and while there must always be a lead professional, a different policing professional put forward that rather than having a lead professional, there should be one person within a care plan nominated as the "information gatherer" (policing professional), and it may be that a police officer would be the most appropriate person to play this role, but that all professionals involved with a client would lead.

It is undeniable that when radicalisation leads to violent action against another societal faction then that becomes a police matter. However, due to nuance of a person being able to hold extremist beliefs without committing actual crime, there appears to be an opportunity for more joint working that is currently being missed. If no crime has been committed, then while the police may need to still be involved in a multidisciplinary team capacity, as in other forms of criminal proceedings, it does not guarantee that they are the most appropriate professional to lead on radicalisation cases.

Moving forward with radicalisation: practitioner-led recommendations

This chapter intends to provide a snapshot of the opinions of professionals who have a governmental defined responsibility to have the understanding and ability to spot the signs of and report radicalisation, for the purposes of proposing that there is not enough support or adequate training for said professionals to complete this duty. It is vital that work exploring the current trajectory of preventative work within counter-terrorism continues. The British government persists in its focus on the prevalence of Islamic radicalisation and with reports such as the recent Shawcross 'Independent review of PREVENT' insisting that PREVENT officers 'ignore the contribution of non-violent Islamist narratives networks to terrorism' (Shawcross, 2023, p 7), and defines Islamist terrorism as the 'primary terrorist threat to this country' (Shawcross, 2023, p 7). However, this is completely nonreflective of the current referral statistics, and it must be noted that Shawcross developed his report on a woefully small cross-section of PREVENT meetings he attended. Since his appointment, 500 civil liberties groups, Muslim-led societies and individuals argued to boycott this review (Holmwood and Aitlhadj, 2023).

The risk of ignoring the ever-growing presence of extreme right-wing, or non-ideological based radicalisation is high, and professionals will feel even less confident in spotting the signs of radicalisation as they are not being shown an up-to-date view of the current face of radicalisation. Of the referrals made to PREVENT for the last available year (2021/2022) 16 per cent were regarding Islamist radicalisation, as opposed to 20 per cent for extreme right-wing ideology and 33 per cent were for individuals with no ideology present (Home Office News Team, 2023). It is impossible and irresponsible to place a legal directive on professionals and arm them with tools that they need.

Discussions around radicalisation are uncomfortable, anxiety-provoking and difficult, and, as mentioned earlier, most of the practitioners asked to take part in these interviews checked multiple times before taking part that they didn't need to be an expert in this field to be able to input into the knowledge base. When discussing terrorism and/or any other kind of mass harm, it is natural for thoughts and feelings to go to the victim. From a policy perspective to protect those at risk so it never happens again and from a practitioner perspective to want to help those that have been harmed by the situation. It is harder to shift that perspective of empathy, compassion and desire to help to the possible perpetrator. It is understandable that policy makers and practitioners have worries around becoming involved in radicalisation work and therefore want to externalise the responsibility onto a group that 'knows what they're doing'. However, just as radicalisation does not have one presentation, neither can its treatment. The UK government has chosen to give reporting and treatment duties to many different sectors and therefore it must provide those it has charged with the appropriate frameworks in which to do this. As the research has shown, the current narratives are ones of confusion, misinformation and a lack of confidence in implementing radicalisation interventions. There needs to be a commitment to creating an evidence base of current radicalisation streams, not only focused on Islamic radicalisation. Professionals also need a clear and inclusive definition of radicalisation to offer clarity around the mythologised journey of a person from 'normal' to 'terrorist'. There must be a clear set of guidance, interventions and frameworks communicated to all practitioners who are responsible. It is not enough for radicalisation to be "lumped in" (healthcare sector professional) to a safeguarding policy informing practitioners to report it to their PREVENT lead. Policy should be designed to offer intervention on all level, a toolkit for the practitioner, a "safety net" (healthcare professional) for them to rely on and an expert to offer guidance and specific help. Finally, a multidisciplinary team should be established where the needs of the person supposedly being radicalised are placed first, they should be viewed through a systemic lens which allows for the analysis of the person's intersectional needs throughout their life and works to understand the drivers behind that person becoming radicalised.

Radicalisation can happen to anyone, as one police officer said it doesn't matter "how much money you have in the bank" or "what postcode you live in" (policing professional), and so an approach that considers all people is needed. An example from Preti Taneja's work on her experiences was used earlier to depict how ignoring radicalisation can damage professionals, however, when asked, all interviewees expressed cautious hope around the future of radicalisation work, if treated from a truly multidisciplinary sense, just as Taneja concludes her work: 'We need a different kind of ship to sail on a collective breath' (Taneja, 2022, p 198).

Summary

- The current definition of radicalisation does not provide clarity for policy makers or practitioners and externalises responsibility for interventions on PREVENT leads/PREVENT teams, disempowering practitioners from offering possible relevant interventions.
- The current definition of extremism being an opposition to 'British values' is not comprehensive and offers no clarity for practitioners on the differences between extremism, radicalisation and terrorism.
- Radicalisation is currently only seen in safeguarding policy, and needs expanding to include more information, sources of advice and interventions for practitioners.
- Overall, practitioners who are outside of the police do not feel confident in their abilities to complete radicalisation work despite having yearly training.
- Practitioners currently feel a lack of connection with radicalisation work. This partly stems from the current inherent association with counter-terrorism work which feels outside their remit and a lack of time within which this could be explored.

- There needs to be a change in the way that radicalisation changes are approached by services, as all practitioners and policy makers discussed it needing a multidisciplinary approach with the person at the centre, however this is not the case in current provisions with all responsibility being placed on PREVENT officers.
- More work needs to be focused on creating alternative radicalisation frameworks that focus on the many push and pull factors that draw people in to being radicalised, such as: systemic oppression, socioeconomic status as opposed to being entirely focused on one type of religious radicalisation.

Suggested directions for future research

The following questions can orient further research and discussion in the area:

- What systematic vulnerabilities, as opposed to person-specific factors, make an individual more likely to become radicalised?
- Is there evidence of public health interventions being utilised in other areas of crime prevention that could be tested and evaluated in radicalisation/deradicalisation work?
- How can information sharing and multidisciplinary working between professionals be improved to strengthen radicalisation/deradicalisation interventions?
- Is the term safeguarding fit for purpose, or is there a better categorisation system for risks of harm?

References

Bael, S.J. (2014) 'Are terrorists "insane"? A critical analysis of mental health categories in lone terrorists' trials', *Critical Studies on Terrorism*, 7(2): 257–76.

Bayoumi, M. (2021) 'Dangerous outsiders and exceptional citizens: Being Muslim American since 9/11', *The Guardian*, 10 September. Available from https://www.theguardian.com/us-news/2021/sep/09/muslim-america-september-11-war-on-terror [Accessed 14 September 2023].

Bell, J.S. (2002) 'Narrative inquiry: More than just telling stories', *TESOL Quarterly*, 36(2): 207–13.

Berger, J.M. (2018) *Extremism*, Cambridge, MA: MIT Press.

Betts, R.K. (2017) *Conflict After the Cold War: Arguments on Causes of War and Peace*, New York: Routledge.

Cabinet Office and Her Majesty the Queen (2017) 'Queen's speech: Her Majesty's most gracious speech to both Houses of Parliament', *GOV.UK*, 21 June. Available from https://www.gov.uk/government/speeches/queens-speech-2017 [Accessed 14 September 2023].

Charity Commission for England and Wales (2023) 'Charities in England and Wales', *Charity Commission for England and Wales*, 24 October. Available from https://register-of-charities.charitycommission.gov.uk/sector-data/sector-overview [Accessed 15 September 2023].

Chisholm, T., Coulter, A. and Kantar Public (2017) *Safeguarding and Radicalisation* [Research Report–Department for Education, Government Social Research], August. Available from https://assets.publishing.service.gov.uk/media/5a81ffd7e5274a2e87dc09d7/Safeguarding_and_Radicalisation.pdf [Accessed 23 September 2023].

Daoust, G. and Dyvik, S.L. (2020) 'Knowing safeguarding: The geopolitics of knowledge production in the humanitarian and development sector', *Geoforum*, 112: 96–9.

DHCS Media Team (2023) 'NHS workforce: Record numbers of doctors and nurses in NHS', *Department of Health and Social Care Media Centre*, 27 April. Available from https://healthmedia.blog.gov.uk/2023/04/27/nhs-workforce-record-numbers-of-doctors-and-nurses-in-nhs/ [Accessed 15 September 2023].

Doosje, B., Moghaddam, F.M., Kruglanski, A.W., De Wolf, A., Mann, L. and Feddes, A.R. (2016) 'Terrorism, radicalization and de-radicalization', *Current Opinion in Psychology*, 11: 79–84.

Elahi, M. and Hargreaves, J. (2022) 'How to define and tackle Islamist extremism in the UK', *International Centre for Counter-Terrorism*, December. Available from https://www.icct.nl/sites/default/files/2022-12/Elahi%20and%20Hargreaves%20Final.pdf [Accessed 23 September 2023].

GOV.UK (2023) 'School workforce in England, Reporting year 2022', *GOV.UK*, 8 June. Available from https://explore-education-statistics.service.gov.uk/find-statistics/school-workforce-in-england [Accessed 15 September 2023].

GOV.UK (nd) Prevent duty training: Learn how to support people susceptible to radicalization, *GOV.UK*. Available from https://www.support-people-vulnerable-to-radicalisation.service.gov.uk/ [Accessed 14 September 2023].

Greater Manchester Combined Authority (2018) 'A shared future', *Greater Manchester Preventing Hateful Extremism and Promoting Social Cohesion Commission*. Available from https://www.greatermanchester-ca.gov.uk/media/1170/preventing-hateful-extremism-and-promoting-social-cohesion-report.pdf [Accessed 23 September 2023].

Hall, J. (2022) *Terrorism in Prisons*, London: OGL

Heath-Kelly, C. (2013) 'Counter-terrorism and the counterfactual: Producing the "radicalisation" discourse and the UK prevent strategy', *British Journal of Politics and International Relations*, 15(3): 394–415.

Heath-Kelly, C., Baker-Beall, C. and Jarvis, L. (2015) *Counter-Radicalisation: Critical Perspectives*, New York: Routledge.

Hill Bailey, P. and Stephen, T. (2002) 'Storytelling and the interpretation of meaning in qualitative research', *Journal of Advanced Nursing*, 38(6): 574–83.

His Majesty's Government (2015) 'Revised Prevent duty guidance for England Wales', *Home Office*, 12 March. Available from https://www.gov.uk/government/publications/prevent-duty-guidance/revised-prevent-duty-guidance-for-england-and-wales [Accessed 20 May 2021].

Holmwood, P.J. and Aitlhadj, D.L. (2023) 'A response to the Shawcross report', *The People People's Review of Prevent*, March. Available from https://peoplesreviewofprevent.org/wp-content/uploads/2023/06/response-to-shawcross-1.pdf [Accessed 23 September 2023].

Home Office (2018) 'CONTEST: The United Kingdom's Strategy for Countering Terrorism – Annual Report', *HM Government*, July. Available from https://assets.publishing.service.gov.uk/government/uploads/system/uploads/attachment_data/file/1186413/CONTEST_2023_English_updated.pdf [Accessed 23 September 2023].

Home Office (2023) 'Police workforce, England and Wales: 30 September 2022', *GOV.UK*, 25 January. Available from https://www.gov.uk/government/statistics/police-workforce-england-and-wales-30-september-2022/police-workforce-england-and-wales-30-september-2022 [Accessed 15 September 2023].

Home Office News Team (2023) 'Prevent and Channel factsheet – 2023', *Home Office*, 7 September. Available from https://homeofficemedia.blog.gov.uk/2023/09/07/prevent-and-channel-factsheet-2023/ [Accessed 14 September 2023].

Horgan, J. (2014) *The Psychology of Terrorism: Revised and Updated Second Edition*, London: Routledge.

Hurwitz, B. and Charon, R. (2013) 'A narrative future for health care', *The Lancet*, 381(9881): 1886–7.

Kundnani, A. (2012) 'Radicalisation: The journey of a concept', *Race Relations*, 54(2): 3–25.

Langdon-Shreeve, S., Nickson, H. and Bright C. (2021) 'Safeguarding and radicalisation: Learning from children's social care' [research report], *Government Social Research*, June. Available from https://assets.publishing.service.gov.uk/media/60cb7679d3bf7f4bd9814f51/DfE_Safeguarding_in_CSC.pdf [Accessed 23 September 2023].

Launer, J. (2002) *Narrative-Based Primary Care: A Practical Guide*, Abingdon: Radcliff Publishing.

National Centre for Domestic Violence (2023) 'Domestic abuse statistics UK', *NCDV*. Available from https://www.ncdv.org.uk/domestic-abuse-statistics-uk/ [Accessed 4 July 202].

O'Kane, G. and Pamphilon, B. (2015) 'The importance of stories in understanding people's relationship to food: Narrative inquiry methodology has much to offer the public health nutrition researcher and practitioner', *Public Health Nutrition*, 19(4): 585–92.

Riley, T. and Hawe, P. (2005) 'Researching practice: The methodological case for narrative inquiry', *Health Education Research*, 20(2): 226–36.

Sandvik, K.B. (2019) '"Safeguarding" as humanitarian buzzword: An initial scoping', *Journal of International Humanitarian Action*, 4(3): 1–6.

Sartori, G. (1984) *Social Science Concepts: A System Analysis*, Thousand Oaks: SAGE.

Savin-Baden, M. and Van Niekerk, L. (2007) 'Narrative inquiry: Theory and practice', *Journal of Geography in Higher Education*, 31(3): 459–72.

Schmid, A.P. (2014) 'Violent and non-violent extremism: Two sides of the same coin?', *The International Centre for Counter-Terrorism – The Hague*, May. Available from https://www.icct.nl/sites/default/files/2023-01/ICCT-Schmid-Violent-Non-Violent-Extremism-May-2014.pdf [Accessed 23 September 2023].

Schmid, A.P. (2018) *Routledge Handbook of Terrorism and Counterterrorism*, New York: Routledge.

Shawcross, W. (2023) 'Independent review of prevent', *Home Office*, 8 February. Available from https://www.gov.uk/government/publications/independent-review-of-prevents-report-and-government-response [Accessed 23 September 2023].

Shepherd, L.J. (2010) 'Women, armed conflict and language: Gender, violence and discourse', *International Review of the Red Cross*, 92(877): 143–59.

Taneja, P. (2022) *Aftermath*, Sheffield: And Other Stories.

Wiktorowicz, Q. (2005) *Radical Islam Rising*, Lanham: Rowman & Littlefield.

7

Restorative justice for preventing and countering violent extremism: some reflections from the Basque Country

Gema Varona

Introduction

Spanish philosopher Adela Cortina (2017) reminds us that we have the power to transform violence into a peaceful legacy and that human beings' identities are constructed by exchange and dialogue, not an imposing monologue. For Cortina (2017), 'it is necessary to argue, and not just feel, to cooperatively discover what is the truest and fairest' (p 22) in every context. Restorative justice (RJ) can be defined as a voluntary step towards that complex discovery of a transformative and precarious truth through addressing harm while engaging those affected to find a common understanding of different ways of reparation (European Forum for Restorative Justice, nd; United Nations Office on Drugs and Crime, 2020b).[1]

This chapter aims to underline the importance of (re)creating the value of restorative dialogues substantiated by evidence of their positive impact on enhanced restorative conversations before, during and after political violence (European Forum for Restorative Justice, 2008; Walgrave, 2015). Acknowledging the difficulties of agreeing on a standard definition, political violence is understood here as a harmful expression of extremism that unlawfully uses force with the intent to achieve political objectives or defend ideas on how a society[2] should be organised. This text will primarily focus on violent extremism (United Nations Office on Drugs and Crime, 2020a), including that of a religious nature (Thijssen et al, 2023) and the so-called pro-state or vigilante violent extremism (Taylor, 2023).

With concern for the global rise in violent extremism (UNESCO, nd) and within the tradition of peace studies (Ford, 2020; United Nations Office on Drugs and Crime, 2020a), civil society and public institutions' will to develop restorative conversations might entail difficult dialogues on how violence affects society and on how society responds in the short, middle and long run. A restorative response entails policies and measures to constructively prevent and counteract individual and collective violence, through inclusive listening and active accountability, based on free will. In this context, the term 'countering' is understood as offsetting violent narratives through restorative ones, serving as a counterbalance to the monologue of political violence. This approach necessitates societal involvement, particularly the engagement of young generations as the main stakeholders. With a longitudinal perspective, a 'stakeholder' can be defined as any individual, group or organisation impacted by violent extremism.

Drawing on RJ and victimology literature, this work offers a descriptive and analytical contribution, supported by some evidence and concrete examples on the qualitative evaluation of some RJ projects conducted by the Restorative Justice Theory & Practice Lab of the Basque Institute of Criminology of the University of the Basque Country (Spain). This includes personal experiences and joint learning drawn from the ongoing Encounter of the Encounters project in regions such as Spain, Italy, Northern Ireland, Scotland, Israel, Palestine, Germany, Belgium and France, supported by the European Forum for Restorative Justice (European Forum for Restorative Justice, 2021; Varona, 2021; Biffi, 2023).[3]

This chapter is structured into five sections. The first section underscores the role of society as a stakeholder, emphasising the concepts of social and political harm, as well as diffuse victimisation beyond a monolithic notion of public order. The second section explores the tension between the confidentiality principle of RJ and its social echo or impact to move beyond victim–offender relationships by drawing on the all-affected principle (Ivison, 2023). Considering victims' needs, the third section highlights the potential of RJ to challenge the conventional understanding of prevention as separate from the reparation process. From this perspective, individual and social reconstruction are inseparable for those impacted and accountable in relation to harm. The fourth section examines the challenges of regarding younger generations as part of the community of conflict in RJ processes. Finally, before summarising the key ideas, the chapter concludes by proposing restorative cities as an avenue for further development.

The political harm on pluralism: society as an indirect victim to be restored

Regarding political violence, society serves simultaneously as an indirect victim and a community of support for those directly impacted by violence. Hence, society plays a double stakeholder's role in RJ. Offenders and victims were born into and belong to the same community, where violence finds the conditions to grow due to the support of certain groups and the spread of feelings and ideas (Heath-Kelly and Shanaah, 2022; Orofino and Allchorn, 2023). Furthermore, the political harm is a fundamental, but usually overlooked, aspect of the victimisation impact of violent extremism and other types of political violence. If the principles of *minimum* intervention and *ultima ratio* (the idea of criminalisation as last resort) are truly respected, any criminalisation of a conduct entails the assessment of social harm. However, in crimes of violent extremism, this social harm is also political because political pluralism, the basis of any democracy, is attacked. Any form of politically motivated violent extremism tries to condition politics through violence. The consequences of that sort of violent extremism on the population as a whole – regardless of its massive or systematic nature – might be less evident than those on direct victims. They include a general fear of participating in public or private life, or simply fear of relating to certain people (including police in the case of state terrorism) or moving around certain places or areas; a lack of participation in public affairs; the absence or difficulties of political representation of the ideas attacked; resentment towards certain social groups; and lack of social understanding of fundamental human rights, together with further conflicts in society, starting within families, groups of friends or work colleagues. Finally, eliminating or violating people's wellbeing through violence to achieve political ends impoverishes society as a whole, depriving it of both victims and the perpetrators who, to varying degrees, end up harmed by the exercise of violence.

In one of our restorative projects, the victims expressed their experience of political harm as follows (Varona, 2020, p 19):[4]

> 'It was not only against me and my family, it was against all citizens, and also against our system of living in democracy because the possibility of freedom of movement or freedom of expression was affected by an atmosphere of imposed fear, silence and actual violence.' (V-1)

> 'If the state is behind state terrorism, the whole system is discredited. They were torturing and killing their own citizens with public money, including those involved in terrorism whose guarantees, no matter the awful acts they had committed, should have been respected for their own value and also to avoid a spiral of resentment and justification of violence.' (V-2)

Individual victims are dehumanised because they are used as a mere channel through which violent extremist organisations want to transmit terror to the whole society, or to a large part of it, to put pressure on governments. Victims are treated as objects within the argument of their collateral character: the end justifies the means, and this violent ideology might make the processes of desistance and reintegration more difficult (Van der Heide, 2018; Garro, 2022). As will be later explained, restorative encounters might provide a chance to rehumanise the victim in the eyes of harm-doers[5] and the society.

Likewise, the fact that politically motivated violent extremism results in political harm implies its victims face heightened risk of continued instrumentalisation after the crime, for example, when they do not receive any solidarity or through secondary victimisation produced by the media or political parties in terms of manipulation or partisan use of their suffering under the notion of ideal victims (Christie, 1986; Maglione, 2017). This often leads to conflict or hierarchies of victims (for example, as seen in Spain among victims of Franco's regime, Euskadi Ta Askatasuna [ETA] or right-wing extremist groups). This constitutes a challenge for restorative encounters in this realm and precaution needs to be taken so that hierarchies of suffering, depending on who is the victim or the harm-doer, are avoided.

Therefore, if the harm is also political, RJ reparations must also address this dimension so that victims are acknowledged as full members of a community from which, one day, someone tried to exclude them. This idea reaches harm-doers too, and the parallel state duty to encourage their return to society as non-violent citizens. Even if they have committed severe victimisation, the legitimate violence of the state, through the *ius puniendi* (state power to punish), cannot operate with the logic of the criminal law of the enemy in the form of total exclusion (Gil, 2023; Maculan, 2023). This would be the ultimate victory of the monologue of extremist violence that draws on the political logic of Carl Schmitt, formulated at the end of the 1920s, dividing the world into friends and enemies, a logic that also favours the expansion and perpetuation of a state of exception or emergency (Agamben, 2005). Moreover, the friend-enemy logic supports the so-called terrorist calculation. The terrorist calculation aims to produce a state illegitimate violence reaction which ends delegitimising democratic institutions and transforming harm-doers into victims.

Thus, the political harm from political violence entails not only the attack on victims and society, but also to democratic pluralism, a complex notion itself in 'superdiversed societies' (Phillimore et al, 2017). Accordingly, RJ aligns with the humanity principle in criminal justice in reacting more peacefully to violence and recognising the possibility for all stakeholders (victims, offenders and society) to engage in a voluntary dialogue for reparation.

Balancing confidentiality and social echo to extend restorative justice beyond interpersonal relations

From its inception, RJ theory has stressed the three pillars needed in the restorative processes: victims, offenders and the community, but it has not reflected enough on the community's role as an indirect victim of political harm and participating stakeholder. Empirical evidence from RJ applied to other crimes and qualitative data from emerging projects in this field can be mentioned. Following the all-affected principle (Young, 2000), because the impact and legacy of political violence affects the whole population and different generations, RJ programmes in this field must involve the community as indirect victim and supporter for those directly affected. This might conflict with the confidentiality principle, understood as a guarantee for a safe space, allowing speaking frankly and with honesty so that public exposure is avoided. Of course, this confidentiality principle can be demanded of participating members of the community as well. Even if extending restorative conversations to large groups is likely problematic, diverse controlled formats for sharing and post-participating in restorative dialogues are possible, as the Encounter of the Encounters demonstrates (Varona, 2023).

RJ programmes have diversified since they started operating in Canada in the mid-1970s under the format of mediation. At first, they focused on minor offences involving juveniles, mainly in Anglo-Saxon countries, but they currently encompass all harm, criminal or not, of varying severity, on all continents (Zehr, 2004). Evidence demonstrates the need for qualified facilitators and an unhurried, intersectional perspective to prevent power imbalance in extreme cases (Wood and Suzuki, 2020). RJ evidence does not justify excluding specific crime categories (D'Souza and Shapland, 2023). However, one must consider the diverse penological impact and optimal timing when implementing RJ programmes, whether within or outside the criminal justice process.[6]

A relationship with the traditional criminal justice system seems critical because restorative values and principles contrast with those embedded within it. Every restorative process is guided by core values of truth through dialogue: justice to prevent or undo wrongs, solidarity to connect people and establish healthy relationships with respect to duties and rights, respect for human dignity, supporting the involvement of those affected in their own voice, and personal and social responsibility (European Forum for Restorative Justice, nd). Principles of restorative practice include the following: voluntary participation based on informed consent, direct and authentic communication; processes designed to fit the participants' needs, capabilities and culture, through non-judgemental and multipartial facilitation; and engagement in agreed actions (European Forum for Restorative Justice, nd).

According to evidence assessment (Why me?, 2019), in a RJ process, beyond political violence, the community would benefit indirectly from the improvement in the victims' wellbeing and perception of procedural justice, even if the result of the dialogue does not meet victims' expectations. It will also benefit from a reduction in repeat offending, although quantifying this in terms of disengagement and deradicalisation is challenging (Ruiz Yamuza and Ravagnani, 2018). Overall, RJ could reduce costs to the criminal justice system and other public services while improving public perception of the criminal justice system (Why me?, 2019). Emerging evidence also suggests that RJ could contribute to the prevention and mitigation of violent polarisation at local and regional levels (Radicalisation Awareness Network, 2019; Pausch, 2020; Gómez et al, 2021; Chapman, 2022).

These principles and evidence supporting RJ need to be reframed for political violence in every country and for the concrete case where it is being implemented. Most research on the effectiveness of RJ stems from Anglo-Saxon contexts, focusing on victims' and offenders' participation, their experience of restorative processes, and outcomes, rather than community involvement. Some studies indicate that victims participate to be heard, ask questions to facilitate healing, obtain reparations, and for prosocial purposes, like preventing further (re)offending or societal harm. RJ appears to address some victims' needs (for instance, recognition, respect, safety and restoration) through a tailored approach.

In some programmes (United Nations Office on Drugs and Crime, 2020b), participating members of the community (or family) are selected and invited to participate by the victim, the harm-doer or the facilitator, and they appear to do so willingly as part of professional or volunteer work or for the sake of supporting any of the key participants in restorative processes beyond bilateral mediation. In some restorative circles, facilitators ask the harmed and the harm-doer if anyone else should join the process, facilitating their inclusion. An offender may want to participate because they want to explain themselves and show the victim and community that they are more than their actions and have changed. Sometimes they seek to make amends and assist the victim, especially if the victim expresses a willingness to meet. In any case, there is an ongoing debate about the instrumental motivation in the process for the offender concerning potential penal or penitentiary benefits that should be clearly communicated to the participating victim and community in terms of the existent legality.

Once more, evidence in victimology shows that victimhood and recovery are complex processes that involve not only interpersonal relationships but also a mixture of personal and social reconstruction. At the same time, criminological evidence on desistance (Walgrave et al, 2021) also points out the need for individualised approaches that involve the merging process of micro-meso reconstruction.

Victims' needs: reparation through social prevention

According to the evidence[7] provided in cases of violent extremism by Biffi (2020, 2021), sometimes there is a need to do justice through understanding and sharing, instead of separating and dividing (Ouferroukh, 2020; European Forum for Restorative Justice, 2021). However, the number of cases that have gone through RJ is negligible so it should be concluded that there are no generalisable results. In some countries (Varona et al, 2016), there is evidence of the communities', offenders' and victims' interest for this form of justice in contrast with limited access to these kinds of programmes. The awareness of this fact demands more equality in access policies, at different moments, according to victims' rights and RJ standards (Milquet, 2019). Some restorative processes have been supported by public institutions, but others preferred to trust in the promotion and implementation of civil society, even if some public funds were available which should justify transparency and evaluation (Clément et al, 2021).

According to some studies (Tedeschi et al, 2018; Lynch, 2023), narratives and personal stories seem to be crucial in these processes and a trauma and post-traumatic growth approach. Support for participating stakeholders should also be provided because they challenge societal constructs of ideal victims or ideal combatants for certain groups in society. The craft of RJ and its unique and complementary tailored approach to the needs of all those affected (including the society for the political harm) should safeguard against the risk of uncritical standardisation and manipulation of participants for other systemic or political ends (Maglione, 2017; Radicalisation Awareness Network, 2023).

In these cases, RJ has shown that reparation of primary and secondary victimisation is needed, victims need the involvement of the community, and, in particular, of younger generations so that their testimonies, together with those of change by harm-doers, can bring to the forefront the principle of 'never again' as a way of reparation (Varona, 2021; Biffi, 2023). Here RJ faces a major problem because mutual understanding cannot mean justification of violence. Otherwise, violence could occur again when justified. At the same time, democracy admits the defence of any political idea, always with the premise of the abandonment of political violence. In this way, restorative encounters work with the notions of parrhesia and agonism (Bean, 2009). Living in a very diverse society, even polarised, does not have to mean political violence, particularly if critical thinking and listening to others' arguments and needs are valued in face-to-face encounters where all senses play a role (McClanahan and South, 2020). Agonism values disagreement to be open to different possibilities for organising society.

One of the ways to expose and criticise the partisan instrumentalisation of any victim of politically motivated violent extremism is to point out the obvious: the diversity of the victims (Alonso, 2020). This evidence is fundamental for a tailored approach in RJ. All victims share two things in common: none of them wanted to be a victim and none of them deserved to be a victim. In conversional spaces, violence justifications can be contrasted, and counter-narratives and transformative truths can emerge without avoiding non-violent conflicts. From the moment they were made victims, they had rights, and the state had responsibilities, as common goods compatible with the rights of the perpetrators and the parallel duties towards them. Some of those victims' rights, like those for truth, justice and memory, express needs (Barker and Dinisman, 2016) and prosocial interests of prevention and reparation that merge beyond individual interests (European Commission, nd). According to the testimony of a victim at one Encounter of the Encounters event: 'I needed what was not obvious. I needed to meet the person who killed my father to be able to escape from a prison of suffering and isolation to construct a better future without violence' (Varona, 2020, p 25).

Somehow, RJ processes operationalise mechanisms of agonistic moral engagement to counteract what Bandura called the mechanisms of selective moral disengagement. Bandura (2004) referred to the variability of moral conscience and its adaptation to the circumstances (and to the harmed subject), so that affection and care can be shown towards some fellow beings and not towards others. In relation to behaviour, moral justification, advantageous comparison and use of euphemisms are usually applied. Within the mechanisms related to responsibility, displacement and diffusion take place. The mechanism of distancing the causes from its effects also comes into play. Finally, reification and blaming of the victims can be observed. Together with other steps in rehabilitation and recovery, RJ offers conversations where those selective disengagement mechanisms present in society can be deactivated. Being confronted with victims' testimonies compels the harm-doer and witnesses to reconsider whether the ends justify the means and whether an idea holds more value than the unique life of a concrete person (Zweig, 2019). Restorative processes produce a certain journey through time, tracing the victim's path and those who dare to take accountability hand-in-hand with the community. When the victim is felt as a real and a concrete person, they are (re)humanised, and mechanisms of selective moral disengagement are much more difficult to apply in relation to past events that shape the present and the future.

Nevertheless, RJ cannot be identified with interpersonal or group therapy, though it may have therapeutic effects (Farber and Erez, 2023). If the need for justice claimed by victims, in the form of active accountability and guarantees of non-repetition, is not met, there is a real risk of instrumentalising victims. That risk could alternatively be interpreted as instrumentalising offenders for punitive drives, if RJ is conceived as a mandatory requirement for obtaining basic prisoners' rights (Varona, 2021).

Procedural justice emphasises the meaning of justice as a process for all stakeholders (Tyler, 1987), key to minimising the secondary victimisation produced by the penal and social response to violent extremism. According to research (Farber and Erez, 2023), procedural justice is related to the concepts of respect, control and participation, legitimacy, and trust. It also underlines a notion of inclusive social control over decision-making in relation to the ethics of care and human rights, and to the so-called interactional justice and the duties of solidarity and memory in the face of violent extremist victimisation, duties that also imply respect for the human rights of the perpetrators. Closely related to procedural justice (Marder and Wexler, 2021), therapeutical jurisprudence can be related to public health and the ethics of care. It is a psychological and pedagogical perspective on the impact of substantive and procedural law on the mental equilibrium and health of individuals, an issue that is particularly relevant for victims of violent extremism, harm-doers and society. The intervention of different professionals and of the criminal justice system as a whole must try to reduce or contain harm, in its different dimensions, through an integrated perspective, with a participatory approach when defining the underlying problems and their response, an issue that is part of the public interest in primary, secondary and tertiary prevention.

In research conducted over the years, RJ has been studied in relation to procedural and therapeutic justice as a medium- to long-term option that can better accommodate the needs of repairing the interdimensional harm produced by violent extremist victimisation, including helping create conditions for post-traumatic growth, understood as interacting individual and social dimensions (Van Camp and Wemmers, 2013). This dimension focuses on a change of vision regarding relationships with others, particularly with 'difficult others', those who have caused the primary and secondary victimisation. Not renouncing the ethical minimum of non-violence for politics in a democracy is comparable with avoiding demonising the political adversary. In the long run, this perspective promotes a vision of coexistence and social reconciliation.

Young generations as engaged post-witnesses, part of the conflict community

According to a technical report from the European Commission (Milquet, 2019), reparation entails various interconnected elements relating to restitution, compensation, support, recognition, truth and guarantees of non-repetition, that is, prevention. In our restorative projects, victims show interest in the participation of young people as post-witnesses (Schult and Popescu, 2015). This provides evidence for the relationship between prevention and reparation in restorative processes, but also for the victims' need to avoid epistemic injustice. Victim testimonies require active, receptive listeners to validate what they have endured. From the perspective of linguistic pragmatics, Miranda Fricker (2017) refers to 'epistemic injustice' as a process produced when a subject's capacity to transmit knowledge and give meaning to their social experiences is negated, for example, because of political violence. Fricker analyses and demonstrates the detrimental impact derived when a subject's discourse is discredited for reasons unrelated to its content. Fricker identifies two types of epistemic injustice: testimonial injustice, produced when an audience discredits a speaker due to prejudice, and hermeneutic injustice, which occurs when a collective lacks the interpretive resources to comprehend the speaker's social experience, thereby placing the speaker at a disadvantage and reducing their credibility. These two processes underscore the intricate relationship between power and ethics. The question we must consider is to what extent younger generations can understand the testimonies of victims and ex-offenders in a humane and contextually meaningful way.

According to one young student participating in RJ projects:

> It is only listening to victims and their direct or indirect dialogue with violence and offenders, that we understand the long and irreparable impact of violence. They want us to remember, in a sort of

restorative memory. It is not only they narrating, it is they questioning us, it is we questioning ourselves about the legitimation of violence after being aware of their devastating and useless consequences as expressed by victims and ex-offenders. (Varona, 2023, p 269)

These ideas can be integrated within the framework of conversational victimology (Varona, 2023). A conversational victimology questions the sufficiency of current victimisation surveys, which are focused on quantitative aspects, since they do not allow us to understand victimisation experiences, which are largely hidden, always subjective, and difficult to classify or reduce into watertight categories (Cook and Walklate, 2020). In this sense, conversational victimology is related to critical theory by seeking to connect individual aspects with social and structural ones to study how the events experienced are understood and narrated, integrating subjective and objective, intimate, interpersonal and group dimensions, with respect to the condition of being a victim, a critical concept that cannot be confused with victimisation.

Ultimately, conversational victimology is an exercise in exploring the concepts of victimisation and victimhood, approached in a complex and dynamic way, where individual agency and structure play an interactive role. As expressed by Pemberton and colleagues (2019), a narrative victimological approach would complement individual agency with the community and the context, and the act of speaking and listening. A conversational victimology, with different stakeholders talking respectfully, would allow us to critically reflect on harm and resistance to it, as well as on personal and collective responsibility.

In the face of cumulative, primary and secondary victimisation (Stauffer, 2015; Holder, 2018), conversational victimology reveals complex stories of suffering, intertwined with processes of resistance and resilience (Stephens, 2021). Only by reinterpreting the notion of resilience as a change of values can it acquire an emancipatory, individual and social sense, as life is forced to transform itself, even within a culture of violence. For some authors (Plough, 2021), to speak of community resilience implies valuing the narratives that exemplify how to act critically in an unconventional way in the face of existing conditions. Resilience, like resistance or emancipation, involves highly variable and diverse processes that call into question the classical notions of crime and harm. It also questions the paternalistic, pathologising essentialist and antagonistic conceptions of victims, which risk idealising or demonising them and, therefore, dehumanising and manipulating them, which can also happen when offenders are classified as abnormal subjects or monsters.

With a certain reductionist character in a study with victims, Discola (2021) classifies the narratives of indirect murder victims into three types: the victim, the survivor, and the transcendent. These narratives can be related to the passage of time (Crawford, 2015; De Haan and Destrooper, 2021), where, at the beginning, their rage appears in response to the injustice suffered, that, with time, requires knowing the truth and demanding the assumption of responsibilities. The survivor is in another phase of searching for meaning and fighting for justice, in this case together with other survivors, while the transcendent seeks to live in such a way that he can get something good out of so much unjust suffering and not be trapped in it. In different understandings, a transcending victim affirms that, despite everything and even with suffering, life is worthwhile for everyone, and attempts to contribute to society to prevent what happened to them from happening again. Transcendent narratives seem to be more general, encompassing more people, more issues and more time segments, and could be related to the concept of post-traumatic growth in enlarged processes of RJ, only if complexity is considered and notions of ideal victims, offenders and communities are rejected.

A victim participating in an RJ encounter (Varona, 2020) recalled how, at that time, being a widow of a politically motivated murder meant dealing with fear and indifference. She indicated that, at that time and still today, she did not only expect something from the law and the courts of justice, but also from society. Therefore, she highlighted the importance of remembering with society, of youth memory. She also wondered how to punish and forgive the irreparability of a life taken away, with all that that has meant for the people affected. Entering the subject of forgiveness (Pemberton, 2014), something optional in RJ and with a great diversity of opinions on the part of the participating victims, "For me the important thing is to have raised my children without transmitting hatred. That is more important than forgiveness. The possibility of living together is the relevant issue" (V-3).

Other recent victims of jihadist violence in France speak in a similar vein about personal reconstruction through social anchoring (Lançon, 2019; Naudin, 2020; Salines and Amimour, 2020). Similarly, considering evidence on the sensitive relationship of victim recovery and social reconstruction processes in other crimes, Loofbourow (2020) points out that society's questions about perpetrators tend to be directed towards the future (for example, 'Will he be stopped?', 'Will he be convicted?'), while questions about victims tend to focus on the past (for instance, 'How did it happen?', 'What did the victim do?'). In the end, both society and research lack sufficient vocabulary to understand not only the moment of the immediate victimisation, but also its aftermath. Although victims' testimonies do not change power structures (Radicalisation Awareness Network, 2020), they do serve to facilitate new intergenerational and preventive spaces where they can be expressed, heard and, perhaps, considered for ongoing social grief and a 'post-traumatic future' (Loofbourow, 2020).

From victimological studies, it can be observed that many victims of serious crimes have shown a capacity for peaceful coexistence, offering keys to integrate in a preventive and reparative way the meaning of the elimination of lives and injustice, as well as the opportunity to respond to ethical loneliness (Stauffer, 2015), marked by epistemic, testimonial and hermeneutic injustice (Fricker, 2017), aspects to be considered in a far-reaching process of social, cultural and political reparation. In this sense, having different narratives of victims, in all their diversity and dynamics, offers the possibility of an intergenerational conversation with them, to reach a situated understanding, though their perspectives might not be shared. However, as mentioned before, to be able to listen, the speaker must be trusted at some level and should adhere to a basic ethical stance of non-violence. In other words, questioning violence in its multifold forms should be shared.

Encouraging victims, ex-offenders and communities to express themselves and be understood entails an act of justice that aligns with the empirically contrasted idea of 'kaleidoscopic justice' (McGlynn and Westmarland, 2019), which is: constantly refracted in the face of new circumstances, experiences and understandings; non-linear (with multiple beginnings and endings); complex, nuanced and difficult to predetermine; a living experience and a changing process, rather than an outcome, thus requiring conversation about consequences, recognition, one's experience, dignity, prevention and citizenship in terms of human rights. RJ seems to offer conditions for suspending an uncomfortable and accelerated present time, taking it back in an ongoing commitment towards non-violence (Baldoli, 2020).

Challenges in the involvement of young generations in restorative processes to prevent further political violence

Drawing from the experience of the Basque Country (Zernova, 2019; Varona, 2021), which did not provide any prescriptions due to the tailored approach needed, certain issues must be addressed when initiating a RJ project involving young people as part of the conflict community in political violence,

- Can young people initiate and have access to RJ projects of this kind?
- What are the requirements for participation in terms of age or attitude towards violence? How many young people should participate in every process? Is there a balance in terms of gender (Rothermel, 2020) and other characteristics?
- What is their role during the whole process?
- How to value dissent and understanding? How to avoid justification of violence while promoting empathy and contextualisation?
- How to manage different agendas in terms of time?
- How is the confidentiality principle implemented?
- What happens if they want to stop participating?
- How are the preparatory meetings organised with the young people to avoid secondary victimisation or stigmatisation?
- In what sense are the participating youth representing the young community or future generations?
- What is the role of public institutions and civil society?

- How are the facilitators selected? What is their cultural and professional background? Do they have intercultural, intersectional and intergenerational training and supervision?
- How are the restorative processes implemented and supervised (follow-up of potential agreements)?
- How is the process related to the justice system, if so?
- Considering the rights of both offenders and victims, as well as democratic values, is there any risk of punitivism? Similarly, is there any risk of impunity?
- Is the programme being evaluated?
- What is the relationship between public opinion and the media?

Restorative cities for promoting peaceful and just democracies

RJ makes it possible to humanise the direct and indirect victims, and also harm-doers, to give them a face, to start a transformation process from the injustice experienced and not only from the breach of the abstract criminal norm, making possible agency that reverses the instrumentalisation of innocent victims used as a channel for the monologue of violence. However, in these cases, RJ not only attempts to start from the concreteness and individualisation of the injustice, giving voice to the most affected, but also to rethink the multiple dimensions of harm produced, including the social and political harm, even when some segments of society may not perceive those. At the same time, we should not understand RJ as a private bilateral mediation between victim and offender or as therapy.

If we focus on the 2021 Basque Country announcement of a restorative penitentiary model, after the Basque government assumed the prisons competences and after the progressive approach of ETA prisoners to Basque prisons, the Collective of Victims of Terrorism of the Basque Country (COVITE, 2021) published a manifesto entitled *Potentiality of Restorative Justice and Restorative Messages for Victims* (Varona, 2022). In this manifesto, COVITE (2021) recognised that 'restorative justice is bidirectional, it must repair both the convicted and the victim' (p 3), but emphasised the need to delegitimise all kinds of violence. Consequently, RJ can be considered a social movement extending beyond criminal justice that should encompass the possibility of educational and community learning throughout society.

In this line of thought, it is interesting to consider the possibility of working on reparation processes for victims of violent extremism within the framework of the network of restorative municipalities promoted by the European Forum for Restorative Justice (Mannozzi, 2019). This idea would require social and institutional support from local authorities and other entities to materialise a concrete possibility to improve local living together. This is feasible through the creation and strengthening of capacities for the use of a restorative approach in everyday life, favouring dialogue on local needs regarding conflictive or hidden but latent risky issues, while facilitating access to RJ in different contexts. In short, a network of restorative cities or municipalities would allow us to address the deeply relational nature of the concept of justice in its different dimensions – not only criminal but also social, delving into the relational complexity of restorative practices to transform everyday life more effectively and with respect to human rights. This would support the capacities for solidarity and cooperation in the face of conflicts and violence, in a relational understanding of justice, to ensure non-violent and less harmful responses to conflicts as a way of prevention, intervention and response (Khalil et al, 2022; Varona, 2022).

Summary

- The value of restorative dialogues must be consistently (re)created across generations, particularly in violently polarised societies.
- Restorative conversations provide a framework for transforming narratives. This requires the involvement of 'difficult others' and participants from the community affected by violence or conflict, driven by the victims' needs and incorporated appropriately into the RJ process.
- Growing evidence demonstrates the positive impact of enhanced restorative encounters in polarised societies recovering from political violence.
- A comprehensive approach, addressing individual, social and cultural reconstruction is necessary as part of the recovery process after violence.

- By amplifying the voices of victims and facilitating conversations between them, ex-offenders and young people, we can challenge the cultural legitimisation and prestige associated with violence.
- The delicate task of respecting individual timelines and autonomy while avoiding the construction of 'ideal victims, (ex) offenders and communities' in standardised RJ processes is crucial.
- Contextualisation is needed, as well as parrhesia (frank speech) and agonism (constructive conflict) in democracy and RJ. However, victims demand a firm stance against the justification of violence, irrespective of its political leanings or whether it stems from violent extremist groups, including any illegitimate form of state reaction.
- Restorative conversations can enhance societal awareness of persistent mechanisms of selective moral disengagement and propose proportionate alternatives for expanded moral engagement.
- Further exploration is needed to promote networks of restorative cities, leading to practical actions in this field.

Suggested directions for future research

The following questions can orient further research and discussion in the area:

- In what sense can RJ merge prevention and reparation of radicalisation and violent extremism?
- How can we complement quantitative and qualitative evidence to develop intergenerational RJ circles?
- What are the benefits of RJ in cases where violence keeps going on and has not stopped, and how can we minimise potential risks?

Notes

[1] The United Nations (United Nations Office on Drugs and Crime, 2020b) defines 'restorative justice' as the use of restorative processes to achieve restorative outcomes. A 'restorative process', including conferences and

circles, is any process in which the victim, the offender and, where appropriate, any other person or member of the community participate together actively in the resolution of issues arising from the crime (including political harm), usually with the help of a facilitator. A restorative outcome is an agreement reached as a result of a restorative process. Such an agreement may include responses and programmes such as reparation, restitution and community service, aimed at meeting the individual and collective needs and responsibilities of the persons involved to achieve the reintegration of the victim and offender.

2   In this chapter, 'society' is equivalent to 'community' without entering the *Gesellschaft-Gemeinschaft* socio-legal debate, full of nuances in different cultures and languages. Occasionally, 'community' refers to the most affected closer society, beyond victim and offender, independent of its common bonds (Bradshaw, 2008).

3   As Biffi (2023) explains, during the July 2018 Criminal Justice Summer Course organised by the Criminal Justice Platform Europe and focused on radicalisation and violent extremism, the European Forum for Restorative Justice (EFRJ) Secretariat invited Claudia Mazzucato, Guido Bertagna (Bertagna et al, 2015) and Gema Varona as trainers. Beyond the Basque and Italian cases, other potential participants were contacted: Tim Chapman (2018), who has facilitated restorative dialogues between Catholics and Protestants in Northern Ireland (Eriksson, 2015), and Robi Damelin, one of the activists of the Parents Circle Families Forum involved in the ongoing Israeli–Palestinian conflict. The first Encounter of the Encounters was held in San Sebastián, Spain, in September 2019, with people participating as victims, survivors and ex-offenders, some with the support or participation of family members, and young people (university students selected by every national group coordinator – and in 2021 and 2022, four young Italian interpreters, and a Ukrainian refugee), restorative justice facilitators and restorative justice researchers, including attendees from Germany and Belgium. In 2021, due to the COVID-19 pandemic, there was a second meeting of the Encounter of the Encounters online and, in 2022, three face-to-face encounters: a smaller one during the International Symposium of Victimology in San Sebastián and two larger ones during the EFRJ Conference and a specific event at the University of the Sacre Cuore of Milano. At the end of 2023, the sixth was programmed in San Sebastián. Restorative dialogues were opened to the general public in these three last encounters. The conversation was also amplified using collaborative art with the help of the Scottish restorative justice facilitator, Clair Aldington, who participated in the entire project.

4   Author's translations from Spanish and Basque.

5   Following some restorative justice trends, the term 'harm-doer' in this text is equivalent to 'offender' or 'responsible person'.

6   Most serious crimes usually require a relatively long time in prison (Weimann-Saks and Peleg-Koriat, 2020). However, this may not apply where a case is under the statute of limitations, the offender has not been sentenced or, in general, during transitional justice processes.

[7] The lack of scientific evidence is also attributable to this confidentiality principle in usually controversial political violence (Pascual and Ríos, 2014). This also happens with other sensitive crimes, like institutional sexual victimisation.

References

Agamben, G. (2005) *State of Exception*, Chicago: University of Chicago Press.

Alonso, M. (2020) 'Víctimas del franquismo, víctimas del terrorismo. ¿Es procedente adjetivar a las víctimas?' ['Victims of Francoism, victims of terrorism. Is it appropriate to adjective the victims?'], Conference at the X Encuentro victimológico en memoria del profesor Antonio Beristain, 26 November, Basque Institute of Criminology, Donostia/San Sebastián (unpublished paper).

Baldoli, R. (2020) 'Fighting terrorism with nonviolence: An ideological perspective', *Critical Studies on Terrorism*, 13(3): 464–84.

Bandura, A. (2004) 'The role of selective moral disengagement in terrorism and counterterrorism', in F.M. Moghaddam and A.J. Marsella (eds) *Understanding Terrorism: Psychosocial Roots, Consequences, and Interventions*, Washington, DC: American Psychological Association, pp 121–50.

Barker, A. and Dinisman, T. (2016) *Meeting the Needs of Survivors and Families Bereaved through Terrorism*, London: Victim Support England and Wales.

Bean, H. (2009) '"A complicated and frustrating dance": National security reform, the limits of parrhesia, and the case of the 9/11 Families', *Rhetoric & Public Affairs*, 12(3): 429–59.

Bertagna, G., Ceretti, A. and Mazzucato, C. (2015) *Il Libro dell'Incontro: Vittime e Responsabili della Lotta Armata a Confronto* [*The Book of the Encounter: Victims and those Responsible for the Armed Struggle Compared*], Milan: ilSaggiatore.

Biffi, E. (2020) 'The role of restorative justice in preventing and responding to violent extremism', *RAN*. Available from https://ec.europa.eu/home-affairs/pages/page/ran-rvt-ran-exit-role-restorative-justice-preventing-and-responding-violent-extremism-dublin-03-04_en [Accessed 25 April 2023].

Biffi, E. (2021) 'The potential of restorative justice in cases of violent extremism and terrorism', *RAN*. Available from https://home-affairs.ec.europa.eu/system/files/2021-03/ran_cons_overv_pap_restor_just_pcve_vot_10022021_en.pdf [Accessed 25 April 2023].

Biffi, E. (2023) 'The encounter of the encounters: Restorative dialogues with witnesses of political violence and violent extremism', *European Forum for Restorative Justice*. Available from https://www.euforumrj.org/en/encounter-encounters [Accessed 25 April 2023].

Bradshaw, T.K. (2008) 'The post-place community: Contributions to the debate about the definition of community', *Community Development*, 39(1): 5–16.

Chapman, T. (2018) ' "Nobody has ever asked me these questions": Engaging restoratively with politically motivated prisoners in Northern Ireland', in O. Lynch and J. Argomaniz (eds) *Victims and Perpetrators of Terrorism: Exploring Identities, Roles and Narratives*, London: Routledge, pp 181–96.

Chapman, T. (2022) 'Restorative justice, an approach that contributes to the prevention and mitigation of polarisation at the local and regional level', *European Forum for Urban Security*. Available from https://efus.eu/topics/restorative-justice-an-approach-that-contributes-to-the-prevention-and-mitigation-of-polarisation-at-the-local-and-regional-level-by-tim-chapman/ [Accessed 10 April 2023].

Christie, N. (1986) 'The ideal victim', in E. Fattah (ed) *From Crime Policy to Victim Policy: Reorienting the Justice System*, Basingstoke: Macmillan, pp 17–30.

Clément, P.-A., Madriaza, P. and Morin, D. (2021) *Constraints and Opportunities in Evaluating Programs for Prevention of Violent Extremism: How the Practitioners See It*, Sherbrooke: UNESCO Chair in Prevention of Radicalisation and Violent Extremism, Sherbrooke University.

Cook, E.A. and Walklate, S. (2020) 'Excavating victim stories: Making sense of agency, suffering and redemption', in J. Fleetwood, L. Presser, S. Sanberg and T. Ugelvik (eds) *The Emerald Handbook of Narrative Criminology*, Bingley: Emerald Publishing, pp 239–57.

Cortina, A. (2017) 'El vigor de la razón dialógica' ['The strength of dialogic reason'], *El País. Babelia*, 27 May, p 22.

COVITE (2021) *Potencialidad de la Justicia Restaurativa y Mensajes Restauradores para las Víctimas* [*Restorative Justice's Potential and Restorative Messages for Victims*], San Sebastián: COVITE.

Crawford, A. (2015) 'Temporality in restorative justice: On time, timing and time-consciousness', *Theoretical Criminology*, 19(4): 470–90.

D'Souza, N. and Shapland, J. (2023) 'The exclusion of serious and organised offenders and their victims from the offer of restorative justice: Should this be so and what happens when the offer is put on the table?', *Criminology & Criminal Justice*, 23(1): 60–77.

De Haan, M. and Destrooper, T. (2021) 'Using restorative justice to rethink the temporality of transition in Chile', *The International Journal of Restorative Justice*, 4(2): 206–28.

Discola, K.L. (2021) 'Emerging narratives in the wake of homicide: Victim, survivor and transcender', *Journal of Victimology and Victim Justice*, 3(2): 202–18.

Eriksson, A. (2015) 'Restorative justice in the Northern Ireland transition', in A.M. McAlinden and C. Dwyer (eds) *Criminal Justice Transition: The Northern Ireland Context*, Oxford: Hart Publishing, pp 341–61.

European Commission (nd) 'Victims/Survivors of Terrorism Working Group (RAN VoT)', *European Commission*. Available from https://home-affairs.ec.europa.eu/networks/radicalisation-awareness-network-ran/topics-and-working-groups/ran-vot_en [Accessed 30 April 2023].

European Forum for Restorative Justice (2008) *Victims of Terrorism: Towards European Standards for Assistance. EU-Funded Project: Literature Review*, Leuven: EFRJ.

European Forum for Restorative Justice (2021) *Restorative Justice in Cases of Violent Extremism and Hate Crimes*, Leuven: EFRJ.

European Forum for Restorative Justice (nd) 'Why restorative justice matters?', *European Forum for Restorative Justice*. Available from https://www.euforumrj.org/en [Accessed 25 April 2023].

Farber, S. and Erez, E. (2023) 'Procedural justice, therapeutic jurisprudence, and reoffending: Adjudicating Palestinian minors in the West Bank's Military Court', *International Journal of Offender Therapy and Comparative Criminology*, 67(15): 1581–6.

Ford, K. (2020) 'A peace studies approach to countering extremism: Do counter-extremism strategies produce peace?', in A. Martini, K. Ford and R. Jackson (eds) *Encountering Extremism. Theoretical Issues and Local Challenges*, Manchester: Manchester University Press, pp 116–35.

Fricker, M. (2017) 'Evolving concepts of epistemic injustice', in I.J. Kidd, J. Medina and G. Pohlhaus Jr. (eds) *Routledge Hndbook of Epistemic Injustice*, London: Routledge, pp 53–60.

Garro, E. (2022) 'Penal policies and terrorist offenders in Spain: A matter of recidivism risk assessment or a matter of de-radicalisation?', in C. Walker, M. Llobet Anglí and M.C. Meliá (eds) *Precursor Crimes of Terrorism: The Criminalisation of Terrorism Risk in Comparative Perspective*, Cheltenham: Edward Elgar, pp 304–15.

Gil, A.G. (2023) 'Extreme legislation and practice against jihadist terrorism in the European Union: The Spanish case', *EuCLR European Criminal Law Review*, 13(1): 53–74.

Gómez, Á., Martínez, M., Martel, F.A., López-Rodríguez, L., Vázquez, A., Chinchilla, J., et al (2021) 'Why people enter and embrace violent groups', *Frontiers in Psychology*, 11: 614657.

Heath-Kelly, C. and Shanaah, S. (2022) 'Rehabilitation within pre-crime interventions: The hybrid criminology of social crime prevention and countering violent extremism', *Theoretical Criminology*, 27(2): 183–203.

Holder, R. (2018) *Just Interests: Victims, Citizens and the Potential for Justice*, Cheltenham: Edward Elgar.

Ivison, D. (2023) 'Democratic trust and injustice', *Journal of Social and Political Philosophy*, 2(1): 78–94.

Khalil, J., Horgan, J. and Zeuthen, M. (2022) 'The attitudes-behaviors corrective (ABC) model of violent extremism', *Terrorism and Political Violence*, 34(3): 425–50.

Lançon, P. (2019) *El Colgajo* [*The Flap*], Barcelona: Anagrama.

Loofbourow, L. (2020) 'The post-traumatic novel', *The New York Review of Books*, 12 March. Available from https://www.nybooks.com/contributors/lili-loofbourow/ [Accessed 25 April 2023].

Lynch, O. (2023) 'Victims and victimhood: The case of terrorism and political violence', in L. Frumkin, J. Morrison and A. Silke (eds) *A Research Agenda for Terrorism Studies*, Cheltenham: Edward Elgar, pp 43–61.

Maculan, E. (2023) *Realidad Penitenciaria y 'Utopía' Restaurativa en las Condenas por Delitos de Terrorismo* [*Penitentiary Reality and Restorative 'Utopia' in Convictions for Terrorist Crimes*], Madrid: Dykinson.

Maglione, G. (2017) 'Embodied victims: An archaeology of the "ideal victim" of restorative justice', *Criminology & Criminal Justice*, 17(4): 401–17.

Mannozzi, G. (2019) 'The emergence of the idea of a restorative city and its link to restorative justice', *The International Journal of Restorative Justice*, 2(2): 288–92.

Marder, I.D. and Wexler, D.B. (2021) 'Mainstreaming restorative justice and therapeutic jurisprudence through higher education', *University of Baltimore Law Review*, 50(3): 398–424.

McClanahan, B. and South, N. (2020) '"All knowledge begins with the senses": Towards a sensory criminology', *The British Journal of Criminology*, 60(1): 3–23.

McGlynn, C. and Westmarland, N. (2019) 'Kaleidoscopic justice: Sexual violence and victim-survivors' perceptions of justice', *Social & Legal Studies*, 28(2): 179–201.

Milquet, J. (2019) *Strengthening Victims' Rights: From Compensation to Reparation*, Luxembourg: European Commission.

Naudin, C. (2020) *Journal d'un Rescapé du Bataclan: Etre Historien et Victime d'Attentat* [*Diary of a Bataclan Survivor: Being a Historian and Victim of the Attack*], Montreuil: Libertalia.

Orofino, E. and Allchorn, W. (eds) (2023) *Handbook of Non-Violent Extremism Groups, Perspectives and New Debates*, London: Routledge.

Ouferroukh, H. (2020) 'The role of restorative justice in preventing and responding to violent extremism', *RAN*. Available from http://www.antoniocasella.eu/restorative/RAN_rj_Ireland_14jan20.pdf [Accessed 30 April 2023].

Pascual, E. and Ríos, J. (2014) 'Reflexiones desde los encuentros restaurativos entre víctimas y condenados por delitos de terrorismo' ['Reflections from the restorative encounters between victims and those convicted of terrorism crimes'], *Oñati Socio-Legal Series*, 4(3): 427–42.

Pausch, M. (2020) 'Polarisation in pluralist democracies: Considerations about a complex phenomenon', in *Bridge Project. Building Resilience to Reduce Polarisation and Growing Extremism, European Forum for Urban Security*. Available from https://efus.eu/tag/bridge-en/ [Accessed 30 April 2023].

Pemberton, A. (2014) 'Terrorism, forgiveness and restorative justice', *Oñati Socio-Legal Series*, 4(3): 369–89.

Pemberton, A., Mulder, E. and Aarten, P.G. (2019) 'Stories of injustice: Towards a narrative victimology', *European Journal of Criminology*, 16(4): 391–412.

Phillimore, J., Sigona, N. and Tonkiss, K. (2017) 'Introduction: Superdiversity, policy and governance in Europe', *Policy & Politics*, 45(4): 487–91.

Plough, A.L. (ed) (2021) *Community Resilience: Equitable Practices for an Uncertain Future*, New York: Oxford University Press.

Radicalisation Awareness Network (2019) 'Preventing radicalisation to terrorism and violent extremism: Delivering counter or alternative narratives', *RAN*. Available from https://home-affairs.ec.europa.eu/networks/radicalisation-awareness-network-ran/collection-inspiring-practices_en [Accessed 26 April 2023].

Radicalisation Awareness Network (2020) *Handbook: Voices of Victims of Terrorism*, Brussels: RAN.

Radicalisation Awareness Network (2023) 'Involving victims/survivors in P/CVE', *RAN*. Available from https://home-affairs.ec.europa.eu/system/files/2023-04/ran_paper_involving_vot_in_pcve_29-30092022.pdf [Accessed 26 April 2023].

Rothermel, A.K. (2020) 'Gender in the United Nations' agenda on preventing and countering violent extremism', *International Feminist Journal of Politics*, 22(5): 720–41.

Ruiz Yamuza, F.G. and Ravagnani, L. (2018) 'Countering Islamic radicalisation in prison through restorative justice-based programmes', *ERA Forum*, 18: 611–26.

Salines, G. and Amimour, A. (2020) *Il Nous Reste les Mots [We Have the Words Left]*, Paris: Robert Laffont.

Schult, T. and Popescu, D.I. (eds) (2015) *Revisiting Holocaust Representation in the Post-Witness Era*, Basingstoke: Palgrave Macmillan.

Stauffer, J. (2015) *Ethical Loneliness: The Injustice of Not Being Heard*, New York: Columbia University Press.

Stephens, W. (2021) *Arranging Resilience: The Role of Social Actors in Preventing Violent Extremism*, The Hague: Eleven.

Taylor, S. (2023) 'Status quo terrorism: State-terrorism in South Africa during apartheid', *Terrorism and Political Violence*, 35(2): 304–20.

Tedeschi, R.G., Shakespeare-Finch, J., Taku, K. and Calhoun, L.G. (2018) *Posttraumatic Growth: Theory, Research, and Applications*, London: Routledge.

Thijssen, G., Masthoff, E., Sijtsema, J.J. and Bogaerts, S. (2023) 'Understanding violent extremism: Identifying motivational classes in male jihadist detainees', *International Journal of Offender Therapy and Comparative Criminology*, 67(15): 1455–73.

Tyler, T. (1987) 'Procedural justice: Future directions', *Social Justice Research*, 1: 41–65.

UNESCO (nd) 'Preventing violent extremism', *UNESCO*. Available from https://www.unesco.org/en/preventing-violent-extremism?TSPD_101_R0=080713870fab2000c7bc47ff2 92f14c56f6c918d1f86371d05122170ffcb9c742a25b1fc3aa6d79 608af15af34143000d4c8a6c74e820475b788f056a376165f8d03 b4f8851511b8ba59d2ac70273da0dd2bcde7ed6870cbe2133fea7 e430f42 [Accessed 29 October 2023].

United Nations Office on Drugs and Crime (2020a) *From Victims of Terrorism to Messengers for Peace: A Strategic Approach*, Vienna: UNODC.

United Nations Office on Drugs and Crime (2020b) *Handbook on Restorative Justice Programmes* (2nd edn), Vienna: UNODC.

Van Camp, T. and Wemmers, J. A. (2013) 'Victim satisfaction with restorative justice: More than simply procedural justice', *International Review of Victimology*, 19(2): 117–43.

Van der Heide, L. (2018) 'Ideology matters: Why we cannot afford to ignore the role of ideology in dealing with terrorism', *Penal Reform International*, 3 April. Available from https://www.penalreform.org/blog/ideology-matters-why-we-cannot-afford-to-ignore/ [Accessed 30 April 2023].

Varona, G. (ed) (2020) *Caminando Restaurativamente: Pasos para Diseñar Proyectos Transformadores Alrededor de la Justicia Penal* [*Walking Restoratively: Steps to Design Transformative Projects Around Criminal Justice*], Madrid: Dykinson.

Varona, G. (2021) 'La red de encuentros restaurativos en casos de terrorismo. Eco social de un proyecto internacional' ['The network of restorative encounters in cases of terrorism. Social echo of an international project'], *Revista de Derecho Penal y Criminología*, 26: 203–35.

Varona, G. (ed) (2022) *Resiliencia y Crecimiento Postraumático Individual y Social. El Eco de la Justicia Restaurativa, en Particular en Víctimas de Terrorismo y la Violencia Política* [*Resilience and Posttraumatic Individual and Social Growth. The Echo of Restorative Justice, Particularly for Victims of Terrorism and Political Violence*], Barcelona: Huygens.

Varona, G. (2023) 'Afterword: Conversational victimology in a wounded planet', in G. Varona, *Victimology and Violence: Connecting with Victims*, Cizur Menor: Arazadi, pp 277–84.

Varona, G., De la Cuesta, J.L. and Echeburúa, E. (2016) 'Víctimas del terrorismo en el País Vasco: paradojas de sus expectativas y demandas en el fin de ETA' ['Victims of terrorism in the Basque Country: Paradoxes of their expectations and demands in the end of ETA'], *Revista de Victimología/Journal of Victimology*, 3: 65–84.

Walgrave, L. (2015) 'Domestic terrorism: A challenge for restorative justice', *Restorative Justice*, 3(2): 282–90.

Walgrave, L., Ward, T. and Zinsstag, E. (2021) 'When restorative justice meets the Good Lives Model: Contributing to a criminology of trust', *European Journal of Criminology*, 18(3): 444–60.

Weimann-Saks, D. and Peleg-Koriat, I. (2020) 'Promoting inmates' positive attitudes toward participating in a restorative justice process: The effects of a victim awareness process', *The Prison Journal*, 100(3): 381–98.

Why me? (2019) *Evidence from Restorative Justice*, London: Why me?

Wood, W.R. and Suzuki, M. (2020) 'Are conflicts property? Re-examining the ownership of conflict in restorative justice', *Social & Legal Studies*, 29(6): 903–24.

Young, I.M. (2000) *Inclusion and Democracy*, Oxford: Oxford University Press.

Zehr, H. (2004) 'Commentary: Restorative justice: Beyond victim-offender mediation', *Conflict Resolution Quarterly*, 22: 305–15.

Zernova, M. (2019) 'Restorative justice in the aftermath of politically-motivated violence: the Basque experience', *Critical Studies on Terrorism*, 12(4): 649–72.

Zweig, S. (2019) *The Right to Heresy: Castellio Against Calvin*, Lexington: Plunkett Lake Press.

PART IV

Thinking critically about evidence-based practice

8

Role of academic researchers in preventing and countering violent extremism policy and practice

Leena Malkki and Irina van der Vet

Introduction

It is virtually universally agreed that effective policies and practices to prevent and counter violent extremism (P/CVE) require multisectoral and multiprofessional cooperation. Cooperation of different actors, such as law enforcement, governmental authorities, non-governmental organisations and public institutions, has become a key feature of P/CVE policies in many EU member states. Some P/CVE initiatives are built upon the designed partnership models, such as the well-known Aarhus model in Denmark (Hemmingsen, 2015). Such models are typically described and highlighted in the national P/CVE policies and strategies. For example, the Belgian counter-terrorism policy arrangement in Strategy T.E.R. (former Plan R) showcases the evolvement of such partnerships and their role in the information exchange and data gathering in both operative and preventive actions at state, regional and municipal levels (Strategic Note, 2023). It details the chain of all the actors involved, including schools, social workers and event sport clubs, where the data might reside. The Finnish National Action Plan (Ministry of the Interior, 2019a), on its part, highlights the Anchor work, a multiprofessional model which brings police officers, social workers, psychiatric nurses and youth workers together to work on, among others, cases of radicalisation. Many sectors are also often represented in groups and networks which plan and monitor the implementation of P/CVE policies.

The multiprofessional and multi-agency cooperation and policy planning typically involves law enforcement and other first-line practitioners such as social workers, mental health professionals and sometimes educators and youth workers. At the same time, academic researchers (especially those based at universities, which are the focus of this chapter) are not equally represented in these cooperation networks and models. While they have been actively invited, for example, to the activities of the Radicalisation Awareness Network (RAN), their role in national and local cooperation networks has been very uneven, often relatively minor or even non-existent. This would seem to be in contraction with the high value given to the use of evidence and scientific knowledge in policy making and practice, especially when it comes to complex 'wicked problems', which radicalisation to violent extremism undeniably is. The importance of cooperation between researchers, policy makers and practitioners, and the challenges involved in it, have been underlined several times (see, for example, Ranstorp, 2018), but there have so far been few elaborations about various forms that the relationship between researchers and those involved in P/CVE policy and practice may take.

This chapter attempts to underpin the position of academia in the P/CVE policy making and practice, describe perceived obstacles to the use of academic research and participation of academic researchers in related policy networks, as well as identify possibilities for an increased role of academic research in this policy field. It does not pretend to provide a comprehensive overview of this matter but rather inspires more conversation about the role of academic research and researchers in the P/CVE field.

The aim is to move towards a more refined discussion which acknowledges diversity in collaboration. There are various ways in which academic researchers can support and be involved in P/CVE policy and practice, and the challenges and possibilities of such cooperation also vary significantly depending on the form of engagement.

The chapter starts by laying the groundwork for the discussion by introducing some research results, observations and models from the literature on evidence-based policy making and practice, as well as knowledge transfer and research utilisation. The focus is on what we know about the use of scientific evidence in policy and practice, as well as cooperation between academic researchers and policy makers/practitioners. Then, we will shortly go into the debates about policy relevance and cooperation with policy makers and practitioners in terrorism studies, from which much of the radicalisation and P/CVE-related research has emerged. After that, we will dive more deeply into what the collaboration of researchers with policy makers and practitioners means – and could mean in the future – in the P/CVE field. Here, we will look at different forms of collaboration, as well as some challenges and potential that each one of them comes with. Finally, we will distil some key conclusions and suggestions on how to facilitate the inclusion of academic researchers in the P/CVE networks, policy making and practice.

Academic research(ers) and policy making

If results and possibilities offered by academic research have not been optimally used in the P/CVE policy making and practice, this situation is not by any means unique to this field only. Insufficient use of scientific evidence in policy making, as well as the failure of academic research to support policy making enough, have been regular sources of complaint by those calling for evidence-based public policy across the policy spectrum, even if relations between academic research and the policy-making process have generally got significantly closer over time (Ranchold and Vas, 2019). Barriers to using research in policy making and cooperation between researchers and policy makers have been elaborately discussed in the literature on evidence-based policy making, research utilisation and knowledge transfer.

A common way to frame the challenges of researcher–policy maker cooperation has been to talk about two communities. This is also how both academic researchers and policy makers often talk about each other. According to this view, academic research and policy making both have their objectives, timeframes, communicative styles and incentives that are significantly different from each other and difficult to combine (for example, Caplan, 1979; Oliver et al, 2014; Newman et al, 2016).

From policy makers' perspective, academic research has often felt too theoretical and not relevant for their work, because it does not directly address those concerns that policy makers deal with. When relevant academic research is produced, it always seems to come too late. Research on contemporary developments takes time, and therefore, research input, especially in the form of publications, may become available much later than policy makers would need it. Moreover, academic research often uses specialised terminology and is communicated in forms that are not very easy to approach for policy makers and practitioners. Academic research is primarily published in international peer-reviewed scientific journals and books, which are intended mainly for fellow academics and often use rather specialised theoretical language. Academic researchers have been blamed for not knowing how to speak about their research with policy-making and practitioner audiences. What may further contribute to the disconnect is the fact that academic researchers tend not to be very familiar with the realities of the policy-making process and, for example, developing grassroots-level initiatives to address various social problems.

Academic researchers, too, have had their own reservations about interacting with policy makers and how to take policy needs into account when planning their research. Even though there are increasing demands for researchers to think about the relevance of their research for society and demonstrate the impact of their research, the academic systems still assess individual researchers mainly based on their scientific merits and especially their academic publication record. Assessment criteria may also include policy impact and science communication, but they are usually considered a nice addition to scientific merits at best. Communication with policy makers has not always been without frustration from the researchers' side either. From the researchers' point of view, policy makers may sometimes seem disinterested in research findings, ignore them when policy decisions have been made and unappreciative of the amount of work that it takes to produce good quality research (for example, Bogenschneider and Corbett, 2010; Gollust et al, 2017).

There are also deeper reasons for why some researchers, perhaps especially in the social sciences, have found cooperation with policy makers challenging. While academic research is expected to be useful for society, that is not the same thing as being in the service of the state. In fact, there are countless other ways that researchers can contribute to society and the common good, and one of these ways is to examine the state's actions critically and independently (Machen, 2020; Gunn and Mintrom, 2021). In order to do that, many researchers think it is recommendable or even necessary to maintain distance from the state and its representatives, including policy makers. Researchers are also often wary of what will be made out of their engagement with policy makers and practitioners. One common fear is that their involvement and even research results will be misrepresented to justify policy decisions that they would not condone.

Even if these concerns and barriers are all relevant, it has been widely called into question whether the two-communities approach is an adequate representation of the relationship between academic researchers and policy makers (for example, Newman et al, 2016). This is because empirical research has shown that these 'communities' are far from homogeneous. Instead, there is great variation in attitudes and forms of cooperation across the divide inside these communities. While some policy makers are disinterested or reserved towards academic research, others reportedly make active use of it in their work. Similarly, some academic researchers have been considerably more open to cooperation with policy makers than others. A second argument against the two-communities model is that, in fact, there is constant interaction between researchers and policy makers, even if its volume and nature vary from one setting to another and do not always meet everyone's expectations.

What has also been typical for the two-communities-based thinking is to see the use of academic research as a one-directional process in which research is brought into the realm of policy and practice. This image is easily provoked by such often used concepts as 'knowledge transfer' or 'knowledge translation', which may provoke a connotation of 'gathering and integrating evidence from research, condensing this into convergent knowledge, and neatly packaging this knowledge for transfer elsewhere' (Davies et al, 2008, p 189). Also, this view needs to be called into question. Davies et al (2008) have, for example, suggested that rather than knowledge transfer, terms such as knowledge interaction or knowledge intermediation would better describe how diverse actors in the policy process engage with evidence, including academic research.

We believe a good way to approach the use of academic research in policy and practice is to see it as a relational process: instead of travelling alone, academic research often travels with people and through human interactions. What kind of evidence gets noticed and trusted depends significantly on interpersonal relations. The use of academic research for policy making is, therefore, to a large part, also a question about the relationship between academic researchers and policy makers. The interaction between them does not happen in a vacuum. Instead, academic researchers are typically part of broader policy networks, which can include a wide range of actors involved in policy making and practice. Whose evidence gets noticed and used depends partly on the trustworthiness and credibility of the messenger. Trust, legitimacy and accountability play a key role in facilitating the use of evidence for policy making (Ranchold and Vas, 2019; Rickinson and Edwards, 2020).

This relational perspective may also partly help understand why academic researchers are not always so easily included in policy making. When policy makers need knowledge and analysis from an external partner, they may often approach a consultancy or a think tank, rather than a university. One reason for this may be that consultancies and think tanks seem more accessible and easier to reach. Their work is often more client-oriented, they are accustomed to conducting relatively short-term projects, and they more openly market their services. Compared to consultancies and think tanks, universities may seem distant, and there may be doubts about whether they will understand policy-makers' needs and realities sufficiently.

What is perhaps good to state here is that the aforementioned challenges should not be taken as discouragement. That cross-sectoral collaboration may come with tensions and difficulties, is hardly unique or surprising. For example, it is well known that the multi-agency collaboration in the P/CVE field has had (and still has) many challenges to overcome. Yet, such cooperation is broadly seen as essential and possible. What is also noteworthy is that many challenges that have complicated multi-agency collaboration have been quite similar to those identified in the cooperation between researchers and policy makers/practitioners: different professional and institutional logics, unclear legal grounds for information-sharing and lack of trust (Solhjell et al, 2022). A multi-agency collaboration is said to rest on 'an uneasy alliance of ideas which do not necessarily sit together comfortably, and when these hybridised elements are made explicit, they invoke broader ideas and practices which are in greater tensions' (Clubb et al, 2021, cited in Solhjell et al, 2022, p 168). If multi-agency collaboration can be made to work, so can constructive cooperation between researchers and policy makers/practitioners.

Policy relevance in terrorism studies

All aforementioned difficulties in the relationship between research and policy making are also visible in the P/CVE field. Considering how quickly violent extremism is evolving as a phenomenon and the pressures that are put on policy makers and practitioners to prevent radicalisation and violent attacks, the pace of academic research may seem hopelessly slow. What has given this discussion its own flavour is that terrorism studies, from which much of the current research on radicalisation and violent extremism emerged, have traditionally been strongly influenced by policy needs. Ever since the research field started to take its shape in the 1970s, it has had close ties with policy makers and practitioners (Stampnitzky, 2013; Ilardi et al, 2021). Much of the research on terrorism has aimed at producing knowledge that would help the authorities fight terrorism and consequently also focused strongly on those manifestations of terrorism that were a concern for Western security authorities at the given time. Especially in the early decades of the research field, the state was a major funder of research and much of the research was conducted in think tanks and research institutions with close ties to the state.

While this may sound great for evidence-based policy making, it did not turn out to be as beneficial as one may think. During the early decades of terrorism studies, the research agenda became excessively dictated by policy needs. This also meant that most studies on terrorism resulted from short research projects that were mostly synthesising already existing knowledge, while more in-depth research projects which would have generated new knowledge remained rare. This meant that the scientific understanding of terrorism advanced very slowly. According to Andrew Silke, terrorism studies existed 'on a diet of fast-food research: quick, cheap, ready-to-hand and nutritionally dubious' (Silke, 2001, p 12). The close relationship between researchers and policy makers/practitioners also led to debates and criticism about the researchers' role in counter-terrorism. A prominent terrorism scholar, Alex P. Schmid, famously complained in 1988 that terrorism researchers had misunderstood their role: they were not supposed to be firefighters but rather students of combustion (Schmid and Jongman, 1988). This experience shows that more policy orientation in the research field does not always mean better possibilities for evidence-based policy making. There is clearly a place, also from this perspective, for independent and 'slow' academic research which builds general knowledge about social phenomena.

The discussion about the relationship with policy making in terrorism studies has continued until this day. Since the 9/11 attacks, the volume of terrorism research has grown exponentially. While policy-facing studies remain common, academically oriented study of terrorism has expanded dramatically. This has led to the rising academic quality of the research (Neumann and Kleinmann, 2013; Schuurman, 2020), as well as the diversification of research approaches and methods. Also, views about the relationship between research and policy have become more diverse. While much of the research on terrorism, radicalisation and violent extremism is still influenced by current developments and many researchers have a positive attitude towards policy relevance, more critical perspectives on terrorism and P/CVE policy cooperation have become increasingly structured and visible. This is especially due to the emergence of critical terrorism studies in the latter half of the 2000s. Critical terrorism studies have blamed 'orthodox' terrorism studies for uncritical acceptance of the state's counter-terrorism agendas and approaching terrorism as a problem to be solved, rather than as a social phenomenon to be studied (see, for example, Gunning, 2007; Jackson et al, 2009). Researchers have expressed differing views about what would be a societally responsible way for researchers to engage with counter-terrorism policy making and whether being 'policy relevant' is an appropriate measure of good research or even its societal significance (see, for example, Jackson, 2016; Toros, 2016; Youngman, 2020). There have also been calls for considering the possible ethical challenges that state involvement in academic research may entail (for example, Massoumi et al, 2020).

At the same time, there are other researchers who generally consider collaboration with policy makers and practitioners as something worth striving for, either in the name of the common good or because of the potential benefits it might bring to research. One key potential benefit is better access to data. Terrorism expert Marc Sageman, who has experience both from the academia and intelligence community, has even polemically argued that the lack of collaboration between researchers and the intelligence community, and thereby lack of access to their data, is a key reason for alleged stagnation in terrorism studies (Sageman, 2014). Having better access to authorities' data would undeniably be helpful for the research field, though, as many researchers have pointed out, such data also comes with its own problems – and terrorism research has many other sources of data to draw from (Morrison, 2022; Frumkin and Ford, 2023).

Given how much influence policy concerns have had on terrorism studies, there has been surprisingly little research on what kind of cooperation researchers have had with policy makers and practitioners. We do not, in other words, have much understanding of what the cooperation and interaction between academic researchers and policy makers/practitioners has actually looked like in different contexts. Neither there are evaluations of such collaboration, so it is difficult to track its impact and effectiveness. There are also only a few studies on what counter-terrorism and P/CVE policy makers and practitioners think about academic research and their interactions with academic researchers. One of the very few studies that look into this topic was conducted by Bart Schuurman (2019). According to his study, many policy makers and practitioners used academic research on terrorism in their work, but the majority also found that terrorism research failed to address many topics that would be relevant to policy and that research was often too theoretical.

Another common feature of the policy relevance debates within terrorism studies is that the cooperation with policy makers and practitioners is mostly discussed only at a very general level. What is typically not reflected in these debates is that there are many ways in which academic researchers can engage in P/CVE policy and practice and that the exact challenges and implications that a researcher may need to deal with depend at least partly on the form of engagement. The rest of this chapter will map these different forms of engagement, some of their implications to the researcher and ways that research can influence policy and practice.

Use and position of academic research in preventing and countering violent extremism policy and practice

To lay some groundwork for discussing the (potential) roles of research in the P/CVE field, it is good to say a few more words about the use and role of academic research in (evidence-based) policy making. Policy studies have convincingly shown that academic research is only one type of evidence that policy makers and practitioners engage with. Policy makers typically understand 'evidence' in much broader terms than academic researchers, including also 'their own knowledge of the policy-making system, as well as the "practical wisdom" of their advisers and colleagues, the professional and "hands-on" knowledge of practitioners, and the insights of service users' (Cairney, 2016, p 23). Moreover, the policy makers' capacity to gather and analyse evidence is always constrained, and therefore, it is impossible to process all available relevant information before making policy decisions. Academic research is, thus, often competing for attention in situations where other sources of evidence are available, and resources for making use of evidence are limited.

When it comes to evidence-based policy making, it is equally important to understand the multitude of considerations that play into it. That policy decisions are not solely based on academic research or even evidence, more generally, is not a glitch, but instead a key feature of the policy-making process. From the point of view of democratic decision-making, it is not even desirable that policy making becomes fully 'evidence-based'. It is actually even an unrealistic goal as evidence alone cannot tell what is actually desirable, because that is ultimately a value question (for example, Cairney, 2016; Parkhurst, 2017). This does not mean that academic research could not have an important role to play in policy making – just that the role is not straightforward, and it has to be seen as embedded in a wider set of complex considerations.

The final point concerns the uses of 'evidence'. The most common way to understand the utilisation of evidence is to think that research results are used to decide on the best course of action. This kind of instrumental use is, however, only one way that academic research can and has been used in policy making. Boaz and Nutley (2019), building on Carol H. Weiss's (1979) classic work, identify three main types of research use: instrumental, conceptual and strategic. Instrumental use means the application of research results to develop policies or solve policy problems. This is, according to Boaz and Nutley, actually a relatively rare form of research utilisation. Conceptual use, on its part, refers to the 'often indirect ways in which research can influence the knowledge, understanding and attitudes of policymakers and practitioners' (Boaz and Nutley, 2019, p 252). Finally, strategic use of research means that research is mainly used to justify and support policy choices that have already been made based on other considerations. It is also possible that research is used tactically to influence the policy process, for example, to delay action around a certain issue or deflect attention by saying that more research is needed before making a decision or taking any action.

Similarly, academic research may also be used in different stages of policy development and serve different functions. Boaz and Nutley suggest four main uses (Boaz and Nutley, 2003, pp 226–229). Again, the first one – design and develop policy – is perhaps the most commonly recognised one. The possibilities for research use do not end here but instead continue throughout the entire policy cycle. Academic research and researchers can have a role in assessing the impact of policy interventions (second use) through evaluations and thereby also help improve policy implementation (third use). Academic research can also contribute by providing alternative ways to address policy issues and look over the horizon (fourth use), and identify emerging new societal challenges and policy issues.

There are a number of implications that derive from our discussion on the role of researchers in the P/CVE field. The first one is that it is beneficial for researchers to have a realistic understanding of the policy-making process and reasons why policy makers may not seem to 'follow evidence' when making policy decisions. This is not necessarily because policy makers would not value academic research, but because policy making is influenced also by other types of evidence and considerations. This is something that the newer literature on the evidence-based approach also explicitly acknowledges. Second, the importance of academic research should not be viewed only in this kind of instrumental terms, but it should also be recognised that it can play an even more important role in shaping policy-makers' understanding of radicalisation and violent extremism and how they can be prevented (conceptual use). This kind of influence may be harder to detect and document, but it can have an even more profound impact on policy (and practice).

Furthermore, researchers seem to be generally very conscious about the third type, strategic use of research in policy making. This possibility seems, in fact, to be one reason why some researchers are wary of engaging with policy makers or practitioners. The main concern, however, does not seem to be strategic use in principle, but that research would be used to justify policy choices that are, in fact, not supported by it. The use of evidence in policy making tends to come with its own politics and various kinds and levels of biases that can be frustrating for researchers (Parkhurst, 2017). At the same time, there is also something that can be called misuse of evidence. This means, for example, 'using findings out of context, stretching findings, distorting findings and rejecting or ignoring findings' (Boaz and Nutley, 2019, p 255). This is something that researchers have no obligation to accept.

It is also important to recognise that the collaboration of researchers with policy makers (and practitioners) will very likely require some negotiation and learning from each party involved. Because policy makers, practitioners and academic researchers do not typically inhabit the same ecosystems, they do not automatically share the same working culture or have detailed knowledge about each other's capabilities, commitments and operating environments (Grossman and Davis, 2021). In the case of researchers, it can mean learning more about the policy-making process. For policy makers and practitioners, it can mean getting to know what can and cannot be expected from academic research. Collaboration should be based on realistic expectations and be guided by clear and shared views about its objectives and possibilities.

Finally, enhancing the cooperation of researchers with policy makers and practitioners does not mean that all researchers would need to take part in it, or that it should take a certain form. Such cooperation may take many different forms and require different levels and types of commitment from the partners involved. We will now move on to identify, describe and discuss some of these forms.

Forms of collaboration of researchers and policy makers/practitioners in the preventing and countering violent extremism field

As it was mentioned earlier, there is a tendency in terrorism studies to discuss cooperation with policy makers and practitioners as a monolith. There are, indeed, questions related to research ethics, power and independence of researchers that are meaningful to discuss on a general level. There are, however, many forms that such interaction can take, and some of them bring researchers to a much closer collaboration with policy makers and practitioners than others. They can also have different implications for the researcher's daily work and allocation of time. Later in the text, we go through various forms of collaboration we have detected in the P/CVE field (Stephens and Sieckelinck, 2019). All of them can contribute to evidence-based policy making and practice. Along the way, we give some examples of collaboration, focusing especially on Belgium, Finland and the European Union (EU) level, as these are the contexts that we are most familiar with.

Sharing knowledge

Perhaps the common type of collaboration is that researchers share their knowledge about the results of academic research. This can take many forms: policy briefs and reports summarising research insights on a given topic, participation in seminars and workshops and smaller bilateral meetings and exchanges between researchers and policy makers/practitioners.

Knowledge sharing can have different objectives and focus. It can concentrate on summarising research results and theoretical insights on a broader topic, for example, processes of radicalisation and the role of different factors in these processes. It can also aim at contextualising ongoing forms of violent extremism and radicalisation by presenting their larger context and historical roots. Focus can also be on what happens right now, and knowledge sharing can support policy makers and practitioners in maintaining situational awareness of the context in which they work and anticipating what may be expected in the future.

This kind of engagement is, generally speaking, a relatively easy and light form of collaboration, as it does not necessarily require a lot of time or resources or a more long-term commitment. It can also often be beneficial for researchers themselves because it can provide useful insights into how the P/CVE policy making and practice works and how professionals outside the academia view these issues. It is also typically through this kind of interaction that possibilities for new partnerships are identified and foundations laid for closer collaboration.

At the same time, there are limits to how much and in what kind of terms researchers can participate in these kinds of activities. One constraint is time; researchers can commit only a certain amount of their time to this kind of activity, especially when they are doing this on top of full academic research and teaching obligations, which tend not to leave much time for other tasks. Another set of limits derives from the implications that this kind of knowledge sharing may have for the research activities. It is not always easy to participate in this kind of interaction at the same time as the researcher is actively doing fieldwork and interviews among those involved in violent extremism, for example, as it can create issues with trust towards the researcher and ethical dilemmas in what kind of information can be shared.

Knowledge sharing in various different forms is very common in the P/CVE field. A major platform for this has been the RAN, and there are also other European platforms which serve this purpose, for example, the European Expert Network on Terrorism Issues. At the same time, there appears to be significant variation in how common and intensive knowledge-sharing activities are in different contexts. Our experience is that there are significant differences by sector and country in how comfortable researchers, policy makers and practitioners are with this kind of interaction.

Research for policy-making purposes

The second form of engagement involves conducting research projects that are explicitly designed to produce information for policy-making purposes or developing P/CVE initiatives. These studies are typically commissioned and paid for by ministries or other government bodies. In addition to universities, this kind of study is also conducted, for example, by think tanks and 'in-house' researchers working in various government bodies.

As it has already come out, this form of cooperation has also been common in terrorism studies, and it is easy to find examples of it (for examples from Finland, see Malkki and Pohjonen, 2019; Malkki and Saarinen, 2019). While commissioning research is a good way for policy makers to get research on topics that are of most relevance for them, this form of collaboration is not without challenges. One obvious significant challenge is the timeline: conducting research projects that produce new knowledge takes time and usually more time than is feasible for the government. Therefore, these kinds of research projects tend to be at their best when there is already at least some previous research to draw from.

Besides the amount of previous research, the usefulness of this kind of research depends also on how the calls for proposals, and thereby requirements for the research project, are set. The research is most likely to produce relevant and high-quality results when the requirements are in line with the allocated time and resources. It is not always easy for policy makers, who do not necessarily have detailed understanding of what kind of research is out there and how much time is required for different kinds of research tasks, to find this balance. Another critical moment comes when the received research proposals are assessed. Evaluating the quality of the proposals and expertise of the research staff is also not always easy for the government. It has been suggested that the governments should more often use similar peer review processes as research councils do (Neumann and Kleinmann, 2013) and use academic researchers as reviewers to assess the quality of research proposals.

Government-funded research can be attractive to academic researchers, because it provides additional funding opportunities in the highly competitive academic environment. Engaging in such research is not, however, entirely unproblematic from the researchers' point of view and requires careful consideration and negotiation of the terms and conditions (Martini and Fernández de Moysterin, 2023). The research project may come with predetermined but perhaps unspoken normative commitments that the researcher may not share. There may also be some expectations about what the results might be and displeasure if these expectations are not met. Many such challenges and ethical dilemmas derive from researchers and policy makers/practitioners having different priorities and commitments that guide their knowledge needs and production. A whole different order of ethical challenges emerges when the research is ordered by a government which is not committed to respecting human rights or suppressed non-violent political protest in the name of counter-terrorism (Massoumi et al, 2020).

Evaluation of preventing and countering violent extremism policies and practices

One very natural role for academic researchers *vis-à-vis* P/CVE policy and practice is to engage in the evaluation of P/CVE initiatives. So far, evaluation has not become an established practice in the field, meaning that evaluation studies have remained relatively uncommon. It is widely acknowledged that advancement of P/CVE policies and practices requires more evaluations and there is increasing interest in getting engaged in evaluations (Fisher and Busher, 2023). This hopefully means that we will see more evaluations in the future.

When evaluations of P/CVE policies and practices have been done, they have not always been conducted by academic researchers. It has been relatively common to commission evaluations from consultancies who often provide such services for a wide range of actors and issues. This may be at least partly because consultancies often offer such services and advertise them, while academic researchers rarely actively search for such opportunities. Consultancies and think tanks have been used as providers for evaluations in both Finland and Belgium. The first – and so far, only – evaluation of the Finnish national plan for preventing violent radicalisation and extremism was conducted by a consultancy (Ministry of the Interior, 2019b). In Belgium, the Action plan for the prevention of violent radicalisation and polarisation (Vlaamse Regering, 2015) was evaluated by the Flemish Peace, a research body founded under the Flemish parliament, in 2020 (Flemish Peace Institute, 2021).

As most evaluation designs are strongly based on general academic research methods, most academic researchers would have the basic skills for doing evaluation studies. What academic researchers also have to offer (that consultancies can so far rarely offer) is knowledge and expertise on radicalisation as a phenomenon and P/CVE as a policy field. Experience has shown that in order for the evaluation to succeed and produce meaningful results, the evaluator should be knowledgeable on the P/CVE field, its special features and how they may have an impact on the applicability of evaluation designs and methods (Malkki et al, 2023).

There are already several cases of P/CVE evaluations conducted by academic researchers which show the potential of what can be done. To give a couple of examples, in the EU-funded EMMA project, academic researchers conducted process evaluation of multi-agency work in Belgium, the Netherlands and Germany to understand how the multi-agency structures work towards their objectives, how well they have reached the objectives and what kind of factors influence their success (Hardyns et al, 2022). Another evaluation focused on a resilience-training programme for young Muslims with a migrant background. The study looked at how participation influenced participants' self-esteem, level of empathy, agency, as well as attitudes and intentions with regard to ideologically motivated violence (Feddes et al, 2015).

To make the most of the collaboration opportunities in evaluations – and conduct high-quality, evidence-based evaluations in general – it is very important to take into account that evaluation requires planning that needs to start well before the actual evaluation begins. This is because many evaluation designs require data that must be collected prior to the initiative's implementation. For example, if the objective of evaluation is to assess the initiative's effect on participants' attitudes, like in the study mentioned earlier, there needs to be some data on the participants' attitudes before participation in the initiative. Ideally, the initiative's evaluation plan should be developed together with the initiative itself (Malkki et al, 2023). It is even better if the prospective evaluators are included in developing this plan and, consequently, the initiative's monitoring and documentation practices to ensure the availability of required data for evaluation.

Acting as an evaluator is a rather natural role for academic researchers because it allows them to maintain their independent position and put their core skills to use. When planned well, there may be significant synergies between evaluating P/CVE initiatives and academic research aiming at advancing the theoretical understanding of radicalisation and deradicalisation processes. At the same time, there are sensitivities related to evaluations that may also reflect on the work of academics as evaluators. Even if policy makers and practitioners agree that evaluations are important, they may still have reservations about conducting them. One reason is that they are concerned about how negative results might reflect on their reputation and resources. This may have an impact on what kind of evaluations they feel comfortable with and whether they allow the evaluation results to be published.

Evaluations also require quite significant resources and cannot be realistically considered as something that is done on top of everything else as a side project. There needs to be separate funding for it. So far, funding for P/CVE initiatives still does not include funding for evaluation, and it is not completely clear who could and should provide funding. This is something that needs to be solved in order for evaluations to become more common.

Co-designing policies and practices

Knowledge sharing, policy-facing research and evaluations can all contribute significantly to the advancement of P/CVE policy and practice by providing it with the necessary scientific evidence and making it more easily available for policy makers and practitioners. Sometimes, the researchers' involvement takes deeper and more elaborate forms and researchers participate in developing policies and practices in a more substantial way. Generally speaking, researchers are experts in knowledge production and not policy planning, but there may be situations in which researchers, due to their research topics and the nature of their expertise, can also give a very substantial input to policy development.

How researchers are involved in drafting policies and practices is difficult to say because there is not always full transparency about such involvement. Our impression is that it may happen more at the level of practices than policies. A light version of this kind of collaboration has been to appoint researchers as members of the steering committee in some P/CVE initiatives. This has been the case, for example, in Finland, where researchers are involved, for example, in the steering committees of the Exit programme for deradicalisation and the Radik project, which has produced learning resources and a risk assessment tool for social and health care professionals. Another limited form of this kind of collaboration is to use academic researchers as trainers in capacity-building courses. This way, they participate in producing the content for the training.

Academic researchers can also be more substantially involved in developing P/CVE initiatives and play a key role in designing them. Many EU-funded projects in this field have, for example, developed many kinds of training on radicalisation and violent extremism for professionals. Sometimes, although in our understanding still quite rarely, academic researchers have acted as the main instigators, developers, content producers and implementers of trainings for policy makers and practitioners. One example of this is P/CVE trainings developed and organised by researchers at the University of Helsinki. These trainings have been financed by several ministries, but their content has been developed by the University of Helsinki researchers. Most of these trainings have been meant for educators, there have also been trainings for other professionals who work with young people. These trainings have not only been about radicalisation and violent extremism as a phenomenon but also about the role of educators in P/CVE, including how educators can do this work in practice as part of their daily work.

When it comes to policy making, perhaps the most common way to involve academic researchers is to hold hearings and roundtable discussions. Informal exchange of views between individual researchers and policy makers may undoubtedly play a role in shaping policies, and especially views about violent extremism that guide policy planning and implementation. One easily demonstrable way that academic researchers have had a profound influence on policy making can, again, be found in Finland. Academic researchers who specialise in P/CVE in education have significantly shaped the way it has been framed in Finland. Based on their ongoing research projects dealing exactly with this topic, they cooperated significantly with the Finnish National Agency for Education, developing the sector's approach to P/CVE, to the point that much of what was written about this sector in the National Action Plan for Preventing Radicalisation and Violent Extremism for the years 2019–2023 is authored by them (Ministry of the Interior, 2019a).

Research co-production

At times, academic researchers have also engaged in deeper collaborations with policy makers or practitioners to co-produce research. This is a significant possibility that has not, to our knowledge, been used very much, but has the potential to produce research that would be otherwise very difficult to conduct. Co-production designs can be particularly useful for solving issues with academic researchers' limited access to security authorities' data. In this kind of collaboration, policy makers and practitioners can play an important role in identifying useful data, anonymising or otherwise transforming it to a form that can be shared with academic researchers and help academic researchers understand how the data was produced and, thereby, what kind of limitations it may have.

One example of research co-production is the study on active shooters in the United States conducted by the Federal Bureau of Investigation in cooperation with academic researchers. Besides the research results, the research team has also produced a description of the co-production process, together with their experiences of being involved in it (Silver et al, 2021). This description can be very helpful for those who plan similar research projects in the future and more descriptions. Overall, it would help the field if more similar descriptions were published.

Looking ahead

To conclude this chapter, it may be good to return briefly to the remarks about the first decades of the terrorism studies we made earlier in the chapter. It was mentioned that the research field was then dominated by state-funded and policy-oriented research and that the lack of basic academic research producing new knowledge was slowing down its development. Is there something we should learn from those decades in order not to repeat the same mistakes?

During the post-9/11 period, public interest in terrorism and violent extremism has remained high, and the states continue to be a significant research funder. There are, however, some important differences between the situation earlier and now. The most important one concerns academic research on terrorism. A huge increase in interest and knowledge needs on terrorism not only leads to more policy-oriented studies but also to the solidification of studies on terrorism and violent extremism as an academic research field. There are many more academic research projects, research institutes, degree programmes and PhD schools that focus on terrorism and violent extremism than ever before. It also appears that the state funding has got a bit more strategic. In addition to projects with a short time span, there are now also funding schemes that fund 'slower' research, like the US Minerva Research Initiative and the National Consortium for the Study of Terrorism and Responses to Terrorism, to mention two well-known examples. This means that the research field is nowadays producing much more new academic knowledge, and the understanding of terrorism and violent extremism has expanded significantly.

The problem with early terrorism research was not only the dominance of state funding and interests but also the lack of attention to research ethics and the integrity of academic research. One important and still relevant learning is that academic researchers should be more mindful and reflective to avoid getting swayed by counter-terrorism agendas and politics. Any kind of collaboration with partners who have different objectives, obligations and normative commitments, requires a good sense of what academic research and research ethics are about. The good news is that there is more work being done on this front, too, and more resources to support researchers to find their way.

Finally, when confronted with challenges and tensions involved in academic researchers collaborating with policy makers and practitioners, it is useful to remember that collaboration is not likely to function well without putting some effort into finding common ground and agreeing on terms of collaboration. Deeper forms of collaboration especially require a different kind of mindset than that of one-directional science communication. One potentially productive way to understand collaboration is that on top of engaging in collaborative work itself, participants are also involved in boundary spanning. By boundary spanning, we understand 'work to enable exchange between the production and use of knowledge to support evidence-informed decision-making in a specific context' (Bednarek et al, 2018, p 1176). How to facilitate this boundary spanning would be a useful area to explore in the P/CVE field in the future.

Summary

Studies on terrorism and violent extremism have a long tradition of doing policy-relevant research and cooperation with policy makers and practitioners. Even so, the role of researchers in the P/CVE field remains rather unclear and uneven, as well as many possibilities for collaboration between researchers and policy makers/practitioners are underused.

- Academic researchers, policy makers and practitioners have a lot to gain from collaboration, but such collaboration almost always requires some negotiation and learning from all parties involved. It needs to be based on realistic expectations and guided by a clear and shared view of its objectives.
- There has been a tendency to discuss the collaboration of academic researchers with policy makers and practitioners

as a monolith, even though such collaboration can take many different forms. Possibilities, challenges and limitations of collaboration depend significantly on the exact form of engagement.
- To facilitate a more finetuned discussion on this collaboration, the chapter introduces a list of various forms of engagement. These include knowledge sharing, research for policy-making purposes, evaluation of P/CVE policies and practices, co-designing and research co-production.
- There is significant underused potential, especially in collaborating with academic researchers, especially in evaluating P/CVE policies and practices. Such collaborations should ideally be created already during the initiative's planning stage.
- Even though collaboration between academic researchers and policy makers/practitioners is needed for advancing evidence-based P/CVE, it is also good to emphasise that academic research does not have to be explicitly designed for policy purposes in order to be useful for evidence-based policy and practice. Basic empirical and theoretical research on violent extremism is also needed to build the necessary evidence base.

Suggested directions for future research

The following questions can orient further research and discussion in the area:

- What kind of collaboration between academic researchers, policy makers and practitioners takes place in different national and local contexts? What kind of factors influence the opportunities for such collaboration and the forms that it takes?
- How to arrange evaluation of P/CVE initiatives so that it improves the evidence base of the field while also taking into account the political and practical realities in which these evaluations take place?
- What kind of boundary-spanning activities could further facilitate constructive participation of academic researchers in P/CVE policy and practice?

References

Bednarek, A.T., Wyborn, C., Cvitanovic, C., Meyer, R., Colvin, R.M., Addison, P.F.E., et al (2018) 'Boundary spanning at the science-policy interface: The practitioners' perspectives', *Sustainability Science*, 13: 1175–83.

Boaz, A. and Nutley, S. (2003) 'Evidence-based policy and practice', in A.G. Bovaird and E. Löffler (eds) *Public Management and Governance*, New York: Routledge, pp 225–36.

Boaz, A. and Nutley, S. (2019) 'Using evidence', in A. Boaz, H. Davies, A. Fraser and S. Nutley (eds) *What Works Now? Evidence-Informed Policy and Practice*, Bristol: Bristol University Press, pp 251–78.

Bogenschneider, K. and Corbett, T. (2010) *Evidence-Based Policymaking: Insights from Policy-Minded Researchers and Research-Minded Policymakers*, New York: Routledge.

Cairney, P. (2016) *The Politics of Evidence-Based Policy Making*, London: Palgrave Macmillan.

Caplan, N. (1979) 'The two-communities theory and knowledge utilization', *American Behavioral Scientist*, 22(3): 459–70.

Davies, H., Nutley, S. and Walter, I. (2008) 'Why "knowledge transfer" is misconceived for applied social research', *Journal of Health Services Research & Policy*, 13(3): 188–90.

Feddes, A.R., Mann, L. and Doosje, B. (2015) 'Increasing self-esteem and empathy to prevent violent radicalization: A longitudinal quantitative evaluation of a resilience training focused on adolescents with a dual identity', *Journal of Applied Social Psychology*, 45(7): 400–11.

Fisher, T. and Busher, J. (2023) 'How can we meaningfully evaluate the effects and effectiveness of programmes to prevent or counter radicalisation?', in J. Busher, L. Malkki and S. Marsden (eds) *Routledge Handbook of Radicalisation and Countering Radicalisation*, New York: Routledge, pp 320–37.

Flemish Peace Institute (2021) 'Lessons learned from the Flemish Action Plan for the prevention of violent radicalisation & polarisation', *Flemish Peace Institute*, 22 March. Available from https://vlaamsvredesinstituut.eu/wp-content/uploads/2021/03/20210322_AnneliesPauwels_LessonsLearned-1.pdf [Accessed 13 November 2023].

Frumkin, L.A. and Ford, P. (2023) 'Collaborative approaches to countering terrorism', in L. Frumkin, J. Morrison and A. Silke (eds) *Research Agenda for Terrorism Studies*, Northampton: Edward Elgar, pp 211–24.

Gollust, S.E., Seymor, J.W., Pany, M.J., Goss, A., Meisel, Z.F. and Grande, D. (2017) 'Mutual distrust: Perspectives from researchers and policy makers on the research to policy gap in 2013 and recommendations for the future', *Inquiry*, 54: 1–11.

Grossman, M. and Davis, N. (2021) 'A bridge too far? An academic-national security practitioner dialogue on research collaboration across the divide', *Journal of Policing, Intelligence and Counter Terrorism*, 16(1): 12–31.

Gunn, A. and Mintrom, M. (2021) 'Where evidence-based policy meets research impact', *Australian Journal of Public Administration*, 80: 544–53.

Gunning, J. (2007) 'A case for critical terrorism studies?', *Government and Opposition*, 42(3): 363–93.

Hardyns, W., Klima, N. and Pauwels, L. (eds) (2022) *Evaluation and Mentoring of the Multi-Agency Approach to Violent Radicalisation in Belgium, the Netherlands and Germany*, Antwerp: Maklu Publishers.

Hemmingsen, A.-S. (2015) *An Introduction to the Danish Approach to Countering and Preventing Extremism and Radicalization*, Copenhagen: Danish Institute for International Studies.

Ilardi, G.J., Smith, D. and Zammit, A. (2021) 'Revisiting the relationship between academics and national security practitioners', *Journal of Policing, Intelligence and Counter Terrorism*, 16(1): 1–11.

Jackson, R. (2016) 'To be or not to be policy relevant? Power, emancipation and resistance in CTS research', *Critical Studies on Terrorism*, 9(1): 120–5.

Jackson, R., Breen Smyth, M. and Gunning, J. (eds) (2009) *Critical Terrorism Studies: A New Research Agenda*, New York: Routledge.

Machen, R. (2020) 'Critical research impact: On making space for alternatives', *Area*, 52(2): 329–41.

Malkki, L. and Pohjonen, M. (2019) *Jihadist Online Communication and Finland*, Helsinki: Ministry of the Interior.

Malkki, L. and Saarinen, J. (2019) *Jihadism in Finland*, Helsinki: Ministry of the Interior.

Malkki, L., Prokic, M. and Van der Vet, I. (2023) 'INDEED E-Guidebook 1. Evidence-based evaluation of PVE/CVE and de-radicalisation initiatives: Principles, challenges and methods', *INDEED*, 19 October. Available from https://www.indeed project.eu/sdm_downloads/e-guidebook-1_eng/ [Accessed 13 November 2023].

Martini, A. and Fernández de Mosteyrín, L. (2023) 'The role of researcher and researchers in counter-radicalisation policy and practice', in J. Busher, L. Malkki and S. Marsden (eds) *Routledge Handbook of Radicalisation and Countering Radicalisation*, New York: Routledge, pp 306–19.

Massoumi, N., Mills, T. and Miller, D. (2020) 'Secrecy, coercion and deception in research on "terrorism" and "extremism"', *Contemporary Social Science*, 15(2): 134–52.

Ministry of the Interior (2019a) *National Action Plan for the Prevention of Violent Radicalisation and Extremism 2019–2023. Government Resolution 19 December 2019*, Helsinki: Ministry of the Interior.

Ministry of the Interior (2019b) *Assessment of the National Action Plan for the Prevention of Violent Radicalisation and Extremism by the Ministry of the Interior*, Helsinki: Ministry of the Interior.

Morrison, J. (2022) 'Talking stagnation: Thematic analysis of terrorism experts' perception of the health of terrorism research', *Terrorism and Political Violence*, 34(8): 1509–29.

Neumann, P. and Kleinmann, S. (2013) 'How rigorous is radicalization research?', *Democracy and Security*, 9(4): 360–82.

Newman, J., Cherney, A. and Head, B.W. (2016) 'Do policy makers use academic research? Re-examining the "two communities" theory of research utilization', *Public Administration Review*, 26(1): 24–32.

Oliver, K., Innvar, S., Lorenc, T., Woodman, J. and Thomas, J. (2014) 'A systematic review of barriers to and facilitators of the use of evidence by policymakers', *BMC Health Services Research*, 14(2): 1–12.

Parkhurst, J. (2017) *The Politics of Evidence: From Evidence-Based Policy to the Good Governance of Evidence*, Abingdon: Routledge.

Ranchold, R. and Vas, C. (2019) 'Policy networks revisited: Creating researcher-policymaker community', *Evidence & Policy*, 15(1): 31–47.

Ranstorp, M. (2018) 'Ex post paper research seminar', *RAN Research*, 17 October. Available from https://home-affairs.ec.eur opa.eu/system/files/2020-09/ran_research_seminar_17102018 _en.pdf [Accessed 13 November 2023].

Rickinson, M. and Edwards, A. (2020) 'The relational feature of evidence use', *Cambridge Journal of Education*, 51(4): 509–26.

Sageman, M. (2014) 'The stagnation in terrorism research', *Terrorism and Political Violence*, 26(4): 565–80.

Schmid, A.P. and Jongman, A.J. (1988) *Political Terrorism: A New Guide to Actors, Authors, Concepts, Data Bases, Theories & Literature* (expanded and updated edition), Amsterdam: Transaction Publishers.

Schuurman, B. (2019) 'Counterterrorism professionals on terrorism research: An end-user assessment', *ICCT Perspective*, 5 December. Available from https://www.icct.nl/publication/ counterterrorism-professionals-terrorism-research-end-user-ass essment [Accessed 13 November 2023].

Schuurman, B. (2020) 'Research on terrorism, 2007–2016: A review of data, methods, and authorship', *Terrorism and Political Violence*, 32(5): 1011–26.

Silke, A. (2001) 'The devil you know: Continuing problems with research on terrorism', *Terrorism and Political Violence*, 13(4): 1–14.

Silver, J.M., Craun, S.W., Wyman, J.V. and Simons, A.B. (2021) 'A coproduction research model between academic and law enforcement responsible for investigating threats', *Journal of Policing, Intelligence and Counter Terrorism*, 16(1): 32–43.

Solhjell, R., Sivenbring, J., Kangasniemi, M., Kallio, H., Wilchen Christensen, T., Haugstvedt, H., et al (2022) 'Experiencing trust in multiagency collaboration to prevent violent extremism: A Nordic qualitative study', *Journal for Deradicalization*, 32: 164–91.

Stampnitzky, L. (2013) *Disciplining Terror: How Experts Invented 'Terrorism'*, London: Cambridge University Press.

Stephens, W. and Sieckelinck, S. (2019) 'Working across boundaries in preventing violent extremism: Towards a typology for collaborative arrangements in PVE policy', *Journal of Deradicalisation*, 20: 272–312.

Strategic Note (2023) *Extremism and Terrorism: Towards a Multidisciplinary Approach in Belgium*, Strategy T.E.R. Available from https://ocad.belgium.be/wp-content/uploads/2023/10/Strategic-Note-Extremism-and-Terrorisme_WEB.pdf [Accessed 13 November 2023].

Toros, H. (2016) 'Dialogue, praxis and the state: A response to Richard Jackson', *Critical Studies on Terrorism*, 9(1): 126–30.

Vlaamse Regering (2015) 'Action plan for the prevention of violent radicalisation and polarisation: Overview of actions and measures', *Vlaamse Regering*. Available from https://preventie-radicalisering-polarisering.vlaanderen.be/preventie-radicalisering-polarisering/sites/preventie-radicalisering-polarisering/files/action_plan_prevention_violent_radicalisation_polarization_20170602.pdf [Accessed 13 November 2023].

Weiss, C.H. (1979) 'The many meanings of research utilization', *Public Administration Review*, 39(5): 426–31.

Youngman, M. (2020) 'Building "terrorism studies" as an interdisciplinary space: Addressing recurring issues in the study of terrorism', *Terrorism and Political Violence*, 32(5): 1091–105.

9

The Atomwaffen Division: the myth of evidence-based policy on the threat of far-right extremism

Simon Fulgoni and Susanna Menis

Introduction

Since 2015, governments, law enforcement agencies and the media across several Western countries have highlighted the threat posed by the Atomwaffen Division (AWD), a neo-Nazi group. Indeed, America's initial considerations to proscribe the group as a terrorist organisation have led Canada, the United Kingdom and Australia to do so. However, some observers have questioned how significant the threat of violence is from the group. While articles and reports are often published to educate and inform the public, scholars contend that the academic and policy literature regarding the AWD and its later reincarnations as the National Socialist Order (NSO) and National Socialist Liberation Front and other similar groups, tends to inflate and sensationalise the actual threat posed. Subsequently, as reflected in Beck's *Risk Society* (1992, p 260), the extensive coverage of such a minor organisation could potentially create a misleading amplification of a risk narrative within the public.

This chapter examines the dynamic between risk and threat and evidence-based policy. It takes the AWD as a case study. The aim is to evaluate the existence of violence and risk the group poses, and whether this informs and justifies counter-terrorism policy.

Counter-terrorism has long been a contested issue, and it seems that governments are driven by the principle of not being taken by surprise; this approach reflects the concern voiced in the quote, 'price paid for omission, is far greater than that paid for an overreaction to a threat' (Beck, 2006, p 336). The importance of this study lies in the need to draw attention to the question of the diversion of resources; it is one thing to prosecute individuals for the threatening of journalists (as in the recent AWD case), while it is another to invest energy, personnel, finance and other resources in preventing risks that do not exist in their current form. This does not suggest that inciting a race war should not be taken seriously. However, given the otherwise high crime rates compared to terrorist acts, a more realistic threat assessment should be constructed.

The chapter opens with a discussion on the construction of risks and threats from terrorism. It draws on Beck's concept of risk society, examining how the media fuel social perception and how this, in turn, drives governmental anti-terrorism policies. Then, a more detailed discussion on the media's construct of threat in the context of the AWD follows. The chapter then provides an overview of the AWD, highlighting its nature, structure and characteristics. The following section evaluates governmental counter-terrorism policies concerning far-right extremism and, second, the effects these may have on the civil liberties of other non-terrorist minority groups. Finally, the chapter concludes by examining the AWD action dynamic; this draws on the perspective of internal brakes and demonstrates the extent to which policy related to countering this group's actions may not reflect the evidence.

Despite the metamorphosis experienced by the group and subsequent changes in name, the chapter will refer to it throughout as the AWD. This is the most recognised feature identified with this small group. According to one of its latest members, Ryan AW, 'You either loved us or hated us. And our name is now more famous than it has ever been, even though we now only exist in the collective imagination' (Ryan, 2017, p 620).

Terrorism: risks and brakes

A discussion on policy, the construction of crime and fear perception must start with acknowledging Beck's concept of the 'risk society'. Beck (2006) contends that over recent decades, societal understanding of risk has transformed from a neutral term that can be quantified positively and negatively depending on the outcome to one predominated by fear. This heightened societal fear has led Beck to argue that we now live in what he labels a 'risk society'. This perspective has been used in different contexts (most recently regarding the COVID-19 pandemic) to define Western society's incessant preoccupation with its safety and commitment to eliminate or minimise future unknown risks. These risks are a socially constructed anticipation of a catastrophic event; risks mainly relate to future incidents, and the constructed fear feeds into a deep sense of threat. Hence the urgent need to prevent it. However, while risks are always considered threatening, they are hypothetical and yet to be experienced (Beck, 2014).

Several characteristics have been attributed to modern societal risk. First, 'delocalisation' refers to new threats that contemporary societies face, such as global warming, man-made pandemics or terrorism, which are not restricted by geographical boundaries, rendering them omnipresent. Hence, risk, directly propagated through the media, becomes visible, tangible and 'real': anyone can become a victim of the threat at any point. Another characteristic, 'non-compensability', reflects the notion that the eventual damage and harm will be irreversible. This taps into apocalyptical fears, such as the extinction of humanity following climate change or the use of biological or chemical weapons of mass destruction (Beck, 2006). The previous two characteristics are fundamental to constructing fear and threat; if the previous are not present in the citizens' perception, there is no case to answer regarding governmental responses to the threat.

Another characteristic that makes the discussion on justifiable governmental response interesting is 'incalculable' risk. This refers to the idea that because risks are hypothetical, they cannot be quantified and calculated (Beck, 2014). However, this notion has not been taken at face value. For example, Richards (2014) contests this perspective; he argues that if the risk is a constructed reality, it does not exist. Therefore, by definition, it is controlled by those who have constructed it. Amoore's study (2014), on the other hand, shows how a risk (in this case, one that seemed predictable: an earthquake) was wrongly 'calculated' and evaluated as 'minor', leading to fatal consequences. Still, the importance of this characteristic lies in its nature; whether the risk can be calculated or not, it places pressure on the government to resolve it, thus justifying intervention. This has allowed the position of 'precaution by prevention', inducing a state of security perception. Therefore, the anticipation and prevention of risks that have not been proven has become the predominant driving factor of restrictive government policies impinging on civil liberties (Da Silva et al, 2022).

Prevention has become even more justifiable in the case of terrorism. As opposed to, for example, ecological or global financial catastrophes (mere by-products of unrelenting modernisation), terrorism is intentional (Beck, 2002). The opening address in the US Department for Homeland Security declaration fatuously stated, 'Terrorists can strike any place, any time, using any weapon' (Mueller, 2009, p 9). However, the disruption is not only physical. As acts of communicative violence designed to challenge usually taken-for-granted values and social order, terrorist incidents dramatically encode the limitations of the state's responsibility to protect its citizens. Stanley Cohen (1985) drew attention to this, indicating that 'there is never the fear of too much control, but of too much chaos. If we are losing control, we must try to take control' (p 235). However, prevention has less to do with 'doing justice' and more with the systematic management of security (Mythen and Walklate, 2008). Therefore, the success of 'prevention' has significant implications on the notion of 'state power' and its successful endorsement by the citizen. This fuels a climate in which certain groups or organisations, in the case of this chapter, the AWD, are systematically overly characterised as a dangerous threat.

However, research has demonstrated that extremist elements or entire groups within the far-right milieu rarely carry out anything like the amount of violent activity their propaganda and rhetoric suggest. Focus has been placed on explaining why these groups are unwilling to initiate violent action, preferring to limit themselves to purely self-defensive measures. An example is the Nordic Resistance Movement's declaration that 'In the future weapons will be decisive ... but as long as we can act legally, there is no reason for the Resistance Movement to arm itself'

(Nordfront forlag, 2016, cited in Bjørgo and Ravndal, 2020, p 37). Furthermore, interviews with far-right extremists identified social or psychological 'barriers' that restricted migration into Mass Casualty Terrorism (MCT). The interviewees viewed MCT as counter-productive; they suggested that members supporting MCT merely demonstrated a predilection for interpersonal violence. Other reasons for leaning towards a non-violent milieu were unforeseeable changes in personal circumstances such as addiction, marriage or employment, organisational infighting, and moralistic reluctance to cross the threshold from low-scale violent behaviour to murder (Simi and Windisch, 2020).

This disjuncture between rhetoric and the employment of violence by extremist groups is also related to internal group policy. Researchers have argued that internal policing exercised by group leaders and advisors accounts for restraint when using violence within various groups, including those that espouse or even engage in serious violence (Dutter, 2011; Bjørgo and Ravndal, 2020; Macklin, 2020). Restraint is understood as 'a process whereby militants choose to drop, downscale or limit an attack or campaign, or adopt tactical or strategic innovations that lead them away from violence' (Busher and Bjørgo, 2020, p 2). Wilson and Halpin (2022) contend that this is primarily in recognition that such acts would be detrimental to recruitment, group expansion and, ultimately, group survival. Expanding on the theory of internal extremist group policing, Busher et al (2019) offer a working framework of 'internal brakes' on violent action. These factors account for restraint when using violence and can be found within various groups (see examples in Macklin, 2020; Wilson and Halpin, 2022).

Busher and Bjørgo (2020) explain that this framework should be examined within the context of 'multi-level ecologies of conflict'. Although the authors identify five categories of internal brakes, this chapter will focus on the first two brakes only. Brake number 1 reflects the 'strategic logic' that aims to identify effective, less violent strategies. The authors define this brake as the '[i]dentification of non – or less violent strategies of action as being as or more effective than more violent alternatives' (Busher et al, 2019, p 9). This indicates several concerns; for example, it might reflect an expression of scepticism about the group's ability to achieve its goals using violence and the recognition that violence can lead to greater levels of repression by the authorities. Similarly, a violent milieu might discourage support for the group's cause and thus limit recruitment. Therefore, opting instead to carry out activities concerning shaping the group's image, such as speeches and publications, is far more favourable. Brake number 2 is the 'moral logic', this functions as an ethical threshold. The authors define this as the '[c]onstruction of moral norms and evaluations that inhibit certain forms of violence and the emotional impulses towards violence' (Busher et al, 2019, p 9). Here, the aim is to encourage a working framework that sets limits, for example, on who and what is a legitimate target for violence (Busher and Bjørgo, 2020). According to Morrison (2020), this framework parallels political-organisational theory, particularly with the notion of organisational survival. Hence suggesting that these brakes are not incidental.

In this chapter, these brakes will be used to guide the analysis of the main instruction manual of the AWD, *Siege,* by James Mason (editions 1993–2021). This text, updated in 2021, is an anthology of Mason's newsletters written and distributed throughout the far-right community during the 1980s; this latest edition was created, edited and written mainly by James Mason, the individual considered to be the ideologue of the AWD; the collection includes photos, pamphlets and flyers, as well as writing by other members.

Media's construct of threat

We find the media playing a fundamental catalyst in the space between the implications driven by a 'risk society' and subsequent governmental policy. This is true for any area of our life, but certainly for what the media deems newsworthy. When it occurs, terrorism dominates the headlines of all mass media, informing the public immediately of incidents as and when they happen. The intensive media coverage serves at least one of the terrorists' aims, to instil fear; however, it also makes contextualising the actual extent of terrorism problematic (Zulli et al, 2022). The 'availability heuristic', a cognitive bias in decision-making based on recent experiences or information readily available (Tversky and Kahneman, 1973, p 207), triggers an unrealistic multiplication of the risk from terrorism as the boundaries between reality and fantasy become increasingly blurred (Kollmann et al, 2022). For example, in the 20 years before the 9/11 terrorist attacks, very few Americans considered the threat of terrorism a critical national concern. Yet the day following the attacks, the threat of terrorism was named by 46 per cent of those asked as the number one concern (Stewart and Mueller, 2016). A Gallup poll conducted in 2006 saw 43 per cent of Americans worried about becoming a victim of terrorism (Woods, 2007). However, by 2017, this had risen to 70 per cent (Mueller, 2021).

The media feeding and enhancing public alarmism has damaging implications. The continuous flow of scaremongering rhetoric across the airwaves affords insignificant terrorist groups an acknowledgement of their power beyond reality (Livingston, 2019). For example, while the potential for far-right use of chemical, biological, radiological and nuclear weapons is considered unlikely, with little or no evidence to support such a hypothesis (Earnhardt et al, 2021), a simple Google Scholar search returns over 78,000 articles suggesting such a threat. Fear, as a commodity (Altheide, 1997), generates profit, and the spectacular theatre offered by terrorism, regardless of the accuracy of coverage, is impossible for the media to resist (Mythen and Walklate, 2008). With the rise of the Internet, the media can rely on the new notion of 'citizen journalism' to get hold of newsworthy, often uncensored material. Subsequently, the thirst for ratings forces other mainstream media outlets to broadcast extreme content they might not otherwise feature. For example, the AWD and other White extremist groups' narrative concerning White farmer genocide in South Africa directly influenced the American television channel Fox News' decision to cover the subject and display untypically gruesome images for which they were roundly criticised (Hendry and Lemieux, 2021). Recuber (2009) has taken further the notion of utilitarian mass media, arguing that 'terrorism today is consumed like a brand, with a host of spin-off products, and terrorists are recognised as a distinct and dangerous social type through advertisements, rumours, and staged public relations pseudo-events' (p 160).

Subsequently, the public understands the threat based on information fuelled by fear. For example, the American Centre for Strategic & International Studies, a non-profit policy research organisation, has recently expressed concerns about the escalation of terrorism, particularly of far-right groups (Jones et al, 2020a, 2020b). However, the authors' colourful charts should be read with caution. For example, research by Jones et al (2020a) suggests that in 2020, 90 per cent of terrorist attacks and plots are attributed to right-wing terrorist groups; however, in Jones et al (2020b), the authors' research suggests only 67 per cent, and of these only one fatality. The previous (Jones et al, 2020a, 2020b) hardly indicates an increase in terrorism threat; also, the AWD is categorised under the umbrella of 'White supremacists'; therefore, there is no real indication of their actions. Jones et al (2020a) describe the AWD threat as the following: 'In January 2018, the AWD hosted a "Death Valley Hate Camp" in Las Vegas, Nevada, where members trained in hand-to-hand combat, firearms, and the creation of neo-Nazi propaganda videos and pictures. In August 2019, leadership members of the AWD attended a "Nuclear Congress" in Las Vegas, Nevada' (p 6). Therefore, it is argued in this chapter that for all the attention terrorism garners, while acknowledging that the threat and potential harm posed by the AWD exists, it is essential to recognise that it has been vastly overstated.

Review of the Atomwaffen Division

On 12 October 2015, founder Brandon Clint Russell formally announced the creation of the AWD (German for 'Nuclear Weapons Division') on the now defunct far-right extremist forum Iron March (Hawley, 2017). Describing itself as a 'revolutionary, national socialist movement', the AWD espouses a violent accelerationist political ideology, aiming to achieve 'purity through revolution' (May and Feldman, 2019, p 26). It has been argued that the AWD's strategy strongly resembles that described in the book by Abu Bakr Naji, *The Administration of Savagery* (2004), also used by Al-Qaeda and Islamic State in their quest to establish a caliphate (Makuch and Lamoureux, 2019). Indeed, the leadership of the AWD has praised the willingness of members of Al-Qaeda and Islamic State to sacrifice themselves for their cause, leading a member to claim that the AWD also wanted 'radicals ... young men willing to put down their lives for our ideas' (Makuch and Lamoureux, 2019). Hence, the AWD has been described as 'violent fetishists' (Ware, 2020; Southern Poverty Law Center, nd).

The AWD employs a 'leaderless social resistance' model espoused by White supremacist Louis Beam in the journal *The Seditionist* (1992) (Ware, 2020, p 6). Accordingly, this operation requires small cells or lone actors to conduct acts of anti-state terrorism independently without oversight or direct communication with the core organisation. Thus, it becomes increasingly difficult for law enforcement to monitor the AWD's operations and communications. The Center for International Security and Cooperation (2023) indicates that the AWD membership included more than 80 members (at its height), divided into 23 cells across the United States; it has grown its international footprint with affiliate groups the Sonnenkrieg Division (UK), AWD Deutschland (Germany), Feuerkrieg Division (Estonia) and the Northern Order (Canada). However, identifying the leadership or the membership of the AWD remains problematic due to the sophisticated online encryption systems employed by the group. More recently, the AWD has profited from the opportunities provided by new social media ecosystems. Adherents use media platforms such as Telegram and Parler to maximise recruitment, manipulate public opinion and intimidate political opponents (De Vynck and Nakashima, 2021).

The AWD continuously releases public statements promising an intensification of its violent activities. The group's chat room logs reveal how power stations, powerlines and other critical infrastructure sites have been earmarked for attack (Thompson et al, 2018). However, counter-terrorism authorities have struggled to accurately assess the group's capacity to carry out its threats. Still, after the arrest and jailing of Brandon Russell, while possessing components believed by law enforcement capable of creating a viable 'dirty bomb' (the combination of radioactive material and conventional explosives), the public espousal of violent intent made by the AWD may now be supported by a capability to do so (Ware, 2020). Compounding this was the AWD's calculated strategy of recruiting members and veterans of the armed forces who often gravitate towards violent extremism. Thus, the AWD's strategy appeared to be the accumulation of combat-hardened military professionals, utilising their expertise in future terrorist attacks (Norris, 2020).

However, despite the AWD's growing reach at home and transnationally, 2020 was challenging for the organisation. In February, 'Operation First Pillar', conducted by the Federal Bureau of Investigation (FBI)'s Joint Terrorism Taskforce, arrested 18 members, and incarcerated five of the AWD's most senior leadership (Norris, 2020). All were found guilty of instigating a campaign of 'swatting', making hoax emergency calls regarding ongoing violent situations hoping to garner a response from law enforcement SWAT teams (Baker et al, 2021) against political opponents and journalists. Furthermore, Max Rose, Chairman of the Subcommittee on Intelligence and Counterterrorism, has been placing increasing pressure on the State Department to proscribe a White supremacist group, with the AWD top of the list (Ware, 2020). Consequently, the increased pressure on the organisation led the AWD's chief advisor, James Mason, to announce the group's disbandment on 14 March 2020 (Makuch, 2020). However, some scholars, such as Bertrand et al (2020), argue that the demobilisation of the AWD was a temporary measure to avoid proscription by the US government. In other words, the group could not be proscribed with the AWD disbanded, leading to the US government proscribing the Russian Imperial Movement instead (Tech Against Terrorism, nd). Indeed, the AWD announced its re-emergence as the NSO in July 2020 (Ware, 2020).

However, the existence of the NSO, created from the residual membership of the AWD, would be short-lived. The NSO was infiltrated and taken control of by the Satanic group Order of Nine Angles. The open promotion of Satanism and sexual violence towards children led neo-Nazi websites and other influential neo-Nazi groups, such as The Base, to distance themselves from the NSO in early September 2022. The NSO was subsequently discontinued; on 12 September 2022, former members announced that a new organisation called the National Socialist Resistance Front had been created (Counter Extremism Project, 2022).

Policy and the myth of threat

There is no doubt that federal law enforcement agencies have recognised far-right violence as a threat to national security (Erlenbusch-Anderson, 2022). Newly elected President Joe Biden introduced America's first strategy to combat domestic terrorism with the National Strategy for Countering Domestic Terrorism 2021. And most recently, the US Congress passed the Domestic Terrorism Prevention Act 2022 (Domestic Terrorism Prevention Act of 2022, 2022). However, it is arguable whether this extensive legal framework is justifiable on legitimate grounds. For example, in 2017, the Trump administration released to the media a catalogue of 78 terrorist attacks between 2014 and 2016. When asked what the aim of the publication was, the White House declared, 'What we need to do is to remind people that the Earth is a very dangerous place these days' (Spicer, 2017). The constructed risk is fundamental to reinforce further the justification and, therefore, the need to invest taxpayers' money in protecting against a (mythical) threat. The recent narrative uses far-right terrorism as the 'poster boy' to justify counter-terrorism campaigns. As indicated by Zenn's research, this has been further facilitated by the media's constructions of new definitions of terrorism that capture lethal and non-lethal acts to reflect the a-typical non-violent political campaigns by far-right groups (Zenn, 2022). Indeed, Dr Miller-Idriss (2020) declared 'a spike in far-right terrorist violence around the world', while the US Bureau of Counterterrorism (2019) claimed that far-right extremism is 'a growing threat to the global community'. Also, President Biden's National Strategy for Countering Domestic Terrorism claimed ideological neutrality but only referenced far-right/White supremacist attacks, overlooking attacks by the far left, incels and jihadists (Zenn, 2022).

The AWD has appeared to be an easy target for politicians and government advisors. When addressing the US Committee for Foreign Affairs, Christian Picciolini (2020), an American former White supremacist, wrongly claimed that the AWD was responsible for five homicides and then likened the group to an Islamic State terror cell. In 2021, the FBI and Department of Homeland Security claimed that the AWD was responsible for a 'significant domestic terrorist incident'. Yet this single incident happening across two years was the mailing of posters meant to intimidate journalists. Although widely reported, no mention was made that the offences were directly linked to terrorism legislation, nor that any of the actions of those prosecuted met the threshold for terrorism as contained within the multitude of its definitions. The AWD also made news when the group's founder, Brandon Russell, was accredited with a terrorist threat against US nuclear power infrastructure, despite no evidence corroborating this (Krill and Clifford, 2022). Indeed, Russell, who received a five-year jail term, was only charged with unlawful possession of a destructive device and explosive materials, all of which were in his apartment and not with him when arrested (Office of Public Affairs, US Department of Justice, 2018). Still, researchers from the National Nuclear Security Administration in Washington, DC, which deals specifically with the risk of nuclear terrorism, have used the AWD logo as evidence of the far-right's 'explicit interest' in nuclear terrorism. For them, the name Atomwaffen, German for atomic weapons, suggests the group's threat. This is despite academic literature indicating that its future use by the far-right is widely adjudged as very unlikely (Earnhardt et al, 2021); significantly, during 2016–2021 the AWD was only connected to the incident mentioned earlier.

Similarly, the international reach of the AWD's threat seems to have been inflated by its proscription. Proscription refers to a suite of legal measures permitting a government or security authority to ban the presence or support of a recognised group within its jurisdiction to limit possible terrorist acts (Jarvis and Legrand, 2018). Much was made of the Australian government proscribing the Sonnenkrieg Division, the UK-based arm of the AWD, in November 2021. Yet, when Peter Dutton, the Australian Home Affairs minister who decided to proscribe the AWD, was questioned, he conceded that the group had no presence or conducted any activities 'on the ground in Australia' (Theodorakis, 2021). The UK government proscribed the AWD in April 2021 (GOV.UK, 2021). Yet Evans (2021) argues that proscription was a symbolic gesture of geopolitical solidarity with international partners rather than in response to the group's threat to the UK, which is described as 'negligible to non-existent'.

Following the disbandment of the AWD, Australia moved on to proscribe the group's new formation, the NSO. Yet, despite the use of proscription, there have been hardly any notable instances of individuals being indicted, prosecuted or convicted for being members thereof (Jarvis and Legrand, 2018).

Indeed, closer scrutiny reveals that no AWD group members' criminal acts and behaviour have ever been prosecuted using the American anti-terrorism legislation indicated earlier (Ware, 2020). Instead, local and federal law enforcement have resorted to employing regular statutes and laws when pursuing the group and its membership. The following indicates the various laws used to charge and prosecute AWD members; none comes specifically under anti-terrorism legislation: Brandon Russell, 2017, 26 US Code 5861(d) possession of a destructive device, and 2023, 18 US Code 842(j) unlawful storage of explosive material; Kaleb Cole, Cameron Shea, Johnny Garza and Taylor Parker-Dipeppe, 2020, 18 US Code 371(d) to mail threatening communications and cyberstalking; John Cameron Denton, 2020, 18 US Code 875 and 371 interstate threats to injure; Brian Baynes, 2019, 18 US Code 922(g)(3) unlawful acts, unlawful transport of a firearm; Benjamin Bogard, 2019, 18 US Code 2252 (US Attorney's Office, Western District of Texas, 2023). Thus, purely in terroristic terms and from legal perspectives, it is argued here that the threat or risk that the AWD represents is, in fact, speculative.

Still, the drive to expand domestic terrorism legislation has not disappeared, and this has raised concerns among minority and marginalised communities and non-violent activist groups campaigning on their behalf. Research indicates many examples demonstrating how the US Department of Homeland Security and the Justice Department already abuse current domestic terrorism laws against protected First Amendment rights (Gibbons, 2019). In 2017, Native Indian Water Protector activist Jessica Reznicek received a three-year sentence for drilling holes into the unfinished Dakota Access oil pipeline. However, applying a 'domestic terrorism clause' within the Patriot Act of 2001 enabled a judge to increase the sentence to eight years (Madeson, 2022). In 2017, despite concerns that the widening of the domestic terrorism framework could be unfairly utilised against minority communities, the state of Georgia changed its definition of 'domestic terrorism' to include property crimes. These changes allowed police to arrest 19 Defend the Atlanta Forest activists who disrupted the construction of a new police training facility in DeKalb County (Brown, 2023). Also, the Joint Terrorism Taskforce targeted Palestinian human rights student activists. In 2016, the Joint Terrorism Taskforce obtained files from the far-right website Canary Mission containing unsubstantiated claims that student activists at two universities campaigning for Palestinian human rights had links to terrorism. Another example concerns the targeting of Black Lives Matter. Throughout 2015, while tracking the group's whereabouts, the Department of Homeland Security conducted surveillance of unrelated Black community events, such as the DC Funk Music Parade. Then, in 2017, the FBI declared a new threat, namely Black Identity Extremism, hence shifting the nature of Black Lives Matter from activism to terrorism (Gibbons, 2019).

Action dynamic of the Atomwaffen Division

Scholars consider terrorist attacks a fundamental communicative strategy designed to dominate mass media, ensuring enormous publicity and facilitating the widespread dissemination of an organisation's message (Hoffman, 2006). Significantly, however, recent research has drawn attention to the importance of attacks as a recruitment tool. Hence these become instrumental to the group's survival (Limodio, 2022). For example, Reid (cited in Grey, 2021) argues that the Capitol Hill riots of 6 January 2021 were a staged publicity stunt by the far-right to bolster recruitment, with the hope that the four far-right activists who died would be considered martyrs, and their deaths will mobilise huge numbers. Therefore, with such a limited membership, a diminutive group such as the AWD would be expected to conduct violent media attention-grabbing terrorist acts.

However, although the AWD has dominated the headlines for several years, the group has not committed any indiscriminate terrorist attacks. Indeed, deadly American far-right terrorist violence has been perpetrated by individuals but not on behalf of the group as such (Ware, 2020). While scholars, media and government continually espouse the threat posed by the AWD, evidence suggests that the group has prioritised instead the promotion of its increasingly violent rhetoric in what Post et al (2014) have labelled a 'virtual community of hatred' (p 306). Indeed, the group has considered its role to be the exploitation of the vulnerabilities of its current members to facilitate their radicalisation in preparation for a future race war, all done via online propaganda (Jackson, 2020).

Scrutinising the AWD's activities highlights the reluctance to engage in violence and freeriding on the back of violence committed by a violent minority within the far-right milieu. The AWD modus operandi suggests that it prefers to distribute its offensive extremist propaganda to garner as much publicity as possible. For example, in 2016, the AWD distributed flyers across the University of Chicago campus containing the message 'Hitler Disapproves'. The group continued this flyer campaign at several American universities in 2017. Flyers appeared at Florida College stating, 'How is a diploma going to help you in a race war? Join your local Nazis'; at Evergreen State College, stickers demanded to know 'Where will you be when the race war begins?'; homophobic leaflets were handed out to students at the University of Western Florida; and members attended the National Front White Lives Matter rally in Tennessee (Jackson, 2020). According to the Southern Poverty Law Center (nd), the AWD has also organised hate camps and uploaded and published their footage. For example, the Doomsday Hate Camp: Mid-West was held in 2017 and provided the attendees with weapons and combat training.

While most of the AWD's activities have been restricted to campaigns that do not deploy physical violence, on occasion, acts of extreme violence, often not approved by the group although celebrated by its members, are attributed to it. Between May 2017 and January 2018, five murders were linked to AWD members (Boghani et al, 2019); while horrific, none of these turned out to be a terroristic event (Jackson, 2020). The shooting of two fellow AWD members in 2017 by Devon Arthurs received mixed reports by the media; while emphasising Arthurs' links to both neo-Nazi and jihadist terrorists' ideologies, it also suggested the killing was 'to prevent an act of domestic terrorism' (Dearen, 2017). However, it transpired that Arthurs had shot his friends because they had continuously ridiculed him regarding his recent conversion to Islam (Norris, 2020); his reaction seemed to have been affected by what later was diagnosed as schizophrenia and autism (Sullivan, 2017). The double homicide by AWD member Nicholas Giampa of his girlfriend's parents and his attempted suicide were attributed to the AWD cause (Schulberg and O'Brien, 2018). However, it seems that a history of mental health issues and his girlfriend's parents' efforts to get the couple to separate were the critical factors in the homicide (Jackson, 2020); more recent reports have even suggested that the act was a suicide pact between Giampa and his girlfriend (Barakat, 2022). Finally, the alleged murder committed by AWD member Samuel Woodward of his Jewish homosexual classmate followed a three-day hate camp organised by the group in Texas (Thompson et al, 2018). The investigation uncovered anti-gay and hateful material in Woodward's possession, yet it was also revealed that he had autism, and evidence suggested that he was 'sexually confused' (Melley, 2018). According to Jackson (2020), Woodward was also diagnosed with Asperger syndrome and expressed suicidal thoughts; thus, not simply ideology would seem to have played an essential role in driving his action.

However, this does not suggest that the group does not glorify violence. For example, James Mason (2021), the AWD's ideologue, describes the racist killing spree in New York state by White supremacist Joseph Christopher in 1980 that left 13 dead and seven seriously injured as 'outstanding news' and 'positively electrifying' (p 274). Another example is that of White supremacist serial killer Joseph Franklin who in the 1990s travelled up and down the East Coast of America, aiming to kill African Americans and Jews; he would later be convicted of murdering eight people and was executed in November 2013. Describing these actions, Mason (2021) succinctly exclaims, 'Bravo!' (p 275). The AWD has celebrated other terrorist acts by, for example, producing a flyer depicting an image of Osama Bin Laden set against the background of the crumbling Twin Towers (Makuch and Lamoureux, 2019). Also, AWD member Samuel Woodward openly promoted rape to terrorise ethnic minorities by referring to the mass rape of Muslim Bosnian women by Serbian soldiers during the Bosnian War in the 1990s (Thompson et al, 2018).

Although this attitude to freeride on other far-right groups' violence is arguably accidental, examining the group's literature suggests a contained, orderly approach to violence and its dissemination. By applying the internal brake classifications Busher et al (2019) offer to the AWD's guiding text and self-produced literature, one finds clear indications suggesting brakes are employed by its author and the group. Earlier incidents in James Mason's life have shaped his views on effective modus operandi for the group's survival. For example, in his introduction to *Siege*, James Mason's collection (for the 2003 edition, 2021), Schuster recounts that Mason considered killing his headteacher and deputy's headteacher in 1968. However, it appears that William Pierce, then editor of the American Nazi Party's magazine *National Socialist World*, dissuaded Mason from entering the 'tunnel of violence prematurely'. Another example was Mason's incarceration in 1974, where he admitted to recognising the threat to his cause from external influences such as law enforcement. Mason decided to leave violence behind in both cases and concentrate his efforts on the political front.

These experiences might have led Mason (2021) to reconsider the effects of direct violence on the strategy for achieving the group's objectives (Brake 1: strategic logic). Mason admits that 'we cannot challenge the government now' (2021, p 104). He matches this expression of scepticism about the success of violent struggle with the recognition of external brakes (Busher and Bjørgo, 2020), that is, the increased repression by the state consequential to violent acts. Mason (2021) states, 'We'd be absolute idiots to attack the Pigs ourselves in any attempt to initiate something of the nature of a general rebellion' (p 81). Moreover, in an essay in *Siege*, AWD member and leader Ryan AW explains that external actions, such as the one experienced by the group in 2017, being betrayed by 'traitors' and their founder, Brandon Russell, being sentenced to prison, would lead any other group to 'go into pieces' (Ryan, 2017, p 616).

Moreover, Mason's book suggests that he focused on refining the group's moral norms (Brake 2: moral logic) to minimise the emotional triggers towards violence. In other words, Mason further encourages members to adopt non-violent moral principles, thus setting boundaries on unacceptable violent actions. For example,

Mason (2021) can be seen to articulate these sentiments, stating, '[t]he objective is not to murder ethnic minorities, rather fan the flames of revolution and bring down the system' (p 64) and, 'assassinating Presidents won't change a damn thing' (p 297). For example, a propaganda pamphlet (Mason, 2021) indicates that 'the key to success in the struggle ahead is self-discipline' (p 46). Against emotionally driven action, Mason (2021) suggests that he would '[m]uch rather run the risk of a tactical, personal set-back at the hands of a sharp, intelligent person, something I would expect I could reverse in time, than to have everything, the whole ball of wax, upturned or destroyed by some flake who loses all better judgment and control' (p 108).

Indeed, research (Jackson, 2020; Ravndal, 2021) indicates that for the AWD, self-discipline and remaining 'legal' in the face of intense provocation by the state are critical to future victory. Additionally, strategic logic and moral logic could be seen as interlinked. Mason (2021) indicates that 'making headlines doesn't work and only reveals our weaknesses' (p 49); he asks members to 'stay out of their way, don't give the authorities the excuse to come after you' (p 63) and urges to carry 'no stunts, no fanfare, only long-term planning' (p 92). He says, '[b]e assured, cooler heads will prevail. It is up to you to make certain that the cooler head belongs to you' (p 113).

Capitalising on growth rather than risking repression, the focus on recruitment also reflects a strategy of survival (Makuch, 2020). Scholars have indicated that 'victory' is connected to group size (Simi and Windisch, 2020). Thus, with a membership estimated at around 80, Mason recognises the futility of waging war against the government, thus dismissing 'minor' attempts to gain publicity, preferring to 'direct ourselves towards recruitment' (Mason, 2021, p 536); also, several pre-2020 AWD flyers in the 2021 *Siege* edition address recruits, encouraging them to join their local group (Mason, 2021). Group member Ryan AW confirms (Mason, 2021) that after the AWD was disbanded in 2017, 'the group plugged along, gaining a slew of members ... our propaganda was really coming into its own' (p 616). Mason (2021) further concedes that engaging in violent struggle would be stupidity without 'sufficient personnel in possession of the necessary expertise' (p 32). This reflects another concern within the strategic logic

(Brake 1), that violence will have a detrimental effect on support for the group, '[f]or sympathy is lost, and condemnation follows' (Mason, 2021, p 189). Group member Ryan AW adds to this, indicating that the 2018 events – the shutting of the website *Iron March*, the Satanic Panic infiltration events, and the leak of AWD group members' private conversations – led to the ruin of the group's public reputation, badly affecting membership numbers. He said that '[t]he old tactic of placing posters at Universities, government buildings, etc., was not netting us nearly as much press coverage as before' (Mason, 2021, p 617). Ryan AW honestly admits:

> I asked myself a simple question – if the version of me from 2016 was transferred to March 2020, would he have joined the group? Sadly, the answer was a resounding hell no. ... I thought to myself, if I wouldn't join this group, how the hell can I ask anybody else to? (Mason, 2021, p 619)

This tendency to restrain from physical violence seems to go against what we have been told about the aim of terrorism, that violence is a critical component of any terrorist organisation. However, Mason's ideology indicates prioritising long-term goals, thus steering away from violence. So far, it seems that this strategy is succeeding. Group member Ryan AW explains:

> What did we accomplish? All in all, we accomplished not nearly as much as we'd have liked, but we accomplished a hell of a lot more than the kikes and white traitors would've preferred. We, so far, have been the most influential National Socialist group of the 21st century. We spread the message further than almost anyone post-Rockwell, and we created an aesthetic that has been copied many times but has never been bested. (Mason, 2021, p 619)

Indeed, a simple Google search of 'Atomwaffen' returns over 2.7 million entries, the 'National Socialist Resistance Front' gets over 8 million hits, and 'James Mason AWD' gets over

5 million hits. Consequently, saturation coverage by media, academia and government amplifies the threat and diffuses fear across a wider audience without the AWD lifting a finger.

To conclude, it is worth copying this lengthy quote from Mason's 1985 entry to his newsletter *Siege* in response to a letter from a 'fan':

> [The letter] was 'standard' all the way except that at the close it had 'READY TO FIGHT!' above the author's signature. It was too much for me. I didn't gag, but I did get steamed and still do whenever I stop to consider it. 'Ready to fight.' 'Ready to fight.' 'Ready to fight.' Kick it around in your mind and roll it over your tongue a few times. I'll bet I could draw you a picture, complete with personal background and history, of that individual … but I won't because that would make me sick for sure.
>
> 'Ready to fight'? Yes, I sent a copy of SIEGE in response – which probably scared the hell out of him if it didn't entirely confuse him – and, no, there wasn't any further communication. … I have vowed to cut waste.
>
> Not everyone is a fighter. That's understood around here. But don't come on like a fool and don't use that term to hide behind. I will show respect for anyone who approaches me in seriousness and who is willing to apply themselves seriously. And a serious approach in this case would have been something like, 'Ready to work.' Or 'Ready to serve.' As it was, this person wasn't even ready to subscribe! This is an insult to all who DO work and serve, in quiet, without fanfare. (Mason, 2021, p 184)

Summary

- Although the AWD has dominated headlines for several years, the group has not committed any indiscriminate terrorist attacks. The few acts of violence initially attributed to being driven by its ideology were proven otherwise. Moreover, no

AWD group members' criminal actions and behaviour have ever been prosecuted using American anti-terrorism legislation; local and federal law enforcement have resorted to employing regular statutes and laws when pursuing the group and its membership.
- The AWD group engages widely with social media and other non-violent forms of political propaganda. Following Busher et al's (2019) perspective on terrorist groups' strategic brakes, this modus operandi seems to reflect the need for safeguarding the group's survival, where the AWD chief advisors systematically discourage members from engaging in acts of violence.
- However, the AWD has featured more widely in the media than any other far-right group. This has led to a misleading amplification of a risk narrative. Subsequently, by paying lip service to the duty of public protection and national security, policies are used to contextualise acts under the umbrella of terrorism.
- Moreover, the drive to expand domestic terrorism legislation has not disappeared. This has raised concerns among minority and marginalised communities and non-violent activist groups that have nothing to do with terrorism. Evidence demonstrates how current domestic terrorism laws have been applied against protected First Amendment rights to safeguard constructed threats. It is arguable whether this extensive legal framework is justifiable on legitimate grounds.
- This, in turn, has several implications: it unnecessarily enhances public anxiety; it incentivises attention-seeking lone wolves to carry out acts of violence; it limits rights and liberties; it antagonises causes worthy of public debate and attention.
- Therefore, it is argued in this chapter that for all the attention terrorism garners, while acknowledging that the threat and potential harm posed by the AWD exists, it is essential to recognise that it has been vastly overstated. The direct attention generated by the media, thus driving the government's policy, appears more damaging than beneficial.
- Instead, the government should carry out realistic threat assessments; it should divert resources back to other areas of social life that are far more tangible, such as high crime rates,

poor socioeconomic conditions, inadequate health services and education.

Suggested directions for future research

The following questions can orient further research and discussion in the area:

- What are some key characteristics of modern societal risk according to Beck's concept of the 'risk society', and how do these characteristics influence governmental responses to threats such as terrorism?
- How does the media's portrayal of terrorism, driven by sensationalism and fearmongering, influence public perception of the threat, and what are the potential consequences of this distorted perception, particularly in relation to far-right extremist groups like the AWD?
- What is the current status of the AWD and its subsequent iterations, such as the NSO and the National Socialist Resistance Front, as of September 2022?
- Is the AWD considered a significant domestic terrorism threat, and how has the application of anti-terrorism legislation been used in pursuing the group's members?
- How does the AWD utilise violence and propaganda according to James Mason's ideology, and how does this contrast with traditional perceptions of terrorism as a communication strategy?

References

Altheide, D.L. (1997) 'The news media, the problem frame, and the production of fear', *The Sociological Quarterly*, 38(4): 647–68.

Amoore, L. (2014) 'Security and the incalculable', *Security Dialogue*, 45(5): 423–39.

Baker, M., Goldman, A. and MacFarquhar, N. (2021) 'White supremacists targeted journalists and a Trump official, FBI says', *The New York Times*, 26 February 2020, updated 4 May 2021. Available from https://www.nytimes.com/2020/02/26/us/atomwaffen-division-arrests.html [Accessed 7 February 2023].

Barakat, M. (2022) 'Suicide pact between daughter and her boyfriend may have fueled Virginia couple's 2017 slaying', *NBC4 Washington*, 8 August. Available from https://www.nbcwashington.com/news/national-international/suicide-pact-between-daughter-and-her-boyfriend-may-have-fueled-virginia-couples-2017-slaying/3128159/ [Accessed 7 February 2023].

Beck, U. (1992) *Risk Society: Towards a New Modernity*, London: SAGE.

Beck, U. (2002) 'The terrorist threat: World risk society revisited', *Theory, Culture & Society*, 19(4): 39–55.

Beck, U. (2006) 'Living in the world risk society', *Economy and Society*, 35(3): 329–45.

Beck, U. (2014) 'Incalculable futures: World risk society and its social and political implications', in U. Beck (ed) *Springer Briefs on Pioneers in Science and Practice*, New York: Springer, pp 79–90.

Bertrand, N., Toosi, N. and Lippman, D. (2020) 'State pushes to list white supremacist group as terrorist organisation', *Politico*, 3 September. Available from https://www.politico.com/news/2020/03/09/state-department-white-supremacist-group-124500 [Accessed 7 February 2023].

Bjørgo, T. and Ravndal, J.A. (2020) 'Why the Nordic resistance movement restrains its use of violence', *Perspectives on Terrorism*, 14(6): 37–48.

Boghani, P., Robiou, M. and Trautwein, C. (2019) 'Three murder suspects linked to Atomwaffen: Where their cases stand', *PBS Frontline*, 18 June. Available from https://www.pbs.org/wgbh/frontline/article/three-murder-suspects-linked-to-atomwaffen-where-their-cases-stand/ [Accessed 23 September 2023].

Brown, A. (2023) 'Documents show how 19 "Cop City" activists got charged with terrorism', *Grist*, 27 January. Available from https://grist.org/protest/atlanta-cop-city-terrorism/ [Accessed 23 September 2023].

Bureau of Counterterrorism (2019) 'Country reports on terrorism 2019', *US Department of State*. Available from https://www.state.gov/reports/country-reports-on-terrorism-2019/ [Accessed 12 May 2023].

Busher, J. and Bjørgo, T. (2020) 'Restraint in terrorist groups and radical milieus: Towards a research agenda', *Perspectives on Terrorism*, 14(6): 2–12.

Busher, J., Holbrook, D. and Macklin, G. (2019) 'The internal brakes on violent escalation: A typology', *Behavioral Sciences of Terrorism and Political Aggression*, 11(1): 3–21.

Center for International Security and Cooperation (2023) 'Atomwaffen Division/National Socialist Order', Stanford University, last update August 2022. Available from https://cisac.fsi.stanford.edu/mappingmilitants/profiles/atomwaffen-division [Accessed 3 February 2023].

Cohen, S. (1985) *Visions of Social Control: Crime, Punishment, and Classification*, Oxford: Polity Press.

Counter Extremism Project (2022) 'Extremist content online: White supremacist raising money on GiveSendGo to support campground to be used for training', *The Counter Extremism Project, CEP*, 12 September. Available from https://www.counterextremism.com/press/extremist-content-online-white-supremacist-raising-money-givesendgo-support-campground-be [Accessed 28 January 2023].

Da Silva, R., Fontana, G. and Armstrong, M. (2022) '"It's about keeping children safe, not spying": A governmentality approach to prevent in primary education', *The British Journal of Politics and International Relations*, 24(2): 259–76.

Dearen, J. (2017) 'Muslim student shot dead neo-Nazi roommates "to prevent act of domestic terrorism"', *Independent*, 24 May. Available from https://www.independent.co.uk/news/world/americas/florida-muslim-student-kills-neo-nazi-terrorist-bomb-plotters-islam-convert-shoots-dead-roomates-a7753676.html [Accessed 23 September 2023].

De Vynck, G. and Nakashima, E. (2021) 'Far-right groups move online conversations from social media to chat apps – and out of view of law enforcement', *The Washington Post*, 18 January. Available from https://www.washingtonpost.com/technology/2021/01/15/parler-telegram-chat-apps/ [Accessed 7 February 2023].

Domestic Terrorism Prevention Act of 2022 (2022) *CONGRESS.GOV*, 117th Congress 2021–22. Available from https://www.congress.gov/bill/117th-congress/house-bill/350 [Accessed 3 January 2023].

Dutter, L.E. (2011) 'Why don't dogs bark (or bomb) in the night? Explaining the non-development of political violence or terrorism: The case of Quebec separatism', *Studies in Conflict & Terrorism*, 35(1): 59–75.

Earnhardt, R.L., Hyatt, B. and Roth, N. (2021) 'A threat to confront: Far-right extremists and nuclear terrorism', *Bulletin of the Atomic Scientists*, 14 January. Available from https://thebulletin.org/2021/01/a-threat-to-confront-far-right-extremists-and-nuclear-terrorism/ [Accessed 3 January 2023].

Erlenbusch-Anderson, V. (2022) 'Historicizing white supremacist terrorism with Ida B. Wells', *Political Theory*, 50(2): 275–304.

Evans, H. (2021) 'All you need to know about the UK proscribing the neo-Nazi group Atomwaffen Division', *Lawfare*, 17 May. Available from https://www.lawfaremedia.org/article/all-you-need-know-about-uk-proscribing-neo-nazi-group-atomwaffen-division [Accessed 3 January 2023].

Gibbons, C. (2019) 'Still spying on dissent: The enduring problem of FBI First Amendment abuse', *Defending Rights and Dissent*. Available from https://rightsanddissent.org/fbi-spying/ [Accessed 23 September 2023].

GOV.UK (2021) 'White supremacist group, Atomwaffen Division, banned in the UK', *GOV.UK*, 23 April. Available from https://www.gov.uk/government/news/white-supremacist-group-atomwaffen-division-banned-in-the-uk [Accessed 3 January 2023].

Grey, E.E. (2021) 'The DC mobs could become a mythologized recruitment tool', *Wired*, 8 January. Available from https://www.wired.com/story/trump-dc-protest-online-extremism/ [Accessed 1 June 2021].

Hawley, G. (2017) *Making Sense of the Alt-Right*, New York: Columbia University Press.

Hendry, J. and Lemieux, A.F. (2021) 'The visual and rhetorical styles of Atomwaffen Division and their implications', *Dynamics of Asymmetric Conflict*, 14(2): 138–59.

Hoffman, B. (2006) *Inside Terrorism*, Columbia: Columbia University Press.

Jackson, P. (2020) *Transnational Neo-Nazism in the USA, United Kingdom, and Australia*, Washington, DC: George Washington University Publications.

Jarvis, L. and Legrand, T. (2018) 'The proscription or listing of terrorist organisations: Understanding, assessment, and international comparisons', *Terrorism and Political Violence*, 30(2): 199–215.

Jones, S.G., Doxsee, C. and Harrington, N. (2020a) 'The escalating terrorism problem in the United States', *CSIS*, 17 June. Available from https://www.csis.org/analysis/escalating-terrorism-problem-united-states [Accessed 25 October 2020].

Jones, S.G., Doxsee, C., Harrington, N., Hwang, G. and Suber, J. (2020b) 'The war comes home: The evolution of domestic terrorism in the United States', *CSIS*, 1 October. Available from https://csis-website-prod.s3.amazonaws.com/s3fs-public/publication/201021_Jones_War_Comes_Home_v2.pdf [Accessed 28 March 2021].

Kollmann, J., Benyamini, Y., Lages, N.C. and Renner, B. (2022) 'The role of personal risk experience: An investigation of health and terrorism risk perception in Germany and Israel', *Risk Analysis*, 42(4): 818–29.

Krill, I. and Clifford, B. (2022) *Mayhem, Murder, and Misdirection: Violent Extremist Attack Plots Against Critical Infrastructure in the United States, 2016–2022*, Washington, DC: Program on Extremism at George Washington University.

Limodio, N. (2022) 'Terrorism financing, recruitment, and attacks', *Econometrica*, 90(4): 1711–42.

Livingston, S. (2019) *The Terrorism Spectacle*, New York: Routledge [original work published 1994].

Macklin, G. (2020) 'The internal brakes on violent escalation within the British extreme right in the 1990s', *Perspectives on Terrorism*, 14(6): 49–64.

Madeson, F. (2022) 'The Feds are using terrorism charges against water protestors', *The Real News Network*, 6 July. Available from https://therealnews.com/the-feds-are-using-terrorism-charges-against-water-protectors [Accessed 23 September 2023].

Makuch, B. (2020) 'Neo-Nazi terror group Atomwaffen Division re-emerges under new name', *Vice*, 5 August. Available from https://www.vice.com/en/article/wxq7jy/neo-nazi-terror-group-atomwaffen-division-re-emerges-under-new-name [Accessed 23 September 2023].

Makuch, B. and Lamoureux, M. (2019) 'Neo-Nazis are glorifying Osama Bin Laden: A new wave of neo-Nazi propaganda glorifies and pulls from ISIS and Al Qaeda, illustrating how the terror groups have some shared priorities', *Vice*, 17 September. Available from https://www.vice.com/en/article/bjwv4a/neo-nazis-are-glorifying-osama-bin-laden [Accessed 23 September 2023].

Mason, J. (2021) *Siege: The Collected Writings of James Mason* (5th edn), Ohio: Storm Books.

May, R. and Feldman, M. (2019) 'Understanding the alt-right: Ideologues, "Lulz" and hiding in plain sight', in M. Fielitz and N. Thurston (eds) *Post-Digital Cultures of the Far Right: Online Actions and Offline Consequences in Europe and the US*, Bielefeld: Verlag, pp 25–36.

Melley, B. (2018) 'Southern California man to stand trial for gay Ivy League student's slaying', *The Associated Press*, 5 September. Available from https://apnews.com/ad9bf9e037e943abb00f9f3e1ffdd9ba [Accessed 23 September 2023].

Miller-Idriss, C. (2020) 'When the far right penetrates law enforcement: America can learn from Germany's response', *Foreign Affairs*, 15 December. Available from https://www.foreignaffairs.com/articles/united-states/2020-12-15/when-far-right-penetrates-law-enforcement [Accessed 23 September 2023].

Morrison, J. (2020) 'Reality check: The real IRA's tactical adaptation and restraint in the aftermath of the Omagh bombing', *Perspectives on Terrorism*, 14(6): 152–63.

Mueller, J. (2009) *Overblown: How Politicians and the Terrorism Industry Inflate National Security Threats, and Why We Believe Them*, New York: Free Press.

Mueller, J. (2021) *Public Opinion on War and Terror: Manipulated or Manipulating?*, Washington, DC: CATO Institute.

Mythen, G. and Walklate, S. (2008) 'Terrorism, risk and international security: The perils of asking "what if?"', *Security Dialogue*, 39(2–3): 221–42.

Norris, J.J. (2020) 'Idiosyncratic terrorism: Disaggregating an undertheorized concept', *Perspectives on Terrorism*, 14(3): 2–18.

Office of Public Affairs, US Department of Justice (2018) 'Neo-Nazi leader sentenced to five years in federal prison for explosives charges', *US Department of Justice*, 9 January. Available from https://www.justice.gov/opa/pr/neo-nazi-leader-sentenced-five-years-federal-prison-explosives-charges [Accessed 30 January 2023].

Picciolini, C. (2020) *Breaking Hate: Confronting the New Culture of Extremism*, New York: Hachette Books.

Post, J.M., McGinnis, C. and Moody, K. (2014) 'The changing face of terrorism in the 21st century: The communications revolution and the virtual community of hatred', *Behavioral Sciences & the Law*, 32(3): 306–34.

Ravndal, J.A. (2021) 'From bombs to books, and back again? Mapping strategies of right-wing revolutionary resistance', *Studies in Conflict & Terrorism*, 46(11): 2120–48.

Recuber, T. (2009) 'The terrorist as folk devil and mass commodity: Moral panics, risk, and consumer culture', *The Journal of the Institute of Justice & International Studies*, 9: 158–71.

Richards, A. (2014) 'Conceptualizing terrorism', *Studies in Conflict & Terrorism*, 37(3): 213–36.

Ryan, A. (2017) 'The decline and fall of the Atomwaffen division', in J. Mason (ed) *Siege: The Collected Writings of James Mason* (5th edn), Ohio: Storm Books, pp 615–20.

Schulberg, J. and O'Brien, L. (2018) 'We found the neo-Nazi Twitter account tied to a Virginia double homicide', *Huffpost*, 4 January. Available from https://www.huffpost.com/entry/nicholas-giampa-neo-nazi-teenager-murder-girlfriends-parents-virginia_n_5a4d0797e4b0b0e5a7aa4780 [Accessed 23 September 2023].

Simi, P. and Windisch, S. (2020) 'Why radicalization fails: Barriers to mass casualty terrorism', *Terrorism and Political Violence*, 32(4): 831–50.

Southern Poverty Law Center (nd) 'Atomwaffen Division', *Southern Poverty Law Center*. Available from https://www.splcenter.org/fighting-hate/extremist-files/group/atomwaffen-division [Accessed 5 October 2020].

Spicer, S. (2017) *Press Briefing by Press Secretary Sean Spicer*, Washington, DC: The White House.

Stewart, M.G. and Mueller, J. (2016) *Chasing Ghosts: The Policing of Terrorism*, New York: Oxford University Press.

Sullivan, D. (2017) 'After treatment, man accused in 2017 Tampa neo-Nazi case returns to court', *Tampa Bay Times*, 10 June. Available from https://www.tampabay.com/news/tampa/2022/06/10/after-treatment-man-accused-in-2017-tampa-neo-nazi-case-returns-to-court/ [Accessed 23 September 2023].

Tech Against Terrorism (nd) 'The designation of the Russian Imperial Movement by the US State Department: Why it matters for tech companies'. Available from https://www.techagainstterrorism.org/2020/05/26/the-designation-of-the-russian-imperial-movement-by-the-us-state-department-why-it-matters-for-tech-companies/ [Accessed 31 December 2020].

Theodorakis, K. (2021) 'Officially a terror organization, religiously or ideologically motivated, online, offline, "onlife"? Recent extremism developments and debates downunder', *Periscope*, April. Available from https://periscopekasaustralia.com.au/officially-a-terror-organization-religiously-or-ideologically-motivated-online-offline-onlife/ [Accessed 23 September 2023].

Thompson, A.C., Winston, A. and Hanrahan, J. (2018) 'Inside Atomwaffen as it celebrates a member for allegedly killing a gay Jewish college student', *Propublica*, 23 February. Available from https://www.propublica.org/article/atomwaffen-division-inside-white-hate-group [Accessed 23 September 2023].

Tversky, A. and Kahneman, D. (1973) 'Availability: A heuristic for judging frequency and probability', *Cognitive Psychology*, 5(2): 207–32.

US Attorney's Office, Western District of Texas (2023) 'New Braunfels man sentenced to 80 months in federal prison for possessing obscene visual representations of the sexual abuse of children', *US Department of Justice*, 5 August, updated 4 September 2019. Available from https://www.justice.gov/usao-wdtx/pr/new-braunfels-man-sentenced-80-months-federal-prison-possessing-obscene-visual [Accessed 12 May 2023].

Ware, J. (2020) 'Fighting back: The Atomwaffen Division, countering violent extremism, and the evolving crackdown on far-right terrorism in America', *Journal for Deradicalization*, 25: 74–116.

Wilson, C. and Halpin, J. (2022) 'Explaining the gap between online violent extremism and offline inaction among far-right groups: A study of Action Zealandia from 2019 to 2021', *Behavioral Sciences of Terrorism and Political Aggression*, 1(1): 1–15.

Woods, J. (2007) 'What we talk about when we talk about terrorism: Elite press coverage of terrorism risk from 1997 to 2005', *Harvard International Journal of Press/Politics*, 12(3): 3–20.

Zenn, J. (2022) 'War on terror 2.0: Threat inflation and conflation of far-right and white supremacist terrorism after the capitol "Insurrection"', *Critical Studies on Terrorism*, 16(1): 62–97.

Zulli, D., Coe, K. and Isaacs, Z. (2022) 'News framing in the aftermath of the January 6 attacks on the U.S. Capitol: An analysis of labels, definitional uncertainty, and contextualization', *American Behavioral Scientist*, 67(6): 702–20.

Index

References to figures appear in *italic* type; those in **bold** type refer to tables. References to endnotes show both the page number and the note number (231n3).

A

academic researchers 15, 275–97
 cooperation with policy makers 277–81, 284–7, 296–7
 forms of collaboration 287–95
 future research 297
 looking ahead 295–6
 terrorism studies 281–4, 295–6
Action Plans 86
activism 315–16
addiction prevention 88–90
Al-Qaeda 220, 221, 310
American Centre for Strategic & International Studies 310
Amoore, L. 305
Anchor work 275–6
Andreasson, T. 34
Andrews, D.A. 34
Ankerloo, B. 36
Anttila, I. 31
anxiety 176
Arthurs, D. 317–18
assessment 128–9, **130**
Atomwaffen Division (AWD) 303, 309, 310–12, 313–15, 316–23, 324
attitudes, extremism enhancing 172–3
Australia 314, 315
availability heuristic 309–10

B

'bad practices' 126, 150–1
Baker, S.H. 33
Bandura, A. 253
Basque Country 245, 249, 260
Baynes, B. 315
Beam, L. 311
Beccaria, C. 21–2
Beck, U. 303, 304, 304–5
behavioural radicalisation 183
behavioural sciences 63–73, **74**
behavioural theory 66
Belgium 275, 291
Bentham, J. 22, 30
Berger, J.M. 219, 220
Bertrand, N. 312
Bhui, K. 173, 176
Biden, J. 313
Biffi, E. 251
Black Lives Matter 315–16
Boaz, A. 285
Bogard, B. 315
boot camps 29, 43n2
Borum, R. 183
boundary spanning 296
Bronsard, G. 173
Buchanan, R. 54
Busher, J. 307–8, 323

C

Cambridge Crime Harm Index 25
Campbell Collaboration 11–12
Capital Hill riots 316
car thefts 37
case-control studies 72
Center for International Security and Cooperation 311
Chen, H.T. 135–6
Chermak, S. 180
childhood experiences 177
Chisholm, T. 217, 221–2
Christie, A. 31, 38

333

Christopher, J. 318
Clarke, R.V. 36, 38
co-production 294–5
cognitive impairment 178–9
cognitive radicalisation 183
cognitive theory 66
Cohen, L.E. 25–6
Cohen, S. 306
cohort studies 72
Coid, J.W. 176
Cole, K. 315
Collective of Victims of Terrorism of the Basque Country (COVITE) 260
Commission for Countering Extremism 219
community resilience 256–7
compensation 40–1
computer programming 88
conceptual research use 285
conclusive evaluation *see* results evaluation
confidentiality v. social impact 249–51
consultancies 280, 291
CONTEST (Home Office, 2018) 216–17, 219, 220, 221, 222–3
  see also PREVENT strategy
control 26, 27–36
conversational victimology 256
correlational indicators *148*
Cortina, A. 244
Counter-Terrorism Agenda 86
counter-terrorism strategy, UK *see* CONTEST (Home Office, 2018); PREVENT strategy
COVID-19 51
crime prevention 4, 21–2
  definitions 23–5, 50
  evidence-based 2, 3–4, 50–1, 52, *53*, 73–4 (*see also* problem-solving criminology)
  and behavioural and social sciences 63–73, 74
  characterisation of initiative's benefits and side effects *60*
  and design science 52–7, 73
  and prevention science 57–63, 73
  future research 42–3
  precaution by prevention 306
scientific basis for 41–2
state's responsibility for 22–3
theoretical and conceptual groundings 7
typology 25–7
  control 27–36
  harm reduction 40–1
  opportunity 36–40
  see also long-term prevention programmes; preventing and countering violent extremism (P/CVE)
crime statistics 71
criminal activity, history of 174
criminogenic indicators 173–5, 184
critical realism 94
critical sociology 94
critical terrorism studies 282–3
cybercrime 39

D

data access 283
data collection 72–3
data elements 123
Davies, H. 279–80
Defend the Atlanta Forest activists 316
definitional indicators *148*
delocalisation 305
denotative definitions 218
Denton, J.C. 315
depression 174, 176
design
  engineering 83
  environmental 38
  see also evidence-based practice design; policy design and development; research design
design models 83
design science 52–7, 73
  see also evidence-based practice design
Dhumad, S. 177, 181
differential association theory 67
dirty bombs 311
Discola, K.L. 257
discrimination 177–8, 183
Disha, M. 123–4
domestic terrorism legislation 313, 315–16, 323
domestic violence 229
Doomsday Hate Campaign 317
Doosje, B. 229

Index

drug addiction 88–90
  see also substance misuse
Dutton, P. 314

E

economic analysis 70
education 39, 123–4, 294
  see also formative evaluation; schools
educational-focused initiatives 61, 65–6
educational programmes *see* 'UNDERSTAND = RESPECT' programme
Ekblom, P. 23
Elahi, M. 220–1
Elias, N. 23
EMMA project 291
emotional impairment 179
employee performance evaluation 124–5
Encounter of the Encounters project 245, 253, 263n3
engineering design 83
environmental design 38
epistemic injustice 255
ethical challenges 290
  see also research ethics
European Commission 5, 86, 253, 255
European Crime Prevention Network (EUCPN) 3, 25, 50, 62
European Expert Network on Terrorism Issues 289
European Forum for Restorative Justice (EFRJ) 244, 245, 250, 261, 263n3
European Monitoring Centre for Drugs and Drug Addiction (EMCDDA) 88, 90
evaluation
  'bad practices' 126, 150–1
  definitions 131–3, 151
  evidence-based 133–5, 151, 152–3
  in evidence-based practice assumptions 141–5, 152
  future research 152–3
  importance, role and functions 122–7, 150
  relationship between objectives, indicators and 146–50
  role of academic researchers in 290–2

types of 135–41, 151–2
v. peer review, measurement and assessment 127–31
  see also impact evaluation; outcome evaluation
Evans, H. 314
Evergreen State College 317
evidence 284, 285, 286
evidence-based crime prevention 2, 3–4, 50–1, 52, 53, 73–4
  and behavioural and social sciences 63–73, 74
  characterisation of initiative's benefits and side effects 60
  and design science 52–7, 73
  and prevention science 57–63, 73
  see also long-term prevention programmes; problem-solving criminology
evidence-based evaluation 133–5, 151, 152–3
  see also evaluation
evidence-based medicine 2–3, 12–13, 133–4
evidence-based practice
  design 81–112
  and evaluation 141–5, 146–50, 152
  future research 112
  and logic models 84–5
  long-term prevention programmes 85–8, 110–11, **136**
  standardisation 88–92, 111, 113–14n4
  step-by-step model 92–109, 111
  systematic approach 82–3, 110
evidence-based practice (EBP) 1–6
  core components 87, 110
  thinking critically about 14–15
  three pillars of 11–14
Evidence-based Prevention and Intervention Support Centre 62
ex-post evaluation 140
Exchange on Drug Demand Reduction Action (EDDRA) 89, 90
extremism 219, 220–1, 223, 238
  see also far-right extremism; psychology of extremist violence, systematic review; terrorism; violent extremism
extremism enhancing attitudes 172–3

335

F

far-right extremism
  Atomwaffen Division (AWD) 303, 309, 310–12, 313–15, 316–23
  future research 324
  media's construct of threat 308–10, 313
  risks and threats from 304–8
  impact on policy 313–16
Farrington, D.P. 35
Felson, M. 37
Finland 291, 294
Finnish National Action Plan 275–6, 291
Fishbein, D.H. 58, 63
'Fishmongers Hall' incident 224
Florida College 317
follow-up evaluation 140
forensic populations 182–3, 185
formative evaluation 137–8
Franklin, J. 318
Fricker, M. 255
frontline practitioners
  expectation to prevent radicalisation 216–18, 221–5
  perspectives on radicalisation 228–31
  perspectives on radicalisation work 231–3, 234–6, 238
  practitioner-led recommendations on radicalisation 236–8
  views on organisational policies 233–4
Fuller, R.B. 52–3
Funnell, S.C. 9

G

Garza, J. 315
gated communities 38
gender 180–1
general incapacitation 29
Gensheimer, L.K. 31
Giampa, N. 318
Gill, P. 177
Giordano, P.C. 26
Gonzàlez, A.L. 181
government-funded research 290
Groppi, M. 180
Grounded Theory Approach 167
group identity 175, 184
group membership 220
Gruenewald, J. 180

H

harm reduction 40–1
hermeneutic injustice 255
Hevner, A.R. 56
history of criminal activity 174
history of violence 173
Horgan, J. 219–20
Horizon 2020 5
housing 37–8
human sciences 54
'humanistic coefficient' 97
humanistic theory 66

I

ideology 164, 172, 183, 187, 236–7
impact evaluation 70, 140
impaired functioning 178–9
impulsiveness 179
incalculable risk 305
incapacitation 29–30
INDEED project 5, 62, 86, 112–13n1, 126, 134, 142–3, 153n1, 153n2
indicated prevention 4
indicators 5, 68, 70, 103, *104*, 147–9, 173–5, 184
instrumental research use 285, 286
International Centre for Counter-Terrorism 6
Islamic State 310, 313
Islamist terrorism 236, 237
Islamists 180

J

Jackson, P. 318
Jacques, K. 180
Joint Committee on Standards for Educational Evaluation 131–2
Jones, S.G. 310
juvenile detention centres 29

K

kaleidoscopic justice 259
Khan, U. 224
Klausen, J. 180
knowledge-based interventions 61
knowledge sharing 287–9
knowledge translation 58–63, 73–4, 279–80
Krout, M.H. 177
Kruglanski, A.W. 183

Index

L
Lab, S.P. 24
labour market 40
LaFree, G. 176
language of radicalisation 218–21
Levin-Rozalis, M. 132
Liem, M. 180
Lindgren, L. 148
Lipsey, M. 34
Lipton, D. 30
logic
  moral 308, 320
  strategic 307, 320
logic framework approach 10
logic models 84–5, 89, 92–109, 111, 144, *145*
lone actors 180, 181, 311
long-term prevention programmes 85–8, 110–11, **136**
Loofbourow, L. 258
Lösel, F. 164
Lub, V. 61

M
Martinson, R. 30, 33
Mason, J. 308, 312, 318, 319–20, 320–1, 322
Mass Casualty Terrorism (MCT) 307
measurement 128, **130**
mechanisms of selective moral disengagement 253
media 308–10, 313
medical practice 2–3, 12–13, 133–4
medical research 226
mental health 176–7, 184, 228, 318
mental hospitals 29
mentorship programmes 61, 66–7
Merari, A. 177
meta-analyses 11–12
Miller-Idriss, C. 313
moral conscience 253
moral considerations 182
moral logic 308, 320
morphogenetic methodology 96
Morrison, J. 308
mortality salience 181
Mulcahy, E. 163, 183
multiprofessional / multiagency working 275–6
  academic researchers and policy makers 277–81, 284–7, 296–7
  forms of collaboration 287–95
  future research 297
  looking ahead 295.–6
  terrorism studies 281–4, 295–6

N
narrative research 225, 226
narratives 256–7
National Socialist Order (NSO) 312, 315
natural sciences 53
needs assessments 56–7
neo-Nazi groups *see* far-right extremism
neoclassicism 32
Nivette, A. 182
non-compensability 305
Nordic Resistance Movement 306
Notice, Check, Share directive 223
Nowak, S. 147
nuclear terrorism 314
Nuclear Weapons Division *see* Atomwaffen Division (AWD)

O
objectives 146–7
observational studies 71–2
opportunity 26, 36–40
Order of Nine Angles 312
organisational policies 233–4
othering 220, 226
outcome evaluation 68–70, 139–40

P
Pahl, G. 83
Palestinian human rights activists 316
Palmer, T.B. 33
paradigmatic non-contradiction 95–6
Parker-Dipeppe, T. 315
Parsons, T. 95
partnership working *see* multiprofessional / multiagency working
Pauwels, L. 179
peer pressure 175–6, 184
peer-review 127–8, **130**
Pemberton, A. 256
personality disorders 177
Picciolini, C. 313
Picciotto, R. 131
Pierce, W. 319

Poland 89–90
  'UNDERSTAND = RESPECT' programme 93–109, 114n8, **149**, 153n4
policy design and development 285–6
policy-facing research 289–90
policy makers 233–4
  cooperation with academia 277–81, 284–7, 296–7
  forms of collaboration 287–95
  future research 297
  looking ahead 295–6
  terrorism studies 281–4, 295–6
political beliefs 172
political engagement 172, 173
political harm 246–8
political violence 245, 246, 248, 259–60
Post, J.M. 317
post-witnesses 255–9
practitioners *see* frontline practitioners
precaution by prevention 306
Preferred Reporting Items for Systematic Reviews and Meta-Analysis (PRISMA) 164, 165, 167
PREVENT strategy 216, 217, 221, 228, 236, 237
  training 222–4, 232
preventing and countering violent extremism (P/CVE)
  design, implementation and evaluation of initiatives 9–11, 69 (*see also* evaluation; evidence-based practice design)
  educational-focused initiatives 64–6
  research methods 70
  and evidence-based practice (EBP) 2, 3, 4–6
  thinking critically about 14–15
  three pillars of 11–14
  role of academic researchers in 275–97
  cooperation with policy makers 277–81, 284–97
  policy relevance in terrorism studies 281–4
  theoretical and epistemological framework 7–9
  see also psychology of extremist violence, systematic review

prevention, precaution by 306
  see also crime prevention
prevention science 4, 57–63, 73
prisons 29, 30, 163, 176
problem analysis 71
problem-solving criminology 50–1
  see also evidence-based crime prevention
procedural justice 254
process evaluation 138–9
professional expertise 12–13
  see also frontline practitioners
programme design *see* evidence-based practice design
programme evaluation 132, 150
  see also evaluation
programme logic models 84–5, 106
programme objectives 146–7
programme theory 9–10, 64, 143, 148
proscription 314–15
prosocial goal obtainment 177–8
prosocial life 39–40
psychology of extremist violence, systematic review 163–212
  discussion 182–6
  future research 187
  limitations 186
  methodology 165–7, *168*
  results 167–82
  study characteristics 188–203
  study references 204–12
psychopathology 177
public health insurance 41
punishment 28–30

Q

qualitative research 225

R

radicalisation 61, 163–4
  cognitive v. behavioural 183
  expectations on practitioners 216–18, 221–5
  four phases of 229–31
  future research 239
  language of 218–21
  organisational policies 233–4
  practicalities of 221–5
  practitioner-led recommendations 236–8
  practitioners' perspective on 228–31
  practitioners' perspective on radicalisation work 231–3, 234–6, 238

Index

research into 225–8
  see also psychology of extremist violence, systematic review
Radicalisation Awareness Network (RAN) 5–6, 62, 86, 125–6, 150, 276, 288
radicalisation cognitions 181–2, 184
Radik project 291
Recuber, T. 309
relational sociology 94, 95, 96
religion 172, 183
research 132–3, 151
  government-funded 290
  medical 226
  narrative 225, 226
  policy-facing 289–90
  see also academic researchers
research co-production 294–5
research design 71–3
research ethics 295–6
  see also ethical challenges
research methods 67–73
resilience 256–7
resilience-training 291
restorative justice (RJ) 244–62, 262–3n1
  confidentiality v. social impact 249–51
  future research 262
  restorative cities 260–1
  society as stakeholder 246–8
  and victims' needs 251–5
  young people as post-witnesses 255–9
  challenges 259–60
restraints 307
results evaluation 139–40, *141*
retrospective studies 72
revenge 182
Reznicek, J. 315
Richards, A. 305
right-wing ideology 236–7
risk society 305, 324
  and the media 308–10
Roschuni, C.N. 55
Rose, M. 312
Routine Activity Theory 25–6
Russell, B.C. 310, 314, 315
Ryan, A. 319, 320, 321

S

Sackett, D.L. 13
safeguarding 222

Sageman, M. 283
Saghal, G. 4
Sahlin, I. 24
Sarnecki, J. 24, 25–6, 28
Saroti, G. 218
Satanic groups 312
scaling 62–3
Scarcella, A. 164
Schils, N. 172
Schmid, A.P. 282
Schmitt, C. 248
schools 39, 65
  see also education; 'UNDERSTAND = RESPECT' programme
Schuurman, B. 283
Scriven, M. 131
selective incapacitation 29–30
selective moral disengagement 253
selective prevention 4
self-esteem 61
self-reporting 72
self-review 127–8, **130**
'shared future, A' (Greater Manchester Combined Authority 2018) 219
Shawcross, W. 223, 236
Shea, C. 315
Siege (Mason) 308, 319
significance, loss of 181
Silke, A. 163, 164, 282
Silva, T. 4
situation analysis 56–7, 70
situational crime prevention 37–9
SMART objectives 57, 91
social bonds theory 67
social engineering 56
social harm 246
social impact v. confidentiality 249–51
social influences 175–6
social psychology 65
social realism 97
social sciences 63–73, 74, 132–3
social security systems 41
social workers 217, 221–2
sociodemographic characteristics 179–81, 183–4, 187
sociology, relational 94, 95, 96
Sonnenkrieg Division 314
Southern Poverty Law Center 317
stakeholders 14
standardisation 88–92, 111, 113–14n4
stories 225, 226
  see also narratives

strain 177–8
strategic logic 307, 320
strategic research use 285, 286
Strategy T.E.R. 275
Strauss, S.E. 1
substance misuse 82, 88–90, 177
Suchman, E.A. 10
suicide 37, 318
suicide bombers 176, 180–1
summative evaluation 139
  see also results evaluation
survivor narratives 257
Sweden 22, 29, 31–3, 66
Swedish Center for Preventing Violent Extremism 6
Swedish Criminal Code 32
Swedish National Council for Crime Prevention 32
systematic reviews 11–12
  psychology of extremist violence 163–212
    discussion 182–6
    future research 187
    limitations 186
    methodology 165–7, *168*
    results 167–82
    study characteristics 188–203
    study references 204–12

T

Taneja, P. 224
teaching-learning process 123–4
terrorism 219, 220, 225–6, 236
  domestic 313
  and the media 308–10, 324
  risks and threats from 304–8
    impact on policy 313–16
  see also violent extremism
terrorism studies 281–4, 295–6
terrorist calculation 248
testimonial injustice 255
theory 64–7
theory-based evaluation 143
theory of change models 84–5, 105–6, 110
Thijssen, G. 173
think tanks 280, 289, 291
threat
  media's construct of 308–10, 313
  from terrorism 304–8
  impact on policy 313–16
Tolerance Project 66
'Total institutions' 29

training courses
  PREVENT strategy 222–4, 232
  on radicalisation and violent extremism 293–4
  resilience-training 291
transcendent narratives 257
transport 38
Träskman, P.O. 31
treatment 30–6
Trump administration 313

U

'UNDERSTAND = RESPECT' programme 93–109, 114n8, **149**, 153n4
United Kingdon, counter-terrorism strategy *see* CONTEST (Home Office, 2018)
United Nations Evaluation Group 124
United Nations Office on Drugs and Crime (UNEDC) 25
universal prevention 4
University of Chicago 317
University of Western Florida 317
utilitarians 21–2, 28, 30, 43n1

V

vaccine development 51
Varona, G. 247
Vergani, M. 164, 183
victim narratives 257, 258
victim testimonies 255–6
victimology 251, 256, 258
victims 40–1, 246–8, 251–5
violence
  among far-right groups 306–8, 310–12, 313–14, 317–22
  history of 173
  see also domestic violence; political violence; psychology of extremist violence, systematic review
violent extremism 58
  social and political harm of 246–8
  and victims' needs 251–5
  see also far-right extremism; psychology of extremist violence, systematic review; terrorism
VIVA model 37

W

Wallner, C. 61, 65–6
Weiss, C.H. 143
Welsh, B.C. 35
White supremacist groups 180
  see also Atomwaffen Division (AWD)
White supremacists 318
wicked problems 54, 276
Wikström, P.-O.H. 23–4
Wilson, C. 307
Woodward, S. 318

worldview 172
Wright, W.E. 31

Y

young people 40, 61, 65, 66–7
  involvement in restorative justice (RJ) 255–9
  challenges 259–60

Z

Zenn, J. 313

www.ingramcontent.com/pod-product-compliance
Lightning Source LLC
Chambersburg PA
CBHW071147070526
44584CB00019B/2694